Secret Hiding Places

Michael Hodgetts

Edited and illustrated by Paul Hodgetts

First published 1989 by Veritas Publications,
Lower Abbey Street, Dublin 1, Ireland
Second edition published 2024 by Pear Branch Press
Text © Michael Hodgetts 1989, Paul Hodgetts 2024
Typesetting Paul Hodgetts 2024
Illustrations © their owners (details p299).
The moral rights of the author have been asserted.

ISBN 978-1-7384270-0-0 Hardback
ISBN 978-1-7384270-1-7 Paperback

Contents

Foreword

When *Secret Hiding Places* was originally published in 1989, Michael Hodgetts presented the first truly scientific overview account of 'priest-holes', a subject which had previously been largely the stuff of legends and romanticism.

The book was complemented by an important body of parallel work published in *Recusant History*, the journal of the Catholic Record Society, recording meticulously the precise location of every hiding place, with historical details relating to each place.*

Taken together, this body of research both debunked theories about certain spaces in country houses which had previously been thought to have been hiding places for priests, while also bringing to the fore the significance, ingenuity, and utility of genuine hiding places.

This subject is important because priest-holes were literally a matter of life and death to priests and their hosts, and they were crucial to the survival of Catholicism, particularly after the Spanish Armada. By a curious twist of fate, these hiding places also played an important subsequent role for hiding royalists during the Civil War, including helping save the life of Charles II after the Battle of Worcester in 1651, and, even later, providing cover for Jacobites, and, in certain places, for smugglers.

During the years of research which came to underpin *Secret Hiding Places*, Michael was encouraged in his quest by the discovery of a hide at Ripley Castle in 1963 and another in the Little Attic at Stonor in 1964. With prescience in 1989, he wrote that 'it would be rash to suppose that no more will ever come to light, even though the discard rate of those reported in local newspapers is very high' (p. 217 of the present edition): and he was delighted when the Chimney Hide at Mapledurham was discovered in 2003.†

Though his death in December 2022 ended sixty years of intensely focused personal research in a highly specialist area, of which, academically, he was the master, his research work lives on and will be built upon by others.

In this context, this new edition of *Secret Hiding Places* is needed as an important continuing reference point for a number of reasons.

First, further hiding places will come to light in the future and these

---

* Michael Hodgetts, "A Topographical Index of Hiding Places (Part 1 of 3)." *Recusant History* 16 (1982): 146–216; "Index" (Part 2 of 3)." *Recusant History* 24 (1998): 1–54; and "Index (Part 3 of 3)." *Recusant History* 27 (2005), pp. 473–520.

† Michael Hodgetts, 'The Chimney Hide at Mapledurham', *Midland Catholic History*, 11 (2005), pp. 4–30.

will need to be integrated within the larger context of Michael's precise recording of the locations of hiding places, their dimensions, and contents, providing essential information for present and future digital mapping. Through the creation of new datasets on hiding places, using his meticulously researched work, there lie ahead exciting new possibilities for linking with existing and future datasets, better to understand the complex world of post-Reformation British Catholic history.

Secondly, increasing public interest since 1989 in Catholic material culture, including works of religious art, vestments, and printed liturgical works, needs locating within a wider context: hiding places form an important part of this, not least because important items of Catholic material culture have long been found in hiding places as they have been re-discovered.

Thirdly, while priest holes were originally created for the protection of priests valiantly serving the perilous Catholic mission to Great Britain, their survival over time and their interpretation has transformed them into the shared heritage of everyone, of all faiths and none.

Fourthly, and sadly, since 1989, a number of authentic hides have been destroyed, largely through lack of ready access to information about what they are, why they are important, and how they contribute to our common heritage. Having this information available will hopefully assist heritage professionals and planning authorities to safeguard these fragile survivals for the benefit of all.

Maurice Whitehead

Emeritus Professor of History, Swansea University

Honorary Research Fellow, Centre for Catholic Studies, Department of Theology and Religion, Durham University

Research Fellow, British School at Rome

Director of Heritage Collections and Research Fellow, Venerable English College, Rome

Rome, November 2023

Preface to the First Edition

This is the first full-length book on its subject for more than half a century, and the first ever to attempt a chronology of it. Any such attempt has to start from Jesuit priest John Gerard's *Autobiography* and *Narrative of the Gunpowder Plot*, which causes problems in counties where he did not work and in the years of his imprisonment from 1594 to 1597. Accordingly, this book consists of three sections, of three, four and five chapters. Chapters 1-3 take the story down to 1594. Chapters 4-7 deal with Warwickshire and Worcestershire, the south-east and the North, and are centred on the searches at Baddesley Clinton (1591), Scotney Old Castle (1598) and Grosmont Priory (1599). Chronological sequence is resumed in Chapter 8 with Gerard's escape from the Tower (1597) and his subsequent work in Northamptonshire and London down to the time of the Gunpowder Plot (Chapter 9). Then follow the years between the Plot and the Civil War (Chapter 10); the escape of Charles II in 1651 (Chapter 11); and the period after the Restoration (Chapter 12), which saw the beginnings of an antiquarian and literary interest in hiding-places at the same time as they continued in use (at least intermittently) by priests, Jacobites and smugglers. In this way, a more or less continuous narrative can be combined with a study of the geographical clusters of hides which Granville Squiers noted in 1933 but could not explain.

In his book, Squiers aimed at a county gazetteer as complete as possible. But many of his shorter entries were tacit corrections of two previous books by Allan Fea, on houses which otherwise would hardly be worth mentioning at all. Apart from that, the need to get several hundred houses into a book of reasonable length meant saying very little about the elaborate network of family relationships that linked them together. This was an unfortunate omission. The recusant gentry who owned these houses and had priest-holes built into them knew one another well. They married one another's sisters and had Mass said in their secret chapels by cousins, who in turn had known one another as students at Oxford and Rome or Rheims. Meanwhile, their conforming brothers-in-law warned them of impending searches and tried not to find too much when compelled to bestir themselves. The actual hiding-places make far better sense in the light of this information, and to leave room for it I have only included half as many houses as Squiers. These do, however, include all the really outstanding examples that he mentioned, together with a number of others which have been discovered or first recorded since 1933.

Like all works of research, the book owes much to those who have been generous with their time and knowledge to assist its author. In particular, I want to record my thanks to the owners and custodians of the many houses where I have crawled through the roof or between the floors with steel tape and camera; to the archivists and librarians, especially at Birmingham Reference Library, who have answered queries and supplied references and photocopies; to my colleagues on the Council of the Catholic Record Society, especially Mr Antony Allison, Dr David Rogers, Mr Philip Harris and Mr Timothy McCann, for much encouragement and for permission to use material which I have previously published in *Recusant History*; to the editorial board of *Eighteenth-Century Life* (Williamsburg, Virginia), in which part of Chapter 12 first appeared; to the governing body of Christ Church, Oxford, who elected me to a schoolteacher studentship for Trinity term 1986 so that I could finish the book; to the governors of the St Thomas More School, Willenhall, for leave of absence; to Dr David Rogers, Dr Christopher Haigh and Prof. J. J. Scarisbrick for reading and commenting on the typescript; to Mrs Rosemary Walters and Mr. C. A. Sawbridge for the artwork; and to Mrs Barbara Britton for the index. Without their varied contributions the book could not have been written, and I hope that they (and others) will enjoy it. Any errors are mine.

Michael Hodgetts 1989

Preface to the Second Edition

One of the great boons of the Internet has been the digitization of out-of-copyright books. For example, almost all the secondary sources for this work can be accessed instantly and free of charge (see p292). The downside is that outdated but public domain information is more readily accessible than recent copyrighted research. Most of what the internet knows about priest holes comes from Alan Fea's books of 1901 and 1931, which are online, but were unreliable even when written. The warehouse stock of Granville Squires' better-researched work was destroyed in the Blitz, and the first edition of this book has been out of print since 1991. My father left a large body of very carefully researched material on this subject, both published and not, and we want to make all of that as widely available as possible. This edition of the book is the first step, but there is also an online map (linked from Wikipedia's entry on priest holes) showing all the currently known hides and a website (www.priestholes.net) is in development.

As Professor Whitehead said in the Foreword, the ongoing loss of hides is destroying irreplaceable heritage. Only around one hundred hides survive in recognisable condition. All are in listed buildings, but listings seldom detail the hides and so planning authorities are inadvertently permitting their destruction. I hope this project will help with this problem.

As the UK becomes a more secular country, differences between the Christian churches may pale somewhat, making the actions and motivations of the people in this book harder to understand. We should understand from

Gerard's *Autobiography* that he and his colleagues had no doubt that the people around them were destined for hell if they did not convert from the Established Church to the Roman Catholic Church. Their mission was to save – literally – as many of those souls as they could. They were willing to face torture and a particularly horrific form of execution to carry out a task they considered themselves privileged to undertake.

We should also remember that, although the searches and the escapes make for eye-catching drama, Recusants were *not* in general living in day-to-day expectation of a knock on the door like members of the Paris Resistance in 1943. There were hundreds of recusant houses, travel and communications were slow, the machinery of government was small compared to today and the Privy Council had many other matters to worry about and only a few skilled pursuivants. Searches might happen at any time and they intensified at times such as the Armada, but otherwise, in most places, years, and even decades, passed quietly by. Fr John Gerard, top of the most wanted list, endured several searches over his fifteen-year ministry, but many priests undoubtedly served out their own ministries without ever using a hide.

I am not competent to update the text in the sense of revising the material, but I wanted this edition to have something newer to say and so I have included as Appendices two of Michael's recent papers. These describe the way that houses were adapted to accommodate and manage the risks of priest-harbouring and the networks that enabled priests to be brought into the country, transported around and stationed. Any errors are now mine.

Paul Hodgetts 22 March 2024, the Feast of St Nicholas Owen.

Editorial Notes

Most of the text, and all the historical argument, is unchanged, but many hide descriptions have been rewritten to exploit the illustrative power of photography. Some technical terminology has been replaced and measurements are in metric. I have added a list of places where hides can conveniently be seen today and a timeline of events. First person speech and comment is Michael's voice unless indicated otherwise.

I would like to thank a new generation of owners and custodians for permission to visit their homes and photograph their hides, Phil Downing, Manager of Harvington Hall, for his company, conversation and much appreciated input on visits around the country, Professors Judith Champ and Maurice Whitehead for encouragement and advice, Liam Temple and the Catholic Record Society for access to copyright material and the Midlands Catholic History Society for financial support. I would particularly like to thank my wife Trish for her love, patience and support during the time I have spent on this project. PH

Where To See Hides

Many of the places in the book are still private houses. The author and editor are very fortunate to have had the privilege of visiting and photographing them and are immensely grateful to the owners for that. However, we would respectfully ask readers to remember that those sites are family homes and to appreciate these hides solely through the pages of this book, its accompanying website and other public information.

The following houses are open to the public, and all have many other features of interest. Please call or check online before travelling as opening times and rooms on show can vary.

Baddesley Clinton (Warwickshire, p61, National Trust)
Two hides, one by Nicholas Owen, both used during a well-documented search of 1591.

Boscobel House (Shropshire, p208, English Heritage)
Where Charles II hid in the oak tree. Two hides in the house, one used by him.

Carlton Towers (Yorkshire, p193)
One large hide, visible from above through glass panels. Tours available by prior booking – search online.

Chastleton House (Cotswolds, p203, National Trust)
A lovely house, with a possible hide used by civil war Cavaliers.

Coughton Court (Warwickshire, p29, National Trust)
One certain hide, not by Nicholas Owen, and one possible one, which might have been by him: he did visit the house. Many Gunpowder Plot and Recusant associations.

Harvington Hall (Worcestershire, p81)
Seven hides, of which four (and a false chimney) are shown to visitors. Children (and small adults) may be able to enter the Library hide, depending on volunteer availability.

Moseley Old Hall (Shropshire, p211, National Trust)
Charles II's next stop after Boscobel with two hides, one used by the King, the other a 'secret corner' (for objects rather than people) and an attic chapel.

Oxburgh Hall (Norfolk, p40, National Trust)
An excellent early Owen hide in superb condition.

Scotney Old Castle (Kent, p103, National Trust)
One hide, and two thrilling search and escape stories. The hide is in a part of the Castle that is not always open to visitors, so please check before travelling.

Speke Hall (Merseyside, p147, National Trust)
A National Trust property with two hides, one partly visible, and other secret features.

Towneley Hall (Burnley, p136)
The largest hide anywhere, visible through a glass plate in the floor of the room above.

Other sites
Ufton Court (Berkshire, p16) is a children's residential outdoor and heritage educational centre: children staying at the house are shown the hides and do activities based on the history. House tours *may* be available by prior arrangement. *Hardwicke Hall* (Durham, p124), *Irnham Hall* (Northants, p158), *Karma Salford Hall* (Evesham, p75), *Naworth Castle* (Cumbria, p192) and *Thurham Hall* (Lancs, p142) are hotels or function venues but *may* allow guests to view their hides by prior arrangement.

Timeline of Events

The "Priest Hole era" is later than is sometimes imagined. Despite the turmoil, there are no records of hides during the reigns of Henry VIII, Edward VI or Mary. The first recorded use of a hide is in 1574, and the main period of building was between the Armada (1588) and the Gunpowder Plot (1605).

1558	Death of Queen Mary and accession of Queen Elizabeth.
1559	Elizabethan Acts of Uniformity and Supremacy: Catholic services made illegal and all non-attenders at (Anglican) Church are subject to a fine of 12p/week.
1568	Foundation of Douai - overseas seminary to train priests.
1569	Northern Earls Plot to depose Elizabeth I and put Mary Queen of Scots on the throne.
1570	Pope Pius V excommunicates Elizabeth I: Catholicism now seen as a political threat to the State.
1574	First seminary priests return to England. First record of a hide.
1577	First seminary priest executed (Cuthbert Mayne at Launceston)
1580	First Jesuits (Campion and Persons) return to England.
1581	Recusancy fine raised to £20/month.
	Search at Lyford: Campion arrested and later executed.
1583	Throckmorton Plot to assassinate Elizabeth I and put Mary Queen of Scots on the throne.
1585	New law against Jesuits and returning seminary priests. Sheltering a priest becomes a felony, for which the penalty is death by hanging. Being a priest ordained abroad becomes high treason, punishable by death by hanging drawing and quartering.
1586	Jesuit conference at Harleyford sets new strategy for the priests, who will now be based long-term in one house. These houses will be equipped with priest holes. A transport network will be established to move incoming batches of priests to centres with multiple hides and onwards when their posting is arranged.
	Babington Plot to assassinate Elizabeth and put Mary Queen of Scots on the throne.
	Henry Garnet and Robert Southwell return to England.
1587	Execution of Mary Queen of Scots.
1588	Spanish Armada – Spanish Fleet threatens invasion of Britain.

	Nicholas Owen begins building hides.
	Jesuits John Gerard and Edward Oldcorne return to England.
1591	Search at Baddesley Clinton; 7 priests escape in an Owen hide.
1594	Search at Braddocks; Gerard escapes but is arrested later.
1597	Gerard escapes from the Tower and moves to work in Northamptonshire.
1598-9	Searches at Scotney Old Castle and Grosmont
	Treasure Hide Search at Ufton
1603	Death of Elizabeth I and accession of James I. Early hopes of tolerance for Catholicism swiftly disappointed.
1605-6	Gunpowder Plot; searches at Harrowden and Hindlip; arrest and death of Garnet, Oldcorne and Owen; Gerard escapes abroad; Afterwards, persecution gradually eases until 1640s.
1625	Death of James I and accession of Charles I.
1642	Outbreak of English Civil War (Roundheads and Cavaliers)
	Renewed persecution
1649	Civil War ends with execution of Charles I; England becomes a republic ("The Commonwealth"), under Oliver Cromwell.
1651	Charles II returns with an army, is defeated at the Battle of Worcester and escapes via an oak tree and a series of priest holes.
1660	Commonwealth fails after death of Cromwell. Charles II invited back as King ("the Restoration of the Monarchy").
	Almost no prosecutions or executions.
1678-81	Fictitious Oates (or "Popish") Plot leads to the last executions
1685	Death of Charles II and accession of Catholic James II.
1688	Glorious Revolution/Dutch Invasion/Protestant Coup*: James II overthrown in favour of William and Mary of Orange.
1698	Popery Act repeals death penalty for being a priest but introduces a £100 bounty for catching one.
1778	Papists Act: first Catholic relief measure.
	Gordon Riots: anti-Catholic riots
1791	Roman Catholic Relief Act makes Catholic worship (under licence) lawful for the first time in 232 years.
1829	Final Catholic Emancipation Act passed

---

* delete according to personal view of this event.

1
Harleyford, 1586

1

Priest-holes and other hiding-places add a spice of mystery and excitement to many a novel. They have a secure, if vague, place in the mythology of the English country house, somewhere between the ancestral ghost and the bed that Queen Elizabeth may have slept in. They are listed by estate agents as features of eminently desirable residences, along with the stables and the swimming pool. Some are on show to the public in houses opened by the National Trust or other owners: King Charles II's hide at Boscobel has been a tourist attraction for nearly 300 years.

But serious historical research on the subject is rare: this book's first edition in 1989 was the successor to a 1933 work of the same name and there have been no others. Among the more obvious reasons for this are the scattered nature of the evidence, both architectural and documentary, the difficulty of interpreting it, and the lack until recent years of the necessary studies in local history. But another is that professional historians have feared to venture into a subject so inextricably entangled with legend and hearsay - perhaps seemingly only a few steps away from ghost-hunting.

Victorian owners of country houses convinced themselves that every old closet was a priest-hole and every old conduit or sewer a secret tunnel but when, after the First World War, archaeology became a rigorous science and the Office of Works cleared away the bats and ivy, grouted the stonework, mowed the lawns and disapproved of the legends, an atmosphere developed in which stories of hiding places were not so much refuted as ignored.

But the proper answer to uncritical acceptance is not uncritical rejection. There were, and in many houses there still are, genuine priest-holes and other hides. Despite alterations and rebuildings, enough evidence remains for truth to be sifted from tradition. The documenting, and still more the dating, of hides does present particular difficulties. There are no building accounts or architects' drawings. No hide-builder scratched his name or the date on his handiwork. Contemporary documents nearly all describe hides which were found during searches and were subsequently destroyed. A hiding-place rarely has any pretensions to architectural style. It is usually an almost featureless space, perhaps 2.5m by 1m and 1.5m high, only identifiable by its flooring and by its entrance, which is most often a trapdoor in a garderobe closet or other dark corner. If the boards above have been renewed because of dry rot, wet rot or death-watch beetle, the proof that the space was a hide at all may have gone for ever. Nevertheless, the difficulties can be exaggerated. There are places where a camouflaged entrance, signs of furnishings and occupation, or an authentic history, are enough to quell all doubts. The two sorts of evidence, those of the hiders and the seekers, are surprisingly copious. From the one side, there are spies' reports, accounts of searches, examinations of suspects (sometimes under torture), lists of aiders and abettors, and so on. From the other side, there are letters, memoirs and reports of the priests and sometimes of the families who sheltered them. These rarely mention names, except of those who were dead or safely abroad, but it is often possible to identify people and places from Government records or from family and other local sources. With such evidence we can recover the pattern of hide-building and date enough examples.

The hides described in this book were built for four sorts of fugitive: for Catholic priests under Elizabeth I and James I; for Cavaliers during the Civil War and Commonwealth; for Jacobites after the Glorious Revolution of 1688; and for smugglers. This is not a rigid classification, because some priest-holes were later used by Cavaliers and Jacobites; some were still in use for their original purpose at the end of the seventeenth century; and the construction of smugglers' hides still goes on today. But of those built before 1800, the great majority are priest-holes. Rather unexpectedly, there seems to be only one possible Protestant hiding place from the Marian persecution of 1555-1558 and only one from the Puritan opposition to the Elizabethan settlement. The latter was at Fawsley in Northamptonshire, where the ultra-Protestant Marprelate Tracts were printed. But even the Catholics took a long time to start building their hides. The earliest recorded priest-hole in the country was at York in 1574 – fully sixteen years into Elizabeth's reign – and the most intense period of construction was between the later 1580s and the 1600s – roughly between the Spanish Armada and the Gunpowder Plot. These two events mark the beginning and the end of the work of the most famous hide-builder, Nicholas, alias Little John, Owen. His remarkable craftsmanship has never been properly appreciated, partly because of its secrecy but also because he does not fit into the conventional pattern of historical textbooks. In these, the Counter-Reformation is dealt with under the 1570s and 1580s, and after the Armada in 1588 we are given a series of chapters on the Elizabethan cultural achievement, which makes an agreeable finale to the reign. The Papists, who might strike something of a discordant note, do not appear on stage again until the Gunpowder Plot in 1605. But this artistic arrangement is obtained only at the cost of omitting a fascinating and important story. It was in 1588 that Martin Marprelate began to attack the 'wainscot-faced bishops'. In the same year, Nicholas Owen began to attack wainscot-faced walls.

2

At sunrise on 14 July 1586, three men rode westwards out of London. The eldest, a tall man with habitually downcast eyes, was William Weston, superior of the Jesuits in England. The month before, a spy had described him as wearing doublet and hose of yellow canvas lined with black. Next in age was Henry Garnet, a fair, rather plump man of thirty-one, formerly a printer, now a priest and an able mathematician and musician. At the Roman College he had not only lectured in Hebrew but had also deputised for the great mathematician and astronomer Christopher Clavius. The youngest of the three, at twenty-five, was Robert Southwell, the poet, who for the last two years had been in charge of studies at the English College in Rome. The three of them were the only Jesuits in England who were not in prison, and Garnet and Southwell had arrived from Rome only the week before.

They were making for Harleyford, a house on the north bank of the Thames two miles above Marlow. The owner, Robert Bold, was a Catholic and harboured a priest, Robert Dibdale, who was later executed. Other Catholics were among the visitors: Sir George Peckham, Lord Compton and Lord Windsor of Bradenham. Bold was a keen amateur musician who maintained a musical establishment in the household; during the week that Garnet and the others stayed there, Mass was sung with a mixed choir, organ and other instruments, conducted by no less a master than William Byrd, who, despite being organist of the Chapel Royal, was also a Catholic. Perhaps one or more of his own settings, such as the bare and haunting Mass for Three Voices, were first performed during this week. Nearly the whole of the mornings, wrote Weston in his autobiography, was taken up with Masses, sermons and confessions. In the afternoons they dealt with what he discreetly calls 'other business'.

In 1559, when Garnet and Weston had been children and Southwell not yet born, the Elizabethan Act of Uniformity had made illegal any forms of worship other than those in the Book of Common Prayer. The Marian bishops had resisted, and all but one had been removed from office. Most of their clergy had conformed, at least outwardly. Monuments of superstition such as wall-paintings, stained glass, rood-lofts and organs had been defaced or destroyed. But few parsons celebrated the Lord's Supper more than four times a year; some still said Mass in secret and kept a suit of vestments in their parlour chambers; many, who could not be trusted to preach according to the mind of the Privy Council, were restricted to reading one of Cranmer's Homilies at Morning and Evening Prayer. The more obstinate had been deprived, like their bishops, or had quietly left their vicarages to live, as the

Bishop of Worcester complained in 1564, 'in corners in gentlemen's houses, where they marvellously pervert the simple and blaspheme the truth'. Some dons from Oxford and Cambridge had fled abroad to Louvain, where they wrote and printed controversial books, which were smuggled into the country from about 1560 onwards, despite spasmodic efforts by the Government to stop them. But for the first ten years of Elizabeth's reign there was fairly general acquiescence in the religious settlement, and the fine of twelvepence a week for 'recusancy' (absence from church on Sundays) was rarely collected and not often incurred.

In 1568 however, when Weston was eighteen, Garnet thirteen and Southwell seven, Dr William Allen, a former Fellow of Oriel College, Oxford, had founded a college at Douai in Flanders for the training of Catholic priests who would be ready to minister in England when the next reaction took place. In 1569 the Northern Earls' uprising attempted to replace Elizabeth with Mary Queen of Scots and in 1570 a Papal Bull, *Regnans in Excelsis*, excommunicated Elizabeth and released her Catholic subjects from their allegiance to her. In 1574, the first of these new priests (called "seminary" priests) returned to England. Opposition to the established religion was no longer a matter solely of middle-aged or elderly survivors from Queen Mary's reign. The priests from Douai were young, ardent and enthusiastic, who in the course of their training in controversy had been put through the New Testament no fewer than sixteen times. Weston went to Douai in 1572, and Southwell in 1576. In 1578, when Douai became unsafe because of the Dutch Revolt, Allen took as many of the students as he could to Rheims in France and sent the remainder to Rome, where another College was established in the buildings of the former hospice for English pilgrims where it remains to this day as the Venerable English College, Rome. Englishmen were also entering the Jesuit novitiate at Sant' Andrea in Rome, including Garnet and Weston during the Holy Year of 1575 and Southwell in 1578. In the summer of 1580, two Jesuits, Edmund Campion and Robert Persons, crossed the Channel with some twenty other priests from Rome and Rheims.

Campion had been the foremost scholar of his generation at Oxford and counted the Queen and the Earl of Leicester amongst his patrons. When he had left the country in 1572, even Sir William Cecil, Lord Burghley, had regretted the loss of one of 'the diamonds of England'. He was an exquisite stylist, a superb preacher and a saint. Persons, a former bursar of Balliol, was a much more robust type: a vigorous pamphleteer with a pronounced gift for diplomacy and for organisation or, as his enemies said, for intrigue. The spy Charles Sledd, who attached himself to the party, described him as 'sometimes a student of physic and at the finding of about forty years of age, tall and big of stature, full-faced and smooth of countenance, his beard thick, of a brown colour and cut short'. During the twelve months before Campion's arrest, Persons and he travelled over much of England: it was estimated that they made 4,000 converts on these journeys, and Campion's Brag (his challenge to the Privy Council to allow open debate) caused him to be regarded as the leader and spokesman of all the 'seminary priests'. The Government's alarm showed in the measures that it took. Reconciling or being reconciled to Rome was made high treason; priests began to be tortured and executed; and the fine for recusancy was raised to £20 a month.

In July 1581, Campion was caught in a priest-hole at Lyford Grange in Berkshire with two other priests, John Colleton and Thomas Ford. In November they and seventeen others were tried in Westminster Hall on a charge of plotting with Allen at Rome and Rheims to murder the Queen. Colleton was able to prove that he had never been to Rome, and that he had left Douai before the College moved to Rheims. But the others were found guilty and executed or banished, and for the next three years all priests whom the Council wished to prosecute were accused of the same plot, only the date varying from one indictment to the next. To avoid any more embarrassments such as Colleton had caused, these indictments also contained the words 'and at divers other places and times, both before and after', which made an alibi impossible. Persons escaped across the Channel and busied himself with political schemes, the smuggling of priests, books and church stuff, and later with the foundation of three more colleges. He died in 1610 as Rector of the English College in Rome, without ever setting foot in England again.

Meanwhile, the Government was making strenuous efforts to find out who had harboured Campion. On 15 November 1581, the day after his arraignment, six suspects were brought before Star Chamber, where they were heavily fined and sentenced to imprisonment at the Queen's pleasure. One of them was William, Lord Vaux of Harrowden in Northamptonshire, who had employed Campion in 1568 as tutor to his son Henry, and whose daughters Eleanor and Anne, and daughter-in-law Elizabeth were to play a crucial part in the story of recusancy for the next thirty years. Another was Sir Thomas Tresham, Lord Vaux's brother-in-law, a scholar and mystic best known today for his three architectural fancies - Rushton Triangular Lodge, Rothwell Market House and Lyveden New Bield. A third, also from Northamptonshire, was Sir William Catesby, father of the Gunpowder conspirator Robert Catesby and a former resident, with Sir George Peckham, at Gloucester Hall, Oxford, a notoriously Papist house. Catesby and Tresham had been reconciled to the Roman Church by Persons in 1580, which made them technically traitors. But it seems likely that they were also singled out for another offence, though it was not mentioned at their trial.

Campion and other priests had been furnished with money and disguises and escorted about England by a group of wealthy young men. These included Henry Vaux, William Tresham (Sir Thomas's brother), Edward Brooksby (who had married Eleanor Vaux), Thomas Pounde (a cousin of the

Earl of Southampton), and Francis Browne (brother of Lord Montague), whose wife later provided Weston with lodgings in Hog Lane. The Privy Council was determined to make an example of such defiance, and by the end of 1581 it seemed to have succeeded. Pounde, who had already spent two years in the Marshalsea prison, was removed in September 1580 to solitary confinement in the decrepit castle at Bishops Stortford, and subsequently to the Tower. In the spring of 1581, the hunt for the leader of the group, George Gilbert, became so hot that Persons insisted on sending him abroad. Edward Brooksby died that summer, and Gervase Pierrepoint, who had guided Campion through Nottinghamshire and Derbyshire, was arrested in August.

Nevertheless, the group, led now by Henry Vaux, was still operating at the time of the Harleyford conference in 1586. Weston recorded tersely that he gave Garnet and Southwell the names of Catholic houses where they could live 'and arranged for reliable guides to take them there'. But by this time the organisation had been infiltrated by a Government spy, Nicholas Berden, who was reporting its activities to Sir Francis Walsingham.

In March 1585, another Act had been passed which made it high treason for any priest ordained since 1559 to set foot in England. The charge of plotting against the Queen was no longer needed. Anyone who sheltered a priest was guilty of a felony and could be hanged. This Act presented the recusants with their gravest challenge yet. Could priests in conscience ask the laity to harbour them at such a risk? Late in April there was a meeting at Hoxton between Weston and other priests and several Catholic gentlemen, including Lord Vaux, Sir William Catesby and Sir Thomas Tresham, who were now out of prison again. Nicholas Berden was also there. According to his report in the State Papers, it was decided that the gentlemen should contribute 100 marks (£66, at a time when a servant would earn a few pounds per year) a year each to a fund administered by Henry Vaux and that 'the priests shall shift for themselves abroad, as in inns or such-like places, and not visit any Papists, especially of the gentlemen, except they be sent for, this summer season'. But clearly things could not go on like that. During the next year or so, nine more priests were hanged, and in March 1586 Margaret Clitherow, a butcher's wife who had harboured one of them, was pressed to death at York.

By mid-July 1586, when Weston and the others met at Harleyford, out of the 300 priests who had returned to England during the previous twelve years, only about 130 were still at work. Some had died of natural causes, some had died in prison and thirty-three had been executed. Another fifty were in prison, and sixty-odd had been arrested and banished or had returned to the Continent of their own accord. Since it took anything between two and seven years to train a priest, and the colleges beyond the seas were always chronically short of money, this wastage rate was unsustainably high. During the five years since the executions had begun in earnest, the Privy Council had gained a commanding advantage over the seminary priests and could hope shortly to eliminate them altogether.

The decisions taken at Harleyford led, among other things, to the building of most of the hides described in this book. But other precautions were needed as well. First, the arrangements for smuggling priests into the country were far from safe. Many of them had been drifting into London, where they had wandered around for a few weeks, getting in each other's way, until picked up by informers and arrested. When Persons had arrived in London in 1580, knowing no one, he had gone to the Marshalsea prison, calculating that there, if anywhere, he would find trustworthy Catholics. He was right, but it was hardly a procedure to be recommended. Apart from that, there were those who were unable to stand the pressure and who, when arrested, almost welcomed the opportunity to confess all that they knew. In recent years, spies had been planted in the colleges abroad, who provided the Government with detailed descriptions of their fellow-students, so that watch could be kept for them at the ports when they returned. One of these was Anthony Munday, a literary hack whose publications included a chronicle play, *Sir John Oldcastle*, a vivid account of life at the English College in Rome in 1579, and a pamphlet on the arrest of Campion at Lyford. If such false brethren were to be prevented from betraying their friends to imprisonment, torture and death, then priests would have to be sifted discreetly when they reached England, and preferably by someone who had recent experience of teaching them in one of the seminaries. For this, Southwell was the obvious choice and, what was even better, he was related (like Thomas Pounde) to the Earl of Southampton and had cousins in Sussex and Hampshire, where many of the priests were landing.

The second precaution concerned the distribution of priests. Until now, they had been constantly on the move; rarely, says Persons, staying more than one night in one house for fear of discovery. That in itself was a heavy drain on their physical and psychological stamina. It had also resulted in their being very unevenly spread. A letter written to Allen on 23 July, just after the Harleyford conference, records that 'There are three or four counties together as yet unfurnished with priests. The tops have been left and only the lower boughs dealt with'. Two days later, on 25 July, Southwell himself said the same: 'In many counties, containing no small number of Catholics, there is not a single priest.... The priests actually at work here make for one or two counties, leaving others without shepherds'. This assessment can be confirmed from other surviving evidence. For nearly 100 of the priests who were at liberty in July 1586 there is some clue to their whereabouts in the 1580s; and of those 100 nearly half were in Yorkshire, Lancashire and Derbyshire. There were a dozen or so around Oxford, in Oxfordshire, Buckinghamshire and Berkshire, and the remaining forty-odd were scattered over the rest of England and Wales, London included. Although these figures do not include the Marian* clergy, the youngest of these were now in their fifties. Ten years later, in 1596, it was to be estimated that there were, by then, only fifty or sixty of them left. The solution had been indicated by George Gilbert in an Italian memorandum which he had written not long before his death in 1583 at the English College in Rome, while Southwell was on the staff there. Priests, wrote Gilbert, would still have to avoid detection by constant changes of name, clothes and horses. But in addition it would be necessary *(sarà necessario)* for them to be distributed in various places and for each of them to live in a gentleman's house, with responsibility for the household and for 'a certain circuit around' *(un certo circuito intorno)*. In such a house, a priest could pass as a cousin, friend or steward of the owner, or hold some honourable sinecure which would not interfere with his real work. Some of the old Marian priests had been doing this ever since the Elizabethan Settlement. Some of the young seminary priests had done so as well, like John Payne, who was living with Lady Petre at Ingatestone in Essex, disguised as her steward, as early as 1577, when he was listed as a recusant by Bishop Aylmer of London. But these had been exceptions, and from now on they would not be. Priests were to be based in the manor-houses of the recusant gentry: in Weston's phrase, they were 'to make their residence there'. That would mean planning and organising. Someone would have to contact Catholics who were ready to risk sheltering a priest despite the Act of 1585. The priests themselves would still have to be met and furnished with disguises, money and horses. There would have to be arrangements for moving them from one house to another, and houses where groups of them could be held for short periods while they were being placed†. Weston had already compiled a list of names, which he gave to Garnet and Southwell. It was agreed that Garnet would contact recusant gentry from somewhere outside London, preferably in the Midlands. At the end of the week he went to one of the Vaux houses, either Harrowden or Shoby in Leicestershire.

A fortnight later, Weston was arrested in a London street. He was kept in prison without trial for the next seventeen years, four of them in solitary confinement in the Tower. But the scheme was put into effect by Garnet, his successor as Jesuit superior. Although there were so few Jesuits (two in 1586, four in 1588, still only sixteen in 1598), they had the support of belonging to an organised Society. They met regularly twice a year, and most of them had known each other as students at the English College in Rome during the 1580s. By the end of 1588, Southwell reported, 'People who up to now would not even speak to a priest, much less admit one to the house, do not only receive us but press us to come and stay with them'. And John Gerard, Sir George Peckham's brother-in-law, who landed that October, noticed that at

---

* "Marian" priests were those who had been ordained in or before Queen Mary's reign. They were exempt from the harshest laws and thus generally safer than their younger colleagues.
† For more details, please see Appendix II: The Elizabethan Catholic Underground (p257).

first

> My hosts could seldom provide the essentials for Mass, and I had therefore
> to bring them myself. But after a few years there was no need to do this. In
> nearly every house I visited later, I would find vestments and everything else
> laid out ready for me. Moreover, before very long I had so many friends on
> my route, and so close together, that I hardly ever had to put up at a tavern
> in a journey of a hundred and fifty miles. In my last two years [1604-1606] I
> don't think I slept in one a single night.

In 1596, Garnet reported to Rome that he and his colleagues had
stationed in fixed residences most of the 300 priests who had landed during
the previous ten years. The number of seminary priests actually at work in
England rose from perhaps 130 in 1586 to 300 in 1596 and 400 in 1610. Some
of these were still itinerant. (In 1615 a specially abbreviated Missal, which
would slip easily into a pocket, was printed at St Omers for their use). Others
might be both stationed and itinerant, like Ambrose Barlow, hanged at
Lancaster in 1641, whose custom was to spend three weeks of every month
at home and the fourth 'in circuit'. But from the 1590s until the early
nineteenth century, a Catholic mission usually meant a country-house
chaplaincy. Garnet and his colleagues were aware of scriptural precedents in
the house churches of Prisca and Aquila, Clement and other early Christians.
What had been good enough for the apostles could be made to work in
Elizabethan England.

But the decision, once taken, had a consequence. If priests were to
stay longer in one house, the risk of arrest there would be that much greater.
So, to protect both priest and owner, hiding places would now have to be
built in such houses.

3

In 1586 priest-holes were not yet a normal feature of recusant houses. A Latin
letter written by Persons in 1581 and first published in 1586 says that Catholic
houses, as in the primitive Church, had 'more retired places' (*loca secretiora*)
to which priests could withdraw, but that nearly all of these, by long use and
occasional treachery, had become known to the searchers. Catholics
themselves, he adds, were accustomed to hide in copses and ditches when
there was a night raid. It might seem as though Persons was referring to
priest-holes, but other parts of the same letter, and much other evidence,
suggest that these places were attics and lofts, rather than purpose-built
secret chambers. That would not only explain their wholesale detection and
why lay Catholics retreated to copses and ditches but would also provide a
more exact parallel to the early Church, since the catacombs, though
sometimes used as refuges in the third century, were originally built as

cemeteries, not places of concealment.

The first seminary priest to be executed, Cuthbert Mayne in 1577, made no attempt to hide. He was sitting in the garden when the posse arrived and came over to the house to see what all the noise was about. On one occasion in 1580-1, Persons himself had to hide in a haystack; on another, he opened the door to the searchers, assured them that there was no one in except himself, and took them round the house to prove it. In the letter just quoted, he describes how priests, 'like deer at the cries of the huntsmen', pricked up their ears and did not dare to make a sound when strangers were heard knocking. He does not say, however, that they fled to the safety of priest-holes.

When Campion was arrested at Lyford in July 1581, there was only one priest-hole in the house. Four facts point to this conclusion. First, he and the other two priests were all in the same hide. Second, Edward Yate, the owner's brother, was also on the run and had to be concealed. But he was put in the dovecot (where the pursuivants soon found him), not in a priest-hole. Third, during repairs in 1959 an Agnus Dei (Fig. 1) and some papers dated 1579 were found in a box nailed to a joist under the slope of the roof. Effective as it had been, this concealment was clearly a hasty improvisation. Fourth, the spy responsible for the arrest, 'Judas' Eliot, says that the searchers 'found many secret *corners*' in the house, even before they discovered Edward Yate in the dovecot, but twice uses the phrase 'secret *place*' for the hole where the priests were. This is a distinction which occurs elsewhere, and it suggests that the 'secret corners' were merely the odd nooks and wasted spaces which are common in Elizabethan houses.

Fig. 1 The Agnus Dei ("Lamb of God") found at Lyford; a disc of wax embossed with the Lamb. This one shows the Transfiguration on the obverse. It probably came from Rome with Campion.

Similarly, when Mrs Jane Griffiths was accused before the Star Chamber of harbouring Campion, Attorney-General Popham made great play of 'sundry secret ways to escape out' of the house, Southland near Uxbridge, which she had rented from Sir George Peckham. There was a cobbled causeway under the water by which the moat could be forded, 'for a place to shift away by if any search should be made'. The house itself was 'so full of shifting-places as it may be that a man may easily shift himself from taking that is acquainted with them'. Popham seems to have envisaged only the possibility of priests getting away from the house into the surrounding woods and not that of secret chambers within the walls. He was not a man to understate his case, and if these 'shifting-places' had been anything more than unobtrusive wickets and back-stairs, he would certainly have seized on this evidence of Papist duplicity.

After the Somerville Plot in November 1583, several houses in Warwickshire were unsuccessfully searched for books and 'Popish trumpery'. But the pursuivant, Thomas Wylkes, did not even consider the possibility that such things had been concealed in hiding-places. Any discoveries, he wrote, had 'been prevented by conveying away from their houses all such things immediately upon the rumour of the apprehension of Somerville'. The 'large and suitable' house near London to which Weston retired in April 1585, when the Treason Act was passed, was not fitted with priest-holes, and when the pursuivants arrived, all he could do was hide in a barn until dusk and then escape on horseback. The agreement at Hoxton a few weeks later, that the priests should 'shift for themselves abroad', makes sense only on the assumption that most recusant houses were not yet equipped to conceal them. Seven or eight years later, in 1592-3, two pursuivants whom we shall meet again, John Worsley and William Newell, searched several houses in the Midlands, including Thomas Lygon's at Elkstone in Gloucestershire. 'And in his own cupboard we found his prayer book in Latin, and we found certain books that, when they saw us coming, they did throw down into the privy' – from which Worsley and Newell retrieved them. In 1591, a spy reported that at Henwick, near Newbury in Berkshire, a priest named Oliver Almond could be found either in the house or in a hollow oak 'in the first close without the gate, upon the left hand in the hedgerow'. In February 1592, Garnet wrote a letter to Rome (which was smuggled out of the country in the French Ambassador's diplomatic bag) asking that no more priests be sent across the Channel for a while, 'since, more often than not, there is simply nowhere left to hide'. In March 1593, Anthony Page was caught near York in a hiding-place made in the bottom of a haystack. 'The entrance thereof not being well stopped, one of the searchers, climbing up upon the hay, fell into the place where Mr Anthony was, and so was he taken'. He was executed the following month, only fifteen months after returning to England.

The link between the building of hides and the stationing of priests in recusant houses after 1586 comes out most clearly in a slightly comic misunderstanding which involved Southwell himself just before Christmas 1586. Philip Howard, Earl of Arundel, was in the Tower, and his Countess, deprived of Howard House and of most of her income, was living at Arundel House in the Strand. A priest, Martin Array, used to visit her there, but he had been captured. So, she sent a gentlewoman to inquire of her relatives the Vauxes and the Arundells about a replacement. They recommended Southwell, who asked 'if her Lady's meaning were whether he should reside with her or no'. To this the gentlewoman replied that he was to reside at

Arundel House. But she had misunderstood her mistress, who had only wanted a priest to visit, 'neither intending that he should make his abode with her nor thinking it possible, by reason of the inconveniency of her house and the small number of Catholics about her'. Southwell accordingly arrived and did not go away. The Countess only realised what had happened a few days later, when Southwell 'began upon occasion to speak of procuring some secret convenience to be made in some part of the house, wherein himself and his few books, together with the church stuff, might be hidden in case any sudden search should happen to be made, as it was usual in most Catholic houses where any priest had residence'. So, Southwell stayed at Arundel House until his arrest in the summer of 1592, and it was not until some years after his arrival that the Countess told him with some amusement that he had originally been an unintended lodger.

Even such proper hides as there were before 1586 had shortcomings. Campion, Ford and Colleton were caught at Lyford because light was shining through the 'wall of boards' which covered the hide. At Ripley Castle (p131) in Yorkshire, perhaps with this incident in mind, the cracks of a hinged panel were chamfered and backed with cloth, but the hide itself is cramped and one thrust with a pike would reveal it. When Lord Vaux's house at Hackney was raided on 5 November 1586, Southwell described himself as 'separated from [the searchers] only by a thin partition, rather than a wall'. And a hide in which Weston spent two days in 1585 was 'constructed with no particular cunning or ingenuity', dark, dank, and so narrow that he was forced to stand, covered in dust and cobwebs, for the whole of the two days. When at last the searchers had gone, he found the ladder so flimsy that he was afraid of snapping the rung beneath his feet as he lifted the heavy trapdoor above him. It must have closely resembled the surviving ladder in one hide at Ufton (Fig. 321) in Berkshire.

There was more to building a 'secret convenience' than the construction of a camouflaged trapdoor. Some ostensible alteration or repair would have to be contrived in the right part of the house as cover, and the hide itself had to be kept secret from everyone except the owner and the priest. Elizabethan country houses had an elaborate hierarchy of servants in the kitchen, the pantry, the brew-house, the dairy, the gardens, the estate-yard and the stables. With the tenants and labourers on the manor, they formed the congregation, and any one of them might be a spy. George Eliot, who arrested Campion at Lyford, was taken up to hear him say Mass and preach by the cook there, who was an old friend of his. There is a report of 1586 on Ufton by a local tailor. A letter written to Persons in 1592 says that servants were being flattered or tortured into revealing what priests their masters were harbouring. In 1594, John Gerard was betrayed by a servant to imprisonment and torture in the Tower. It is easy to understand why priests had been reluctant to spend more than one night at a time in the same house.

Now that they were doing so, certain parts of the house must not be too easily accessible.

Many great houses, from medieval times onwards, had private chapels on the ground or first floor, with obvious ecclesiastical fittings like the carved screens at Compton Wynyates and Ightham Mote. Even the Act of 1581 imposing the £20 fine for recusancy had allowed such a household to attend service in its own chapel, as long as everyone was present in the parish church at least four times a year. But a recusant chapel had to be in the attics, as far as possible from the main staircase, and with nothing left about to betray it. Close by there would also be the quarters for the priests. These might be one room or several, and it is in this part of the house that priest holes are most often to be found*. Both priest and Massing stuff might have to be hidden at very short notice - how short is shown by a raid in London on Maundy Thursday 1606, when the Lord Mayor and his men found the congregation and the smoke from the extinguished candles, but nothing else. So, the nearer the hides were to the chapel and the priest's room, the better. At Braddocks in Essex, the hide is actually entered through the hearth of the chapel fireplace. In the later layouts, of which Harvington is the finest surviving example, chapel, priests' rooms and hides were planned in conjunction, and the hides themselves were designed to be usable for much longer than the day or two of earlier searches. In 1581, Campion had been found at Lyford in less than twenty-four hours, but there were several searches in the late 1590s and 1600s which lasted for more than a week. From this later period there are also records and survivals of hiding-places with brick or stone seats; rush mats to sleep on; feeding traps or tubes for nourishment; ventilation, sometimes in the form of false chimney-flues; and even sanitation, in the form of close-stools or of earth-closets chiselled out of the solid masonry or brickwork. Eventually, the passage of time and changes of fashion brought opportunities to design hides into the structures as houses were remodelled instead of working with the existing fabric, to the benefit of comfort and security.

4

Such devices were needed to counter the increasing sophistication of the searchers. Justices of the Peace were often reluctant to intrude on their Catholic cousins and neighbours, whom indeed they sometimes warned of impending raids. But they could be induced to act by orders from the Privy Council, by pressure from a powerful nobleman, such as the Earl of Huntingdon in the North, or by pursuivants from London with a warrant.

---

* More information about Recusant Chapels and Priests' Rooms is given in Appendix I, p239.

Although it was usual for magistrates to be present when pursuivants conducted a search, there was no doubt in anyone's mind about who was in charge; an insult which rankled the more because of the difference in social standing between the pursuivants and the gentry.

To gain complete surprise, the searchers might surround the house in silence or at night. The first warning of the raid would then be a hammering on the gates and shouts of 'Open in the Queen's name!' as at Baddesley Clinton in 1591. Those within would stall as long as they could, keeping the doors barred while everything incriminating – priests, Massing stuff, clothes, books, boots and swords – was hidden. To prevent this delay, the searchers might knock gently, hoping that some sleepy servant would open up without first scrutinising them through the wicket. If they were kept waiting too long, they would break down the gate, though that might take time if, as at Hindlip in 1606, it was 'very strong and answerable to the greatness of the house'. Once in, they would fan out all over the house in search of overlooked evidence. The priest might have disappeared, and his bed might have been made, but the mattress would still be warm unless someone had turned it over. In time this trick became known. During a search at West Hallam near Derby at the time of the Oates Plot, 'the mattress was cold in the upper part but I found it warm beneath, for they had turned it'. Next, the family would be locked up in one part of the house; guards would be stationed at the doors, 'that none should escape out, but such as were known'. Then the hunt would begin in earnest.

The searchers, says Gerard, would begin by going round the house on the outside, noting any unexplained stretches of blank wall. They would measure the inside with rods to locate any spare space and examine dark corners with candles. Panelling would be probed with swords, 'in which case' (Gerard again) 'some priests have escaped very hardly of being wounded or slain'. If these methods were unsuccessful, the searchers would then sound walls and chimneys with hammers, pierce floors, panelling and ceilings, and open up the roof-space, 'where sometimes nothing but mice or birds have come of many years'. Chimneys could be tested by climbing to the tiles and dropping stones down them; hollow spaces between rooms could be detected by ringing a bell and listening for variations in the sound, as at Thornley, Durham, in April 1593. Masons and bricklayers were sometimes called in to identify sections of walling that had been tampered with, as at Scotney Old Castle in 1598. At Hindlip in the same year, the searchers found in the Long Gallery a point for trussing hose which the priest, Edward Oldcorne, had dropped as he went into hiding. They checked this against all the men's clothes in the house and, on discovering that it did not match any of them, they concentrated on the panelling in the Gallery, behind which Oldcorne was in fact hiding. But on that occasion, he escaped, only to be caught with Garnet in the later search of 1606.

There were techniques more subtle even than these. Sometimes the searchers would lie absolutely still, listening for any movement or cough or sneeze. Then they would suddenly make a great clatter and stampede, shouting 'Here they are - we've got them!' in the hope of provoking some involuntary movement from the hidden priest. Or, with much stamping and banging of doors, they would pretend to abandon the hunt and leave, after which one of them would come round the house and say quietly that the heretics had gone, thanks be to God, and it was safe to come out. At a pinch, they could simply sit down and wait until the fugitive was starved out. Children could be wheedled and threatened. Margaret Clitherow was given away by a twelve-year-old whom the searchers had threatened to thrash until he talked; John Mush, one of the priests whom she had concealed, remarks that her one mistake had been letting the children know where the hide was. But some Elizabethan children were tougher. When Lord Vaux's house at Hackney was raided in November 1586, the pursuivant, William Newell, and his men were held up in the hall for several vital minutes by eleven-year-old Frances Burroughs. 'Put up your swords', she cried, 'or else my mother will die, for she cannot endure to see a naked sword!' Rather sheepishly, the officers did so, while Frances, on the excuse of fetching some wine for her swooning mother, ran back upstairs (shutting the doors behind her) and helped to hide the priests. On another occasion, a pursuivant held a dagger at her breast and threatened to stab her unless she told him where the priests were. In a phrase that would have done credit to Lord Vaux's company of players, she retorted: 'If thou dost, it shall be the hottest blood that ever thou sheddedst in thy life!' Later on, she became a nun of St Monica's at Louvain, in whose usually sedate chronicle both incidents are recorded.

In the last century, some hiding-places have been destroyed by fire or demolition, but many new ones have come to light and much more has been discovered about others. Apart from the immense advances in local history and the wealth of archival material now available, there are many instructive parallels in the accounts of escapers and evaders during the Second World War. Corrie ten Boom's *The Hiding-Place*, for instance, supplies a useful piece of information which is not in any Elizabethan source - namely, that a hide large enough for several people, concealed by a false wall and entered through the sliding back of a fixed bookcase, could be built, complete with the necessary redecoration (right down to coving and fifty-year-old water-stains), within a week.

Another Dutch woman who visited Harvington about 1956 observed that she had a hide in her own house similar to the one under the stairs (p89): it had been built during the Occupation for black market food, but had come in useful when an Allied airman had been shot down nearby.

At Colditz, the famous high security prisoner of war camp in Germany, right at the end of the war, the inmates constructed a large hide in the castle roof, in design near-identical to two of the places to be described below, and in it they built a glider. The castle was liberated before the glider could be used, but at least two replicas have been built and test flown successfully.

Even some of the jargon was the same. Despite its reputation, several successful escapes were made from Colditz and the fox hunting term 'gone away' was used by the inmates to mean 'escaped'. It appears in this exact sense in a document dated December 1591.

Fig. 2 Ufton Court, Berkshire. (Upper) Modern render masks the original timber framing of the front of the house. (Lower). Rear of building. Lady Benyon's Room (p22) is marked in green and its hide (Fig. 7) in red. A void below the hide continues to ground floor level but despite the presence of cellars, a roomy sewer and an icehouse beneath the terrace, there is no evidence that this was an escape route.

2

Garnet and Southwell
1586-1588

On 22 July 1586, the last day of the Harleyford conference, there was a banquet in the Marshalsea prison. At it there were priests, gentlemen and three ladies dressed in the height of fashion, as a spy disapprovingly reported. Two of them were daughters of Sir John Arundell of Clerkenwell and Chideock Castle in Dorset. The guest of honour was Southwell, who had had to miss the closing sung Mass at Harleyford because of this prior engagement. During the evening he preached a sermon on St Mary Magdalen, whose day it was; almost certainly the one that he later published as *Mary Magdalen's Funeral Tears* and dedicated to Dorothy Arundell. For the next five months his base was at Lord Vaux's house in Hackney. The site of this is not known, but it may have been where Hackney House stood in the eighteenth century, just east of the church and between Tresham Avenue and Brooksby's Walk. The priest's chamber, according to a report of 1584, was 'beyond the hall, on the left hand the stair that leadeth to the chambers'. The chapel was 'right over the port entering into the hall, and the way into it is up the stair aforesaid, on the left hand at the further end of the gallery, and there is a very fair crucifix of silver'.

From this base, Southwell started networking. He had recusant cousins in Sussex and Hampshire: the Shelleys of Petersfield, the Copleys of Roffey, the Gages of Firle, the Cottons of Warblington. Southwell himself used the alias of Cotton, and it seems likely that it was from Warblington Castle on Chichester Harbour that he, together with John Cotton, had crossed to France in 1576. Southwell was also connected by marriage with the Earl of Southampton, who, with his father-in-law Lord Montague at Cowdray, was the most powerful protector of Catholics in those parts. The house at Hackney had been leased by Lord Vaux from Lord Montague. Among those noted as frequenting Southampton House in London were a Mrs Gage and a Mrs Banister who was probably Southwell's sister Mary. The Arundells' chaplain, John Cornelius, was a friend from Roman days. Close by, in St Andrew's Holborn, lived Swithin Wells, a former tutor in Southampton's household and one of the laymen who escorted priests about the country. From some time before Christmas 1586 until the end of February 1587, Wells was living with his nephew Francis Perkins at Ufton Court in Berkshire, after which he set out on an unexplained journey to the Sussex coast, spending a night at various recusant houses on the way and ending at Warblington and Michelgrove, another home of the Shelleys. It is not surprising that by

January 1587 Southwell was able to assure the Rector of the English College in Rome that he had 'reliable friends' who could bring packages from Paris into England.

Meanwhile, Garnet had gone either to Harrowden or to Shoby in Leicestershire, the home of Lord Vaux's daughter-in-law Eleanor Brooksby. In February 1587 he met Southwell in London. During the summer he visited 'several counties', which probably included Yorkshire, Nottingham and Derby, and was in London again at the end of August, when he visited Weston in the Clink. From February until July 1588, Garnet took Southwell's place in London while Southwell himself rode through counties which Garnet had not yet visited. In the late summer of 1588, Garnet went on another 'long excursion', either to the Midlands or to the west country. In October, Garnet returned to London, and in November and December Southwell in turn travelled 'on horseback round a great part of England'.

Despite the discreet omission of names from their letters, it is possible to make some intelligent guesses about houses which they visited and where they stationed priests. After 1588, when John Gerard landed in Norfolk, his autobiography makes identification and dating much easier. But of houses with hides which can reasonably be associated with the work of Garnet and Southwell in the two years from 1586 to 1588, five are worth describing in detail: Ufton, Stonor, Compton Wynyates, Coughton and Padley.

1

Ufton Court in Berkshire is a long, many-gabled house of about 1560, seven miles south-west of Reading and close to the River Kennet and the Bath road. It was the home of the Perkins family, who were notorious recusants. On 5 September 1586, seven weeks after the Harleyford conference, it was raided after a local tailor named Roger Plumpton submitted this report:

> There resorteth unto the dwelling house of the said Francis Parkyns a certain unknown person, which is commonly lodged in a cock-loft or some other secret corner of the house and is not commonly seen abroad, but coming abroad he weareth a blue coat. Which person so unknown he vehemently suspecteth to be some seminary priest, for that on divers Wednesdays, Fridays and other festival days he hath seen most of the family of the said Parkyns, one after another, slipping up in secret manner to a high chamber in the top of the house and there continue the space of an hour and a half or more. And this examinate, hearkening as near as he might to the place, hath often heard a little bell rung, which he imagineth to be a sacring bell, whereby he conjectureth that they resort thither to hear Mass.

> Item, he further and lastly saith that one George Tettersoll and other unknown persons, which he suspecteth to be Papists, resorteth to the house of the said Francis Parkyns in secret manner, sometimes by day,

sometimes by night.

The three local Justices who took this statement sent it, and Plumpton, up to Sir Francis Walsingham, explaining that they had 'forborne to stir until your honour's pleasure further known'. They thereby drew attention to their own punctilious devotion to duty, whilst ensuring that Perkins would have a few days in which to dispose of the evidence. On receiving Walsingham's instructions, the Justices 'made present repair' to Ufton. Perkins was out hawking, but they went through 'his study, closets and all other secret places of the house, perusing all the books, letters and writings in chests, cupboards and boxes there remaining, but found nothing contrary to the laws wherewith he might be charged, neither any stranger or unknown person'. But a subsequent report of Plumpton's implies they did not look very hard:

> George Lingam... travelled about at James-tide last [25 July] with another gentleman whom he called his cousin, and had then letters to deliver at Bath, about Bristol and in Gloucestershire.... The said Lingam harboured and lodged sometimes at one Mr Wilscot's and at Englefield; who is at these places called James Lingar, and under colour of teaching on the virginals goeth from Papist to Papist; is thought also to be a priest, so made in Queen Mary's time, and like to be the man that was kept in the top of the said Parkins' house at a time when her Majesty was but ill served by her officers in a search there made.

Thirteen years later, on the night of 17 July 1599, Ufton was searched again. This is one of the best-documented searches that we have, because during it £1,300 (about £200,000 in 2023 prices) in gold and plate was found in one of the hiding-places and confiscated. It was later claimed that there had been a further £751 15s 7d in silver (£120,000) in the hide, which has never been found.

The story begins with the arrival from London of two officers, George Bland and Edmund Duffield, with a warrant signed by Lord Hunsdon for the apprehension of Garnet and Gerard, the two best known Jesuits. They went to Reading Abbey, the home of Sir Francis Knollys, and required him to turn out with a search party – but without telling him where they were going. Although it was already dark, Sir Francis did so, but it was not until they had ridden past the road to Ufton that Bland and Duffield revealed their destination.

When the company arrived at Ufton Court, it was more than three quarters of an hour before they were let in. Eventually, 'after much knocking', Thomas Perkins, the owner's brother, appeared with a light. On learning what they had come for, he and his wife offered to take the searchers round the house. Accordingly, 'at every outward door one man was set to watch' and then the party began its tour. All the doors were open or were unlocked by the obliging Thomas Perkins, except for one to which he claimed not to have a key. The searchers kicked the door down and found a room furnished with stools and cushions and containing what Bland described as

> divers relics and Popish trash, as namely holy water, as he thinketh, with a
> sprinkler therein, and candles half burnt out, such as usually Mass is said
> withal, and such cakes as are used in saying Mass, and divers pictures and
> such other things whereby it seemed unto them that some Mass had been
> there said or sung not long before.

No Jesuits, however, were to be found, and 'after a pretty while' the party returned to the hall. Here they were rejoined by Duffield, who had been unaccountably absent for at least part of the search. He announced that 'he had found the nest', and produced a second warrant from his pocket, which he gave Sir Francis to read. This referred to a 'great store of treasure and money' deposited in the house 'for the relief of ill-disposed persons' and authorised Sir Francis to seize any such treasure that was found. If none was found, this warrant was to be suppressed. Sir Francis, realising he had been tricked out of a night's sleep was 'very angry' and said that he had come to look for Jesuits and would continue to do so. He could not, however, ignore Duffield's 'nest' and followed him to a hiding-place, in which they saw two small chests. Lights were fetched and the chests were raised and placed on the floor in the nearest chamber. Thomas Perkins, who had denied all knowledge of the hide, went away to find a smith to open the chests and failed to return. Eventually, Sir Francis grew impatient and had the chests broken open.

One chest contained a quantity of plate. The other contained bags of gold, which were laid in Mrs Perkins' lap as they were taken out and afterwards counted on a table in a closet in the chamber. It came to a total of £1,300. Next morning, all the treasure was taken to Reading Abbey, where Bland and Duffield left Sir Francis and returned to London to report to Lord Hunsdon. What happened to the £751 in silver was never established, but there was a strong suspicion that it had previously been stolen from the hide by two servants, in collusion with Richard Perkins, the third brother. The denunciation that led to the search was made by the servants and the intention would have been that the confiscation of the remaining treasure would cover their own previous theft.

Mr Perkins sued in the Exchequer Courts to recover the whole sum, and it is from the witness statements in that case that the story is known. These depositions are so detailed that it is possible to follow the participants round the house, identifying the rooms which they searched.

The treasure hide can be identified and dated to the 1580s by the evidence of one of the witnesses, John Vachell, who

> knew the said secret place in the interrogatory mentioned above twenty
> years since, by reason that he was brother unto Thomas Vachell, whose
> money was that was found in the said place. And further saith that he and
> his said brother did carry certain gold to the said house and left the same in

a chest in the custody of one Richard Perkins; and that afterwards about a quarter of a year he this deponent was sent to the said house by his said brother to remove the said chest into the said secret place. Which he and the said Richard Perkins did, letting it down into the said place by a cord and putting the board over the place again as they found it.

Of the four hides at Ufton, only two are entered through trapdoors, and one of these is only about 1.2m deep, which would mean that Vachell and Perkins would not have needed a rope to lower the chest of gold into it. n Fig. 3, fits

the descriptions exactly. It is entered through a single oak plank in one corner of a dark landing, which explains Vachell's reference to 'the board'. It is about 2.70m deep, which would explain the need for a rope. The original rough ladder is still in place but, even in 1599, it would hardly have been safe to use while carrying a chest which must have weighed at least 20kg.

On the underside of the trapdoor is a very rare form of spring bolt (Fig. 4). The spring (orange) is a long, tapering, strip of wood nailed firmly in place

Fig. 3 The Treasure Hide with original ladder: a single tree branch split in half along its length.

Fig. 4 Spring Bolt – detail of operation

at the wide end and with its other end against the bolt (yellow). When the cord (blue) is pulled, the strip bends as the bolt opens. Upon releasing the cord, the spring pushes the bolt closed. Further along the trapdoor is

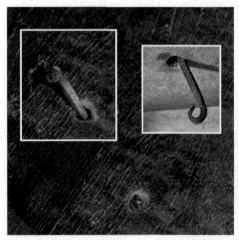

Fig. 5 Detail of trapdoor and the nail that operated the spring. A cord ran from the loop in the nail to the bolt which was opened by raising the nail.

a nail (Fig. 5) which, when the trap is closed, looks like any other nail fastening a board to the joist below. But there is no joist below, and a piece of cord was fastened through a loop in the end of the nail and through a hole in the butt of the bolt. When the hide was shut, the wooden spring kept the bolt in position. But by pulling up the head of the nail and then moving it sideways, the cord and bolt could be drawn back against the pressure of the spring and the trapdoor opened. This curious device occurs in two other hides at Ufton and one at Mapledurham, seven miles away

(see p189). It is otherwise unknown, and the inference is that the same builder was responsible for the hides in both houses. It is the nearest authentic approach to those intricate springs so popular in fiction - and it shows why they do not seem to have

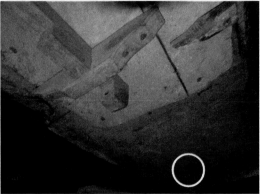

Fig. 6 Underside of trapdoor with bolt and remains of spring. The circled object is the nail shown in Fig. 5

been used elsewhere: the wooden spring was liable to snap. In all the Ufton examples only the thick end is left, while at Mapledurham only the nails which held it remain (Fig. 141).

The second hide at Ufton is a hole under the closet (Fig. 7) off the first-floor room known as Lady Benyon's room. Without its original trapdoor, it is identifiable only by the plaster lining which extends for 1.20m down, with evidence of a former floor at that level. There is a void below the hide which

Fig. 7 Hide in Lady Benyon's room. The shaft is 3.5m deep, but the hide was only the top 1.2m of the shaft.

reaches down to ground level and nearby there is a vaulted sewer tall enough to walk in, but there is no evidence that they ever connected or that this was an escape route. Its similarity to such places elsewhere makes it clear that the plastered portion at least was a hide, but in a house with so much else to show it is not of great importance.

The other two hides at Ufton are in the roof space, between the slope of the gables and the vertical plaster partitioning of the attics. These hides are simply concealed entrances to the roof voids rather than self-contained enclosed spaces. Each is entered through a pivoted panel of lath-and-plaster. The use of a pivot causes the door to rotate about a vertical axis, which allowed the join between the door and its frame to be hidden much more effectively than would have been possible with an ordinary hinge. The door

Fig. 8 Ufton: door to small roof hide. (Inset) Remains of door-opening spring on front sill of doorway.

to the smaller (Fig. 8) is about 1.2m off the floor and awkward to climb into, which suggests that it was for vestments or prohibited books. The full height door to the larger affords more convenient access, though it is not much more comfortable inside. It may have been here that George Lingam 'was kept in the top of the said Perkins ' house' during the search of 1586.

Both hides have spring-bolts of the same type as the hide under the landing. The operating cords ran through holes pierced in the upright pivoting posts and then through holes in the timber studding. They could have been concealed either by nails, as in the Treasure hide, or by removable dowels. Both doors have remnants of a second spring (Insets of Fig. 8/Fig. 11) that nudged the door open slightly when the bolt was released – a necessity in the case of the smaller hide, as the cord is pulled from the adjacent room.

The doors are thickly plastered and backed with wood, but the lath-and-plaster panels around them are not. This meant that neither of these hides, despite their remarkably ingenious bolts, can have been very safe. One is reminded of Southwell's comment on his hide at Lord Vaux's house at Hackney in November 1586: that it was concealed by 'a thin partition rather than a wall'. The Treasure Hide, being between two chimneystacks and surrounded by solid stone, was undoubtedly the most secure of the four. John Vachell had known it 'above twenty years' when his evidence was taken in March 1608-9. That means that it cannot be later than 1588, and the two roof hides, which are less safe, may be even earlier. The place off Lady Benyon's room, which is the most conventional of the four, is hardly likely to be any later.

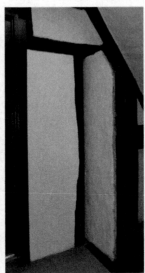

Fig. 9 Large roof hide door, closed and open

Fig. 10 Upper half of inside face of door showing bolt, remains of spring and cord holes.

Fig. 11 (Left) View into large roof hide – little more than access to the eaves.
(Inset) Remains of door-opening spring.

2

Six miles north-west of Harleyford across the Chilterns, and four miles north of Henley-on-Thames, is Stonor, one of the most notable recusant houses in England. Here, from April to July 1581, Campion and Persons had their headquarters, and here Campion's pamphlet *Rationes Decem* ('Ten Reasons') was printed on a secret press. The house had been put at their disposal by the widowed Dame Cecilia Stonor, who was then living at the dower-house in the village, known as Stonor's Lodge. Her elder son Francis, a Church Papist*, remained discreetly at Blounts Court, about five miles away, but her younger son John was at Stonor and took charge of the illicit printing.

Fig. 12 *"Ten Reasons" by Campion, clandestinely printed at Stonor.*

At the end of June, Fr William Hartley, a former Fellow of St John's College Oxford, smuggled copies of Campion's book into Oxford and left them on the benches in the University church before the Commencement ceremony. On 11 July, Persons and Campion rode away from Stonor together and parted for the last time on the common. Less than a week later, on 17 July, Campion was arrested at Lyford. On 4 August, the Privy Council ordered a search of Stonor. The magistrate, Sir Henry Neville, found books, papers, Massing stuff and the press, and arrested not only Hartley and John Stonor but also the printer, Stephen Brinkley, and his four workmen. On 13 August, all seven were committed to the Tower. But, even so, the haul was not quite complete, and on 30 August Neville was ordered 'to have a diligent regard for the apprehending of Hartwell, a priest who much resorted to the Lady Stoner's house, or Persons, or one Robert, his man, or one Robert Seely, servant to John Stonor, now prisoner'. It seems likely that 'Hartwell' was an alias of William Morris, a Marian priest who is mentioned by Persons as having also been involved in the printing.

The press itself was taken up to London and given, 'in part of reward', to David Jenkins, a pursuivant who, with Eliot, had been responsible for Campion's arrest. Meanwhile, Cecily Hopton, daughter of the Lieutenant of the Tower, fell in love with John Stonor, became a Catholic under his influence and began to take messages and letters between prisoners in the Tower and the Marshalsea. This sounds like the plot of Gilbert and Sullivan's *Yeomen of the Guard*, but it did not end so neatly. On his release in 1582, John

---

* The term for a Catholic who avoided the penal laws by attending service at the Parish Church.

Stonor went to the Low Countries where, after a spell of soldiering, he settled in Louvain, married locally and spent the rest of his life there. Cecily continued to carry secret

Fig. 13 Stonor. Due to the slope of the ground, there is only one storey at the rear, so an escape way from the roof is quite plausible.

messages in and out of the Tower until 1584, when she was caught and her father, Sir Owen, was nearly dismissed from his office.

The secret press at Stonor is believed to have been set up in a small room behind the top chamber over the porch, in the roof of the fourteenth-century hall, one truss of which sticks up through the floor. In the west wall of this room, low down in a corner of the next truss, is a triangular door of softwood. It seems likely that it is the successor to a secret door of the same sort as the two at Ufton. Behind it is not a hiding place but the immense and confusing roof-space, nearly 90m long. It is said that the ramifications of this roof-space included an escape to the beechwoods at the back of the house. This is quite possible, since, owing to the steep slope of the hillside along which Stonor is built, there is only one storey, containing the Long Gallery, at the back. But no one can be sure now. Stonor is a house with a complicated and baffling architectural history spanning nearly 700 years, and the ordered sequence of Georgian state rooms which the public sees is loosely fitted inside a much older and much more untidy shell, with unexplained void spaces everywhere.

In the bedroom called the Little Attic in the west wing is a wall of timber and brickwork moulded in a pattern of hearts and flowers, which in 1417 was the kitchen gable. In 1964, it was discovered that most of one panel of the brickwork was a pivoting door. This has been replaced by cement rendering on metal mesh, but the upright timber on the left-hand side of the frame is scooped out to allow the door to pivot, and at the bottom, in the sill, is the hole where the pivot turned. The space behind can still be reached through a trapdoor in the ceiling of the Little Attic, which gives into an adjoining gable and so through a hole (knocked in 1964) in a wall of brick and clunch. Behind the place where the pivoting brickwork was found is the sloping side of a chimney, but there is room to squeeze past it. Both this detail and the size, shape and position of the secret door are reminiscent of the roof-hides at Ufton, though here there are no signs of a bolt on the inside. Behind the chimney is a large space in the roof. Whilst it would be satisfying to think that this place goes back to 1581, the arrest of seven men in a house which would be so difficult to search thoroughly suggests that there were then no prepared hiding-places.

At the end of November 1581, Lady Stonor was allowed to move back from Stonor's Lodge into the main house, where, after a suitable interval, she again harboured priests. Anthony Sherlock, who landed in 1586, confessed that he 'grew into acquaintance first with one Lady Stonor near Henley-upon-Thames and continued there for the most part of three or four years, saying Mass in her house many times.' That brings the story up to 1590. By 1592 Lady Stonor was in prison and her son Francis, as Sheriff of Oxfordshire, was accountable for her arrears of recusancy fines. By 1600 Francis was living at Stonor and making considerable alterations. He was still a conformist at this date, but his wife Martha was a recusant and in 1612 Francis himself was indicted. Although the next priest known for certain to have been at Stonor is John Duckett in 1667, it is safe to say that the hide is as likely to date from the late 1580s or even from the early seventeenth century as it is from 1581.

3

In the southernmost tip of Warwickshire, only a mile from the Oxfordshire

border, is Compton Wynyates, which has been described as the most beautiful Tudor house in the whole of England. It is a quadrangular building of mellow brick in a green hollow of the Cotswolds (hence its other name of Compton-in-the-Hole),

Fig. 14 Compton Wynyates

and is still home to the Comptons, Marquesses of Northampton, who were first recorded there in 1204. On the ground floor is the early sixteenth-century chapel, with a carved screen representing the Seven Deadly Sins and a chamber organ by Father Smith. But in the highest part of the house is a small room known as the Priest's Room, from the fact that a number of crosses are carved on the window sill. The Priest's Room can be approached from the Council Chamber below by no less than three staircases. For this reason it has long been supposed that this room was used as a secret chapel, and Mass said on the large elm window ledge, a conjecture which is made more plausible by the existence under a closet off the Council Chamber of what looks like a hole-under-the-garderobe.

Henry, first Lord Compton, was listed as a Catholic as early as 1574 and is said to have been imprisoned in 1581 for attending Mass. Campion admitted under torture that he had met him once at Lord Vaux's, 'though not mentioning conference with them or the like'. According to Persons, he yielded under pressure and conformed in 1581-2. But by 1586 he was being reported again for harbouring priests, including William Weston, at his house in

Fig. 15 Priest's Room, used as the secret chapel.

London; and it is possible that he was at Harleyford that July. His second wife, Anne Spencer, was a lifelong recusant. But in October 1586 Compton was appointed one of the twenty-four Commissioners for the trial of ry Queen of Scots – an effective way of forcing him to declare himself. He died in 1589 and, although two of his children by his first wife were Catholics, there is no evidence of priest harbouring thereafter. So, if it could be proved that there was a priest-hole at Compton Wynyates, it could be dated to before 1589 and probably to before 1586.

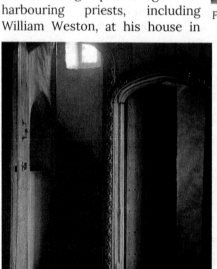
Fig. 16 Council Chamber showing (L) staircase from Chamber to Priest's Room and (R) Closet with hide below.

The place under the closet off the Council Chamber is, as usual, between the floor and the ceiling of the closet below. It measures 1.91m from east to west, 1.55m from north to south, and 1.30m from its floor to the underside of the joists. The floorboards of the space and the boards and joists of the closet above, including the trapdoor, have been renewed. But there seems no reason why such a space should have a floor at all unless the boards are replacements of originals - which would indicate that it was put to use - and the same point can be made about the trapdoor.

Perhaps Compton Wynyates might have become a major centre for priests if Lord Compton had not died, aged forty-six, in 1589. A mile from the county boundary, surrounded by a double moat and with no village close by, it would have been ideal for the purpose. In 1644, it was taken by the Roundheads and, according to family tradition, the widowed Countess of Northampton remained there after the surrender, nursing wounded Cavaliers in the roof until they were sufficiently recovered to make their escape. But there is no suggestion that they were concealed in any form of hiding-place. There is another tradition that about 1770 Lady Frances Compton, while playing as a child in one of the turrets, fell against some plasterwork that sounded hollow. Behind it were the skeletons of a woman and two children. But there is no documentary confirmation of this Gothic story, and even the supposed site is uncertain. A few years later, after a financially ruinous Parliamentary election, all the original furniture was sold, the windows were bricked up to avoid tax and the Comptons left Compton Wynyates for sixty years. By the time they returned, there had been ample time for legends to take root, and it is a lucky chance that even one possible hide has survived.

Fig. 17 Coughton Court

In the Arden country of Warwickshire, nine miles north-west of Stratford-upon-Avon, is Coughton Court, still the home of the Throckmortons, who have lived there since 1409, though it has belonged to the National Trust since 1945. It now consists of three sides of a sixteenth-century courtyard, with what Dugdale in 1656 called 'that stately castle-like gatehouse of freestone'. The fourth side, which in the reign of James II contained a Catholic chapel, was badly damaged in anti-Papist riots of 1688 and finally cleared away in 1790, together with the moat. But the earlier secret chapel survives on the top floor of the gatehouse; and elsewhere in the house there are many recusant relics, including the chemise which Mary

Queen of Scots wore at her execution in February 1587.

Sir Robert Throckmorton, who died in 1586, was a first cousin of Lord Vaux of Harrowden, and his sons-in-law included Sir Thomas Tresham (who had been brought up at Coughton) and Sir William Catesby. His niece Elizabeth, daughter of his brother, Sir Nicholas, married Sir Walter Raleigh. There had been a flourishing Mass centre at Coughton as far back as the 1570s, as we learn from a Latin panegyric written by Southwell in honour of Edward Throckmorton, Sir Robert's nephew, who died as a student at the English College in Rome in 1582. Edward was familiar not only with Coughton but also with Park Hall, near Castle Bromwich, the home of his uncle Edward Arden, with whom both Persons and Campion had stayed in 1580-1581 and who was executed after the Somerville Plot in 1583. Southwell mentions that one of Edward Throckmorton's favourite sports was fishing in the pool (which still exists) close to Coughton Court. He also describes how, when a priest arrived, Edward would take his horse to the stable, pull off his boots, and even clean them. Any such priest (or priests) must have been a Marian survivor, since no seminary priest is known to have reached Warwickshire by 1575, when Edward went to school at Douai. It was there that he met Southwell; later they were together in Rome, and an intercepted letter of April 1582, now among the State Papers, includes commendations from Southwell in Rome to Robert Throckmorton at Coughton.

There can be no doubt, therefore, that Coughton was a likely house for Garnet and Southwell to fix on as soon as they began work in 1586; it may indeed have been a Catholic centre continuously from the accession of Elizabeth onwards. In March 1593, when Thomas Throckmorton was in prison and his sister Mary Arden (Edward's widow) was mistress at Coughton, the Court was searched. According to a disapproving entry in the Acts of the Privy Council,

> 'it should seem by your letter to Mr Topcliffe that there was resistance offered at such time as you did search the house, and that they of the household there did not carry themselves with that dutiful course and obedience they ought to do, and that divers superstitious things and furniture for Mass was there found, and it was confessed that a priest being a seminary was harboured there at that time, who was conveyed out of the way or lieth hid in some secret place'.

It was ordered that Mrs Arden was to be committed to prison and strictly examined, along with 'the rest of her servants whom you shall think fit to be restrained'.

A hiding-place which probably existed at the time of the 1593 search can still be seen at Coughton. In the north-east corner of the Tower Room (the former secret chapel) is a small closet inside a hexagonal turret. The closet floor is of modern boards, with a hole in the middle. Beneath is a secret compartment 1.24m high and 1.2m by 1.17m at its widest. This also has a floor of modern boards, under which again is a lower secret compartment, the same shape and size as the upper one and 1.91m high. When it was found in September 1858, the lower section contained a Spanish leather altar, a rope-ladder, and a palliasse which were given to a convent in Bradford and a small piece of coarse tapestry in faded blue and yellow, now on show in the Tower Room.

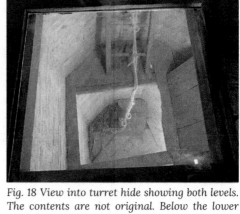

Fig. 18 *View into turret hide showing both levels. The contents are not original. Below the lower level is a newel (spiral) staircase, disused and blocked since the 1780s but never secret.*

Fig. 19 *Courtyard side of gatehouse. The double hide is indicated by the red box, accessed from the turret (green). Blank stretches of wall were a possible sign of a hide that priest hunters would investigate.*

The floor of this lower hole is made of four solid baulks of oak, each 130mm thick. One of these is movable and below again is a newel staircase, blocked about 1780 when the present Great Staircase was built on the other side of the gatehouse but still with glazed windows and blocked doorways into the first-floor tower room and the north wing (the block to the right of the tower in Fig. 19).

Whilst this may appear to be an ingenious and complex place, it is in fact an elongated hole-under-the-closet and the two sections, one above the other, would, if anything, make it more liable to detection from the outside, where it shows as 3.5m of windowless turret (Fig. 19).

The first documentary reference to a double hide is in December 1591 (at the house of one Mr Mompesson in Clerkenwell), but I would be inclined to put this place at Coughton as earlier rather than later than that. At Oxburgh in Norfolk (p40) soon after 1589 Nicholas Owen made a far more cunning use of a very similar position, and it is perhaps reasonable to think in terms of the later 1580s for this hide.

A plausible date for the concealment of the rope ladder and other contents would be 1643. On 20 October that year, Coughton was occupied by a Roundhead force from Warwick, which remained until the following year and then set fire to the house before abandoning it. Sir Robert Throckmorton retired to Weston Underwood in Buckinghamshire, where he died in 1650 and the estates were sequestrated and not recovered until 1651 by his trustees. His heir, Sir Francis, was aged two in 1643 and did not return to Coughton until after the Restoration of the Monarchy in 1660, when he carried out considerable repairs and alterations. The first known resident priest at Coughton was Alban East alias West, who died there in 1671. There were later occasions when evidence of illicit worship would have to be concealed, but no reason why it should not have been recovered again when the crisis was over. So perhaps the secret of this hiding-place died with Sir Robert in 1650.

This hide is often said to be by Owen, but there is no specific reason or evidence for the attribution and the location and similarity to other simple hides would make it a very atypical example of his work. He certainly visited Coughton at least once, for in 1606 under torture in the Tower he confessed:

> that he was at the house of Thomas Throgmorton called Coughton in the beginning of November last, when the Lady Digby was there. . . That on All Hallow Day last Garnet did say Mass at Coughton House, at which Mass this examinant [i.e Owen] was and some others to the number of half a dozen.

But that was twenty years later. There are two other possible hides at Coughton. One, which if it was a hide would be much more typical of Owen's work, is next to the Dining Room and the Tribune which leads from the Dining Room and overlooks the Saloon. It is a space 1.07m by 2.21m high, lined with panelling (not original). Of the 2.3m length, 700mm is taken up by four steps, since the floor is 1.2m above the level of the Dining Room and Tribune outside. During repairs in 1956, a space beneath was discovered in which there were signs of occupation, so this also may have been a double hide. At the inner end, the wall next to the Tribune has been cut away and one of the Carolean panels of the Tribune, 480mm by 530mm, can be removed from inside. If the gap through which the space is now entered had been bricked over, this would have formed a roomy and safe hide, in the middle of the wing, not in a projection on the outside. A secret entrance could have been contrived from some other point, such as the Tapestry Bedroom on the other side of it from the Dining Room or the roof-space above. On the surviving evidence it is impossible to be sure, though in a house such as this, where there is proof of priest-hiding and political conspiracy, it is by no means unlikely.

The other supposed hide is a small space on the ground floor below, opening off the anteroom under the Tribune. The panelling which lines this anteroom was brought from Harvington and fitted here in 1929, when a new approach to the Saloon was created from a former wine-cellar. One panel was made to slide and provide a view of the space, which is, however, labelled 'Bins' on a plan of 1782-1791, a use confirmed by its tiled floor. What it may have been in the sixteenth century cannot now be known.

It is worth adding that two priest-holes were found at Weston Underwood when it was demolished by Sir Charles Throckmorton in 1827. One was next to a chimneystack in a garret near the chapel in the west wing. It was about 1.2m wide, 2.1m long and 1.5m high, and was entered by a trapdoor. In it was a piece of matting, an old box and a short ladder cut from one piece of wood. The other was behind a movable section of wainscot, with a bolt on the inside. Like Coughton, Weston Underwood was a quadrangular building, the work of Sir Robert Throckmorton about 1578 with later alterations. There is no evidence for the dating of the hides, but it is fair to assume that priests were harboured at Weston Underwood from the 1580s onwards, and perhaps the priest-holes were forgotten when Coughton, and later Buckland in Berkshire, became the principal residences of the family after the Restoration of the Monarchy.

4

A very different form of hiding-place from the mid-1580s is a cave in the limestone cliffs of the Little Orme, one hundred metres above the sea near Llandudno. Here was produced Y *Drych Cristianogawl*, ("The Christian *Mirror*") the first book to be printed in Wales. On 13 April 1587, a local man came across 'twelve or more Jesuits, seminaries and recusants' in this cave, some of them armed with pistols. He spoke to them, 'found them strangers and such as cared not for officers' and reported his discovery to the nearest Justice of the Peace, Thomas Mostyn. Mostyn collected forty or so men and came to the spot. 'He durst not or took on him not to dare to enter the cave, the mouth thereof was so narrow, but left a watch there overnight to the number of twenty'. Next morning, however, all the strangers had disappeared from the cave, leaving behind them weapons, food and 'prints of lead and spaces, as I take it, to put between the prints, the which the foresaid seminaries and recusants upon their flight did cast into the sea'. The watch found that the cave was 'boarded', with a wainscoted altar in it, and that it was 'about three fathoms deep'.

Fig. 20 and Fig. 21 show (from slightly different directions) a cave on the Little Orme. Its mouth is 25m below the top of the cliff, in a steep grassy slope which later becomes precipitous. The opening, facing north, is only

Fig. 20 *Little Orme from the north-west showing cave location and (inset) cave mouth.*

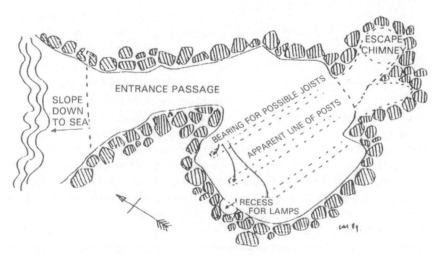

Fig. 21 *Little Orme: Plan of cave made during excavations.*

600mm high and a low entrance passage continues for about 3m. Including this passage, the cave is 6m deep and 4.5m high. At the innermost end is a natural chimney, 4.5m high, which could explain how the printers escaped on the night of 13 April 1587. In 1961 this cave was excavated by Mr Douglas Hague. He only had 1½ days on the site, so concentrated on finding some evidence of the boarded floor, which would have been essential to provide a flat, firm, clean and dry surface upon which to stand the press and which he thought would be the most identifiable feature. Beneath 500mm of modern humus he found a dark horizontal layer which he considered might have represented the floor level, beneath which there were hollows of the same colour, looking like the imprints of floor joists, which aligned with artificial-looking notches cut in the curved part of the wall. No daylight penetrates the interior, and a niche in the north wall in which his team placed their lamps may have been cut for that purpose. Having approached the project with some scepticism, and despite not having found conclusive archaeological evidence (e.g., pieces of lead type), he left "strongly inclined" to believe that the cave was the site of the illicit printing press.

Close by is Plas Penrhyn, which in 1587 was the home of a recusant named Robert Pugh. It is likely that the printers slept there, keeping the press in the cave and retiring there in times of danger. In 1589 and again in 1590 Garnet mentioned his urgent need of a Welsh Jesuit. He was probably thinking of John Bennett, who before joining the order at Verdun in 1586 had worked in Caernarvonshire from 1578 until 1582. After the discovery of the press, Robert Pugh took refuge with Lord Montague at Cowdray Park in Sussex, and the 'seminaries and recusants' may have transferred their activities to Plas Mawr in Conwy, five miles away. This stately stone house in the middle of the town was built in 1577-1580 by Robert Wynne, who in 1585 defiantly added the IHS and other Catholic symbols over the hall fireplace. Gloddaeth, where Bennett was arrested in 1582, is just across the Conwy estuary, and there is a hiding-place at Plas Mawr, between the Lantern Room and the Reception Room or withdrawing room on the first floor. It is within the thickness of a huge chimney stack and seems to have been entered from the attics. But, unlike the cave in the Little Orme, its use cannot be dated.

5

Henry Garnet was born at Heanor, which is nine miles north-east of Derby and ten miles north-west of Nottingham. His father, Brian Garnet, became master of Nottingham Grammar School in 1565, and Henry was a pupil there until he went to Winchester in 1568. His letters after his return to England in 1586 show that he kept in touch with the family at Heanor. On the feast of the Assumption (15 August) 1593, he reconciled his widowed mother, and he arranged for two of his sisters to go over to Louvain, where they became nuns: Margaret in 1593 and Helen in 1595. In the late summer of 1588 he seems to have travelled through the east Midlands, and on 29 October he wrote to Rome describing the execution of three seminary priests at Derby on 24 July.

Two of these, Nicholas Garlick and Robert Ludlam, had been arrested

Fig. 22 Padley: exterior of surviving (gatehouse and chapel) block. The hide may have been in the further buttress, which is also a chimney.

only twelve days before at Padley, about seven miles north of Bakewell, the home of Mr John Fitzherbert. The Fitzherberts were one of the most strongly recusant families of Derbyshire and Staffordshire, and John's brother, Sir Thomas Fitzherbert, was one of the few to pay the full £20 a month under the Act of 1581. He spent nearly thirty years in various prisons; he shared a cell in the Fleet prison with George Cotton of Warblington and in 1590 was interned at Broughton Castle, near Banbury, together with Sir William Catesby, Gervase Pierrepoint, John Towneley of Towneley (p136) and Thomas Throckmorton of Coughton. The internment centres at Broughton, Ely and Wisbech must have encouraged the exchange of ideas about hide-building, and they are aptly commemorated by a painted cloth which hangs in the Tower Room at Coughton. Known as the *Tabula Eliensis* and dated 1596, this depicts Ely Cathedral with its spire, together with portraits of all the sovereigns from William the Conqueror to Elizabeth and the arms of all the Catholic gentry who were imprisoned during her reign, grouped under their various places of imprisonment. John Fitzherbert died in the Fleet prison in 1590 and Sir Thomas in the Tower in 1591.

The arrests of Garlick and Ludlam at Padley were the outcome of an unsavoury contract between Richard Topcliffe, the most notorious of all priest-hunters, and John Fitzherbert's son, another Thomas, a weak and pitiful young man who was badly in debt. Topcliffe, who wanted Padley for himself, persuaded Thomas Fitzherbert that the entire estates were likely to be forfeited for recusancy unless he succeeded soon. Fitzherbert therefore 'entered into a bond to give £3,000 unto Topcliffe if he would persecute his father and uncle to death, together with Mr Basset', another uncle from whom he had expectations. On Candlemas Day (2 February) 1588, on the instructions of the Earl of Shrewsbury, Padley was searched but without success. But on 12 July Shrewsbury took charge himself and captured the two priests along with John Fitzherbert. All three were condemned to death but Fitzherbert was reprieved on payment of £10,000. Young Fitzherbert accordingly refused to pay Topcliffe his blood money and, when sued for the £3,000, argued that the terms of the bond had not been fulfilled, since his father and Sir Thomas had died of natural causes and Mr Basset was still alive and prosperous. In fact, Topcliffe had done his best to find evidence of treason against Sir Thomas and had been responsible for his transfer to the Tower. Not long before his death, Sir Thomas made a will disinheriting his nephew, but Topcliffe removed it from his cell and destroyed it. In the end, although young Thomas got his hands on some of the Fitzherbert estates, Topcliffe established himself at Padley, which he described as 'a delightful solitary place'. He remained there, quarrelling with the tenants and suspecting Lord Shrewsbury of intriguing to kick him out again, until his death in 1604, when Thomas's younger brother Anthony recovered Padley for the Fitzherberts.

Fig. 23 Padley: Interior of surviving block.

Any surviving hide could therefore be dated to before 1588 or after 1604. Of three sides of the courtyard, only foundations remain, but the thirteenth-century block which formed the gatehouse and chapel is still standing and was rescued in 1933 from use as a cowshed. There is a hammer-beam roof with angels and shields; the medieval altar-top has been restored to use; and at the north-east corner is a blocked doorway to the now-vanished east wing, which almost certainly marks the position of the medieval priest's chamber. On the south side are two large buttresses which also served as chimneys, and it is said that one of them contained the hide in which Garlick and Ludlam were found. There is no contemporary evidence for this, and it is doubtful whether any discovered hiding-place would have survived Topcliffe's tenure. But if the traditional site is genuine, this was another hide of the 1580s in a projection on the outside of the building. The significance of Padley is not in any hiding-places but in the date and consequences of the executions.

Between April 1587 and July 1588 only two priests had been executed. But Garlick, Ludlam and Richard Simpson (who was executed with them) were the first of twenty-one priests, nine laymen and one woman to be hanged during the next three months. The motive for these executions was to discourage any Catholic support for the Spanish Armada, which was sighted off the Scillies on 19 July. On the night of 28 July it was driven out of Calais Roads by fire-ships and sustained heavy damage from a tempest. By 2 August, running before the wind, it was as far north as the Firth of Forth, and Admiral Lord Howard was satisfied that there was no longer any possibility of a landing. But there was still the Duke of Parma with his troops and barges at Dunkirk, and it was not until September that reports of Spanish ships wrecked on the west coast of Ireland showed conclusively that the Armada was no longer an effective fighting force. From the Privy Council's point of view, the executions were a necessary precaution.

Since, however, none of the thirty-one victims was actually sentenced for treasonable activities on behalf of Spain but merely for being or harbouring priests, any propaganda success would depend on convincing the public and, in particular, gentry with latent Catholic sympathies, that all seminary priests were political agents in disguise.

Lord Burghley had attempted to make this identification by means of the 'Bloody Question' – that is, if the Pope commanded you to support an invading army, whose side would you be on? But the Crown lawyers, Recorder Fleetwood and Solicitor-General Egerton, ruled firmly that if suspects refused to answer this question, that in itself was no crime. So the executions had to take place under the Act of 1585. Even Fleetwood was repelled by the case of Margaret Ward, the one female victim, and according to Garnet he successfully interceded with the Queen for reprieves for some others who had been condemned. Fleetwood was an active pursuer of Papists, but he stood firm for the principles of the Common Law. If he thought the verdicts rigged, it is likely that the same conclusion was reached by many others. When Southwell rode round England that winter, he found secret Catholics even in the households of Protestant sheriffs and, as already mentioned, that people who before this would not even speak to a priest were now pressing him to come and stay with them. He also reported that during the executions of 28 and 30 August in London (of which he was an eyewitness), people were arrested for shouting out in sympathy. The violence was excessive, and there was a reaction.

So the arrest of Garlick and Ludlam at Padley on 12 July 1588 was perhaps a greater service to their cause than fifty years of ministry in the moorlands would have been. But that argument could hardly be applied to every single priest. The events of the Armada summer, apart from creating a backlash in favour of Catholicism, must have made it clear once and for all that there was a need for more and better hiding-places. It was at this time that Nicholas Owen became Garnet's servant.

3

John Gerard in East Anglia 1588-1594

1

At the first watch on the night of Friday 28 October 1588, 'whilst it rained a good pace', a boat put off from a French ship anchored off Happisburgh, between Great Yarmouth and Cromer. Two men splashed ashore, the boat shoved off and the ship weighed anchor. After a sleepless night in a wood, talking in whispers for fear of rousing the dogs at a nearby farm, the two men parted at dawn. One followed the shore north-west to Mundesley, where he fell in with a party of sailors on their way to London. The other struck out across country to the south, asking the occasional labourers whom he met whether they had seen a stray hawk or heard the sound of its bell. Not surprisingly, none of them had, but they were sympathetic enough, and by evening, although soaked and hungry, John Gerard was eight or ten miles inland without being stopped and questioned. At Stalham or Sloley, he put up for the night at the inn. The people, he records, were very agreeable, especially when he offered to buy one of the horses from the stables. Early on Sunday, mounted and in dry clothes, he took the road to Norwich.

The newly ordained Jesuit had just turned twenty-four. His father, Sir Thomas Gerard of Bryn, near Wigan, was a cousin of Sir Gilbert Gerard, the Attorney-General, and had been Sheriff of Lancashire in 1558. But he had also spent two years in the Tower for scheming to rescue Mary Queen of Scots from Tutbury Castle in Staffordshire, and in October 1588 he had just been released after another two years in prison for supposed complicity in the Babington Plot. John himself had been through an interrupted and adventurous education at Oxford, Douai, Paris and Rheims, as well as spending a year in the Marshalsea Prison. In the summer of 1586 he had gone to the English College in Rome, where he was ordained in July 1588 and admitted to the Jesuits on 15 August, together with Edward Oldcorne, the priest who landed with him. In the next two and a half months they travelled the 1,200 miles from Rome to Norfolk, via Basle, Lorraine, Rheims, Paris and Eu.

There is a vivid description of Gerard in a 'wanted' notice drawn up by Topcliffe in 1597. It runs:

John Gerrard the Jesuit is about 30 years old. Of a good stature somewhat higher than Sir Tho. Layton and upright in his poise and countenance, somewhat staring in his look or eyes, curled hair by nature & blackish & apt not to have much hair of his beard. I think his nose somewhat wide and turning up, blubbered lips turning outward, especially the over lips most upwards towards the nose curious in speech if he do now continue his custom and in his speech he flowers & smiles much and a faltering or lisping, or doubling of his tongue in his speech.

A later description, of 27 August 1601, says that he was

of stature tall, high-shouldered, especially when his cope is on his back, black-haired and of complexion swarth, hawk-nosed, high-templed, and for the most part attired costly and defensibly in buff leather garnished with gold or silver lace, satin doublet and velvet hose of all colours with cloaks corresponding, and rapiers and daggers gilt or silvered.

It is understandable that some of Gerard's converts found it hard to believe that this richly dressed and well-armed gentleman with his passion for hunting and falconry was really a priest in disguise.

Later on the Sunday, 30 October, in Norwich Cathedral, Gerard was introduced to a recusant named Edward Yelverton, of Grimston near Kings

Fig. 24 *Oxburgh Hall Gatehouse: the hide is entered from the room indicated, but on the side opposite the window. The rectangular turret containing this room houses the garderobes (lavatories) for the gatehouse.*

Lynn. On learning who Gerard was, Yelverton promptly got him a change of clothes and a better horse and took him out to Grimston, where they arrived on the Monday. Gerard had to report to Garnet in London, but before he left, Yelverton made him promise to come back to Grimston. Garnet was delighted to approve this arrangement, and so for 'six or eight months' from December 1588 Gerard was based at Grimston. During this time, he says, Yelverton introduced him 'to the house and circle of nearly every gentleman in Norfolk'.

Among these gentlemen must have been Thomas Bedingfeld of Oxburgh, a dozen miles south of Grimston, whose sister, Nazareth, Yelverton later married. Oxburgh Hall is a fifteenth century moated manor with a magnificent brick gatehouse, and now owned by the National Trust. On the first floor of the gatehouse, over the gateway arch, is a large finely proportioned room with linenfold panelling which has been known since at least 1554 as the King's Room, after Henry VII, who slept there in 1487.

This room has a door to an octagonal room in the north-east corner turret of the gatehouse, which opens onto a small garderobe (latrine) closet in the rectangular turret extending from the east wall of the tower and visible in Fig. 24. The garderobe is brick-vaulted and has a tiled floor. In one corner of it is a recess about the height of an ordinary door which is likely to have been the location of the original garderobe seat. There is no garderobe or

Fig. 25 Hide entrance showing pivot, bolt socket and trapdoor. The use of a pivot (rather than hinges) balances the weight, making the heavy trapdoor easier to operate. The blue marker shows how this view relates to Fig. 26.

seat now however, and the floor is tiled right into the recess.

A section of this tiled floor, (Fig. 25) 760mm long and 480mm wide, swings open on a pivot. This secret entrance is 230mm thick and made of two solid blocks of oak bolted together, while the tiles that camouflage it are held on by a thin iron

Fig. 26 (Left) looking back at the entrance – what looks like a fireplace is the entrance. The dotted line indicates the outside floor level. The blue arrow is in the same location as the one in Fig. 25 and the blue dot as in Fig. 27. (Right) General view of hide interior, with a seat!

frame. Its fit and balance are still perfect. The space beneath it is about 800mm deep, which is enough to allow a person to scramble beneath the back wall of the recess and emerge at the bottom of a hide which is far more solid, secure, and comfortable than anything yet described in this book. The ingenious and unique entrance and the provision of a seat, above which is a plastered-in hole that

Fig. 27 Detail of hide entrance from inside, with bottom half of trapdoor visible at right. Two Owen trademarks are visible here: cut away (chamfered) beam and mortice slots cut for hand grips. Both these features assist entry. The blue spot matches that in Fig. 26.

may have been a feeding point show an able and thoughtful designer.

The brickwork at the rear of the vaulted recess where the lightbulb in

Fig. 28 is mounted is not bonded into the wall, indicating it was a later insertion. This area is close to the chapel, and there are 19th century descriptions suggesting there may have been a second entrance here. Access to a hide from a chapel would be more typical (and useful) than via one of the principal bedrooms, and if there was one there, then the present entrance may have been a backup or even an escape route.

Most important of all however, is the siting of the hide at the junction of the tower, the garderobe turret and the gable of the adjoining wing, so that from outside it is completely masked. It is likely that we have here one of the earliest examples of the work of 'Little John' Owen, whom Gerard certainly heard of, and may

Fig. 28 Detail of vaulted recess. There may have been a second entrance and a feeding trap here.

well have met for the first time when he reported to Garnet in London in November 1588.

2

Nicholas Owen was born in Oxford about 1555. His father, Walter Owen, was a carpenter, to whom Nicholas was apprenticed. There were three other sons, all of them active in different ways, in the Catholic underground movement. Henry became a printer and later set up a press in the White Lion prison in London while he was detained there. John was a scholar of Corpus Christi College and subsequently a Fellow of Trinity. In July 1583, he and the fourth brother, another Walter, went abroad to the seminary at Rheims. Walter eventually died in 1591 at the college at Valladolid, but John returned to England as a priest in October 1584. Five months later, he was captured and banished. In 1586 he returned to England again and only a month later was again arrested. Although he recanted in 1588, he and Henry were both still in prison in 1596. But in the next few years Henry was running an illicit press in Northamptonshire, and he was still at work in 1616. The Owens are a useful reminder that recusancy was not confined to the gentry.

Nicholas himself was imprisoned in 1581 for denying that Campion was guilty of treason. In 1588 he became Garnet's servant. It is not known how they met, but there are several likely conjectures. Garnet, like Henry Owen, had been apprenticed as a printer and retained contacts within the trade. Security at the Marshalsea, where John Owen was imprisoned from 1586 to 1588, was notoriously lax: Mass was said in prisoners' cells, and a search in 1584, when John Gerard was confined there, had led to the discovery of enough books and altar-plate to fill a cart. It would have been easy for Garnet to make contact with John Owen there. Or he may have come across the family in Oxford itself. William Weston was there during the last week of July 1586 (the week after the Harleyford conference and the week before his arrest), and as a young man he had been at Christ Church for six years from 1564 to 1570. Many other seminary priests had been at Oxford (many fewer at Cambridge) before going on to Rheims or Rome. In any of these ways, Garnet could have become aware of Owen's skill as a carpenter and of the other qualities of character that made him ideally suited for this peculiar employment.

However that may be, Owen was employed by Garnet for nearly eighteen years, from 1588 until they were both arrested at Hindlip in January 1606 in the aftermath of the Gunpowder Plot. In his *Narrative of the Gunpowder Plot*, Gerard described Owen and explained the value of his work:

> This man did for seventeen or eighteen years continually attend upon Fr Garnet and assist him in many occasions. But his chief employment was in making of secret places to hide priests and church stuff from the fury of searches. In which kind he was so skilful, both to devise and frame the places in the best manner, and his help therein desired in so many places, that I verily think no man can be said to have done more good of all those that laboured in the English vineyard. For, first, he was the immediate occasion of saving the lives of many hundreds of persons both ecclesiastical and secular, and of the estates also of those seculars which had been lost and forfeited many times over if the priests had been taken in their houses. Of which some have escaped not once but many times in several searches that have come to the same house; and sometimes five or six priests together at the same time. Myself have been one of the seven that have escaped that danger at one time in a secret place of his making. How many priests, then, may we think this man did save by his endeavours in the space of seventeen years, having laboured in all shires and in the chiefest Catholic houses of England?

> ... One reason that made him so much desired by Catholics of account, who might have had other workmen enough to make conveyances in their houses, was a known and tried care he had of secrecy, not only from such as would of malice be inquisitive, but from all others to whom it belonged not to know. In which he was so careful that you should never hear him speak of any houses or places where he had made such hides, though sometimes he had occasion to discourse of the fashion of them for the making of others. Yea, he did much strive to make them of several fashions in several places, that one being taken might give no light to the discovery

of another. [After his arrest in 1606] he might have made it almost an impossible thing for priests to escape, knowing the residences of most priests in England, and of all those of the Society, whom he might have taken as partridges in a net, knowing all their secret places which himself had made, and the like conveyances in most of the chief Catholics' houses in England, and the means and manner how all such places were to be found, though made by others.

Several points of great importance occur in this passage. First, it gives dates for the beginning and the end of Owen's work. Before he became Garnet's servant, he could hardly travel round England, introducing himself to 'all shires and the chiefest Catholic houses': if he had tried to do so, he would have been shunned as a spy. But from 1588 his hide-building was directed and continuous.

Secondly, the statement that 'sometimes he had occasion to discourse of the fashion of them for the making of others' can only mean that 'sometimes' Owen acted as consultant designer for hides which others constructed: in Gerard's distinction, he devised them but did not frame them. While, as will appear, it is possible to identify some of Owen's trademarks, some hides which have them may have been the work of his 'studio'. This point must also be borne in mind in any estimates of how many hides Owen was responsible for altogether.

Thirdly, Gerard's statement that Owen knew the residences of *all* the Jesuits in England, 'whom he might have taken as partridges in a net, knowing *all* their secret places which himself had made', gives an essential clue for a system of dating. Garnet's system was that a Jesuit (or sometimes two Jesuits) would move into a certain house in a county and, working from that, establish other centres in the surrounding countryside to which incoming priests, secular* or Jesuit, could be directed. Gerard's *Autobiography* is invaluable here, for it records at first hand and in vivid detail how the scheme worked. Now it is usually possible to find out when the first Jesuit centre was established in a given region, and where it was. Therefore, for many houses one can give a date soon after which Owen would have been building hides there; though that is not the same as saying that all the hides in that house (or any, that survive) are his.

This hypothesis is confirmed by the curiously patchy distribution of hides. Hide-clusters do not coincide, as might be expected, with strongly Catholic regions; nor, as might be expected, with strongly Protestant ones. What they do coincide with is the work of Garnet and his colleagues between 1586 and 1606. Even allowing for subsequent demolitions, especially in

---

* "secular" in this context means a priest who is (unlike Jesuits, Franciscans, etc.) not a member of a religious order. It can also be used (as on p44) to mean anyone who was not a priest and in the 21st century usually means "non-religious".

industrial areas, no other hypothesis will explain why, for instance, there are so many hides in Worcestershire and Warwickshire and so few in Staffordshire, which was just as strongly recusant but was not served by Jesuits until about 1613. Fourthly, there is Gerard's statement that Owen 'did much strive to make [his hides] of several fashions in several places, that one being taken might give no light to the discovery of another'. This commendation of what seems obvious common sense is an implicit criticism of the practice of some other hide builders: it enables us to rule out as Owen's work that very common form of hide, the hole-under-the-garderobe, and (less confidently) that less common but still widespread form, the lath-and-plaster hutch-in-the-roof, as at Ufton.

While it is obviously more difficult to search an Elizabethan roof than to take up the floorboards of a garderobe, the fact remains that roof hides were a common and known form. The Earl of Salisbury's instructions for the search of Hindlip in 1606 include the sentence: 'If there be a loft towards the roof of the house, in which there appears no entrance out of any other place or lodging, it must of necessity be opened and looked into, for these be ordinary places of lurking'. On the other hand, in a sufficiently large and complicated roof it was possible to foil the searchers even when they know what to look for, as was shown at Colditz in 1944; and in the London houses which Gerard mentions, on restricted sites and probably built mainly of timber-and-plaster partitioning, Owen would not have so much choice of position as in a country manor-house. It must be remembered that he was usually obliged to make use of some existing feature of the house, not to design a house to hold his hiding-places. Another reason for thinking that Owen avoided holes-under-the-garderobe is Gerard's observation that the searchers used to 'measure the walls of the house and go round about the house on the outside to see if one part do answer to another, in hope to find some void part left hollow, wherein a man may be hid'. Since holes-under-the-garderobe are in projections on the outside, they are easily located in this way; and the double hide at Coughton (p29) only produces an even more conspicuous stretch of blank wall. It is significant that at Oxburgh this fault was completely avoided.

3

Gerard remained at Grimston until midsummer 1589. During his six or eight months there he reconciled between twenty-five and thirty Norfolk gentry and 'a large number of servants and poorer people'. Among these converts were Richard Cornwallis of Coxford and Yelverton's brother-in-law Sir Philip Wodehouse of Kimberley, who made his confession to Gerard in the library there. Michael Walpole of Anmer, whose brother Henry had become a Jesuit after witnessing Campion's execution and was later executed himself, acted as Gerard's servant on his journeys. In the next few years, he, his brother Christopher, their cousin Edward Walpole of Houghton and Richard Cornwallis all followed Henry Walpole out to Rome. According to the seventeenth-century Jesuit historian Bartoli, the now-demolished Anmer Hall, three miles east of Sandringham, already had a 'reliable hiding-place' as early as 1582; and it is a fair guess that others were added by Nicholas Owen.

Breccles Hall, an Elizabethan house of brick five miles west of Attleborough, was the home of Sir Philip Wodehouse's cousin Francis. At the time of the Queen's progress through Suffolk and Norfolk in the summer of 1578, Francis Wodehouse had reluctantly conformed and gone to church. He later described to William Weston the anguish that this decision caused him, 'like a raging furnace within his bowels'. He rapidly returned to his former recusancy, spent the next four years in gaol at Norwich and in 1599 was obliged to sell Breccles. In 1598 orders were given for the house to be searched, because on 19 March there was to be a meeting there 'of divers and sundry recusant Papists with certain lewd and traitorous Popish priests; also to search there for seditious books and writings and for superstitious and Popish vestures, garments, books, superaltares*, pyxes, crosses, chalices, paxes, beads and other Popish things'.

A *Country Life* article in 1909 mentioned a hiding-place in a chimney at Breccles, entered from the attic above. This is not known to the present owner, but a report of about 1598 gives an excellent description of a hole-under-the-garderobe there:

> In Breccles House, where Mr Woodhouse dwelleth, there is a chamber over the boltings house, whereto there is a way by a door which is in the floor of a privy house. Which door is covered with mats and is so close that it cannot easily be found out; and, the door being opened, there standeth a ladder to go down into a close chamber, and no other way unto it. There are also many secret places about the gallery of the house at Breccles, where they used and do use (as it is thought) the Mass. Great company often resort thither very late in the night, and great provision made for them two or three days together and depart away in the night.

There is a remarkably ingenious place at Snore Hall, three miles south of Downham Market. This is a late fifteenth-century brick building with a great central chimneystack inserted in the sixteenth century. The hiding-place is next to this stack and is entered from the attics, under the slope of the roof. The entrance is now only a simple hole in the floor, but this is said to have been covered by a mock chimney, removed in 1903 during the repairs which led to the find. From here a narrow shaft, tucked away beside the stair-

---

* A superaltare (Latin 'over-altar') was a small rectangle of stone incised with five crosses and used to convert an ordinary table into an altar. Itinerant missioners took light ones of slate on their journeys.

well, descends about 2.7m to a chamber measuring 1.5m by 1.7m but only 1.2m high. This chamber is partly concealed in the thickness of a wall and partly under the stairs. It can now be entered by lifting a shelf or ledge at the side of the stairs, but though this would have made a convenient exit into the first floor, it seems to be a later alteration made so that the hide could be seen more easily.

The floorboards of this chamber can be lifted, and beneath is an inner hide of the same width but only 900mm high. Here a small hole had been made in the wall to provide a spy-hole or feeding trap, as at Oxburgh. It looks into the parlour on the ground floor, where it appears as a small hole about 75mm square over the door. It was perhaps covered by a movable panel.

This hide is comparable to that at Coughton, with the important difference that it is in the centre of the house, not on an outside wall. Edmund Skipwith, who inherited Snore from his father William in 1588, is not known to have been a recusant himself. But on Twelfth Night 1598 he married Anne Guybon or Gibbon of Kings Lynn, whose father, William Guybon, certainly was a recusant. Guybon's name first occurs in a return sent to the Privy Council in 1577 by the Bishop of Norwich. During the royal progress of 1578 the opportunity was taken to arrest a dozen or so recusant gentry who had come to welcome the Queen and demonstrate their loyalty. One was Edward Rookwood of Euston in Suffolk, under whose roof the Queen had spent the night of 10 August; another was William Guybon. A note in the Cecil Papers dated 22 August 1578 records what happened to them. Some were committed to gaol in Norwich. Others were bound over at £200 apiece to confer with the Bishop and not leave Norwich without his licence. Sir Henry Bedingfeld of Oxburgh, William Guybon and two others failed to appear, and the Sheriff was commanded to commit them also if they failed to answer a second summons. The priest-hole at Snore Hall is good evidence that, even if Edmund Skipwith was a Church Papist, his wife had inherited the convictions of her father. It is no surprise to find that their daughter Anne Skipwith married a grandson of Sir Henry Bedingfeld.

In the middle of 1589, Gerard was approached by Henry Drury of Lawshall in Suffolk, whose sister Bridget had married Edward Yelverton's half-brother Henry. Drury maintained a priest, William Hanse, and had been imprisoned in 1587, when he was described as 'a most obstinate receiver of priests and suspected persons, who refuseth to be conversant with any preacher'. In 1594 he sold Lawshall and went to Antwerp to become a Jesuit lay-brother. He now, in 1589, proposed that Gerard should come to live at Lawshall, six miles south-east of Bury St Edmunds. Realising that he was becoming dangerously well known in Norfolk, Gerard agreed, and, having consulted Garnet and arranged for a successor, he moved to Lawshall, which was to be his base until the spring of 1591.

It is not easy to identify any hides which can be associated with Gerard's two years in Suffolk. Part of Lawshall itself still stands, an early Tudor building of diapered brickwork, but no hiding-places are known there. A mile away is Coldham Hall, the home of Drury's brother-in-law Robert Rookwood, whose son Ambrose was one of the Gunpowder Plotters. It is an H-shaped house of red brick dating from 1574. Gerard described it as 'a continual receptacle for priests and a place wherein many other Catholics did often find great spiritual comfort, the house being a very fair great house and his living very sufficient'. One of the priests at Coldham was Garnet's nephew Thomas Garnet alias Rookwood, who was arrested on his way there in 1608 and executed at Tyburn. But the only hide that survives today is a rather obvious one over the porch, entered through a trapdoor and with the remains of a boarded floor.

Five miles south of Lawshall is Melford Hall, which now belongs to the National Trust. This contains a void immediately under the threshold of the room in which the Queen slept during her progress of 1578, but the picturesque notion of Her Majesty walking across the trapdoor of a priest hole is sadly unfounded: the space was created when the east wall of the Blue Drawing Room was squared up for the Georgian panelling to be fitted in the 1740s. John Thorpe's plan of about 1606 shows that it did not exist then. All the same, Sir William Cordell, who built Melford soon after 1554 and died in 1581, was a patron of recusants, despite being Master of the Rolls. When Henry Russell, principal of Gloucester Hall, Oxford, was obliged to resign in 1580, Cordell offered him the post of steward at Melford, 'wherein his only pains shall be to control and oversee the clerk of my kitchen and my other officers that have charge of my house'. Russell had been a friend of Edmund Campion since they had gone to St John's College together in 1555, and when Campion was arrested at Lyford, Russell and two other dons from Gloucester Hall were among the congregation there. More will be said of him later, in Worcestershire.

Four miles north-west of Bury St Edmunds is Hengrave Hall, an imposing quadrangular mansion of pale-yellow brick and stone with a spectacular gatehouse. Both Sir Thomas and Lady Kitson were recusants by 1588, and a Jesuit, William Wright, was arrested there in June 1607 after eight months as chaplain. Two and a half months later he escaped from the White Lion prison in London and spent the next twelve years working in Leicestershire. There were undoubtedly hides at Hengrave but, as at Lawshall, none is known today.

In the spring of 1591 Gerard moved again, this time to Braddocks, between Thaxted and Saffron Walden in Essex. This was the home of William Wiseman, who had inherited it in 1585 and laid out a deer-park round it. The household consisted of himself, his wife Jane (Huddleston) , their daughters Dorothy and Winifred, and his widowed mother Jane (Vaughan). All four of his sisters became nuns on the Continent and two of his brothers joined the Jesuits in Rome under Gerard's influence. William Wiseman himself had been in trouble for hearing Mass in 1586 and he maintained an old Marian priest named Richard Jackson, but until he met Gerard at Lawshall he had exercised a certain discretion about his religion. Now, however, he put Braddocks at Gerard's disposal and it rapidly became a vigorous centre of recusancy. For safety, Protestant servants were replaced by Catholics, but the Wisemans made the mistake of trusting to some extent a Protestant named John Frank who had attended Thomas Wiseman before he went abroad. Gerard often lodged at Frank's house in Lincoln's Inn and 'saw no reason for distrusting a person whom everyone else trusted'. 'But I was careful', he adds, 'not to let him see me acting as a priest or even dressed in a way that would give him grounds for saying I was one'. Frank, however, had guessed the truth from the deference with which Gerard was treated at Braddocks, and he informed the Government of his suspicions.

For a time nothing happened. Frank's apparently friendly visits to Braddocks became more frequent, though he could do nothing beyond mark the comings and goings of mysterious strangers whose movements were curiously difficult to keep track of. But after a while he was able to report sufficient suspicious circumstances to arouse official interest, and in the autumn of 1592 the house was raided.

According to the report of the search, 'three horsemen's armours, seven other armours, two muskets and two culvers, bows and arrows, a jack and a suit of mail with all things complete to the said armours were in a vault behind a door and finely kept'. Possession of such equipment was, of course, perfectly legal, and the phrase 'behind a door' probably only means that it was locked up, not that it was kept in a hiding-place. It may have been stored there by Robert Wiseman, the fourth brother, who was an officer in the Flemish wars. But the searchers also found Richard Jackson in a priest hole behind a false wall. Hidden with him were the vestments and Mass furniture and much incriminating correspondence from priests, many of whom were by then in gaol. There is no mention of Gerard, who seems to have been away in Lancashire at the time.

A month or two later, Nicholas Owen was called in to build another hiding-place and was duly noted by John Frank, who remembered him when he made his full report in May 1594.

> Item, he saith that Nicholas Owen, who was taken in bed with Mr Gerard the Jesuit, was at Mr Wiseman's house at Christmas was twelve months and called by the name of Little John and Little Michael, and the cloak that he wore was Mr Wiseman's cloak a year past, and was of sad green cloth with sleeves, caped with tawny velvet and little gold strips turning on the cape.

Two-thirds of Braddocks has been pulled down, but the remaining wing still contains the hide that Owen built, in almost perfect condition. It is entered from the secret chapel, the usual long low room at the top of the house. Here Owen took up the tiles from the fireplace and constructed a false hearth. Under this he excavated a space in the solid brickwork of the chimneystack. The space is within the wall of the great chamber below and

Fig. 29 Braddocks: reconstructed entrance (originally a simple trapdoor) and hide below.

is situated high up and slightly to the left of the Renaissance fireplace (Fig. 30). It was separated from this room only by lath-and-plaster covered with panelling (Fig. 33). The finished hole is 600mm wide, 1.57m long and 1.68m tall at its highest point. At the end under the hearth, there are two brick steps, which could be used for a seat, and to one side a space that may have been an earth closet.

Altogether, more than five cubic metres of brickwork was quarried out and secretly disposed of. The traditional idea of how this was done is that the hide was quarried from above, but it may have been

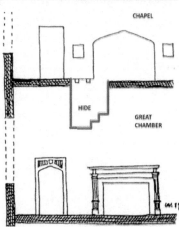

Fig. 30 Hide Location. The searchers stripped the plaster and panelling from the walls of the lower room – except directly in front of the hide.

done from the lower room. Upon the pretext of repairing some fictional problem with the chimney brickwork, (or even something as simple as redecorating the room), scaffolding could have been set up in the great chamber below. Owen could then have stripped the plaster at the top of the wall and removed the bricks to create the hole before reinstating the plasterwork. Some evidence for this is that from within the hide it can be seen (Fig. 33) that

Fig. 31 (Above) view down into the hide and (Right) looking out from within. The beam at the entrance has been cut away to ease entry. This is a feature of several Owen hides, including at Oxburgh (Fig. 27) and Harvington.

the vertical battens to which the laths and plaster are attached now sit inside the hide, not in front of it. It is impossible to be sure now, as several of them have been reused at some time – possibly when the Great Chamber overmantel was removed, a change which would have necessitated replastering the wall. In any case, it would have been very difficult for Owen to remove all the bricks from behind the plaster without disturbing it.

Moreover, creating this space from outside, as a kind of wall cupboard, would have been safer and easier than mining bricks by candlelight from within the confined space of the hide itself.

At the end furthest from the entrance, the hide is close to the stairs up to the chapel, and while there is a narrow extension in that direction, there is no evidence of a second entrance.

This hide is the Rosetta Stone of this book: it is the only certainly identifiable surviving hide for which we have a contemporary attribution (Gerard's) to Owen, the only one for which we have both a first-hand description of its use and the spy's report which led to the search, and the only one of Owen's for which there is documentary

Fig. 33 *Inside the hide, view of rear of Great Chamber wall. This thin lath and plaster wall was all that stood between Gerard and discovery.*

Fig. 32 *Structure inside hide that may have been an earth closet.*

evidence of its date (Christmas 1592). At some point between the search and the mid-19th century the hearth floor was bricked over and later the fireplace itself was bricked up and the exact location of the hide forgotten until in 1932, Granville Squiers, following the hints in Gerard's autobiography, relocated and reopened it. Gerard's account of the search says he got into the hide by "raising part of the floor under the grate", so the sliding hearth stone which he built for it is a somewhat romantic gloss, but everything else about the hide is original.

4

Richard Jackson's arrest at Braddocks in 1592 was only the beginning. On 26 December 1593, the Wisemans' dower-house of Bullocks at Northend was raided by the pursuivants John Worsley and William Newell, (whom we have already met retrieving Papist books from Thomas Lygon's privy). Mrs Wiseman took refuge with Lady Penelope Rich at Leighs Priory. The pursuivants found preparations for Mass, but not the priest, 'a tall man with a waxen beard' named Brewster, 'who was hid in a privy place in a chimney in a chamber'. The search cannot have taken more than a single day, for at five o'clock on 27 December William Suffield, a steward of William Wiseman, came to fetch Brewster and take him back to Braddocks. On 12 January, Mrs Wiseman senior was indicted at Essex Assizes for attending a Mass said by Richard Jackson and was ordered to be taken up to London.

She was imprisoned in the Gatehouse, where she passed her time embroidering vestments. Later, at Topcliffe's instigation, she was indicted on the much more serious charge of 'receiving, comforting, helping and maintaining priests'. The evidence for this was that she had applied a cere-cloth to the inflamed leg of a Franciscan, John Jones, who was subsequently executed, though he had come to her cell in disguise, and she did not know that he was a priest. Nevertheless, she was found guilty and, like Margaret Clitherow, sentenced to be pressed to death. But the Queen, on hearing how 'for so small a matter she should have been put to death, rebuked the Justices of cruelty and said she should not die'. Mrs Wiseman was therefore kept in prison for the next ten years until the accession of James I, when she was released, whereupon she returned to Northend and resumed her interrupted harbouring of priests there.

Meanwhile, John Frank was still trying to have Gerard arrested. On 15 March 1594 he was responsible for a raid on a house in Golding Lane, Holborn, which Wiseman had recently rented for Gerard's use when he was in London. There had not been time to build any hides there, and Gerard's servant Richard Fulwood was caught in a dark corner. But Gerard himself had gone to visit Garnet at a house four or five miles away, and the latter, with a strong premonition of danger, had insisted that he must not go back that night. Next day, Mr Wiseman arrived at Golding Lane and was promptly arrested. He was taken to the Counter in Wood Street, where only Frank was allowed access to him. Fulwood was put in solitary confinement in the Bridewell and threatened with torture. On hearing the news, Gerard returned to Braddocks to confer with Mrs Wiseman and to prepare for Holy Week, which that year fell in the last week of March. During Holy Week, Frank arrived from London with letters from Wiseman to his wife and from Fulwood to Gerard. Gerard read his out to Mrs Wiseman and added that he wished he could endure some of Fulwood's sufferings. After his arrest he was questioned about this remark – a slip on the part of the examiners which enabled him to identify the traitor. But for the time being Frank was unsuspected. On his return to London, he made a full report, and Worsley and Newell were given a search warrant for two local Justices. On Easter Sunday Frank returned to Braddocks with another letter to give him an excuse for keeping an eye on Gerard and the Wisemans.

On Easter Monday, 1 April, while it was still dark, the household were preparing for Mass when suddenly they heard the sound of galloping hooves. The next moment, the house was surrounded. Certain of his prey but still anxious to conceal his treachery, Frank ran downstairs, where he made a great show of resisting the intruders. Upstairs, the altar was stripped, the hiding-places opened, and all Gerard's books and papers thrown in. For his own refuge he wanted to use a 'safe and well-built place' near the great chamber: it was further away from the chapel, there was more chance of overhearing the searchers' conversation from it, and it was provisioned with a bottle of wine, biscuits and other food that would keep. Mrs Wiseman, however, insisted that he should use the Owen hide under the chapel hearth, where he and the Massing stuff could be packed away more quickly. This hide had not been provisioned and, as the pursuivants battered at the doors below, she hastily passed in a couple of biscuits and a little quince jelly. There was no time to find anything else but she expected the search to last no more than a day. As it was, she had barely replaced the logs on the false hearth before the doors gave way and the searchers fanned out through the house.

Their first move was to lock Mrs Wiseman up in her own room with her daughters, and the Catholic servants in different places in the same part of the house. Then they set to work, methodically and ruthlessly. Using candles in dark corners, they lifted the tiles, measured the walls, knocked on walls and floors, and smashed open anything that sounded hollow. They knew that Gerard was in the house, and they meant to have him. For four days, Gerard himself lay sleepless and starving in the dark and cramped hiding place, expecting discovery at any moment. Through the plaster and panelling he could hear anything said in the great chamber, and through the false hearth above him he could listen to the searchers in the chapel. Here he describes an incident of the second day's search:

> They had been in the room above and had examined the fireplace through which I had got into my hole. With the help of a ladder they climbed into the flue and sounded it with a hammer, and I heard one of them saying to another: 'There might conceivably be room for a person to get down here into the wall of the chimney below if this grate was raised.' 'Hardly', said the other, whose voice I recognised .... 'But there might easily be an entrance at the back of the chimney'. As soon as he had said this, he gave the place a kick. I was afraid he would notice the hollow sound of the hole in which I was hiding.

Mrs Wiseman spent her time in prayer and fasting, refusing all food, wishing to share the priest's sufferings and to gauge how long he might hold out. By the end of the search she was so haggard that Gerard doubted whether he would have recognised her, but for her voice and dress.

After two days, however, the magistrates concluded that Gerard could not be in the house and must have left on the Sunday. That evening they departed, leaving Worsley and Newell to take Mrs Wiseman and the Catholic servants up to London for interrogation. Frank and the other Protestant servants were to remain at Braddocks to report anything suspicious. Knowing that Gerard would rather starve to death between two walls than come out while it would incriminate her, Mrs Wiseman decided to take a calculated risk. She instructed Frank to wait until the pursuivants and their prisoners were well away, and then to go to the great chamber and call Gerard, who would answer from behind the panelling and plaster. Immediately, Frank divulged what she had told him, and at dawn on the Wednesday the magistrates returned.

The measurements and soundings were all taken again with extreme care, especially in the great chamber, but nothing at all was found throughout this third day. The searchers decided, therefore, that on the fourth day they would strip the panelling and plaster from the Chamber. Certain of the rough location of the hiding-place, they set guards in all the adjoining rooms, in case Gerard tried to escape that night. He heard the password given and would have attempted to get away by using it, but there were two guards in the chapel, who would have seen him emerge.

That night, the two men felt cold during their vigil and, finding logs ready in the fireplace, they set them ablaze. Before long, the bricks, which (as at Oxburgh) were only camouflage on a wooden trapdoor, worked loose, and a shower of sparks fell through. Gerard was obliged to leave his seat and crouch at the back of the hole to avoid the hot embers*. The guards noticed the loosened bricks and, probing the cracks with a stick, found that the bottom of the hearth was made of wood. Gerard heard them remark that this was odd and expected them to break the place open there and then, but in the end they decided to wait for daylight.

They must have forgotten all about it while asleep and when called down next morning to resume the search in the great chamber cannot even have glanced at the hearth, for the fire had burned a hole in the trapdoor, through which Gerard could have been seen plainly by anyone who came into the chapel. Purely by luck, no one did, all day.

---

*When Granville Squiers rediscovered the hide, he found some tiny fragments of wood-ash on the floor of the hide, the remains of those very embers. They are now at Stonyhurst, an odd and evocative piece of evidence.

All the fourth day was spent in stripping the rooms below. The searchers found the hiding-place which Gerard had originally wanted to use, and he heard their gleeful shouts as they broke into it, but all that they found there was the store of provisions. The location of this hide is still unknown, but it was close enough to the great chamber for the searchers to suspect it was the place mentioned to Frank by Mrs Wiseman, and that Gerard must have escaped after all. Nevertheless, they stuck to their original plan of stripping the great chamber.

This is 4.3m high and had a frieze of panelling at the top, below which the plastered walls were hung with tapestries. With the help of a carpenter, the pursuivants began work close to the ceiling on the right-hand side of the elaborately carved and inlaid overmantel behind which Gerard lurked. They continued right round the chamber, removing the plaster back to the brickwork, until they came again to the overmantel. There, despairing of finding Gerard, they gave up. They knew there were two flues in the stack; that in the chapel had been checked two days before and there did not seem to be enough spare space in the brickwork to justify the considerable labour of removing the overmantel. Convinced that Gerard was not in the house, the party withdrew without taking any prisoners.

The doors were barred, and Gerard, like Lazarus, was called out after four days from what would indeed have been his tomb if the search had lasted much longer. Almost immediately, he encountered the still-unsuspected John Frank, whose acting abilities must have been strained to the utmost to conceal his annoyance. But even he knew that it was pointless to recall the magistrates for a second time. Pausing only for a meal and a short rest, Gerard left Braddocks for a house nearby, where he lay low for a fortnight and then made his way to London, where he stayed in complete safety with the Countess of Arundel at Arundel House.

Safe as it was, however, Arundel House was inconvenient, as the Countess had thought more than seven years before when Southwell first came to live there. Gerard began to look for a lodging of his own and wrote to the Wisemans. This proved his undoing, for the reply was brought by John Frank, who lost no time in informing the authorities. At midnight on 23 April, Gerard and Nicholas Owen were arrested at a house in Holborn by Worsley and Newell. Two days later, Gerard was examined by Sir Thomas Egerton, the Solicitor-General already mentioned with Recorder Fleetwood in the last chapter, after which he was committed to the Counter in the Poultry, 'a very evil prison', according to Garnet, 'and without comfort'.

His capture, just three weeks later, might suggest that his ordeal at Braddocks was all for nothing. However, he points out himself that his capture at Braddocks could have led to the Wisemans' executions whereas his arrest in a rented house implicated no-one else.

Some wealthy Catholics contrived to purchase the release of Owen, whose importance was not yet known to the Government, and after three months and some bribery Gerard was moved from the Counter to the Clink – a change which he called a translation from Purgatory to Paradise – where we must leave him until Chapter 8.

It seems likely that winter 1592-3, the date of the construction of the Braddocks hide, was also the date of what is undoubtedly the finest hiding-place in the country, on account both of its ingenious design and construction and of its excellent preservation.

Fig. 34 Sawston Hall from the North-West. The location of one of the two early hides is indicated in the turret on the right of the picture. The other is in the corresponding turret on the other side of the house, but one storey higher up.

Sawston Hall, seven miles from Cambridge and a dozen from Braddocks, is a quadrangular building of stone, begun in the 1550s. It was the home of Henry Huddleston, whose sister was Mrs Wiseman of Braddocks. Henry had returned to Catholicism under Gerard's influence earlier in 1592 but the family had been reported for recusancy as early as 1577, and there are two early holes-under-the-garderobe, still with their boarded floors, in parts of the house completed by Sir Edmund Huddleston in 1584. As at Braddocks, Gerard's influence led to far more zeal and enthusiasm: he records that Henry and Dorothy Huddleston always had at least one Jesuit in the house, sometimes two or three. It is reasonable, then, to suppose that Henry's conversion in 1592 was the occasion for the building of the third hide, and that Owen may have moved direct from Braddocks to Sawston.

On the upper floor of the south block is a beautifully panelled Long Gallery, with large mullioned and transomed windows facing south on to the garden and north into the courtyard. Halfway down the Gallery on the

courtyard side is a door, which opens into a polygonal stone turret (Fig. 35) containing a newel staircase. At the top of this, close to the original chapel, is a small landing (Fig. 36) made of a single layer of oak boards. At the side of it, under the slope of the roof, two of the boards form a trapdoor beneath which is a dark hole in the stone wall on which their south ends rest. It is contrived in the corner, where the circular inside wall of the turret meets the polygonal outside wall and the straight wall of the Long Gallery, leaving a quadrant of what should be solid stone. The hide below is in the thickness of the Gallery wall, behind the panelling over the door to the turret, and though 2.59m long and 1.5m high is only 500mm wide. At each end of the hide there are stone seats, as at Oxburgh and Braddocks, in one of which a latrine has been chiselled. At the latrine end, there is a gap in the mortar of

Fig. 35 The difference between the straight external walls of this tower and the circular plan of its internal staircase created the space for the hide entrance. The hide is in the wall between the turret and the main building.

the outside wall, which provides a little light and fresh air. All the rest of the wall in which the hide is made is masked from the courtyard by the turret. The twist of the staircase and the different levels are exploited brilliantly: most of the underside of trapdoor can be seen from the stairs below, and when standing on the trapdoor you can see between its cracks to the stairs below. To prevent any betraying rattle, the two boards that form the trapdoor are nailed to blocks of wood that fit into hollows gouged out of the joists below. The real thickness of the Gallery wall is not obvious as you go through the doorway to the stairs because it has been tapered back to appear quite

Fig. 36 (Above) hide closed. (Below) View into hide showing earth closet.

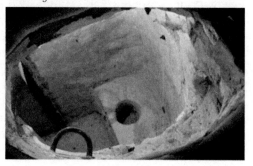

thin immediately above the door.

The contrast between Owen's work and a conventional hole-under-the-garderobe is more striking at Sawston than anywhere else in England. All three hides there are much the same size, all are single, and all were entered through camouflaged trapdoors. Owen was using the same elements as his

predecessors of the 1580s, but his use of them was far more intelligent. The holes-under-the-garderobe are designed in straight lines and in two dimensions. The Gallery hide is by someone who could think in three dimensions and in curves.

Another reason for thinking that this place was built soon after Henry Huddleston's reconciliation in 1592 is that little time was lost when the opportunity arose for stationing a priest. In the same year, Gerard persuaded Mrs Wiseman senior to return to her dower-house, Bullocks, at

Fig. 37 Hide open. The circular stairwell is clearly visible through the gaps between the joists.

Northend, and 'maintain there a priest I had recommended to her'. There she introduced Gerard to her neighbour at Leighs Priory, Lady Penelope Rich - sister of the Earl of Essex, the 'Stella' of Sir Philip Sidney's sonnets, estranged wife of Lord Rich (later Earl of Warwick), and mistress of Lord Mountjoy, with whom she had five children. Only Mountjoy's arguments stopped her from becoming one of Gerard's converts, and in 1606 she was reconciled by another Jesuit on her deathbed. Leighs Priory gatehouse still stands, two miles east of Northend, and even nearer is Felsted, where Nicholas Owen was reported by John Frank to have been at a Mr Emerson's. Another seven miles east of Leighs Priory is Faulkbourne Hall, a stately fifteenth-century building of brick. The owner was Edmund Fortescue, whose wife Isabel was a sister of Henry Huddleston of Sawston and Jane Wiseman of Braddocks. No house is more likely to have contained an unrecorded hide by Nicholas Owen. Only a mile from Faulkbourne is White Notley Hall, which belonged to Lord Vaux of Harrowden. There are probably half a dozen more Owen hides waiting to be found within a ten mile radius of Thaxted.

4

Baddesley Clinton, 1591
Warwickshire and Worcestershire

Fig. 38 Baddesley Clinton, Warwickshire

1

T he hair-raising incident at Braddocks was not John Gerard's first adventure in a priest-hole. Two-and-a-half years previously, he, Garnet, Southwell, Oldcorne and three other priests had all been concealed by the Vaux sisters at a house in Warwickshire 'almost a hundred miles from London'. This was the occasion when Gerard was 'one of the seven that have escaped that danger at one time in a secret place of his [Owen's] making'. As usual, he does not name the house, nor does Garnet, who also wrote an account of the raid, and identifying it is a fascinating exercise in historical detection. It was a custom of the Jesuits to meet twice a year, in spring and autumn, for spiritual renewal and a discussion of their work. This particular meeting lasted for three or four days, ending on Monday, 18 October 1591, the feast of St Luke. The house in Warwickshire had been Garnet's headquarters since 1588 or 1589 and had been used several times before for these conferences. Some information about it is given in the confession of a priest named George Snape, who was arrested in Berkshire about this time:

> Moreover I have heard for a truth, and I do verily persuade myself that it is so indeed, that in Warwickshire dwelleth one of the Lord Vaux his daughters, whose husband's name I marked not, and yet I think I heard him named. She is not far from one Mrs Brookes, a recusant too if I be not deceived. This Mrs Vaux entertaineth commonly a priest or two in her house and is resorted to by divers others, so that sometimes there are to be found in the house at one time five or six priests together. They have very safe and close places of conveyance in the house for them to lurk in, as it should seem, for Mr Hodgkins hath been there divers times and searched the house when there hath been three or four together, and yet could find none of them.

Not long before, Mr Hodgkins the pursuivant had nearly caught William Hopton at Buckland in Berkshire (see p268), and a few days before the conference was due to assemble he turned up at the house in Warwickshire and knocked on the door. Annoyed at being kept waiting while the evidence was concealed and, according to Garnet, drunk as well, he announced that since friends could not be received in a civil fashion, he would return within ten days with others and pull the place apart. There was no time to warn the other Jesuits, who arrived as planned. They decided to take the risk of holding the meeting, but as soon as business was finished, at dinner on the Monday, Garnet urged them to leave as soon as possible, as there were not enough hiding places for them all in the event of a raid. Four of the nine Jesuits present rode off immediately after dinner, leaving the other five and two secular priests who had only arrived that day.

At five o'clock next morning, Southwell was beginning Mass, the other priests were at prayer and the servants were busy with preparations for departure. Suddenly there was a great uproar at the main gate, where four priest-hunters with drawn swords were battering at the doors. Two servants armed with pitchforks came running from the stables and threatened to use them unless the pursuivants moved away. Inside, the altar was stripped, mattresses turned cold side uppermost, and the seven priests stowed away in a hiding-place with their books, vestments, chalices, boots and swords. One of the Vaux sisters, Eleanor Brooksby, was concealed in another hiding-place. Then the pursuivants were admitted and the other sister, Anne Vaux, gave a fine display of aristocratic indignation at being disturbed in this boorish fashion so early in the morning. Possibly they were overawed by the great lady, for Anne Vaux remarked afterwards that, despite much sound and fury, they missed several obvious clues and had no more idea of what they were about than children playing Blind Man's Buff. Breakfast and a bribe gave her a further psychological hold over them, and after four hours they made off without finding anything. After waiting until there was no danger of them doubling back, Anne Vaux released from the den 'not one but many Daniels'.

Where was this house? As already mentioned, it was in Warwickshire, 'almost a hundred miles from London' and run by Eleanor Brooksby and Anne Vaux. Beyond that, it is clear from the accounts of Garnet and Gerard that the hide was big enough for seven men but not for eleven or more; that it was below ground level; and that the floor was covered with water. Gerard complains of standing with his feet in it the whole time. Garnet calls the place a *specus*, a word which in classical Latin can mean either a natural or an artificial cavity, channel or pit. Both the size and the position are very unusual: hides are normally only big enough for one or two men and are sited towards the top of the house so that the priest would not have to run downstairs, towards the searchers, to reach them. Finally, after the search Oldcorne stayed on for a while, as Hindlip in Worcestershire, where he was then living, was 'not far away'.

Two certificates of Warwickshire recusants dating from 1592 mention several times, under Tanworth-in-Arden, a Mrs Elizabeth Brooksby alias Edwards of Leicestershire. Since Edward was the Christian name of Eleanor Brooksby's husband, and she had formerly lived at Shoby in Leicestershire, there can be no doubt that this was Garnet's housekeeper. Tanworth is seventeen miles north-east of Hindlip, an easy day's ride. The Throckmortons owned an estate there called Ladbrook Park, 'in circuit by the pale about two miles, replenished with roes [and] furnished with a great number of timber trees'. But when Thomas Throckmorton sold it in 1603, there was 'no house meet for the habitation of a gentleman' there, and so it seems that the fairly small moated site cannot have contained a house big enough to be the setting of this escape. However, just five miles east of Tanworth-in-Arden is a place which exactly fits the descriptions.

Baddesley Clinton, which now belongs to the National Trust, is a beautiful fifteenth-century moated manor-house, six miles north-west of Warwick and ten miles north of Stratford-upon-Avon. It was originally quadrangular, but now consists of only three blocks: the east, which includes the gatehouse and the Great Parlour; the south, which contains the hall; and the west, which has always contained the kitchen and other offices. The gatehouse and office ranges are of grey sandstone; the hall range was refaced with brickwork during the eighteenth century. Inside, there is fine plasterwork and panelling and a wealth of heraldic stained glass. Much of this dates from the time of Henry Ferrers the antiquary (1549-1633), who was a first cousin of Weston's friends Henry, fifth Lord Windsor (1562-1605), and his brother Edward. The dossier on Baddesley Clinton begins in January 1584, when William Skinner of Rowington, a mile and a half south, had been in trouble for entertaining an old Marian priest named Robert Baker. Thurstan Tubbs, a tanner of Rowington, deposed that he had met Baker or another priest 'with his chalice and a book in his hand going towards Baddesley'. At least three other priests were still working within five miles of Baddesley in 1592. They were Robert Whateley, 'an old Massing priest resorting often' to Henley-in-Arden; Hales, 'a very old Massing priest', resorting commonly to Mrs Brooksby's; and John Appletree, a seminary priest, at Rowington. John Grissold of Rowington, 'a most wilful recusant and a wandering rogue', was in fact one of Garnet's servants, while Thomas Bates of Lapworth, who was Robert Catesby's servant and later one of the Gunpowder conspirators, had brought a son to be christened at Mrs Brooksby's. It is not surprising to find evidence of two hides at Baddesley Clinton.

The first of these, which may be where Eleanor Brooksby sat out the search, is a lath-and-plaster hutch in the roof above a closet off a bedroom

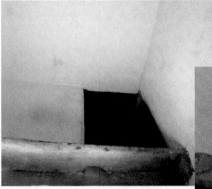

in the gatehouse block. It measures 1.91m by 1.22m and is 1.14m high. This is cramped, but there are two wooden benches,

Fig. 39 View up into Eleanor's hide, showing the gap into the roof space which is probably the original entrance.

and the hide is lined with fine hair-plaster. One section of the plaster is missing, which makes

Fig. 40 One of the two seats in Eleanor's hide

it possible to climb into the roof-space: presumably there was some form of camouflaged plaster door here, like those at Ufton. Although some of the adjoining roof-timbers are modern, the hutch itself is plausible enough as a hide of the 1580s. It is now approached through a hole in the ceiling of the closet below.

The second place is much more intriguing. In the west wing, just above the waterline of the moat (Fig. 41), is a row of loopholes in the stonework at regular intervals of about 1.8m. These loopholes average 430mm high and are splayed through the 600mm thick wall so that although only 58mm wide on the outside they are 300mm wide on the inside. They light a narrow passage, 560mm wide and for most of its length 1.25m high, which runs the full length of this wing and then turns east and runs for 3.7m under the north end of the

Fig. 41 Baddesley Clinton, west elevation showing position of hide and entrance shaft. The central rectangular projection is a later addition and the loopholes behind it are still blocked.

wing. Altogether, there are twelve loopholes, one in the end of the wing and eleven in the west side of it, though only eight can now be seen from outside. At the south end of the wing, the passage terminates in a square hole, just above the water-level. The total length (excluding the brick steps to be mentioned below) is 26m, but there are signs that the passage originally extended further under the now-demolished north wing, and possibly as far as the east wing. Visitors can now look down into the passage through a glass panel in the kitchen floor. Upstairs, in the room (green in Fig. 41) now used as a sacristy next to the chapel, is a modern trapdoor, beneath which is a shaft, 560mm by 1120mm, leading down in the thickness of the stone wall to the passage.

There can be no doubt that this tunnel was originally built as a sewer discharging into the moat, and little doubt that the sacristy shaft was originally a

Fig. 42 (Left) View out of re-opened loophole to moat. (Right) view of inside of one of the two still-blocked loopholes.

garderobe flue. But some curious alterations have been carried out since. 50cm from the south end of the tunnel is a groove or slot, 75mm wide, in the stone walls and roof, at the top of which is jammed a broken slab of stone.

When complete, this slab would have completely blocked the end of the sewer. 12m further along, the entire tunnel from floor to roof has been filled at some time with a plug of brick and stone 500mm thick which is not bonded into the roof or walls. The bottom 600mm of it have been removed, presumably about 1870, when the tunnel was opened again for work on the drains, but traces of stone and mortar on the walls prove that the blocking extended right down to the floor. The only

Fig. 43 Inside the hide: (Left) looking south [to the right of Fig. 41] showing the drain opening to the moat. A plug of masonry near this end which blocked the passage when it was used as a hide has since been removed. (Below) looking north. The vertical partition marks the end of the portion used as a hide and previously extended down to the floor.

way into this isolated 12m section was down the sacristy shaft. Moreover, all the loopholes along the whole tunnel also show signs of having been blocked. Four are still blocked, two of which have been covered over on the outside since the late seventeenth century by a projecting garderobe turret. The other two can be seen from outside to be perfectly camouflaged over in imitation of the surrounding stone. The loopholes were probably created to ventilate the passage in its role as a sewer, and carefully blocked to avoid drawing attention to it as a hide. The fact that there are blocked holes behind the later turret show that the loopholes and their blocking pre-dates that turret. The unblocking was done at the end of the 19th century.

The result of these various alterations was a *specus* or, as Gerard calls it, 'a very cleverly built sort of cave', below ground level; big enough for seven men and their Massing stuff and baggage but not for twice that number; accessible only from the upstairs room next to the chapel; cunningly disguised from outside at least 300 years ago; with a floor that is still covered with pools of water; and in a house already under suspicion of priest-harbouring. Unless evidence is found of another such place nearer to Tanworth-in-Arden, it is difficult to avoid the conclusion that this was the scene of the escape, and that Baddesley was the house at which Gerard was 'one of the seven [who escaped arrest] in a secret place of [Nicholas Owen's] making' (p44). If so, then this hide joins Braddocks as one of only two surviving attested examples of Owen's work and

Fig. 44 View up the shaft from the hide to the underside of the entrance trapdoor.

dateable to between 1588 (when Owen started building) and the 1591 search.

2

On Wednesday 20 October 1591, the day after the search, Gerard and Southwell rode off together, as they had come. It was perhaps the last time that they met. On 7 November, Swithin Wells' house in Holborn was raided during Mass and in the ensuing scuffle Topcliffe was thrown downstairs. Seven people were executed on one day in consequence. In February, Garnet wrote his previously quoted letter to Rome asking for the supply of priests to be halted, since there was nowhere left to hide. The Jesuit meeting at Easter 1592 seems to have been cancelled. On the night of 25 June, Topcliffe arrested Southwell at Uxendon, eight miles north-west of Tyburn.

Topcliffe had laid his plans carefully. Uxendon was the home of the Bellamys, who had sustained priests since the days of Campion and Persons. Their daughter, Anne, was in prison in the Gatehouse where Topcliffe raped her, and then blackmailed her into telling him when Southwell would be at Uxendon. At midnight he was caught there in a hiding-place 'under the tiles'. Topcliffe tortured him ten times in his own house, as he had been authorised to do the previous year, 'because the often exercise of the rack in the Tower was so odious and so much spoken of the people'. But he failed to get the names of any of the houses where Southwell had been harboured, or even the colour of his horses. After a month, at the intercession of his father,

Southwell was moved to the Tower, where Lady Arundel was allowed to send him clean linen, a bible and a copy of the works of St Bernard. Here he remained until his trial and execution in February 1595.

Meanwhile, Edward Oldcorne had stayed on at Baddesley Clinton for a day or two longer. He had been living at Hindlip, three miles north-east of Worcester, since about February 1590. After parting from Gerard that wet morning on the Norfolk coast, he had travelled to London with the sailors whom he met at Mundesley. He found their foul language distressing, but they quite liked him, and at every village they passed through the watch assumed that he was one of them. On arriving in London he made contact with Garnet, with whom he had spent the following year and more at Baddesley Clinton. Early in 1590 he had converted Dorothy Habington, a Protestant who had been mistress of Hindlip since the arrest of her Catholic brothers over the Babington Plot in 1586. Edward Habington was executed,

Fig. 45 Hindlip: view from south-east. This house had eleven hides.

but Thomas was only imprisoned in the Tower, a favour which he may have owed to the fact that he was one of the Queen's godsons. The priest at Hindlip, James Taylor, was also arrested and would remain in prison until the accession of James I in 1603. Garnet was anxious to recover Hindlip as a Catholic centre and, after several other priests had failed, Oldcorne succeeded and moved in. He went under the alias of Parker, which was Mrs Habington's maiden name and that of her brother Lord Mounteagle. The fiction that he was some cousin of Mounteagle's would be a plausible excuse for his presence and his authority in the household.

Hindlip House was built of brick with stone dressings and tiled roofs. The walls were diapered with black brickwork. There were four blocks, built round a courtyard about 22m square, which was entered through a gateway in the middle of the north block. From Gerard's *Narrative of the Gunpowder Plot* we know that at least part of the courtyard was turfed; other parts may have been paved or cobbled. The hall, parlour and original kitchen were in the south block, and the offices on the ground floor of the west block. Upstairs, on the first and second floors, were bedrooms, and above them, in the roof, a Long Gallery, which Gerard describes as 'wainscoted' and as 'four-square going round about the house'. The windows were square-headed, with dripstones, and most of them kept their mullions and transoms until the house was demolished in 1814.

A Jacobean Catholic, writing soon after the Gunpowder Plot, called Hindlip 'the most famous house in England for entertainment of priests'. Gerard says that it was exactly like a Jesuit house on the Continent. In 1592, Thomas Habington was transferred from the Tower to Worcester Castle and in 1593 he was released. His incarceration at Worcester was not a severe one. Worsley and Newell, who carried out an unsuccessful sweep through Herefordshire and Worcestershire that year, discovered that he was riding around the countryside with his gaoler for up to a fortnight at a time before returning to the Castle. Having failed to find him there, they rode to Hindlip, 'a place as fit to harbour a priest as any is in England'. A gentlewoman, either Dorothy or Mrs Mary Habington, told them through the wicket that Habington was at Worcester gaol and refused to let them in. Squinting through the keyhole, the pursuivants recognised the gaoler from Worcester in the courtyard but 'were fain to be gone, for in we must not come by no means. But in truth it is thought that there were in the house at that time some bad persons'.

It was Oldcorne's job, as Gerard puts it, 'to station priests in many places' throughout Worcestershire and the Marches; there are mentions of him in Herefordshire and even in Wales. That explains the extraordinary number of eleven hiding-places that were found at Hindlip during the great search in 1606. Communications with the Continent being what they were, young priests might land before arrangements had been made for them. They would need somewhere to stay in safety for the time being, just as Oldcorne himself had stayed with Garnet for fifteen months 'because he had no home of his own to go to'. In fact, the name of one of these young priests who were at Hindlip in transit has been preserved: Richard Broughton alias Rowse, who was ordained in Rome in 1592 and came across from Douai in 1593. According to the confession of one Edward Pemberton, he was 'sent, as this examinate thinketh, for Worcestershire, because he told this examinate that he should find him, the said Rowse, at Mr Abington's house at Hindlip with Mrs Abington. He is a tall man, with black hair and a black beard with some white hairs, cut close... some thirty years'.

Because Oldcorne was so often away stationing priests, after a while Garnet sent him an assistant, Thomas Lister, so that there would always be a priest at Hindlip to provide Catholics with Mass and the other sacraments. This posting was a mixed blessing. Lister was a brilliant scholar who had taken a doctorate before returning to England in 1589, but he suffered from claustrophobia and could not bear confinement in priest-holes, For this reason, Garnet moved him from Hindlip in 1594 and kept him as his own companion, since he was unwilling to impose such a liability on anyone else, Lister was replaced at Hindlip by Richard Banks, who crossed the Channel in 1595 and worked in Worcestershire until 1598, when Garnet transferred him to Braddocks. Banks in turn was succeeded at Hindlip by Oswald Tesimond alias Greenway, who had landed in 1597. Like Oldcorne, Lister and Banks, he had studied at the English College in Rome; before that he had been at school in York with Guy Fawkes. The proclamation for his arrest after the Gunpowder Plot describes him as

> 'of a reasonable stature, black hair, a brown beard cut close on the cheeks and left broad on the chin, somewhat long-visaged, lean in the face but of a good red complexion, his nose somewhat long and sharp at the end, his hands slender and long fingers, his body slender, his legs of a good proportion, his feet somewhat long and slender. His apparel of cloth, hose and jerkin much after the Italian fashion, the jerkin buttoned on the breast, his cloak buttoned down before with ribands hanging down on his breast, his hat narrow-brimmed with a small band and a broad full crown, as now the fashion is'.

It would be hard to mistake Tesimond if one met him making his way across the woods and streams of the Forest of Feckenham in his Italianate jerkin and narrow-brimmed hat.

In 1596, Lister was persuaded to leave England for Flanders, but having got as far as Antwerp changed his mind, out of a misguided sense of duty, and came back again. In 1597, he was induced to cross to Flanders a second time, where he managed to get himself arrested with another priest, Edward Coffin, and shipped back to England. By 1602, however, he had almost recovered from his phobia, and by 1605 he was back at Hindlip. There were now, therefore, three Jesuits working from there: Oldcorne still opening up new centres in the Welsh Marches; Lister serving at Hindlip itself and at Beoley a few miles away; and Tesimond travelling on foot to other Worcestershire houses. Gerard applies to Oldcorne the comment of St Jerome about St John: that 'he founded and governed all the churches in those parts'. From the other side, there is an unintentional tribute to the effectiveness of the Jesuit mission in a report on his diocese by Bishop Bilson of Worcester in 1596. 'In that small circuit', he wrote, 'there are nine-score recusants of note (besides retainers, wanderers and secret lurkers) dispersed in forty several parishes, and six-score and ten householders. Whereof above forty are families of gentlemen that themselves or their wives refrain the church, and many of them not only of good wealth but of great alliance, as the Windsors, Talbots, Throckmortons, Habingtons and others, and in other respects, if they may have their forth, able to prevail much with the simpler sort'.

No part of England is richer in hiding-places than Worcestershire and the adjoining counties, and in them Oldcorne's work may still be detected. The eleven at Hindlip itself, the greatest number on record in any single house, will be discussed in Chapter 9, at the time of their discovery after the Gunpowder Plot. But even so, the rest of this chapter and the whole of the next will be needed to deal with other houses within a mere fifteen or twenty miles of Worcester.

3

Fig. 46 Huddington Court, Worcestershire

Huddington Court is a beautiful half-timbered building just four miles east of Hindlip. Now a private house, it was the home of three of the Gunpowder plotters (p. 169): Robert, John and Thomas Wintour. They were a family with distinguished recusant connections. Their grandmother had been a Throckmorton from Coughton; one of their uncles, Francis Ingleby of Ripley Castle, was a priest harboured by Margaret Clitherow and, like her, executed at York in 1586. Robert's wife, Gertrude Talbot, was a sister of the future ninth Earl of Shrewsbury; one of their daughters, Mary (d. 1624), became a nun at Louvain; another, Helen (d. 1670), worked two splendid sets of vestments which still exist (they are at Douai and Stonyhurst). At the time of the Plot, the Wintours had a Jesuit chaplain at Huddington, Nicholas Hart alias Hammond, 'a little man with a whitish beard' who had come back from Rome in 1604.

Two interesting hides survive. A third, found in a search following the Gunpowder Plot, is likely to have been destroyed shortly afterwards. In the chapel, a square of the panelling (Fig. 47) can be removed revealing a dark cavity between two heavy beams. These beams are chamfered to allow easier access down two steps into a gable 3.5m long and 1.8m wide, though only 1.2m to the apex. On the left side of this gable is a heavy plaster-covered door, hung on iron hinges fastened by nails behind which is an inner hide in a smaller gable under the tiles. At the far end of the main gable was another plaster-covered door

Fig. 47 (Above) Chapel panelling in place and (right) removed to give access to the hide.

concealing an emergency exit, signs of which survived into the C20. The entrance panel from the chapel is a modern restoration, with a latch kept shut by a weight and released by treading on a floorboard linked to the latch by a chain, but there is no way of telling how far this represents the original mechanism.

Fig. 48 Huddington Court:
Chapel Hide.

Above: View of interior of hide.
The pink plaster door at left
gives access to the inner hide.
Editor's apologies for resorting
to a mosaic – hide interiors
can be tricky locations to
photograph!

Left: View back towards hide
entrance.

Below: Location of hide. The
Chapel is indicated in green
and hide in red, with the
inner hide in the small gable
running parallel to the
Chapel.

The larger surviving hide was only found during repairs at the beginning of the 20th century. Its entrance is in a corner, under the slope of

Fig. 49 Hide door closed and (R Top) open (archive photo). The door is low – about 650mm at the hinge. (Centre) interior side of door: the hide has a modern full-sized door as well and is big enough to be a very useful storeroom!) (R Bottom) the hide location is shown in red.

the roof in a room opposite the chapel. Two sections of lath-and-plaster, together with the vertical post between them which appears to support the principal rafter above, are mounted on hinges and swing open when pushed. The room beyond is 3.7m long by 3.2m wide and 2.1m high - very large for a hide. The space was created by sealing off the end of the attic space with a false wall. When discovered it had no window, (though one, visible in Fig. 49, has been cut since) and no door except the secret one, which was bolted on the inside. It must therefore have had a second secret entrance, and there are signs of a former trap door. Resemblances to Owen's hides in East Anglia, to the large attic hide at Harvington and to the Colditz glider hide are noteworthy.

Ten miles south-east of Huddington, between Evesham and Stratford-

upon-Avon, is Abbots Salford Hall, now trading as the Karma Salford Hotel, a picturesque stone structure of ogival gables and turrets with a detached stone gatehouse and barn. It was built by John Alderford, whose second wife Elizabeth and son-in-law Charles Stanford were both returned as recusants in 1610. The house chapel was not replaced by a local church until 1948. On the top floor is a shallow cupboard let into the thickness of the wall. It is lined with oak and has two stout oak shelves. The whole of the back panel, together

Fig. 50 Abbots Salford Hall and cupboard hide.

with the shelves, swings inwards on hinges concealed at the top. Beyond is a hide 1.5m long in the angle between the wall of the attic and the tiles of the roof. It could be secured

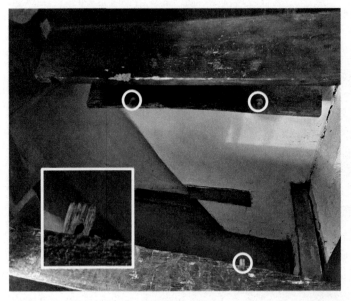

on the outside, except from those in the know, by two oak pegs which would look like any normal dowel and which could also be removed from inside. It is easy to climb into, but the slope of the roof inside it makes a dignified exit impossible.

Fig. 51 Looking into the hide. The circles mark the holes through which dowels could be pushed to lock the fake shelves in place. (Inset) detail of locking hole.

There is an interesting resemblance here to the now-lost hide at Lyford in which Campion, Colleton and Ford were found in 1581. Anthony Munday described this as opening off

> a chamber near the top of the house, which was but very simple, having in it a large great shelf with divers tools and instruments both upon it and hanging by it, which they judged to belong to some cross-bow maker. The simpleness of the place caused them to use small suspicion in it and were departing out again; but one in the company [David Jenkins] by good hap espied a chink in the wall of boards whereto this shelf was fastened, and through the same he perceived some light. Drawing his dagger he smit a great hole in it, and saw there was a room behind it, whereat the rest stayed, searching for some entrance into it, which by pulling down a shelf they found, being a little hole for one to creep in at.

On 19 January 1606, Oldcorne 'met with Mr Garnet two or three miles on this side Evesham' and came back to Hindlip with him. It is not clear which side of Evesham is 'this side': Oldcorne's examination was taken in London but he might easily be thinking of the Worcester approach to the town. Either way, their encounter was close to Abbots Salford.

Only a mile from Abbots Salford as the crow flies, but on the other side of the Avon and so more like five by the bridge at Bidford, is Cleeve Prior Manor, the seat of the Bushell family in the 16th and 17th centuries. Sir Edward Bushell, a cousin of the Wintours of Huddington, was seen just before the Gunpowder Plot with Robert Catesby at Clopton House, near Stratford,

Fig. 52 Cleeve Prior Manor in 1989 before renovation. (Above) The hide is marked in red and the closet in green. The windowless expanse of the turret would attract immediate attention from any experienced priest-hunter. Below (L) Closet with hide entrance – the room marked in green. (R) underside of trapdoor with original bolt and view into hide.

which Ambrose Rookwood had rented at Michaelmas 1605. His son Thomas was farmer of the Welsh mines under Charles I and supplied money to the King's army at Oxford when the Roundheads held the Tower mint. After the Civil War he went into hiding until his friends could make his peace with Cromwell.

The hide is the usual hole-under-the-closet and was very well preserved until recently with a heavy trapdoor of boards running the full length of the closet, and a wooden bolt on the underside which was in perfect condition when these pictures were taken. The hole below is 1.8m long, 1.2m wide and 4.6m deep. It was originally a garderobe with an outlet at ground level which was blocked up when the space was converted to a hide.

The Manor was converted into three houses in 1989 and the hide became a downstairs bathroom – reverting to its original function, in one sense. Whilst reutilisation of otherwise void space is entirely reasonable, it is very sad that the builder did not preserve the historic and rare trapdoor and bolt and that the planning authorities allowed this. This irreplaceable piece of heritage could simply have been left *in situ* or even turned into a feature.

Four or five miles south-west of Evesham, on the slopes of Bredon Hill, are two more houses which had hiding-places. Woollas Hall is a stately stone house with a roof-chapel which still retains its barrel ceiling and screen. The hiding-place no longer exists but was described by Cobbett in *Rural Rides* after a visit to Woollas on 25 September 1826:

> Mr Hanford's house is on the side of Bredon Hill, about a third part up it, and is a very delightful place. The house is of ancient date, and it appears to have been always inhabited by, and the property of, Roman Catholics, for there is in one corner of the very top of the building, up in the very roof of it, a Catholic chapel as ancient as the roof itself. It is about twenty-five feet [7m] long and ten wide. It has arch-work, to imitate the roof of a church. At the back of the altar there is a little room which you enter through a door going out of the chapel, and adjoining this little room there is a closet, in which is a trapdoor made to let the priest down into one of those hiding-places....

Elmley Castle House, which was demolished in 1962, was originally Elizabethan but also contained a fine Queen Anne staircase and some early Georgian ceilings. One of the hides, mentioned in the Victoria County History (1913), seems to have been a hole-under-the-closet beside a great chimney, but with an exit below to the ground floor, by the side of a door next to the staircase. The other, roughly 1.8m square, was above the low ceiling of an ante-room and entered through a trapdoor in the floor of a chapel-like attic above. It was found early in the 20th century when the owner noticed the difference in ceiling levels.

Ten miles south-west of Worcester and three miles south of Great Malvern is Little Malvern Court, the great hall of which formed part of the medieval Priory. It has been claimed that Mass was said continuously at Little Malvern from the twelfth to the twenty-first century. It was the home of Henry Russell, the friend of Campion and former Principal of Gloucester Hall, Oxford, who succeeded to the estates when his brother John died childless in 1588. There is a report in the State Papers which lists together as priest-harbourers John Halsey, (the Russells' family physician), some servants of Lord Lumley, (John Russell's father-in-law), and some servants of Lord Compton. After the death of Sir William Cordell of Long Melford in 1581 and the arrest of Campion in the same year, Henry Russell appears to have been living at Lowches Farm in Long Wittenham, eight miles from Oxford, an estate of St John's College. Here, it was alleged, he and the President of St John's, Francis Willis, had harboured Campion and other 'traitorous Papists'.

When Willis became Dean of Worcester Cathedral in 1586, he kept in touch with his old colleague, and after his death Mrs Willis consulted Russell about a possible second marriage. A gallery partitioned off at the end of the great hall was used as a secret chapel, and a total of six hides have been recorded or suggested: two 'secret corners' in the floor of the Priest's Room, one above the ceiling of the Priest's Room, one in the roof of the round tower next to the Priest's Room (then a garderobe and now containing a staircase), one next to a chimney on the first floor (apparently the former garderobe off the Cedar Room) and one in the roof above the Cedar Room. No (known) hides survive now.

Three and a half miles south-east of Little Malvern is Birtsmorton Court, a quadrangular moated house of various dates from the fourteenth to the twentieth century. Soon after 1580, the owner, Giles Nanfan, married Robert Southwell's sister Elizabeth, and he was returned as a recusant from 1592 onwards. Among the Little Malvern papers is a letter from him to John Russell about finding a priest: 'I am in great distress for christening my children and have sent divers ways and can hear of none. If you can help me, I shall be much bounden to you'.

The traditional hiding-place is a closet off the beautifully panelled Council Chamber on the ground floor of the west block. All round the cornice are coats-of-arms of the Nanfans' connections, including those of the Baskervilles of Eardisley, one of whom married another of Southwell's sisters. The door to the closet is part of this panelling, and no attempt was made to disguise it. There are legends that it sheltered the Lollard Sir John Oldcastle about 1415 and Queen Margaret of Anjou after the Battle of Tewkesbury in 1471, but neither of these be substantiated. Whilst it is reasonably certain that the Nanfans harboured priests, and that Birtsmorton had – and may still have - hides, this is not one.

Twelve miles west of Worcester and a mile north of Bromyard in Herefordshire is Buckenhill, the home of the third Habington brother, Richard. Worsley and Newell had no better luck there: they complained that 'he doth go from one shire unto another so that they cannot come by him... and so there was none found but his wife and her servants'. An exceptionally vivid spy's report in 1607 mentions a priest named Russell who was here: 'a proper man of a middling stature, a full face and seemly colour, and wanteth a tooth or two before. He frequented Clark's house of Millington in Herefordshire and Habington's of Worcestershire or Herefordshire, but whether he knoweth not, for that they were both recusants'. The present Buckenhill Manor is early Georgian, but Duncumb (1812) records that 'foundations to a much greater extent are to be met with near the house', which evidently were the remains of Richard Habington's manor-house.

Fifteen miles north of Worcester, on the road from Kidderminster to

Hagley, is Harborough Hall, Blakedown, a timber framed building with Jacobean plaster ceilings. Mrs Margaret Pen was listed as a recusant by Bishop Bilson in 1596, and in the early nineteenth century a hiding-place containing books was found in the garrets. There is no record of what it looked like, but from its location it was perhaps the usual lath-and-plaster hutch, snuggled down among the chimneys, trusses and other lath-and-plaster partitions. The date is likely to have been after the Pens' marriage in 1590, since she was one of 'the gentlewomen that refuse the church though their husbands do not'.

Grafton Manor, just outside Bromsgrove, was the home of John Talbot, Robert Wintour's father-in-law and one of the most notorious recusants in the country. As early as 1577 he was marked down for his great wealth and his armoury. He spent much of the 1580s and 1590s in and out of prison and was one of the few recusants to pay the full £20 a month. In 1586, he was reported for harbouring priests at Mitcham in Surrey. To the original 'fair manor place' recorded at Grafton by Leland he added a great chamber, a Renaissance porch dated 1567 and a new wing at right angles to the old one. The west front of this is still a fine example of Elizabethan brickwork, diapered in black and with irregularly placed garderobes and chimneys like Hindlip. There were Jesuits at Grafton for most of the seventeenth century and in 1687 they had a library there. But any hides (and there must have been several) were destroyed in a fire in 1710: the porch and great chamber survived intact but the internal woodwork of the Elizabethan wing is all early Georgian, and part of the older block had to be rebuilt from the ground up in the nineteenth century.

All ten of these houses are nearer to Hindlip than Baddesley Clinton is, and the list could be extended. How strong recusancy was in Worcestershire, even before Oldcorne began his founding and governing, is shown by the examination of John Felton, an old Marian priest who was brought before Bishop Whitgift at Worcester on Christmas Eve 1582. He listed by name thirteen places in Worcestershire where he had ministered during the previous ten years, together with one in Herefordshire and one in Gloucestershire. A few of these places, like 'Mrs Talbot's of Grafton' have been mentioned already, but most have not. He had, for instance, 'said Mass sundry times within this twelve-month at Thomas More's of Ripple, and namely on Tuesday last was a fortnight'. The Mores of Ripple were watermen and seem to have run a ferry service across the Severn. The previous July or August, he had said Mass at Strensham, the home of another branch of the Russells, 'finding at Strensham such vestments and other furniture as is usually occupied in the celebrating of Mass'. He had reconciled penitents by authority received 'by word from Dr Allen beyond sea'. And the previous Christmas he had been with a Mrs Pakington of Chaddesley Corbett. The full implications of that will need a chapter to themselves.

5
Harvington Hall

Fig. 53 Harvington Hall, Worcestershire. The secret chapel is the top floor room of the tower bottom centre, and the former escape route to the attics was through a gable joining this tower to the place where a small skylight is visible just behind it.

1

The finest surviving series of hiding-places under one roof is at Harvington Hall in Worcestershire, which lies a mile from Chaddesley Corbett, off the road from Kidderminster to Bromsgrove. Outwardly it seems unremarkable, and it is certainly no prodigy house - simply an irregular pile of red-brick chimneys and gables rising from a reedy moat fringed with trees. But inside is one of the most complex and cunning examples of manipulated space that even Owen ever devised.

The Hall was built or completed by Humphrey Pakington, who inherited the estates in 1578 and is first recorded as living there in 1583. A portrait of 1599, now at Coughton, shows him in ruff and black doublet, with receding hair, goatee beard and dark, slightly protruding eyes. There had been a medieval timber-framed house on the island, part of which is incorporated into the present building. But it is likely that Humphrey's father John Pakington lived at Chaddesley House, a mile away, which became his widow's dower-house, and that it was there that she harboured the Marian priest John Felton at Christmas 1581. The 'mansion house of Harvington', as it was called in 1595, was originally quadrangular but now consists of only two sides: the main south block and the lower east wing containing the medieval solar and the gatehouse, with a four-storey tower at the north end. Humphrey Pakington was a 'deare frynd' of Thomas Habington of Hindlip, ten miles away, and a brother-in-law of Roger Pen of Harborough and Henry Russell of Little Malvern and Gloucester Hall, Oxford. There are continuous references to his recusancy from 1585 onwards, and in 1591 Harvington and his Shropshire estate of Ditton Priors in Corvedale were sequestrated, leaving him only with Chaddesley House. But this legal formality, which went so smoothly that it was probably prearranged, made no difference to his ability to live, and to shelter priests, at Harvington. The estates were assessed at a fraction of their value by a commission presided over by a neighbour, Edmund Broad, who was a friend of Humphrey's and had made John Pakington's probate inventory in 1578. A month later, they were leased by the Lord Chancellor to another friend of Humphrey's, William Sebright of Wolverley near Kidderminster, who was Town Clerk of London and sat for Droitwich in Parliament. In return for an annual rent of £26 13s 4d, paid to the Crown through Sebright, Humphrey continued, as the deeds show, to be the effective owner of all his estates. Such devices were common practice but are rarely so well documented.

Despite this, Humphrey held a post in the household of Lord Chancellor Ellesmere (formerly Solicitor-General Egerton), whose wife, the dowager Lady Derby, was herself a recusant. It was probably in London that he met his first wife, Bridget (Kingsmill), the widow of Sir Thomas Norris, who was killed fighting in Ireland in 1599. About then she was described as 'a great recusant and takes great pains to convert her sisters', while her brother-in-law, Sir Henry Norris, was 'well known' to John Gerard. The Pakington letters refer to politics, London fashions and rare plants acquired from the royal gardener John Tradescant, as well as to coach mares, the bribing of juries, medical treatment by Dr John Halsey, and lamprey pies.

After Bridget Kingsmill's death in 1606, Humphrey married Abigail Sacheverell, one of the daughters of Henry Sacheverell of Morley and Hopewell in Derbyshire. Like Campion and Henry Russell, Sacheverell had been at St John's College, Oxford, and on the Wednesday after Twelfth Night 1581 Campion stayed with him at Hopewell and 'said one Mass'. Later that year, he was said to be keeping both a minister and a priest, William Harrison, who was 'short of stature and very decent of body and behaviour, his beard of a flaxen colour cut short'. A spy's report of February 1595, which led to searches in Derbyshire by William Newell, mentions an old carpenter and mason named Green who was then dwelling on Mr Sacheverell's land at Morley. He 'made a secret place in Mr Bentley's house at Lea, with a door of freestone that no man could ever judge there were any such place, and he made all the secret places in recusants' houses in that country'.

The first priest recorded at Harvington was Samuel Smallman, who was ordained in Rome in 1603 and buried at Chaddesley Corbett in 1613, after 'falling off his horse on Holy Thursday [Ascension Day], being a Roman Catholic and a great traveller'. He was probably one of the Smallmans of Wilderhope, an Elizabethan stone house in Corvedale in Shropshire, not far from Ditton Priors. The next was Humphrey Pakington's nephew Humphrey Lutley, of Broncroft Castle, also in Corvedale, who was back in Shropshire or Worcestershire by 1631 and was described as a 'domestick man servant' of Abigail Pakington on a passport of 1642. He died at Harvington in 1653.

Humphrey Pakington had no children by Bridget Kingsmill, and his elder surviving daughter by Abigail Sacheverell, Mary, was not born until 1610, when he was fifty-five. In 1630, the year before his death, she married Sir John Yate of Buckland, where Mr Hodgkins had failed to catch William Hopton in 1592 (see p268). Sir John, their son and their grandson all predeceased her, so that upon her death in 1696 Harvington passed to her grand-daughter, another Mary, who had married Sir Robert Throckmorton of Coughton. The new owners demolished two sides of the quadrangle but confined other changes to the redecoration of the North Tower in Georgian style and the conversion, in 1743, of a range of farm-buildings in the garden into a larger chapel. This was restored in 1987 with a Georgian chamber-organ and mahogany-fronted altar of about 1780. An inventory of 1826 suggests that by then the top floor and part of the first floor were already unfurnished, and during the 1840s and 1850s the Throckmortons removed the tapestries, the brass door-locks and most of the furniture and panelling, after which the shell rapidly fell into disrepair.

By 1930, when restorations were begun by the present owners, the Roman Catholic Archdiocese of Birmingham, the floors were unsafe, parts of the roof were collapsing, the building was smothered in ivy, and a gaping chasm from ground floor to attics marked where the Great Staircase had been taken out in 1910. But, paradoxically, two centuries of suspended animation and neglect had ensured the survival of the hides and a remarkable series of wall-paintings which were found under layers of whitewash in 1936. The unique value of Harvington for the study of priest-holes is thus due to a succession of historical accidents.

The simplest of the hides (Fig. 54) is the 'secret corner' for vestments under the floor of the chapel. Two boards in one corner lift up together, and beneath is a space 1.1m by 460mm and 180mm deep. The trapdoor is the original and in good condition. The space would have been adequate for one suit of Massing stuff but not much else: a fact which in itself suggests that this hide was made before Harvington became a major centre for priest-harbouring.

By contrast, there is an inventory of this chapel made in 1696 which lists eleven sets of vestments in tabby, damask, sarcenet, silk, velvet, 'crimson plush' and 'carnation Indian satin', most of them with altar frontals to match, and a variety of altar linen and plate which included 'one thurible'. The brickwork of the chapel is whitewashed and painted with a decoration of vines and pomegranates which has been dated to about 1670, in Lady Yate's time.

Fig. 54 Harvington Hall: Chapel Hide

There appears to have been a bolthole, or at least access, through the chapel ceiling to the attics. The Rev. J. R. Burton's *History of Kidderminster* (1890) refers to 'the chapel, from which a narrow doorway gives an outlet to the roof and many little secret rooms' - by which he means the maze of timbers and partitions in the roof-space. This 'narrow doorway' appears to have been above the normal door to the chapel from the Nursery. Since the chapel had only the one door and no hiding-place except the little one under the floor, such a bolthole would make good sense. In 1957, a Mr Leonard Parkes who was then living at Coughton Court but who had known Harvington as a boy seventy years previously was recorded as being:

> very emphatic that over the short stair leading up to the chapel used to be a movable plaster panel, set at an angle. When pushed back, this let you into a hide in the roof. After the restoration [of 1930-1] he went to look for it, and his first remark was that they had done away with it. He had often entered the place as a boy.

The gable through which it would have passed certainly existed: it appears in old photographs but was replaced by a lead flat (see Fig. 53).

However, a second 'secret corner' (Fig. 55) still does exist, in the apex of the gable next to where that bolthole would have emerged. It is a sealed-off section of the triangular space above the garret ceiling, 900mm wide at the base and 900mm high to the underside of the ridge-beam. Nails in the collar-beams show that it had a boarded floor. These nails continue for only 2.5m of the space available, at which point there are signs of another false wall of lath-and-plaster. This use of only part of the gable would lessen the risk of discovery if the ceiling below was pierced during a search. The door was a movable panel of plaster, on the lines of those at Ufton. It is now

Fig. 55 Harvington: Small Attic Hide.

(Above L) hide exterior wall.
(Above R), hide interior. The first four joists from the 300mm wide doorway have nails for a floor.
(R) detail of door frame interior showing signs of fixings for hinges and bolts.

missing, but the inside of the door frame retains mortices for hinges (Fig. 55). The small size, and the difficulty of climbing up to it, indicate that it also was intended for objects - Massing stuff or prohibited books – rather than people.

Of the hides large enough to take a person, the simplest (Fig. 56) is beside the gateway. At the side of the Renaissance fireplace in the Withdrawing Room (the upper half of the medieval block) is a door opening on a short passage to the room over the gate. In the floor of this passage is a modern trapdoor, which covers a hole 600mm wide, 1.3m long and 2.6m deep. The space it takes up shows in the ground-floor room below as a prolongation of the chimneystack on the side opposite the window, though since there is 500mm of sandstone between the room and the hide it was at least proof against any sounding hammer.

The original ladder, with six steps (two renewed), each 500mm wide and 130mm deep, is still preserved in the house, though too fragile to be used. It took up most of the limited space, so that the occupant could only stand or sit on the second or third step. The hide floor is of bare earth, but two sides are lined with panelling of the same design as that in the Withdrawing Room and painted green, as that formerly was. The third wall is formed by the chimneystack and the fourth is the wattle-and-daub outside wall by the gateway.

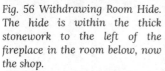

Fig. 56 Withdrawing Room Hide. The hide is within the thick stonework to the left of the fireplace in the room below, now the shop.
(R) The original ladder – no longer in a usable condition.

From outside it can be seen that in one of the diagonal timbers there is a circular depression 230mm across, in whose centre is a smaller hole, 75mm across, cut right through the beam. A person inside the hide can reach between the chimneystack and the outside wall to this opening, a fact which gave rise to theories that it was a feeding-trap. But since there would certainly be a sentry on the bridge during any search, and people would constantly be crossing the courtyard, it is difficult to imagine a less likely position for one. The hole may mark the site of the winch for the drawbridge or it may have been covered with an iron plate and ring to which a horse might be tied up.

There is a very similar hide (Fig. 57) under the garderobe closet off the South Room over the kitchen, on the same floor as the Withdrawing Room but at the other end of the house. This room still has some Georgian panelling and until the nineteenth century was lined with tapestries showing scenes of hunting, with horses, men and hounds. The trapdoor above the hide is the original, 75mm thick and made of three layers of oak boards. The top layer runs the full length of the closet, so that there is no betraying break in the flooring. The space below is 1.5m deep and 800mm by 1.14m, contrived over the bread-oven in the kitchen. This oven may be a later insertion, but there is a layer of earth in the hide, which would insulate it from the heat and perhaps serve sanitary purposes as well. Three of the walls are lined with plaster, and for this reason it is hard to say whether the space was left in the original construction or quarried out of the solid brickwork of the stack.

At the back of the stack, next to this hide, is a tall hollow brick turret with its own gabled roof, with a pulley-wheel at the top. A weight descending in the interior shaft of this turret pulls a cord which turns the kitchen spit. Spit-jacks of this type came into use towards the end of the sixteenth century and began to be superseded in the time of Charles II by smoke-jacks, whose motive

Fig. 57 South Room Hide, open and (inset) closed and (below left) interior. The archetypal hole-under-the-closet: the commonest early form of hide. The trapdoor is the original. The brick garderobe on the left of the main picture would originally have had a wooden seat and is still an open shaft falling straight into the moat.

power was provided by a fan in the chimney. The shaft was added not long after the original building was finished, since the brickwork is almost identical. Two of the walls of the hide were then pierced, so that the pulley cord could be taken through it from the shaft on the one side to the kitchen on the other. Once this had been done, the hide would no longer have been secret, and it seems therefore to have been in use for only a few years between the building of the house and the shaft. That would also confirm the view that this hole-under-the-garderobe is earlier than the more cunning hides elsewhere in the house.

2

Fig. 58 (Above) Replica Great Staircase at Harvington.

Fig. 59 (Right) Original Great Staircase, now at Coughton Court.

The places described so far are comparable with the four at Ufton, though without their curious bolts and copious documentation. But the four to be described now show a far deeper grasp of the possibilities of the structure and, unlike the first four, cannot be appreciated fully without reference to the plan and sections of the entire building. They are all close to the Great Staircase, which was clearly an afterthought to the original building and from its open-well construction cannot be earlier than about 1600. That may have a bearing on the date and function of the hides themselves.

The original was removed to Coughton in 1910 but between 1936 and 1947, as part of the restoration work, an exact copy of the staircase was built by William Fowkes of Droitwich. Apart from the remodelled original, the restorers were also guided by photographs of it taken by Sir Benjamin Stone in 1896, by a Victorian oil-painting which now hangs on the first landing, and by the Elizabethan decoration of the staircase well. This consists of a stippled trellis pattern in red, yellow and black, over which newel-posts, strings and balusters were painted to match those of the staircase itself. (The design is similar to, though cruder than, the decoration of the Great Staircase at Knole, which was built between 1604 and 1608). Consequently, the modern staircase is an authentic reconstruction of the original and, with its five mullioned windows and the interplay of planes and levels, can be appreciated as an impressive piece of Elizabethan or early Jacobean design. For all effective purposes it can be treated as if it was the original.

It is apparent at the top landing that this staircase was not part of the original design of the house. The west wall of the stair-well is set back as if to support joists, and at the same level in the east wall there are mortices and notches in the horizontal beam which indicate that a floor once rested here.

Five steps (Fig. 60) lead up from this landing to the second-floor corridor called (from its wall paintings) the Nine Worthies Passage. Two of these steps can be lifted to reveal a space under the treads of 1.21m wide and 480mm by 510mm at its deepest. The back of this space is formed by a brick and timber wall, the middle panel of brickwork of which is missing. Through this gap one can climb down into an inner space 1.5m by 1.75m and 1.8m high, built under the end of the Worthies Passage and above the ceiling of the 'Butler's Pantry' next to the Great Chamber.

Fig. 60 *The Staircase Hide, closed, and open showing the small outer and larger inner hides.*

The present hinged steps (two treads and one riser) and the fixed riser below them are a reconstruction: the original was vandalised while the Hall lay derelict during the 1890s. It is uncertain how closely this reconstruction matches the original design, but it is clear from accounts written by people who saw the original before its destruction that there was some form of moving stair, hinged or pivoted.

The missing centre panel was in fact an secret door, 530mm by

580mm, which must have been plastered and camouflaged to look like brickwork. Fig. 61 shows the rarely seen view of the back of this false wall looking outwards from within the inner hide. The square door space has an iron socket for a bolt, and halves of two iron butterfly hinges, nailed in place. The jewel boxes in the outer hide are for decoy purposes! There are signs of a false ceiling of lath-and-plaster, which would have lessened the risk of discovery if the floorboards of the passage above had been torn up during a search. The oak floor of the hide was formerly covered by a rush mat, a fragment of which survives in the Hall.

Fig. 61 (Above) Rear of entrance to inner hide. (Inset) detail of bolt socket and remains of hinges. (Below left) interior of inner hide, showing about half of the floor area.

The hide is on an outside wall, but one with at least ten windows in it, and before the demolition of the adjoining west side of the courtyard it was at an inner angle and so even less conspicuous. On the inside, the difference in ceiling levels between the Great Chamber and the pantry was masked by a panelled porch in the Chamber which screened off both the door from the Great Staircase to the Chamber and that from the Chamber to the pantry.

There is a deduction of general importance to be made from fact that the hinges were nailed in place. On a storey which internally consists mainly of timber, this would have made a noise fit to wake the dead, especially if the Staircase well had already been constructed, to provide a highly effective echo-chamber and resonator. It shows that the common idea of Owen working secretly by night cannot always have been the case. Elizabethan squires frequently owned multiple manors and it seems likely that the entire household moved out to either of Packington's other properties (Chaddesley or Ditton Priors), while the hide-builders were given vacant possession for a period which may have run to some months. No suspicion would be roused by such a migration: in Elizabethan conditions the sanitary arrangements might make it necessary.

Along the Nine Worthies corridor is a room decorated with broad

bands of red and grey and known as the Marble Room. In one corner, in the angle formed by the outside wall and the partition which divides the room from the Staircase well, is a triangular fireplace built of brickwork.

There is no chimneystack on the two floors below at this point, so that the whole weight of the fireplace is carried on the floorboards. It goes only as far as the ceiling (2.1m from the floor); and in the attic above it can be seen as a circular brick shaft in the corner with a thick roof timber across the point where the flue should go through the tiles;

Fig. 62 Marble Room: This fireplace appears to have been a concealed escape route to the attics above.

and in any case the high chimney stack needed to throw the smoke clear of the roof would have been far too heavy for the floorboards. At the level of the garret floor, the brickwork is smoothed off with mortar, so that two boards could rest snugly across it. It appears that this was never a genuine fireplace at all, but a camouflaged exit from the second floor into the attics, like the one that is said to have existed in the chapel. A projecting brick in the back of the flue, just out of sight, provides a practical foothold for climbing up and down the chimney,

Fig. 63 The exit to the attics at the top of the False Chimney.

and the very convincing blackening of the back and sides of the fireplace must be artificial camouflage. There is still debated: the diagonal timber visible in Fig. 63 is a later addition so there may have been a short flue and chimneystack at some time.

A dozen paces from the top of this chimney is a place where two roofs meet. Here, above a plaster partition about 1.5m high (Fig. 64), parts of two rafters have been removed to make an opening 900 by 1100mm giving access to the triangular space right under the roof ridge. Upon climbing into this space and turning left, a low passage, or catwalk (Fig. 65) can be followed for ten metres to a lath-and-plaster wall through which a doorway opens into the second largest hide anywhere: 5.2m by 3.8m and 2.1m to the ridge.

Fig. 64 Above - the entrance to the catwalk before remediation work in the 1990s and (inset) as it might originally have appeared when hidden by a plaster hatch. Arrow shows how this picture relates to Fig. 65.

Fig. 65 Above - looking south along the catwalk towards the hide. Arrow shows how this picture relates to Fig. 64

Fig. 66 Left - hide interior wall and view back along the catwalk from inside the hide. Oak planks lining the wall deaden sound and provide insulation and security.

The opening at bottom right was made during the 1930s: until then the only access to this space was via the catwalk.

(Inset) detail of door jamb showing latches: evidence that this space was intended to be secured from within.

Fig. 67 Harvington, The Large Attic Hide: A secret room 5.2m long, 3.8m wide and 2.1m high.

On the inside of the entrance are a wooden catch and a socket for a door latch (Inset of Fig. 66). The plaster wall is lined on the inside with planks of oak 20mm thick (Fig. 66 main picture) and the sloping sides of the roof are still partly lined with rough boarding (Fig. 67). There are square iron nails in the joists, indicating a boarded floor.

It is impossible to stand in this space and not marvel at the sheer audacity of a hide of this size. One might also wonder whether it really was a hide, and if so, whether it was just too big to have withstood a search. There can be no serious doubt that the space was at least intended for habitation and to be secured from within, and the absence until the 20th century of any entrance other than the catwalk means that simplest explanation for the space – in this house above all others - is that it was built as a hide.

As to its security, events at Hindlip in 1606 showed that a long enough search by properly trained and briefed pursuivants could uncover even Owen's finest work, (although Gerard had survived a nine-day search just a few weeks previously), but such searches were not typical: most lasted just one or two days. Captain Michael Burn, MC, who worked on the construction of the Colditz glider hide (p16) examined this hide at Harvington in the 1950s and commented that the fundamental idea of both was the same, but that the Harvington hide was safer, partly because of its split-level design, and partly because of the oak lining of its false wall, as opposed to canvas covered with clay, sand and grit at Colditz. The glider hide remained undiscovered for the last ten months of the war, despite continual searches by the guards, who - unlike priest hunters - lived on site, knew the Castle and had plans of it, and were able to conduct their searches under electric light.

We have already seen that the top landing of the Great Staircase is five steps lower than the second floor which it serves, and this mismatch necessitated a series of other alterations to this block of the Hall. It seems probable that all of this was deliberate, and that these alterations were both the cover for the hide-building and the opportunity for the creation of the spaces themselves.

Fig. 68 shows (lower) the present-day layout of the second floor and attics and indicates how they may have been altered from a simple layout (upper) of four attic rooms (A-D) above four second-floor rooms (1-4) The original arrangement is slightly conjectural but is consistent with the fabric.

At the south end of the wing (left of the diagrams), the ceiling of Room 1 (Priest's Room) / floor of Attic A was raised half a floor level, making Room 1 a much more imposing room than it would have been. What had been the upper half of Attic A became the hide. Attics B and C, and Rooms 2 and 3, were unaltered except for the insertion of the False Chimney route from (Marble) Room 3 to Attic C. The ceiling of Room 4/floor of Attic D were lowered half a level to become the room now known as the Pilate Room* and Room 4 disappeared completely, its lower half becoming the top of the well of the Great Staircase. The doorway between Attics C and D was stranded halfway up the south wall of the Pilate Room and so was blocked up, meaning that the route from the Pilate Room to C involved a descent of six steps, a right turn, a short walk, a left and a right turn, an ascent of one level of an unlit spiral staircase and finally one more left turn. This would have helped mask the absence of A by enormously complicating the task of measuring and comparing the lengths of the second and attic floors. If (as seems likely) the wing originally continued to the north there would also have been attics E, F, G, etc..., making the missing space proportionately even smaller and harder to find.

It seems likely that the Marble Room and the two rooms beyond it, which form an interconnecting suite, were those used by the priests. One of them is known as the Priest's Room and may be the 'P- Room' discreetly referred to in an inventory of 1714. All three, together with the chapel, the Nursery and another small room to the west of it, could be isolated from the rest of the house by the doorways on the Worthies Passage and the adjoining newel staircase, but with access via the false chimney to the hide. In fact, on this floor, only the outside walls are of brick, all internal partitions being of timber and plaster, so there would be difficulties in finding sites for hides.

---

* This room is reached by a flight of six steps up from the Worthies Passage and has a plaster porch with wall paintings that may depict Christ before Pilate and the Resurrection.

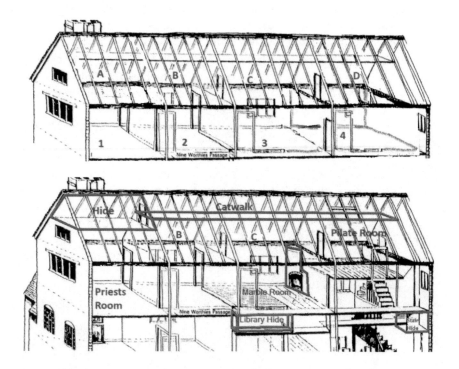

Fig. 68 Harvington, west wing, second floor and attics before (conjectural) and after the Great Staircase was added, including the hides attributed to Owen. The Large Attic Hide is at top left and the Stair Hide at bottom right. Also visible are the Marble Room containing the False Chimney and below it, Dr Dodd's Library with its Hide (p96).

The small room next to the Nursery also seems to have been used as a chapel or oratory. It is decorated with red and white drops, for the blood and water of the Passion, with a frieze of scallop shells above. This design continues around the room except for a rectangle opposite the window, where some piece of furniture 1m high stood against the wall and splashes of candle-fat still adhere to the painted plaster just above.

The last and most ingenious of the hiding-places at Harvington is in the first-floor room known as Dr Dodd's Library, below the Marble Room and next to the Great Chamber and the Great Staircase, but on the opposite side from the stair hide. The room is named for historian and priest Hugh Tootell, alias Dr Charles Dodd, who was at Harvington from 1722 to 1743 and wrote a famous *Church History of England* there. His one sentence on Nicholas Owen runs: 'John Owen, his [Oldcorne's] servant, suffer'd [was executed] at the same time [as Oldcorne]'. Those nine words contain three errors. 'Little John' was a nickname, not Owen's real name; he was Garnet's servant, not Oldcorne's; and he was tortured to death in the Tower five weeks before

Oldcorne and his servant Ralph Ashley were executed at Worcester. If this was Dodd's workroom, he wrote those words oblivious to the fact that he was sitting right outside one of Owen's masterpieces.

Fig. 69 shows a raised platform, originally a panelled cupboard, 2m wide, 1.63m high and 1.0m deep. This is built over part of a corridor known (from a wall painting) as the Mermaid Passage. This cupboard originally had a panelled front with a door in the middle. On the right-hand side an upright beam hangs on a pivot and on being pressed at the top will swing outwards, opening a gap slit 1.5m high and 250mm wide, through which an adult can just squeeze. An oak stop at the bottom on the inside

Fig. 69 Library Hide. The space at the top of the ladder was originally panelled all round and had a cupboard front with a central door, which could not be opened unless the room door was shut, further helping mask the differences in ceiling levels of the landing and the Library.

prevents it moving unless pressure is applied above the pivot. The secret room beyond, built over another part of the same corridor is 2.45m long, 900mm wide and 1.5m high.

This hide was rediscovered in 1894 by a young man, Bernard Lloyd, staying with his grandfather at the Hall Farm.

One day I was cutting the ivy on the old Hall when it began to rain rather heavily, so I went in the Hall to wait for it to stop, and, as always, wandered about inside, looking at this, that and the other. I went up the spiral staircase. On the right of this was a dark space. Out of curiosity, I got inside this and found that one panel of bricks resting on an oaken base swayed a little when touched. This made me curious to know what was on the other side, and after pulling a few bricks away I discovered there was a small dark chamber beyond, and in the left-hand corner of the entrance from this position was a stool. I also noticed the entrance to this chamber was from the Library. The panel at the right end of the Library cupboard previous to dismantling was never *in situ*. I went round to the

Fig. 70 Original stool found in Library Hide.

Library and, lifting up a perpendicular beam in the cupboard, disclosed the proper entrance. Then, getting into the hide, I found the stool, which must have lain undisturbed for at least some ninety years, had a coating of dust quite half an inch thick on the seat and also on the runnels. The base of one leg had dry-rotted away. Some people tried to extract the stool, but the splay of its legs was too wide, fortunately, for it to come though the beam opening; otherwise it would have disappeared as a curiosity.

Fig. 71 Library Hide Interior. (L) The stool is a replica of the one found here in 1894. (R) The swinging beam from the inside of the hide. The beam is also not the original.

Lady Yate had died in 1696 and the Hall passed to her granddaughter Mary (Throckmorton). By then, priest-holes were no longer needed and it may be that this was the time that some of them were forgotten. Whilst the stool had in fact probably lain undisturbed for at least 200 years, Lloyd's misgivings were prophetic. It was eventually removed from the hide, and duly disappeared, (as did the original swinging beam) but not before the photograph (Fig. 70) upon which the replica was modelled was taken.

From the landing outside the Library (Fig. 72) it can be seen how the space was contrived. The rooms on the first floor are generally nearly 4m high, but a mezzanine floor (pink outline), was inserted over this landing and over the passageway leading from it to the Great Staircase. This level was then divided into three, almost equally sized, spaces. The space above area A is the raised cupboard in the library from where the hide is entered (Fig. 69). (The bottom of the ladder to it is just visible through the library doorway centre left in Fig. 72). The hide itself is above area B and above area C is the cupboard via which Lloyd rediscovered the hide, entered from the spiral staircase, the underside of part of

Fig. 72 First floor landing with mezzanine level ABC. L-R part of bedroom door; steps up to Library; passage leading to Great Staircase; closed door to Great Chamber; newel staircase (first landing and underside of treads to second floor visible top R)

which can be seen to the right of C. Thus, most of the mezzanine space is occupied by the two cupboards, one in the Library and the other on the staircase, which between them mask the location of the hide.

If searchers had pierced the ceiling at the point where it suddenly becomes lower, (blue outline in Fig. 72) they would only have found the staircase cupboard. The floor of the Library is higher than that of the passage outside, with a short flight of steps curving through 90 degrees. On the opposite side of the passage is the newel staircase, and the southern end of the passage, (behind the camera) is four steps higher than the rest, a confusion of levels and directions that makes it very hard to retain an accurate sense of direction. Finally, the hide is in the middle of the house in all three dimensions, so that it could not possibly be located from outside. Altogether, a brilliant handling of space.

Although other houses, like Sawston and Braddocks, have single hides which are more dramatic than any of these places, the west wing at Harvington as a whole is the most outstanding architectural record of the Counter-Reformation anywhere in England. Apart from the hides, the contemporary wall paintings vividly evoke the atmosphere of the 1590s or 1600s (and prove that the internal partitions of the first and second floors have not been altered since that time). The finest are the six surviving figures in the Nine Worthies Passage: Hercules and Cerberus, Guy of Warwick and Pompey the Great on the east wall; David and Goliath, Samson and the Philistines, and Joshua or Judas Maccabaeus on the west. The costumes date them at around 1600 and are reminiscent of Shakespeare's Roman plays: Samson with an imposing handlebar moustache brandishing the ass's jawbone; a Philistine officer in a steeple hat with a feather in it; Joshua in plumed helmet and Elizabethan armour riding into battle. They have an imaginative fascination of their own, made all the keener by the knowledge that within a few feet, sometimes only a few inches, are these ingeniously devised priest-holes. The siting of the hides round the Great Staircase suggests strongly that they were inserted at the same time as it was, and it is at least possible that the wall-paintings were part of the making good which followed both the ostensible and the secret alterations. Outstanding as domestic art, they are even rarer for their context.

3

The suggestion that the hides at Harvington, or some of them, were the work of Nicholas Owen was first made in 1903 and the second group of hides are certainly good enough to be his work. The Staircase and the Library hides can each hold three people comfortably and the large Attic hide many more. What can have necessitated such lavish provision, with Hindlip only ten miles away?

It has already been explained that these hides appear to have been designed into the building as part of the alterations made when the Great Staircase was added. The best answers to the questions of why they were needed, and of who built them, and when, seems therefore to depend upon the exact date of this Staircase, which is not currently known. Its style is of 1600-1610 and the Gunpowder Plot, which led both to the discovery of Hindlip's hides and Owen's arrest and death was in 1605.

There are two main possibilities: either the Staircase postdates the Plot, and the hides were built to replace those lost at Hindlip, in which case they are not Owen's. Alternatively, if the Staircase predates the Plot, then the quality of the hides and the close friendship between the Pakingtons of Harvington and the Habingtons of Hindlip makes Owen to be by far the likeliest builder, and a possible answer to the duplication of the facilities of Hindlip could be found in the acrimonious dispute known as the Archpriest Controversy, and particularly in the Papal adjudication of it in October 1602. After the death of Cardinal Allen in 1594, there were demands for an English bishop whose authority could supersede Garnet's unofficial arrangements. Garnet's own letters show that he was much busied with questions of faculties and dispensations which would normally be the business of a bishop or of his vicar-general; and to some it appeared wrong that the Jesuit superior, who had only a dozen of his own men in the country, had been responsible for placing 300 secular priests in ten years.

Garnet himself favoured the appointment of a bishop. But the Roman officials concerned took the view that a bishop would merely provoke worse persecution without being able to do anything useful. In 1598, the Cardinal Protector of England, Caetani, compromised by appointing instead an Archpriest, George Blackwell, who had been one of the first Douai priests to return to England. Not a bishop, and with no authority over the laity or the surviving Marian priests, he was to co-ordinate the work of the seminary priests, consulting Garnet over major decisions. He inherited an almost impossible position and made it worse by severity and lack of tact. Right from the start, his authority was challenged by the 'Appellants', who regarded him as the nominee and tool of the Jesuits, meaning Persons. Some of the rancour went back to the 1570s, when the Appellants' leading spokesman, Christopher Bagshaw, had been first a colleague of Persons at Balliol and then of Blackwell and Henry Russell at Gloucester Hall. Blackwell retaliated by censuring and suspending a number of priests, including John Mush, who had written a biography of Margaret Clitherow, and John Colleton, who had been captured at Lyford seventeen years before in the same priest hole as Campion.

After four years of bitter and tedious pamphlet warfare and representations to Rome, Pope Clement VIII issued a ruling that the controversy was to cease, that Blackwell was to include three Appellants among his Assistants, and that he was not in future to consult Garnet or any other Jesuit (priest or layman) in England. When Blackwell had been appointed in 1598, he had asked Garnet to continue his services to newly landed priests, an obvious piece of common sense. But now, according to the strict interpretation of the Papal brief, Blackwell had to make his own arrangements for smuggling priests into the country, for placing them, and for building priest-holes. He could not ask Garnet for Owen's services, nor could he even take advice from Owen, who had recently become a Jesuit lay-brother, though this was kept so secret that even John Gerard was not sure of it.

Whilst all this may have been something of a self-indulgent distraction from the serious question of how priests could exercise their ministry with the least risk of being disembowelled, it seems clear that after 1603 Garnet and Blackwell each ran their own organisations: Garnet for the Jesuits, whose numbers increased to forty in the next four years, and Blackwell for the seculars. The hypothesis is that Owen was called upon to equip Harvington as a secular counterpart to Hindlip, so that priests like Richard Broughton who had formerly been told to report to Hindlip would no longer need to do so. In support of this explanation, it is worth pointing out that all the priests known to have resided at Harvington were seculars, and that later in the seventeenth century a library for the Midlands secular clergy was established at Harvington, of which Dodd made use in writing his *History*.

Granville Squires closed his chapter on Harvington with the words:

Other investigations are still pending, which perhaps goes some way to explain the fascination Harvington Hall has for me. But even did I know that every inch of it had been thoroughly explored, I should never tire of walking its empty echoing rooms and speculating about the builder of these ingenious hides and the many thrilling hunts and escapes that this great house must have seen.

In a talk given to Harvington staff and volunteers in 2015 to mark his sixtieth year as a volunteer and thirtieth as Historical Director at the Hall, the author of this book quoted Squiers' remark and added his own postscript:

Today, the rooms are no longer empty, the Hall has been thoroughly explored, and we know far more about the hides. But after sixty years I too am still walking and speculating, and we all know what Squiers meant by 'the fascination [of] Harvington Hall'.

Of the many unsolved mysteries of Harvington, the most tantalizing is that we do not in fact know whether there were any hunts (thrilling or otherwise) or escapes: no record of any search has yet been found. The most we can say is that while successful searches left a paper trail of letters and trial documents, unsuccessful ones were written up much less conscientiously. So perhaps it is safe to say that if these hides were ever used for real, then they held their secrets well.

a · Great Kitchen
b · Pantry
c · Spit Shaft
d · Buttery
e · Tea-room Kitchen
f · Parlour (tea-room)
g · Gateway
H · Priest Hole

a · South Room
b · Mermaid Passage
c · Great Chamber
d · Lady Yate's Bedroom
e · Withdrawing Room
f · Room over Gateway
H · Priest Holes

← up → down

a · Priest's Room
b · Marble Room
c · Nine Worthies Passage
d · Small chapel
e · Lady Yate's Nursery
f · Chapel
H · Priest Holes

Garret · a Hide
Garret · b
Garret · c
Garret · d Pilate Room
e Catwalk
f False Wall Remnant
g Entrance
H Hide over

Fig. 73 *Harvington Hall. It appears that the building was originally quadrangular, and that the North wing and the northern half of the West wing were demolished around 1700.*

6
Scotney Old Castle, 1598
The South-East

Fig. 74 Scotney Old Castle, Kent

1

Among the priests at Baddesley Clinton in 1591 was one 'of a reasonable stature, much beard auburn'. He was Richard Blount, a Leicestershire man educated at Oxford, Rheims, Rome and Valladolid. In the early spring of 1591, he and several other priests came back to England disguised as sailors who had been captured by the Spanish during the Earl of Essex's campaign of 1589. Evidently they had been well coached in their cover stories, for when two of them, Blount himself and James Younger, were taken up to London and interrogated by Admiral Lord Howard in person, they were able to convince him that they were what they claimed to be. Then, having been sent off to collect the Queen's bounty for distressed seamen, they presented themselves to Thomas Wiseman of Braddocks, who was studying law at Lincoln's Inn. There they lay hidden for three days and were fitted out with money and clothes, including 'a white satin doublet and black-tuffed taffety hose'. Younger then made his way to Upton Park, Lady Throckmorton's house in Essex, and Blount to Scotney Castle on the borders of Kent and Sussex. Here, seven years later, he made a thrilling and well-documented escape.

Scotney Old Castle is built on two islands in the River Bewl, in a steep valley now landscaped with masses of trees, rhododendrons and waterlilies. The approach is from the land to the smaller and more westerly island, on which the boathouse now stands, and then across a masonry causeway to the larger island and the surviving buildings of the Castle. At the inner end of the causeway are the remains of the fourteenth century gatehouse. On the right is the Ashburnham Tower, also fourteenth century, with a Georgian conical roof and a little glazed cupola.

Although there are remains of three other towers at the other corners of the island, this seems to have been the only habitable one even in the sixteenth century. When the new house was built higher up the valley during the 1840s, parts of the old castle were deliberately ruined to create a picturesque and romantic composition.

Like Ufton and Braddocks, Scotney has the rare distinction of a still-extant hide which is mentioned in a contemporary account of a search.

Fig. 75 Staircase, cupboard in wall and hide entrance (red).

Fig. 75 shows a small wall cupboard on the second landing of the Elizabethan dog-leg staircase. In the right-hand wall of this cupboard is an opening to a second space under the roof whose floor level is slightly higher than that of the cupboard. Below this second space is a hiding-place 1.2m high, 1.0m wide and 1.45m long, lined with brick and stone and devised over a bend in a chimney. The hide cover is an oak block which slid back on oak runners beneath the second space, although it has been removed and is presently on the floor of the hide. When the hide was rediscovered, about 1860, it contained a copy of a Cromwellian proclamation against Jesuits, priests and Popish recusants.

Early in 1598, this hole sheltered Richard Blount and his servant Bray for a week. A pursuivant and two Justices raided the castle, and sent Mr Darell up to London to Newgate prison, his wife to another house and most of the servants to the county gaol, leaving one maid to look after the children for the duration of the search. Like Gerard at Braddocks, the two fugitives had 'very small provision', and after a week they escaped by a bold ruse. Bray slipped out of the hide and gave himself up, claiming to have been concealed in another hole, which he showed to the searchers. He was taken away on suspicion of being a priest, but his examination showed clearly that he was not one, and so he was

Fig. 76 *Hide, with cover in situ, in open position (1964).*

released. Meanwhile, Blount escaped, and Bray soon rejoined him.

Fig. 77 *Hide with cover closed (1964).*

The evidence that the hide shown here was the scene of this adventure is in an account written by Thomas Darell's son William, who was one of the children in the Castle at the time and grew up to reconstruct the hall block in the 1630s. He describes it as 'a secret place under a stair', which would have been a fair description when the staircase continued above the hide into the hall block, instead of ending abruptly at a blank wall as it does today.

Nearly a year later, at Christmas 1598, the Castle was searched again by Sir George Rivers and two

Fig. 78 Hide interior in 2023: cover on floor.

other Justices with a pursuivant and other men. This time they knew that Blount was at Scotney, from information given by a former servant there named Henbury. They surrounded the Castle at night and waited until a servant emerged just before dawn whereupon they seized her and ordered her to light a candle and take them to Mr Darell's chamber. (He was in fact away from home, but they did not know that.) Not intimidated, instead of complying, she called up the stairs to Mrs Darell, and the noise and the delay gave Blount and Bray just enough time to avoid immediate capture. Blount was in breeches and cassock, but both were barefoot, and Bray only had time to slip on his breeches. It was December, but there was no time for anything warmer. Grabbing the church stuff and books, a loaf and a small bottle of wine, they were just able to tumble into a hide in the nick of time.

This hole, whose location is unknown today, is described by William Darell as 'another secret place, digged in a thick stone wall', off 'a little court with stone buildings about it' and separated by two walls about 3m high from a ruinous tower at the corner of the garden where the moat was 25m broad and set with sunken piles. These piles were found in 1863 below the south-eastern tower, and in any case the moat is much narrower than 25m on the north side of the garden. Another, anonymous, account says that to reach the moat from the hide Blount and Bray, 'coming to the court..., passed along by the house side and so to the moat-wall'. Although this 'little court' may not be the same as the present courtyard, it seems clear that it was on the same side of the Castle and that Blount and Bray had to scale first a wall running northwards from the hall block to get into the garden, and then the curtain wall on the far side of the garden, next to the south–east tower. The entrance to the hide was 'a broad stone' at the bottom of a little turret, 'in show not differing from the rest' and, most unusually, in the outside wall - a quirk to which the fugitives would owe their lives.

Mrs Darell and her two children, William and Rose, were shut up in one room over the gatehouse and the searchers took possession of the Castle for ten days. The hunt continued after dusk by candlelight, and carpenters and bricklayers were on hand to detect any apparently pointless alterations. Nothing, however, was found, and at the end of the ten days Mrs Darell was allowed out of the gatehouse, eventually making her way to the little court from which the hide was entered. Here she was horrified to see that in their haste Blount and Bray had left the tassel of a vestment girdle hanging out of the crack in the stonework. She managed to cut off the tassel and called to Bray and Blount to 'Pull in the string'. But she was overheard and asked what string, and to whom she was talking. Flustered, she replied that the door of the next room was shut against her and that she was asking for someone to pull the string of the latch to open it. This did not pass muster and suspicions

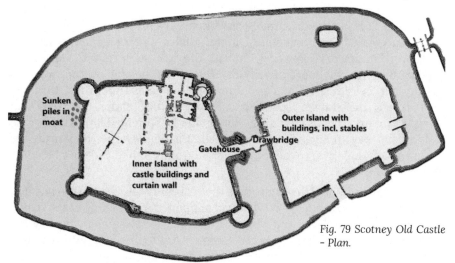

Fig. 79 Scotney Old Castle - Plan.

were aroused. Searchers poured into the courtyard and began to beat the walls with mattocks. A bricklayer among them noticed that one of the stones was not original and sounded hollow. Soon the hinges began to give way and Blount and Bray had to set their backs to the door to keep it in place. They could hear all that the searchers said and see the light of their candles through the cracks, for by then it was growing dark.

Fortunately, it began to rain heavily and soon the gutters were pouring icy streams on the searchers, who decided to leave off until daylight. They were not certain that there was anyone behind the stone and must have supposed that in any case no one could escape from the moated island, so they retired to drink and dry themselves out by the hall fire without posting even a single sentry by the suspicious stone.

A little after midnight, the two men crept out of the hiding place and closed the door behind them. The Massing stuff they hid amongst the weeds. Then, waiting until two men chatting in the courtyard had their backs turned, they stealthily made their way to the south-east tower. Blount climbed on

Bray's back and managed to scale the wall and then haul Bray himself up. Below the tower the moat was covered with thin ice. Bray could not swim, and the plan had been for Blount to tow him over. But both were so weak from hunger, lack of sleep and exposure that Blount now realised that the attempt would probably end with both of them drowning. Instead, he told Bray of a fordable point below a watergate in the stables on the outer island, and arranged that if he could get over there, they would meet at the house of a Catholic servant of the Darells half a mile away. Then, stripping off his cassock, he leapt over the piles into the water and 'with much difficulty' swam across to the other side.

To reach the stables, Bray had first to get across the causeway between the two islands, which was guarded at its inner end by the gatehouse. Tucking the discarded cassock into his breeches, he ran into the hall, shouting that there was a noise in the stables, and someone was stealing Sir George's horses. Sleepy and fuddled, the searchers roused themselves and ran out into the courtyard crying 'Thieves in the stable!' The two men already out there heard them and unbarred the gates to let them through. Bray ran to the stables, splashed across the ford under the trees and disappeared into the darkness. On the far side he stumbled into Blount, who had lost his way and wandered back to the Castle. Together they made for the farm half a mile away, where they were fed and clothed and their bleeding feet washed.

When the hubbub had subsided, the searchers returned to the hall fire. It then occurred to them to ask what had happened to the oddly dressed man who had raised the alarm, and what had caused the splashing by the stables. But by then it was too late. That same night, despite the privations they had already endured, Blount and Bray trudged another fourteen miles, sometimes in mud up to their knees, to the Gages' house at Bentley in the parish of Framfield, just outside Uckfield. Towards the end of their journey, they met a milkmaid with a pail and begged her to give them a drink, only to be told to wash their dirty faces first. As soon as it was light, the searchers were back in the courtyard. They found the hide and put a bloodhound on the scent, and also began to drag the moat by the stables in hopes of finding the priest's body.

While they were doing so, a dishevelled figure crept out of the barn and was sighted. He was a Protestant ploughboy who, terrified of the pursuivants, had been hiding there throughout the search and was now foraging for some food. He was pursued back to the barn, where he burrowed under the straw until prodded out with pitchforks. On his return, Mr Darell was told of this incident, and sometime later, when he was accused of harbouring priests, he put forward the defence that the whole affair had been blown up out of the panic of this harmless country boy.

Since no priest had actually been found, the case was dropped, but that was the end of Blount's residence at Scotney. He spent the remaining forty years of his life living very discreetly at the house of a still-unidentified gentlewoman in London. For fifteen years he kept out of sight of the servants, going out only at night. Despite these precautions, it is said (perhaps unreliably) that George Abbot, the Jacobean Archbishop of Canterbury, was aware of his address, but would not act on the knowledge for the sake of old times together at Balliol. In a list of Jesuits and their places of abode drawn up by Sir Robert Cecil in 1603, Blount is still described as 'with Mr Torell in Sussex', but here at least Mr Secretary's information was out of date.

2

Whatever the hazards at the ports, there were many recusant gentry in the south-east, the region of England closest to the Continent. Between 1586 and 1592, Southwell made good use of his kinship with the Gages, Copleys, Shelleys and Banisters; and Blount was able to profit by his contacts. Blount was, in fact, on his way to Uxendon when Southwell was captured there, and only escaped being taken with him because of a delay when a horse was not ready. So, as in the midlands, it is instructive to follow a clockwise circuit of a dozen or so houses in Kent, Sussex, Hampshire and Surrey.

Fourteen miles north-west of Scotney, at Sevenoaks on the road to London, is Knole, the largest private house in England with its seven courtyards, fifty-two staircases and three hundred and sixty-five rooms. In 1603 it came into the possession of Thomas Sackville, Viscount Buckhurst and Earl of Dorset, who rebuilt it in its present form. Although he was reconciled formally, by Richard Blount, only shortly before his death of a stroke at the Council table in 1608, he seems to have been discreetly sympathetic towards Catholics for some time before that. One of his daughters-in-law was Margaret, , the Earl of Arundel's half-sister and a close friend of the Countess. Another was Anne Spencer, a lifelong recusant who was the widow of Lord Compton of Compton Wynyates. There was formerly a hide in the garrets at Knole, which was destroyed when a chimneystack was reconstructed. Though the place itself was of no great interest, it can at least be dated between 1603 and 1608.

Three miles east of Knole is Ightham Mote, an exquisite, moated manor-house of Kentish ragstone and timber-framing which, like Knole, now belongs to the National Trust. The oldest part, about 1340, is the east wing, which contains the hall and solar and a chapel. The west wing, containing the gatehouse, and the south wing were added about 1480, and the quadrangle was completed about 1520 by a north wing which includes another chapel with a barrel ceiling and carved oak screen. When a blocked doorway at the buttery end of the hall was opened up in 1872, the seated skeleton of a young woman was found inside. But it is likely that Ightham was also the scene of more conventional concealments.

'The Lady Allen of Kent' was listed as a recusant in 1588, and even before that, on 21 September 1585, the house had been searched by a local Justice of the Peace, Thomas Willoughby. Information had been laid that Sir Christopher Allen kept 'a vile and Papistical house' and that 'my Lady Allen, Mr Gerrott and his wife, and her sons and daughters did refuse to go to the church, or to use any open or public or private prayers, as Sir Christopher Allen himself was wont and accustomed in his own house'. More serious still, a certain Mr Christopher Lassels had stayed at Ightham on the night of 16 September – 'a reasonable tall man with a yellow-reddish beard, about thirty-five years of age, in a white doublet, a leather jerkin and a dark greenish cloak'. He had been a servant of Lady Waller's at Groombridge, to which he departed next morning, taking with him Lady Allen's son Charles. By the time that Willoughby had ridden to Groombridge, both had left, supposedly for Lady Waldegrave's in Essex. But Groombridge is ten miles south-west of Ightham, hardly on the way to Essex. It is tempting to wonder whether the mysterious Mr Lassels was the man of the same name who arrived at Rheims in November 1587 and returned to England as a priest in the following year.

Twyssenden Manor, a mile and a half east of Scotney, is a U-shaped

building with two sides of timber-framing and a third of stone in Jacobean classical style with an originally crenelated porch. In the roof of the centre block is a large garret, typical of those used for secret chapels. During repairs about 1880, an opening which had been blocked with a picture was discovered in the slope of

Fig. 80 Twyssendon Manor, picture from a postcard

the roof of this garret, near the floor. This led to a secret room about 3.65m long by 2.45m wide and high enough to stand in.

The entrance had been contrived by cutting away the lower part of a timber and rounding it off to ease passage through the low opening. It is high in the gable end of the secret room, so that a ladder would be needed to reach the floor. When found, the room had no other entrance but was clearly inhabited at some time, since it had a fireplace with a flue visible from outside. It had, however, no windows, the small skylights on the inner slope of the roof being subsequent additions. The general idea is reminiscent of

Huddington or Harvington.

Battle Abbey, thirteen miles south of Twyssenden along the A21, was one of the houses of Anthony Browne, first Viscount Montague, whom even the Queen acknowledged to be a firm Papist but a good subject. After his death in 1592, his widow Magdalen retired there, where she erected a pulpit and a choir for singers and maintained a full round of Catholic liturgical services with considerable splendour. 'A visible church or company of Catholics' numbering eighty or more was 'assembled and preserved' there until her death in 1608. For nearly all this time, her chaplain was Thomas More, a great-grandson of the Lord Chancellor. Battle Abbey must have been almost search-proof, consisting as it did of substantial remains of the medieval Abbey, including the Decorated gatehouse, with massive Tudor additions by the Brownes, all on a twenty-acre site surrounded by a precinct wall. According to a report of 1586, Lord Montague's brother Francis Browne was 'altogether governed' by William Weston and Southwell's friend John Cornelius, who was chaplain to the Arundells. A later list of those present at a Mass begins: 'Mr Browne (my lord's brother), Mr George Cotton, Mr Banister and his wife' - who was Southwell's sister Mary. By the time that Garnet and Southwell arrived in England in 1586, Francis Browne had set up a secret printing-press at his house in St Mary Overies, at the south end of London Bridge, and it seems likely that it was there that they said their first Masses in England on 10 July. It is a fair assumption that Southwell came to Battle Abbey.

Ten miles west of Battle, just outside Hailsham, is Hellingly. Here, in Yew Tree Cottage (also known as The Priest House), the former parsonage, was a long narrow chamber between the wall of a passage and the lower slope of the roof with two (restored) entrances, one at each end, both consisting of hinged plaster panels between heavy beams, as at Ufton and Huddington. When the hide was found, an ancient straw mattress was laid out on the floor at one end of it. Sadly, this hide was wantonly destroyed in 2015 by the owners of the house – one of whom was chair of the local council planning committee. They were prosecuted and paid a total of £200,000 in fines and costs, but the hide is gone forever. A plausible theory for the unexpected location of a priest hole in the house of the Anglican vicar is that it was built for the Massing stuff and illicit ornaments of an Elizabethan incumbent who hankered after the old ways, as so many did. There certainly were such places. At Culworth in Northamptonshire it was reported in 1576 that 'the foresaid churchwardens do keep a rood in a secret place adjoining the steeple and will not deface it'; and as late as 1569 at Arundel 'certain altars do stand yet still to the offence of the godly', while 'in many places' in Sussex there were 'images hidden up and other Popish ornaments, ready to set up the Mass again within twenty-four hours' warning'.

Three miles south-west of Hellingly is Michelham Priory, which until

1897 was another house of the Sackvilles. The Augustinian priory was founded in 1229 on an island site in the River Cuckmere. At the Dissolution, part of it was destroyed, but the rest became the nucleus of a fine Elizabethan house built about 1595 by Herbert Pelham, who bought Michelham in 1587 and sold it to Lord Buckhurst in 1601. It now belongs to the Sussex Archaeological Society and is regularly open to the public.

Behind the panelling beside the main staircase is a series of ladders and platforms, beginning in a cupboard on the ground floor and ending two storeys up in another cupboard, whose door is part of the panelling. At the first landing there is a movable panel which serves as a spy-hole. Unfortunately, in consequence of a fire in 1927, the panelling and staircase are modern, and so is most of the carpentry behind them, though scorched timbers can still be seen there. No records of the original arrangement have survived, so it is impossible to say whether this is a completely modern fancy or a reconstruction, accurate or inspired, of a real hide.

In West Sussex, eight miles north of Worthing, was Ashington House, which was owned by the recusant Nicholas Wolfe. In 1594, a spy named Nicholas or Benjamin Beard reported that both it and Wappingthorn nearby were 'receptacles for priests and have great convenience for hiding them. In Wolfe's house in a little gallery there is a place for an altar and the Massing stuff, and a cover of boards over a great cupboard which can be taken off'. But Ashington House has not survived, and the oldest part of Wappingthorn is dated 1609, fifteen years after this report. Five miles west of Ashington, between Storrington and Pulborough, is Parham, an E-shaped house of grey stone begun in 1577 by Sir Thomas Palmer, who died there in 1582. In 1569, he had been accused of harbouring a Marian priest named Stephen Hopkins and of receiving communion at Easter in his own chapel, choosing priests from a distance. Parham has been altered, but the Great Hall is substantially in original condition, and so is the Long Gallery at the top of the house, with its panelling and bay-windows with views of the Downs. In one of these bays, both the top and the front of the window-seat formerly opened to reveal a rough hole quarried through the outside wall into the apex of a small gable beyond. This gable has now been replaced by a flat roof, the hole filled in and the floorboards under the seat renewed. Two large hinge-marks survive on the underside of the seat, which is much older and rougher than the modern veneered top surface. The rooms beneath the former gable may have been a C.19 addition, in which case the 'hide' was a romantic reconstruction. The chapel and sacristy at the NE corner of the Gallery survived until 1924, and at the SE corner are 'the Priest's Room' and 'the Priest's Dressing Room'.

Further north, in the neighbourhood of Horsham, are three houses which all belonged to the Caryll family and which between them give a picture of recusancy from the sixteenth to the nineteenth centuries and, indeed, down to the present day. The earliest is Bentons Place, Shipley, a double-L-shaped building of timber, brickwork and tile-hanging with a Horsham stone roof. Under Elizabeth and James I it was the home in turn of Edward

Fig. 81 Benton's Place, Shipley in 2024

Caryll and of his son, Sir Thomas. In West Sussex Record Office is a certificate, dated 8 January 1581 and signed by the parson of Shipley, that he and the village constable had searched 'throughout the chambers of the said house as diligently as we might devise to our discretion' without finding anyone. The two men they were looking for, Robert Hampton and Richard Stratford, were not seminary priests and were probably Marians. But this was before many priest-holes existed; and if there had been any at that date, it is unlikely that the parson and the constable would have found them. This level of policing is more reminiscent of Shakespeare's Dogberry and Verges than the ruthless and professional searches of the 1590s.

Newbuildings Place, a classical house of sandstone and brick, was built by Philip Caryll in 1683 according to a date formerly on a down-spout on the south front. Nevertheless, an 18th century note in the Burrell Collections in the British Library records that 'in a closet belonging to the garret is a of concealment through a false top of the cupboard'. According to a report in the early 20th century, this hide was at one end of the house, in the thickness of the wall on the second floor: 'there is little doubt that this place still exists, but it is now covered with loaded bookshelves'. There is, however, no sign of it today.

The Elizabethan manor-house of West Grinstead was acquired by the Carylls about 1638, early enough to have been furnished with hides. In 1671 John Caryll gave £600 to support three priests, one of whom was to live at West Grinstead and serve the neighbourhood, while the other two acted as riding missioners in Sussex and Hampshire. His descendants sold the house about 1750, and both it and its Regency successor by Nash have since been pulled down. But instead, about 1758, Edward Caryll gave a small building in Park Lane which still serves as the Priest's House today. Behind the Georgian front and Ionic porch is an older timber-framed building, but the recusant associations of the house only go back to the mid-eighteenth century. All the same, the former chapel on the second floor still contains a seventeenth-century Italianate altar, beneath which was found a small slate altar-stone, and in 1925 there was also discovered a chalice of French workmanship dating from about 1600.

Roffey or Roughey, now part of Horsham itself, was the home of Southwell's cousins the Copleys and the scene of the arrest of a priest named Nicholas Smith on 9 September 1586. But here again it is clear from Margaret Copley's examination that whatever hiding places it had then would not withstand any rigorous search:

> Item, she saith that he being a timorous person and hearing that Sir Thomas Browne, knight, and John Apsley, esquire, were here at Roghey: he therefore, leaving the company of Edward Gage of Ifield and John Gage, gentlemen, came to her, desiring her help. Who bolted the door of the said chamber after her and afterwards hid himself in the place where he was found. But she spake aloud to him (after that he had bolted that door), saying that he was known to be within the house, and therefore it were better for his own safety to come to them than otherwise, or else to go forth of the chamber into the park.

Nicholas Smith, a cousin of the Copleys, had travelled with Southwell from Paris to Rome in 1578. John Gage was engaged to Margaret Copley. In 1591, the couple were both condemned to death for priest-harbouring but reprieved at the last minute when they were already in the cart that was to take them to the place of execution. By then, no doubt, the facilities at Roffey had been brought up to date. Smith was committed to the Clink and then banished but returned and died working in England as a Jesuit in 1630.

The most important Catholic house in west Sussex was Cowdray Park near Midhurst, the principal seat of Lord Montague. Cowdray is an imposing quadrangular mansion built in the reigns of Henry VII and Henry VIII in a style which had much in common with Hampton Court. In 1793 it was burnt out in a fire that raged for three days. But the organ gallery and eighteenth-century altarpiece in the ruined chapel can still be seen, while a catalogue of the pictures published in 1777 makes it possible to reconstruct the disposition and furnishings of many of the rooms. A vivid picture of the state and ceremony maintained there is given by the Book of Orders and Rules drawn up for the household by Lord Montague's grandson, the second Viscount.

In 1591, the year before the first Viscount's death, the Queen visited Cowdray and was magnificently entertained there for a week, but it was also a major centre for harbouring priests. In 1590, a priest named William Harris was reported to be there, 'a tall man, blackish hair of head and beard'. He was a former bursar of Lincoln College, Oxford, and had been with Campion at Mr Dormer's in Buckinghamshire in 1580. About the same time, another priest, Robert Gray, who had been ordained in Rome in 1586, was conducted to Cowdray by Sir George Browne. He was 'of a black complexion and of a

Fig. 82 Cowdray Castle ruins – destroyed by fire in 1793

mean stature and speaketh broad after the Northern manner'. At Great Todham, a mile away, they found 'a man sitting in his chair, of about forty years old, long, slender-faced, black hair of head and a little beard, whom since he heard was Father Curry the Jesuit'.

In July 1593 Topcliffe obtained a warrant to search Cowdray for Gray, four other priests and three laymen. By August, Gray and one of these other priests, Anthony Garnet, were under arrest and described as 'belonging to the late Lord Viscount Montacute'. Evidently the comparative immunity which the Queen's favour bestowed upon Cowdray in the time of the first Viscount was not to continue. Gray contrived to escape from Windsor, only to be arrested again in October and sent to the Counter in Wood Street. But Curry was still at large in Kent and Sussex a year later, and more will be heard of him in Chapter 8. Later still, in the early seventeenth century, two former servants from Cowdray were ordained in Rome: Anthony Fletcher, who had been Lord Montague's steward, and Anthony Lamb, who had been one of his pages. Another priest, Anthony Whitehair alias Rivers, studied for five years at St Omers at the expense of the second Viscount, who after the Gunpowder Plot was himself imprisoned in the Tower and heavily fined.

In the park, where the Queen went hunting in 1591, was a Keeper's Lodge which after the fire of 1793 was first enlarged for the owners to live in and then pulled down to make way for the much bigger Victorian house. This Lodge contained a hiding-place behind a bedroom fireplace, entered by a movable panel in a cupboard - perhaps like Abbots Salford or other examples to be mentioned later. It was two storeys high but so narrow that opposite the stone bench in it the wall was hollowed out to make room for the occupant's knees. All these details suggest a blocked-up chimney-flue which had been converted to secret use. There were probably other hides in Cowdray itself and in Mr George Denis's house at Great Todham; during the nineteenth century a box was found in the chimney of a house in Midhurst containing rosaries and a deed dated 1634 leaving money for the support of a priest at Midhurst.

A few hundred yards into Hampshire, on Chichester Harbour opposite Hayling Island, is Warblington Castle, almost certainly the point from which Southwell and John Cotton crossed the Channel in 1576. George Cotton of Warblington was one of the few recusants to pay the full fine of £20 a month and eventually died in prison. Thomas Lister from Hindlip was here in 1603, and so at other times were two other Jesuits, William Baldwin and Thomas Singleton. In 1606, George Jetter, 'a low man with a yellow beard', was at Warblington as Cotton's chaplain; and during a search in 1613 part of the body of the martyr Mark Barkworth was found in a reliquary of crimson damask in John Cotton's study.

Fig. 83 All that survives of Warblington Castle

A survey of 1633 describes the Castle as 'two hundred feet [60m] square, with a fair green court within and buildings round the said court; with a fair gallery and divers chambers and two towers covered with lead; a very great and spacious hall, parlour and great chamber with a chapel and all other offices'.

Christopher Devlin suggested that the aesthetic impact of such a setting on the adolescent Southwell was important for his later poetry, leaving 'memories of a casement window opening in the early morning on tree-tops and meadows and a walled garden; of brocaded dresses in the afternoon like moving rose-bushes; of a golden sunset fading over mellow walls and feathery orchards'. But all that remains of the Castle today is one tower and a few other fragments of a quadrangular brick building of the C.15.

In Winchester there is a sixteenth-century house in St Peter Street which is now the Royal Hotel. In the time of Elizabeth it was the home of the recusant Lady Mary West, and during a search in December 1583 three hides were found there, all of them containing books or Massing stuff:

In a secret place enclosed with boards were laid divers new and old Papistical books, printed and written. In another place, more secret, vaulted underground, was found a chest bound with iron, wherein was all kind of Massing apparel; a chalice of tin; a box full of singing-cakes; a rich canopy of silver, of goldsmith's work; needlework cloths upon velvet for the altar; Corpus cakes; a pax of ivory set in wood. There was also wrapped in green silk two Agnus Deis enclosed in satin, broken in many places.... And also in the same chest were divers new Mass-books, manuals and catechisms. In one other place of the same house were found above forty old Mass and Latin service books.

Fifteen miles north-west of Chichester and ten miles west of Cowdray, near Petersfield, was Mapledurham - not to be confused with the Mapledurham in Oxfordshire. This was the home of the Shelleys, yet another family of Southwell's cousins. Here, Nicholas Beard reported in 1594, was

'a hollow place in the parlour by the livery cupboard where two men may well lie together, which has many times deceived the searchers....In Mapledurham House, under a little table, is a vault with a grate of iron for a light into the garden, as if it were the window of a cellar, and against the grate groweth rosemary'.

Nothing of this remains, however, since the house, a large gabled building approached by an avenue of elms, was demolished in the nineteenth century and replaced by a farmhouse.

Records of hiding-places in Surrey are very scanty, and only two houses call for mention here. The first is Sutton Place, just north of Guildford, a brick and terracotta house built by Sir Richard Weston about 1530. In the time of his grandson, Sir Henry, who died in 1592, it was searched at least twice, and during the nineteenth century two hiding-places

Fig. 84 Sutton Place, Guildford

were found there. One was in a cupboard behind the panelling of the chapel in the east wing and contained a beautifully embossed casket of leather bound with iron, in which there were relics. The other contained a much-corroded chalice and paten of pewter. About the same time, a copy of a book printed at Douai in 1618, *The Safeguard from Shipwrack*, was found between a floor and a ceiling. Sir Richard Weston III (1591-1652), two of whose sons married Copley girls, was an agriculturalist and initiator of projects as well as a recusant and Royalist. His most enduring memorial is the Wey Navigation from Guildford to Weybridge, but he also took the opportunity of his exile during the Civil War to make observations of Flemish farming methods, which he published in England just before his death.

The other house in Surrey is Little Santon Farm, two miles south-west of Reigate and close to Leigh Place, another home of the Copleys. The original house was a fairly small T-shaped building of brick and timber with chimney stacks of Reigate stone topped with brick shafts. In 1933 a space was recorded here, 2.45m deep, 900mm long and just over 600mm wide. It was entered through the garret floorboards and tucked away between the angle of two chimneys, the back of a cupboard on a landing and the wall of a bedroom. When discovered, it contained the remains of a chicken or pheasant. But it no longer exists, thanks to alterations in the 1930s when the house was doubled in size by additions at each end and the first-floor landing and passage moved from the south side to the north. With those dimensions, if it ever was a priest hole, confinement in it would only have been tolerable for a few hours at a time.

Devlin was probably right in thinking that the Gages, Copleys, Banisters and Shelleys were already harbouring Marian priests in the 1570s. At that time, it might reasonably be supposed that the safest thing to do when the Justices arrived was to go forth from the chamber into the park. But the arrest of Nicholas Smith in 1586 should have made it clear that times had changed. The point was made even more brutally two years later, on 1 October 1588, with the executions at Chichester and Canterbury of five priests and a layman. Two of these, Ralph Crockett and Edward James, had been arrested even before landing, when their boat ran aground at Littlehampton. John Owen, brother of Nicholas, was also set down for trial in Sussex but saved his life by recanting. After that, it is likely that Nicholas's services were much in demand in the south-east during the 1590s. Priest-holes as cunning as those at Scotney may still await discovery elsewhere in Kent and Sussex.

7

Grosmont Priory, 1599
The North

1

A lthough the northern counties, and especially Lancashire, were notorious for recusancy, not many authenticated priest-holes have survived there. Many examples are known in houses that have been lost due to industrialisation or development but in any case, hides may never have been so common in the North as the numbers of recusants recorded might suggest. In 1593, the spy Anthony Atkinson reported to Sir Robert Cecil that hunted priests in these six counties were 'conveyed into caves in the ground or secret places not possible to find them'. There is other evidence for this use of the natural cover provided by the moors and fells, and in the parts of Lancashire where the whole countryside was Catholic and people would kneel and ask a priest's blessing in the street, prepared hiding-places may have seemed hardly necessary.

Whatever the reason, although many houses have odd spaces which are claimed to be priest-holes, few of them can be authenticated. Some of the genuine ones, as in other parts of the country, are holes-under-the-garderobe. A good example, and the only one that need be mentioned here, is that at Birchley Hall, which was found to contain a pewter chalice, vestments and altar-stones. The wall-cupboard for Massing stuff at Duckworth Old Hall near Claughton-in-Brock, its doors beautifully carved with grapes and ears of wheat, is a fascinating recusant relic but not a hiding-place. These and other eliminations leave us with seventeen houses which, either for the hides or the documents or both, are worth describing here. Some others will be mentioned in Chapter 10, on the early Stuart period, and in Chapter 12, at the time of the Jacobite risings. Of the seventeen, three were in the city of York, four in the rest of Yorkshire and five each in Durham and Lancashire.

2

The earliest datable hide in the country which is known to have been used for sheltering a priest is in the city of York. This was at the house of Dr Thomas Vavasour, in Ogleforth, near the eastern end of York Minster. For the details we are indebted to William Hutton, a draper of Christ's parish, who was in trouble for the same offence himself: on Christmas night 1582 a priest named William Hart was caught in his house, and three months later, in March 1583, the High Sheriff found there 'a secret hiding-place which contained a trunk full of Catholic books'. On 5 November 1574, the Vavasours' house had been raided, and the searchers' behaviour had been so violent that Mrs Vavasour became temporarily insane. According to Hutton,

> the secret place being so politicly devised, they could not find [Vavasour], and being made certain that he was in the house, they did not depart until the Lord Mayor was willed to command watchmen with halberts to be set about the house, thereby to make him yield by famine, which so remaining that night and next day, he yielded himself to the watch the sooner for saving a priest which was with him.

This priest must have been a Marian, since it was only in 1574 that the first four seminary priests returned to England and none of them had got as far as York. The story confirms the impression given by the places at Hellingly and Culworth that some hiding-places were built in the 1560s and 1570s, even though they were exceptional until the 1580s. But the circumstances in York were also exceptional. The rebellion of the Northern Earls in 1569 was followed in 1570 by the appointment of a new and energetic Archbishop, Edmund Grindal, and in 1572 by the arrival of the Earl of Huntingdon as President of the Council of the North, a position which he held until his death in 1595. Grindal was translated to Canterbury in 1575, but Huntingdon found an even closer friend and collaborator in Matthew Hutton, who was Dean of York from 1570 to 1589, Bishop of Durham from 1589 to 1596 and then Archbishop of York and Huntingdon's successor as Lord President from 1596 onwards. The records of the Council of the North and the High Commission are full of recusants who were fined, imprisoned or compelled to give bonds for good behaviour; and in the ten years from 1582 to 1591 there were twenty-two executions at York of priests and of lay-people who had harboured them.

The most famous of these is Margaret Clitherow, who was pressed to death in the Ousebridge prison on Good Friday 1586. A butcher's wife, she had become a recusant through the influence of the Vavasours and welcomed priests to her house at 10-11 The Shambles. But in this narrow street with continuous rows of timber houses on either side, the hiding-place was in fact not in her own house but in the roof of the house next door. John Mush, one of the priests whom she harboured, and later a leading Appellant, says that it was 'in the next neighbour's house' and 'without her own house'. He also says that 'the entry was painful to him that was not acquainted with the door, by reason of the straitness thereof'. If the case had proceeded, her neighbours would have been incriminated as well, and she therefore refused to plead either guilty or not guilty. But Mush says further that when the house was searched, 'the priest... and some other persons with him... were all safely shifted away into a lower chamber of *her* [my italics] house' and were not found there. Since the house was too small for several strangers to have been simply overlooked, it seems clear that the 'lower chamber' was another hiding-place, on the first floor rather than in the roof. In this house in The Shambles, therefore, there were at least one and probably two hiding-places, which can be dated between 1577, when Margaret Clitherow was first recorded as a recusant, and 1585.

Fig. 85 The Shambles, York. The whitewashed building is today a shrine to Margaret Clitherow and may have been her house.

Between 1578 and 1603, more than fifty Marian and seminary priests were imprisoned in York Castle, which became what has been called 'to some degree a Catholic pastoral centre'. Recusant gentry found that they could practise their religion more easily there than in the country; the ramshackle pile of buildings by the Fosse was fairly easy to get into or out of, while the gaolers, who depended on fees and bribes, 'touted for prisoners like seaside boarding-house keepers' and were sometimes in trouble for recusancy themselves. In 1582, Thomas Bell, a friend of the priest William Hart, said Mass in the Castle every day for a fortnight, hearing confessions, preaching and giving great consolation to the prisoners. He then collected three other priests, and all four, together with some laymen, made their way along the moat from the Fosse and scaled the walls with ropes. They then assembled the recusant prisoners for a High Mass with deacon, subdeacon and music. This, however, seems to have attracted the attention of the Keeper, John Burley, and the Castle was beset to catch the priests on their way out again. One, William Lacy, was caught and executed, but the others got away, though Hart was arrested at William Hutton's a few months later. Bell is next heard of in Lancashire where, according to Persons, during a raid in September 1584 he had to flee barefoot and in his night-

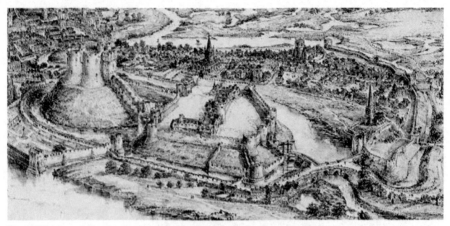

Fig. 86 York and Castle precincts in the C15, from a watercolour by E Risdale Tate. By 1600 the walls were crumbling, and security was very lax.

clothes, and suffered so much that he needed a month in bed to recover. Eleven years later, in 1593, there was a search in the Castle itself, which is also described in vivid detail by William Hutton:

> In the house of Mr Fletcher the Keeper they found a secret passage, sufficient for a man to pass towards the water. They broke open several places, including the ceiling over the outgate and in the new chamber above. They searched for three days. They broke and beat down walls, ceilings, floors, hearths, boards: yea, they untiled the house and, breaking down all within the chambers, tossed and trod under their feet our clothes and bedding: lime, plaster, dust and dirt falling upon it. They found a great store of books and church stuff. A great spite they had about chimneys and kept much ado about them: climbing up to the tops, [they] cast down stones to see if there were any false ones.

Fletcher had not long been appointed, through Huntingdon's influence, but despite such rigorous action, effective control of the Castle was impossible. Within a year or two, Fletcher had been replaced by Robert Redhead, who further weakened the walls by selling masonry for lime. Despite cold, hunger and gaol fever, there continued to be obstinate recusants imprisoned in the Castle throughout the seventeenth century. One was William Clitherow, Margaret's stepson, who was ordained at Douai in 1608. As late as 1680, the Jesuit Fr Pracid was saying Mass daily in the Castle and preaching to fellow-prisoners on Sundays and holy days. No doubt he too had a store of books and church stuff. In 1745, a priest committed to the Castle at the time of the Jacobite rising continued the tradition of Bell and Lacy by conducting a wedding there.

3

Yet another of the survivors of the search at Baddesley Clinton in October 1591 was Richard Holtby, 'a little man with a reddish beard'. A graduate of both Oxford and Cambridge, he had returned from Rheims in 1579 to work in the North. When Campion came to Yorkshire in January 1581, Holtby harboured him and gave him facilities for working on the *Ten Reasons*. Profoundly moved by Campion's sanctity, Holtby decided after the execution to join the Jesuits himself, which he did at Verdun in 1583. In 1590, he landed in the North again, and together with John Mush built up a regular system for smuggling priests from the Continent and sheltering them at Thornley in Durham and Grosmont near Whitby until they had houses of their own to go to. This operation may have been the model for Oldcorne's at Hindlip; no doubt it was one of the matters discussed when the two met at Baddesley. Apart from his abilities as an organiser, Holtby was a skilled needleworker who made his own vestments, and a talented carpenter and mason who made his own priest-holes. Indeed, the seventeenth-century Jesuit historian Henry More says that no pursuivant ever found a hide of his making.

Thornley Hall, five miles south-east of Durham, is now a farmhouse. It is a Georgian building both inside and out, with some fine panelling and brass door furniture. But in the fields to the north of the house are extensive stone foundations which must mark the site of the much larger Elizabethan building. According to the Catholic writer Richard Verstegan, one hiding-place large enough for six people was below ground, and if he was right, its walls and floor may still exist, though it is doubtful whether they could be identified now.

In January 1593, Thomas Clark, a priest from Rheims, was interrogated at Canterbury. He confessed that he had been ordained at Michaelmas 1590 and sent on the mission soon afterwards with two other priests. They had come over in a French ship to a point near Newcastle-upon-Tyne and made their way to Thornley, where they met Holtby, 'to whom they were specially directed'. Clark stayed there for a week or so and had a frieze jerkin made for him by Holtby's procurement. Then he travelled on to Grosmont, where he met another dozen priests, including Mush. Grosmont, he explained, was 'a place where they are specially directed when they come over from Rheims'.

A few weeks later, on 1-2 February, the Earl of Huntingdon organised a massive search 'all over Yorkshire, Richmondshire, Cleveland and the Bishopric of Durham and Northumberland. It was in this search that Anthony Page was captured at York, 'in a conveyance made in the bottom of a haystack'. Both Holtby himself and his brother John had very narrow escapes. In view of Anthony Atkinson's report of that year (p257), it is significant that the pursuivants 'did also seek the grounds and woods in many places'. Three weeks later, 'the like search was made again all over the Bishopric' for four days, from Thursday 22 February to Sunday 25 February.

On the Monday in Holy Week, 9 April 1593, Huntingdon himself took charge of a raid on Thornley. Mr Trollope concealed himself, his wife, one of his sons, a niece aged thirteen and two maids in the hiding-place mentioned by Verstegan, leaving one Catholic maid to face the searchers. Like John Gerard at Braddocks a year later, the fugitives found the hide unprovisioned and had nothing to eat or drink for two days. Holtby and Trollope's eldest son were away for a baptism, but on returning on the Monday evening they nearly blundered into the sentries and were pursued into the woods. Young Trollope's knowledge of the terrain enabled them to get away, but they had to spend that night in a tree and the next in a cave. Meanwhile, the searchers had broken down doors, forced locks and looted silver plate, clothing, saddlery and firearms. They measured the house inside and out and tried to detect any hollow spaces by ringing a little bell and listening for variations in the sound from the next room. Then they scattered throughout the house and remained completely silent while they listened for any betraying cough or sound of breathing. They also tried calling out 'Here they are, mates: we've got them!' in the hope of provoking some involuntary movement. But all these tricks were unsuccessful; the maid who had been left to keep the house slipped out to avoid being taken off to prison, and on the Wednesday evening the searchers abandoned the hunt.

Five miles east of Thornley, and less than a mile from the sea, is Hardwicke Manor Hall (not to be confused with the famous Hardwick Hall in Derbyshire or the nearby Hardwick Hall), a much-altered fragment of the original Elizabethan mansion.

Between the chapel, which, although now divided into two hotel bedrooms, still retains its Georgian ceiling mouldings and other features, and one of the garrets is a large brick chimney-breast, 2.3m wide and 760mm deep. More than half of this space is a hiding-place, not made in the chimney but added on to it. The real chimney is only 965mm wide, but to this was built on another 1320mm of wall, so cleverly blended into the

Fig. 87 Hardwicke, showing the position of the hide, entered from the left-hand end of the chimney breast.

original brickwork that it is impossible to detect the join, built against the actual chimney. Quite conceivably the entire façade, one brick thick, is fake:

the right-hand end of the stack is plastered and so it is hard to be sure. This false wall, like the false chimney at Harvington, is supported on the floorboards only, a fact concealed by a ridge of mortar at the base of the chimney breast.

The hide entrance is a door under the slope of the roof at the left-hand side of the 'chimney'. This door opens inwards and can be fastened on the inside by a rough iron bolt. Although there is plenty of headroom, the hide is only 690mm wide by 1.32m long. There is a wooden seat attached to the real chimney and a wooden shelf head-high above it. Being directly under the tiles, the hide would be hot in summer and cold in winter, though perhaps the heat of the chimney would make up for that.

Fig. 88 Hide door from outside, closed. Note the contrast between the 'bricks' on the door and those on the fake part of the chimney breast.

The door is covered on the outside with a thick coat of plaster, painted and camouflaged to look, and feel, like brickwork, and it is very well done. But there is a puzzle here. The outline of the door is very clear under electric light, and the plaster 'bricks' do not match those in the chimney stack (real or false). Moreover, the door has a frame visible outside the hide and its inner face is panelled in Georgian style. The implication is that, although the hide must originally have been built around 1595, it was refurbished at some time during the heightened tensions of the eighteenth century. A possible occasion is in 1746, when the house was attacked and plundered by a mob in the aftermath of the Jacobite

Fig. 89 View into hide, with seat and shelf.

rising. Although the existing door would not have deceived Elizabethan pursuivants, it might well pass muster in a casual and disorderly incursion. The rest of the hide is in mint condition and is almost certainly one of Holtby's. If it is, then More's compliment about Holtby's work is understandable.

Close to the Hall is a brook, the Hardwick Dene, at the bottom of a precipitous and thickly wooded ravine. In the left bank of this, five hundred yards downstream from the

Fig. 90 Hide door from inside showing Georgian style woodwork, iron bolt and brickwork of Elizabethan false wall.

Hall in the face of a sandstone promontory round which the brook bends, is an artificial cave which appears to have been used as a hide-out and secret chapel. The trees and undergrowth are so dense that it is completely invisible until you have scrambled down to within a few feet of it.

In 1933 the entrance was 'a hole a yard wide ... under an overhanging tree' and

> The mouth of the cave slopes slightly upwards to allow one to crawl in, and the top and sides of the narrow entrance are covered with the marks of implements, proving that the whole cave was dug out for a purpose and is not of natural origin. Within the entrance one can stand upright, for it is 2.5m high, though only 2.7m deep and 2.1m wide. At the entrance a stoup has been hollowed out of the stone, and there are two large recesses cut in the walls, one obviously made to contain an altar.

The last of these remarks is confirmed by Fordyce (1857), who said that at that time 'the mouldering remains of a rude crucifix [were] still visible in the wall'. But the 'narrow entrance' has now collapsed, presumably because of the roots of the overhanging tree, so that the opening is now much wider and only part of the stoup remains. The crucifix, exposed to weathering, is not now identifiable. But the marks of implements can still be seen in the rest of the cave and confirm that it is artificial.

The recusancy of the Maires of Hardwicke began, most unusually, on a precise and known date - 27 May 1590. On that day, four young priests were executed in Durham. Among the crowd were Robert Maire of Hardwicke and Grace, daughter of Henry Smith, a rich lawyer in Durham. What they saw so moved them that both became Catholics. On 24 March 1592, they were married at Monk Hesledon, the parish in which Hardwicke stands. Henry Smith disinherited his daughter unless she would consent to come to a quarterly sermon at Durham Cathedral, which she never did. The Maires were returned as recusants in 1596, and references to their fines and debts are continuous from then until 1636, when the arrears were transferred to the Exchequer as 'hopeless'. In April 1598, Hardwicke was sequestrated but, as at Harvington, that seems to have made little difference to the Maires' ability to shelter priests.

It must have been in a place like this that Holtby and young Trollope took refuge near Thornley on 10 April 1593. After a visit to Holtby about the same time, Garnet described another such place, in which Holtby's colleague John Nelson had lived for six weeks together with a nobleman and his wife, who was shortly expecting a child. It had two apartments, with a latrine and a place for storing food, which was brought to them secretly each day from their house. It had been dug under a large oak-tree, with an entrance camouflaged by a cleft root and covered with a thin layer of turf. When the rain came and the snow melted, it collapsed on them.

Five miles west of Durham were two other houses which had hiding places. One was at Waterhouses, 'a straw-thatched house and containing scarce an honest lodging for one of mean estate'. John Boste, who was executed at Durham in 1594, was arrested here on 10 September 1593. The searchers 'broke up the boarded floor of the parlour where the Lady Margaret [Neville] lay and found a conveyance below; found their church stuff in the bottom of a cupboard in the chamber above but could not find the man they sought for'. Then Francis Eglesfield, a traitor whom the owners had trusted, 'assigned them to break about the chimney and they should have him'. This account is by Holtby, who as a hide-builder himself would appreciate the technical details.

The other house, a mile and a half away, was Esh Hall, an E-shaped building of rubble, roofed with stone slates and containing much panelling and a well staircase. During its demolition in 1857, a small secret chamber was discovered, in which was an iron box containing vestments and church plate. These are now in the possession of the Fitzherberts and are still used occasionally. They may have been hidden in 1644, when the Scots army was besieging Newcastle after the Battle of Marston Moor.

One other house in County Durham should be mentioned: Sledwich Hall, which is near Barnard Castle, half a mile from the River Tees and the North Riding of Yorkshire. In 1622, four of the Clopton girls of Sledwich became nuns of St Monica's at Louvain on the same day, and the convent chronicle, which had earlier recorded the defiant spirit of young Frances Burroughs at Lord Vaux's house in Hackney, now includes a note on the Cloptons and their priest-holes:

> These two constant Catholics were very charitable in relieving of priests and maintained always one of residence in their house, besides receiving those who came, so that at one time there hath been no less than a great table full.... They had an excellent place which was made all the length of a little garden underground and could have held a dozen priests. The going

into it was by a device in the parlour, and it had another going forth beyond the said little garden, where if the secret place should be descried on the inside, they might get forth on the outside and make haste to step into great woods or copses.

Sledwich was originally a medieval house, extensively altered about 1584 and restored in the 20th century. The nuns' parents, William and Anne

Clopton, only became recusants sometime after their marriage, which took place in the 1590s. That gives a limiting date for the construction of the hide. Like the one at Thornley, it may still exist underground: both are parallels to the place at Baddesley Clinton.

Fig. 91 Is there still an underground hide here?

4

Forty miles along the coast to the south-east of Thornley and Hardwicke is the little town of Whitby, wedged into the mouth of the River Esk. The great church of the former Benedictine abbey is still a magnificent ruin, dominating the town from its windswept site on the East Cliff and visible from far out to sea. After the Dissolution of the Monasteries under Henry VIII the buildings were bought by Sir Richard Cholmley, near to which his son Francis built a timbered house on three sides of a courtyard, known as Abbey House. Between 1593 and 1598, Francis' brother Sir Henry Cholmley allowed his wife and his mother to use Abbey House as a major centre for priest-harbouring. Sir Henry's grandson, Sir Hugh, describes how Sir Henry

> married Margaret, daughter to Sir William Bapthorpe, knt. This wife at this time was a Roman Catholic and, he living then at Whitby, it was a receptacle to the seminary priests coming from beyond seas and landing frequently at that port; in so much as I have been told there have been in his house three or four together at a time, and, most coming bare of both clothes and money, have, at his lady's charge, been sent away with a great supply of both, some in scarlet and satin with their men and horses, the better to disguise their professions. All which Sir Henry connived at, being a little then in his heart inclining that way, though he went to church.

The convenience of Whitby and of Abbey House was that Holtby's stronghold at Grosmont Priory, to which the priests were specially directed when they came over from Rheims, was a mere half dozen miles inland, up the valley of the Esk. As at Whitby, the monastic buildings had been bought by Sir Richard Cholmley at the Dissolution, and Clark's examination shows that it was being used for incoming priests by Mr John Hodgson by the autumn of 1590. In 1599, there was a search at Grosmont which, if not on the scale of Ufton or Hindlip, is nevertheless very well documented.

On 27 April that year, John Ferne, secretary to the Council of the North, wrote to Sir Robert Cecil saying that for almost two years he had been entertaining a spy with the intention of raiding the house. But that was easier said than done. Grosmont itself was 'strong, large, and many conveyances underground to a brook running near'; Cholmley would be obstructive, and men for the search would have to be brought from York, since no one for twenty miles along the coast could be relied on. The original date that Ferne had in mind was 3 May, but he was unable to meet it, and on 14 June he wrote to Sir Robert again, describing in vivid detail how the week before five officers had been thrashed and wounded on the moors near Grosmont. Indignant as he was, he felt that any arrests should be deferred 'in respect of the greater service' of raiding Grosmont, since 'a connivancy for a time will make them more secure'. In the end, the search was fixed for two in the morning of 30 June.

By then, Ferne had had to change his plans again. He had realised that it was impossible to bring from York 'such a number as was sufficient to compass the house and able to resist their violence, but it would discover the attempt'. To maintain secrecy as long as possible, he waited until the evening of 29 June and then wrote for assistance to Lord Sheffield at Mulgrave Castle, three miles from Grosmont. Although Sheffield did not receive the letter until ten at night, he immediately roused thirty-six of his servants and rode off to Grosmont, arriving there half an hour before Ferne himself. After such elaborate precautions, it was something of a let-down to find the back doors open, the house empty and the spy nowhere to be seen. He had, however, previously supplied a plan of the building, armed with which Ferne began his investigations - only to discover that it was deliberately misleading. Nevertheless, he persevered, though with little success.

> There was found in this search all things for the furnishing of a Mass and divers Popish books, but nothing else could be found, although all floors, ceilings, pavements and double walls were broken up and divers vaults of strange conveyance were found out. Amongst which, one at a stair-head, within a thick stone wall, was covered with a great post of the bigness of a man's body, which seemed to bear the house but indeed did hinge only and was removable to and fro. Being locked beneath with iron-work [it] did stand fast, but being unlocked would remove from the hole which it covered at the nether end, at which hole a man might easily descend.

The 'conveyances underground' to the brook at Grosmont must have been monastic drains, though they might have been adapted for secret purposes, like the one at Baddesley Clinton. The hide behind the great post is a remarkable parallel to the swinging beam at Harvington, not only in the form of the secret door but also in the bolt, the position next to a staircase, and in the fact that the post opened from the bottom end. It must have been one of Holtby's devices, and it would be interesting to know whether the one at Harvington was suggested by it. Since there is no mention in Ferne's report of an outer door of panelling, as at Harvington, it seems that the one at Grosmont was the less ingenious of the two. Whether that makes it earlier would depend on what knowledge the two builders had of each other's work.

It is hard to say whether Grosmont was abandoned after this search, though at the least some time would have to be allowed before it was safe to use it again. Oddly enough, the main result of the search may have been Sheffield's appointment as Lord President. The Council of the North wrote to Cecil, rehearsing his energetic part in the hunt and suggesting that he should be made a member. Four years later, in 1603, he became President, and for the next sixteen years pursued a vigorous if unsuccessful policy of repression. Perhaps, as a former recusant himself, he felt he had a past to live down. Holtby died in 1640 at the age of eighty-seven, still at large in the North. There are still Hodgsons farming near Grosmont.

One of the priests harboured in The Shambles by Margaret Clitherow was Francis Ingleby, an uncle of the Wintours of Huddington, who was executed at York on 3 June 1586. 'He was a short man but well made, and seemed a man of thirty-five years of age or thereabouts. He was of a light complexion, wore a chestnut beard, and had a slight cast in his eyes'. He was one of the Inglebys of Ripley Castle, a few miles south of Fountains Abbey and Ripon, in which an interesting hide was found in 1963.

This is in the Knight's Chamber on the top floor, which was built in 1555 and has its original panelling. The panels are large, each consisting of four planks with clearly defined cracks. In one panel, the two right-hand planks move on hinges fastened with iron nails, making a secret door 860mm high and 580mm wide. Behind is a space 1.5m high, 610mm long and 1.02m wide, with a seat and a gap in the mortar of the outside wall for ventilation. It is in a quadrant of stone formed by the junction of this outside wall, the internal wall of the Knight's Chamber and a spiral staircase behind, which is entered by a doorway 1.5m from the hinged panel.

Fig. 92 Hide, closed and open.

The hinge edge of the door is chamfered and backed with cloth glued across the join, presumably to prevent any light from escaping, as

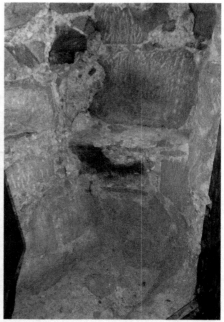

Fig. 93 *Stone seat and construction toolmarks. The floor level of the hide is only slightly below that of the threshold making access easier than might be imagined.*

Fig. 94 *Detail of door showing (above) hinge and remnants of light-blocking cloth and (below) sockets for 'snecks'.*

had happened when Campion was caught at Lyford (p.76)

Inside the frame of the secret door, at the top and bottom, are holes for catches operated by dowel-pegs outside to hold the panel closed when the hide was not in use. The estate carpenter who made the discovery described these catches as 'snecks'. One of them fell down inside, between the panelling and the stone wall, and it is still there in 2024, though the panelling would have to be taken off to retrieve it.

The position of this hide is reminiscent of the one at Sawston (p58), and a good deal of thought has gone into the design of the door. But the place is cramped and at the point of entry there is nothing but the panel between the fugitive and the searchers. So, although it may have been light-proof, it was not sound-proof, and one thrust with a pike would reveal it. It is therefore probably earlier than the time of Owen and Holtby, and the dates of Francis Ingleby's work in Yorkshire, from 1584 to 1586, would fit very well.

The Battle of Marston Moor (2 July 1644) took place just 12 miles away

Fig. 95 Ripley: position of hide in relation to staircase. The staircase continues downwards from this level and occupies much more of the space behind the panelling than is evident here.

from Ripley, and Sir William Ingleby took the field at the head of a cavalry squadron of which his redoubtable sister Jane was also a fighting member. The Parliamentarian Ironsides destroyed the Royalists and Cromwell billeted himself and his immediate entourage at Ripley that night. Jane, armed with two pistols 'for her safety' sat up all night with Cromwell in the castle library to discourage him from venturing up to the Knights Room, where Sir William had taken refuge, presumably within this very hide. Their caution was justified: Cromwell's troops shot several prisoners against the castle wall and had Sir William, who was later declared a traitor and heavily fined, been found, he would doubtless have shared their fate.

Burghwallis Hall, seven miles north-west of Doncaster, was the home of the Anne family, one of whom was executed for priesthood at York in 1589. George Anne, who died in York Castle in 1660, was one of Holtby's successors in the Jesuit mission in the North Riding, and the family were still paying compositions in respect of Burghwallis as late as 1685. The house and estate passed to the Charlton family in the 19th century and became a convent and later a nursing home during the 20th century. It is now privately owned and under restoration.

Fig. 96 Hide exterior in attics. Photo taken from Door B of Fig 87 with Door A visible at right. The door into the hide is modern.

In the Tudor part of the building is a spectacular case of hiding in plain sight. Rather than being concealed behind a wall or under a floor, the hide, 1.5m by 2.1m and 2.45m high, is clearly visible as a blocked off area of the attics (Fig. 96 – the door is modern!). Despite this, it kept its secret even from the residents of the house for at least the 250 years before 1907. In that year some alterations were required in the attics. When the builders tried to translate the drawn plans onto the floors, they were found not to fit. After retaking the measurements and finding that the plans had indeed been drawn accurately, this plaster enclosure was pierced, and the hide found.

It has a floor of lime concrete and reed-and-plaster walls (Fig. 97). It was approached via a catwalk as at Harvington (although here it would be a crawl) and entered from above. The catwalk runs from the chapel about 10m away and is entered via a triangular gap, originally hidden by a plaster door, over the chapel doorway (Fig. 100).

This chapel was superseded about 1820 when a more commodious one was opened elsewhere in the Hall, but altar-

Fig. 97 Hide interior walls of lath-and-plaster and reed-and-plaster.

stones, a chalice which unscrews into several pieces and narrow stoles of thin ribbon which could be put away with the ladies' dresses remained in the Hall down to the 1930s.

The reason that so many people (including the architect and builders of the 1907 works) passed unsuspectingly by for so long, is that it is cleverly disguised as the headroom required at the top of the attic staircase. This staircase occupies a protruding turret (blue in Fig. 101) and the top flight of steps into the attic is twice the length of the flights forming the rest of the staircase (Fig. 98).

Fig. 98 Attic stairwell. The long final flight of stairs masks the distance between the staircase and the main structure.

That extra length, and a short landing at the attic threshold, means that by the time a person climbing the stairs reaches doorway A (Fig. 99), they are rather further away from the stairwell than they may

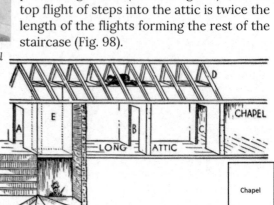

Fig. 99 Burghwallis: Section and Plan. A–C: doorways; D: entrance to catwalk; E: hide.

Fig. 100 View from chapel of catwalk entrance D (dark triangle), above doorway C (lower right).

realise. The result is that subconsciously they expect, on passing through A, to see a blocked off area of attic (as headroom for the stairwell) at position E. Coincidentally or not, the staircase turret has no side windows, making it harder to judge from the staircase how far away the stairwell is from the main building.

Fig. 101 Burghwallis. Positions marked of chapel (green), catwalk (yellow), hide (red) and staircase (blue). The absence of side windows in the staircase turret conceals the distance between the staircase and the main structure of the house.

In 1610, the Jesuit James Pollard alias Sharpe wrote of his experiences in Yorkshire:

> Among my friends and acquaintances, the most of them, if not all, being gentlemen of good account, I can travel from this side Lincoln to York, and so thirty miles further, which is above eighty miles, and within every six miles come to a Catholic house, and for the most part within three miles, all or the most of them gentlemen or gentlewomen's houses of good account; and for all this I will not in all the way go six miles out of the ready and nighest way.

For reasons explained at the beginning of this chapter, not all these houses would have contained hiding-places. But it is likely that many of them did, and so we can form some impression of how many there must have been in Yorkshire as a whole. This one quotation suggests an interesting project for further research.

5

On the other side of the Pennines, the first house for mention is Towneley Hall, near Burnley, only four miles on the Lancashire side of the boundary. This is a building with a long and complicated architectural history of at least 600 years. In the reign of Elizabeth I it was a conventional courtyard house, with the hall on the west, staterooms and Long Gallery on the south, kitchens on the north and gatehouse on the east. Two surviving plans show this disposition and the chapel and library in the gatehouse. In 1628, Richard Towneley constructed a panelled dining-room in the office block. Early in the eighteenth century the gatehouse block was demolished and the chapel, with its furnishings, moved to the north-west corner of the house, with an approach at first floor level next to the dining-room, through what had been

Fig. 102 Towneley Hall. The Gallery and bedrooms occupy the top floor of the left-hand wing. The Staircase hide is within the left-hand one of the two square towers in the central block.

the top half of one end of the kitchen. According to Whitaker's *History of Whalley*, this alteration was made by Charles Towneley, who succeeded in 1706 and died in 1712. Between 1725 and 1730, his son Richard Towneley (1687-1735) removed the floor above the Great Hall and made the block into one room the full height of the building, with stuccoing by Vassali, whose bill, dated December 1730, mentions the decoration of the stone cantilever staircase that had been inserted at the south end of the Hall. Richard Towneley was also responsible for creating three large rooms in the south block below the Long Gallery. In 1817, Peregrine Towneley employed Jeffrey Wyatt to make these into two rooms and to embellish the whole building with turrets and castellations. In 1907, Burnley Corporation, which had acquired the Hall in 1902, completely reconstructed the top two floors of the north block, above the chapel and the dining-room, in order to make a series of art galleries out of what had been bedrooms and nurseries.

Towneley has the unique distinction of possessing a list of its hides from when they were still a closely guarded secret. It was written by Ursula Fermor, who married Charles Towneley in 1685 and died in 1748; the reference to 'the stairs to the garret' suggests that the date was after the present Georgian staircase was inserted but before the attics above the Great Hall disappeared in Richard Towneley's reconstruction. If Whitaker is right in his dating of this alteration to between 1706 and 1712, the Note was probably written when Charles Towneley succeeded in 1706, before the Jacobite risings of 1715 and 1745, in both of which the Towneleys were active.

It details a total of no fewer than nine hides. (Headings are editorial.)

A Note of the Private Places at Towneley

[Library]

In the library, over against the closet door, the middle panel slides back, and the same over against the window. On the floor over against the door, the base slides up and takes out: in the floor is a hole in which an iron hook is to be put and will open to a large place by lifting up the whole floor.

At the back side of the library door, the side wainscot may be taken out and lets you into a place where some boards may be taken up, which will let you into a large place which held all the library books.

[Chapel]

At the chapel door, taking up one board which is not nailed fast will let you into such another. In the chapel, the altar table draws out, and also the upper steps, which will let you into a large place in which may be laid all the gilding, which is only put on with pegs and takes to pieces. Care must be taken not to knock the gilding in taking down or putting up.

Over the canopy of the altar in the library lies a door for the tabernacle, balls for the top of the pillars, instead of the flower-pots, and also capitals and bottoms instead of the gilding, so that the place may be made use of though the gilding be taken down.

[Staircase]

At the steps going from the stone stairs to the garret, a step may be taken out, where there is a large place over the Green Parlour.

[Gallery]

In the second room in the Gallery, the wainscoting opens in the middle of the chimney upon hinges, where there is a hole in the wall, not very big.

In the third room in the Gallery is the close-stool closet: the panel towards the garden has a latch within, which is opened with an iron pin at a hole in the door, which lifts up the latch, which may be made fast by those within. It has a seat and will hold two persons.

No servants should be trusted with this, but upon some occasion some trusty servant may be made use of for some of the places to be used, but not made acquainted with them all.

This fascinating document, with its references to hinged and sliding panels, secret latches, bolts, seats and the double hide behind the library door, shows that Towneley was equipped for concealment on a grand scale. Unfortunately, the four places mentioned in the library and the two in the chapel were all lost when the gatehouse block which completed the original quadrangular plan was demolished and the chapel moved.

The one surviving hide has the further distinction of being the largest one known to exist today: 5.5m by 4.57m and 1.75m high. From the top landing of the stone staircase, a door ahead (Fig. 103) leads to a short flight of stairs, the ones described as "going from the stone stairs to the garret", under which

Fig. 103 Staircase Hide: (L) top landing of staircase. Behind this door are the stairs (C) where originally "a step may be taken out" to enter the hide. (R) The same stairs from within the hide.

is the "large place over the Green Parlour". The entrance is now through a modern trapdoor and the steps are fixed, but the location of the original entrance is evident from within the hide. The whole of the floor is covered with a sound-deadening layer of clay and rushes about 150mm deep. There

Fig. 104 Towneley: the largest hide anywhere. (Inset) Members of staff give an idea of scale!

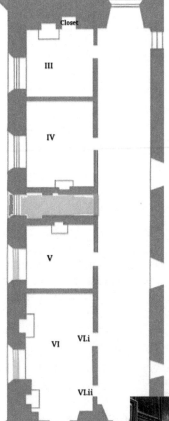

are said to have been four air-holes in the south wall, but if so, they have been pointed over. The hide can be viewed through a pane of glass in the floor of the room above. Its survival through the Georgian alterations, when the Great Hall to the north of it, the stone staircase to the east, the Green Parlour below and the little room above were all constructed or reconstructed, is due, no doubt, to the Jacobite loyalties of the Towneleys.

The only possible other surviving hides from the *Note* would be the two mentioned as in the Gallery. Of the four bedrooms off the Long Gallery, only Room III still has eighteenth-century panelling or a closet but this closet has no hide off it. However, investigations made in the preparation of this edition of this book have identified the location of the two-person hide in the Gallery as occupying part of the area shaded pink on Fig. 105. As this is the first time that this theory has appeared in print, the evidence will be laid out in detail.

Fig. 105 Plan of Gallery

Fig. 106 Gallery looking South – (same orientation as Fig 95

The Gallery is the upstairs of the block nearest the camera in the aerial photo (Fig. 102). Fig. 105 and Fig. 106 show the Gallery from the same direction, looking from north (bottom of plan) to south. To the east of the Gallery are four bedrooms with the Roman numerals III, IV, V and VI painted above each door. These are modern labels (I and II are on the floor below) but they will be used here to identify the rooms and. (Room VI has two doors, here labelled VI.i and VI.ii because until the 1920s this space was two rooms).

The area shaded pink in the plan above is now a storeroom and was from the early 19th century a maid's bedroom. But what it was used for before that is rather more of a mystery!

Fig. 107 East elevation today and in 1750 when there was no window above the doorway.

Fig. 107 shows the east facade today, with the window to this space above the central doorway: (blue on the plan) and the chimney stack for the fireplaces in both bedrooms IV and V directly above this window. However, this window is not shown in the 1750 drawing – which was made precisely because window alterations to tidy up the façade were being planned and so should be reliable on this point.

The presence of the ground floor passage leading to the door makes it very unlikely, for structural reasons, that the fireplaces and chimney stacks of the middle two upstairs rooms ever directly backed onto one another, and therefore the space in question between them must have existed at that time, but it did not then have a window.

On the inside of the block, the current access to this space is from a door in the Gallery panelling (Fig. 108) which is clearly a later alteration. This door (marked orange on Fig. 105) was created by simply cutting straight down the panelling, without even attempting to neaten, let alone conceal, the join by following one of the verticals of the panelling. Moreover, although the panelling is 17th century, the door frame behind it is much later – 19th century.

So it seems that this space existed in the 17th century but without a window or access from the Gallery. The space itself is too large for a hide that we know held just two people, but if most of its area was occupied by closets, then a small space between the fireplaces could be used as a hide. A suggested layout is shown opposite in Fig. 109. The pink shaded areas are closets or cupboards and the hide itself is indicated in yellow. The masonry bulk of the chimney stack would very effectively mask the small amount of missing space as it would just look as though the chimney stack was solid across the whole space. This plan shows two half-depth closets in each room but there are several alternative possibilities, any of which is equally likely and all of which could work to create the space for a 2-person hide accessed from a closet in the third room on the Gallery, exactly fitting the description in the *Note*.

Fig. 109 shows the space today, looking towards the Gallery. The design of the fireplace on the left is consistent with its having been added at

Fig. 108 (Above) Doorway from Gallery to hide area: such butchery of fine panelling was unlikely to have been done by the craftsman who originally built it nor by the Towneley who paid for it!

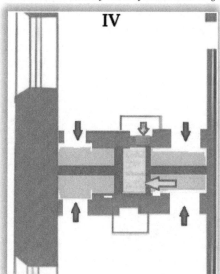

Fig. 109 (Left) Conjectural plan of former hide area with hypothesised closets in pink and hide in yellow. The orange block indicates the likely location of the small hide mentioned as in the second room. (Below) Current appearance of presumed hide location.

the same time as the window and

door. In this hypothesis, the closets and hide were amalgamated to make this space and the window, the doorway and the fireplace added at the same time. There is one further piece of evidence: this whole space has been known as the Priest's Room. This could be an oral memory of the hide having been rediscovered when those alterations were made. The small orange area in Fig. 109 marks what would then be the likely location of the other Gallery hide (a small hide for objects).

If this theory is correct, then this is rather a good hide, with similarities to those at Carlton Towers and Hardwicke Hall, and located exactly in relation to the two fireplaces as at Ufton Court but even better camouflaged by the outer closets. A two-person hide need only have occupied a small fraction of the space – perhaps 1.5m square – and a searcher would find it very difficult to estimate how much of the space behind and between the closets should be solid brickwork. It is away from outside walls, which are often vulnerable spots to locate hides. The door from the close-stool closet into the hide had a latch on it, which could be unlocked from either side. This door was inside a windowless closet, so any searcher inspecting it would be doing so by candlelight.

Bedrooms IV, V and VI have all been repanelled since the 16th century, and unless any archive plans emerge, it is not possible to verify this theory without removing panelling or floorboards, so unless and until that ever becomes necessary for other purposes, the mystery will remain, at least in part, unsolved. Were the panelling to be removed, it is very likely that the location of the small hide in the mantelpiece would be apparent, unless the whole of the chimney breast had been rebuilt. The two-person hide is a different matter: the walls of the maid's bedroom might show evidence of blocked doorways into the hypothesised closets, but the location of the hide itself would probably only be apparent if there was evidence under the floorboards of a lateral partition of the space.

Five miles south of Lancaster is Thurnham Hall, which behind its Regency Gothick facade goes back to the 15th and 16th centuries. Now a hotel, it still contains a hiding-place which is a remarkable parallel to the one in the courtyard wall at Scotney Old Castle (p106) albeit indoors.

Fig. 110 Thurnham Hall, Lancs.

In a first-floor bedroom, to the right of the four-centred stone fireplace, is a small room with a window. To the left of this, a narrow stone doorway opens into a windowless space

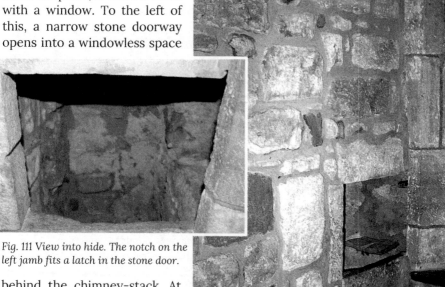

Fig. 111 View into hide. The notch on the left jamb fits a latch in the stone door.

behind the chimney-stack. At the far end of this, on the left, one stone about 900mm from the floor is missing, and behind is a space in the thickness of the stack, 900mm deep, 760mm wide and 1.88m high. Inside the door jamb are two iron L-pins which

Fig. 112 View of hide from outside.

Fig. 113 Stone hide door: the inner face (R) retains an iron latch.

supported iron bars about 20mm in diameter driven into the thickness of a movable stone to act as hinges. The upper bar is still attached to its pin.

The inside of the stone was left rough; the outside was made to look like the smooth ashlar of the rest of the wall. It still has one circular hole in the edge where the iron bar fitted into it; the other has

Fig. 114 View of entrance from inside hide, showing hinges.

broken away at the weak point, perhaps when the stone was removed. Although such a device is recorded at Longhorsley Tower in Northumberland as well as at Scotney, this is the only example remaining and is therefore a survival of very great interest and importance.

In the wall opposite this hide, another, much smaller, stone slides out, not on hinges, to reveal a cavity which might have been used for incriminating papers or other small items. The Daltons of Thurnham were Royalists and Jacobites as well as recusants, and would have had need of such places well into the eighteenth century. The windowless stone-floored space from which

Fig. 115 Thurnham: wall hide for objects.

both hides are approached was itself bricked up when found at the end of the 19th century and could only be entered by a trapdoor from the lead roof. There are no records to show whether this was a later alteration or was intended as an outer hide. My guess would be the former, though (as will be seen in Chapter 12) there are at least two instances on record of hides below trapdoors from the leads.

Salmesbury Hall, near Preston, is about seventeen miles west of Towneley and nineteen miles south-east of Thurnham. In the reign of

Fig. 116 Samlesbury Hall.

Elizabeth I it was the home of Sir John Southworth, a former High Sheriff and a notorious recusant. At that time it was a quadrangular building within a moat, but the moat has since been filled in and the gatehouse and office blocks demolished. The remainder, consisting of the Great Hall and one wing which included the chapel, was neglected for a long time and used in turn as a school, a public house and labourers' tenements. In 1835, much of the timberwork was restored after the pattern of Rufford Hall, a dozen miles west. This was an appropriate model, for more than one reason, but it does mean that much of the detail of Samlesbury is in keeping rather than authentic. It is now owned by a trust, which has repaired and furnished it.

Edmund Campion stayed at Samlesbury about Easter 1581, a few months before he was captured. Southworth subsequently professed to have conformed and was pardoned, but in September 1586 a list of priests harboured in Lancashire included

> James Cowpe, a seminary priest receipted, relieved and maintained at the Lodge of Sir John Southworth in Samlesbury Park by Mr Thomas Southworth, one of the younger sons of the said Sir John, and at the house of John Ward, dwelling by Samlesbury Park side. And the said priest sayeth Mass at the said Lodge and the said Ward's house, whither resort Mr John Southworth; Mrs Anne Southworth; John Walmesley, servant to Sir John Southworth; Thomas Southworth, dwelling in the Park.... At the Lodge in Samlesbury Park there be Masses daily and seminaries resort thither, as James Cowpe, Harrison, Bell and suchlike. The like unlawful meetings are made daily at the house of John Ward by the Park side of Samlesbury.

Evidently Thomas Bell was still undaunted by his adventures at York Castle and his midnight escape in Lancashire two years before. A few months later, at the beginning of 1587, Sir John's son Christopher, who had been ordained in Rome in 1583, was arrested in London, where he 'was now purposed to ride down to visit his father and friends'. The meeting never took place, for Christopher did not escape from prison until thirteen years later, and Sir John's will includes the clause: 'My son Christopher, being now prisoner in the Castle of Wisbech, shall have yearly paid unto him £20 towards his charges and expenses in prison, if the laws and statutes of this realm will permit'.

On 21 November 1592, Samlesbury Hall was raided on the instructions of the fourth Earl of Derby, as Lord Lieutenant of Lancashire. The magistrate in charge, Richard Brereton, was ordered to make 'very diligent, exact and careful search in all chambers, lofts, studies, cellars, vaults and all other rooms and secret or suspicious places of the said house or other houses adjoining to the same [in other words, Samlesbury Lodge], for any Jesuit, seminary priest, unknown or suspected person that may be found there'. The searchers found various printed and manuscript books containing 'much Papistry', and various items of clothing belonging to one Edward Sager, including 'a frieze gown without a pocket and yet devices secretly to keep letters in'. They also discovered

> lmprimis, one canopy to hang over the altar, found in a secret vault over the dining-chamber and another chamber. Item, two candlesticks of brass of the fashion used in the time of superstition, found in the same place. Item, fourteen images of divers fashions, found in the same vault.

There is a place, sometimes identified as this one, in the roof of the bay at the inner angle of the two blocks, between the wall of a little parlour which occupies the upper half of the bay, and the sloping roof of the Great Hall. The modern floor measures 900mm by 3.34m, and the space is entered through a modern door 635mm square, high up in the wall of a closet leading to the gallery of the Great Hall. But, although this place is close to the dining-room, it is not over it 'and another chamber'; and this end of the building has been so much altered that caution is advisable. All the same, extant hides mentioned in contemporary documents are so rare that even possible examples are noteworthy.

Fig. 117 Samlesbury: the gable marked may be the hide found in the search of 1592.

A similar place was found during repairs in 1949 at Rufford Old Hall, between Preston and Liverpool, which was given to the National Trust by the first Lord Hesketh in 1936 and is open to the public. All that remains of the original building is the magnificent heavily-timbered Great Hall, which probably dates from the time of Robert Hesketh, who died in 1490. His great-grandson Thomas Hesketh succeeded in 1539, was knighted by Queen Mary in 1553 and was High Sheriff in 1563. In the 1570s he rebuilt Martholme Tower, a stone building with a fine gatehouse about halfway between Towneley and Samlesbury, and it seems that he and his immediate successors made it their chief residence. In 1591, his widow Alice was alleged to have harboured at Martholme a priest named Thomas Barcroft or Crofts, who had also been reported as staying at Mr Mompesson's in London, a cousin of the Perkins of Ufton. At Rufford, there is a priest-hole in the timbered canopy over the dais of the Great Hall. In it were found three leaves of Greek printing, each 150mm by 100mm. The canopy and its position are similar to that at Samlesbury, and the hide is lined with clay and rushes like the staircase hide at Towneley. These resemblances do not seem to be accidental. Sir Thomas Hesketh's mother was Grace Towneley of Towneley; his cousin Bartholemew Hesketh of Aughton, with whom Campion stayed in 1581, married first Elizabeth Norris of Speke and then Margaret Southworth of Samlesbury.

Fig. 118 Speke Hall north side. The hides are next to the chimney-stacks centre and right.

Speke Hall, seven miles south-east of Liverpool, is a magnificent sixteenth-century house of sandstone and half-timber on the north shore of the Mersey estuary, which is here almost three miles wide. Despite the noise from the airport, the park retains something of its former dignity. The house is built on four sides of a cobbled courtyard dominated by two huge yew-trees and is approached by a bridge across the now dry moat on the north side. The Great Hall is in the usual position opposite the gatehouse, with the offices in the east wing and the state rooms in the west. The interior is justly famous for its panelling, plasterwork and furnishings. Since 1943 Speke Hall has been owned by the National Trust.

Edward Norris, who succeeded in 1568 and died in 1606, was a notorious recusant, and there are three reports on the house, of 1586, 1599 and 1629, which show that it was regularly used for priest-harbouring. But, although it has not been altered as much as these other Lancashire houses, Speke is by no means in its original state. Towards the end of the eighteenth century, most of the furnishings were dispersed and the house itself lapsed into a state of dereliction, from which it was rescued by Richard Watt, whose great-great-grand-uncle, a wealthy West India merchant, had bought it in 1796. As *The National Trust Guide* puts it, "Throughout the house these two complementary influences of the sixteenth and the nineteenth centuries, are juxtaposed and contribute to the richness of cultural texture. Few Tudor houses are structurally so little altered, yet few so convincingly exemplify the affinity which 1850 felt for 1550". Where priest-holes are concerned, such a feeling of affinity can be misleading. An inventory of 1624 includes four places of interest, but none of them can now be identified for certain. They are:

   i.   The chamber over the old chapel, called Sir Thomas Gerard's chamber;
  ii.   The chapel chamber;
 iii.   The new little chapel;
 iv.   The old chapel.

It is, however, significant that the 1599 report mentions 'two priests, of whom the one is called Little Sir Richard or Sir Richard Norris and the other Sir Peter, for the most part lodged in a chamber over the parlour, and at what times strangers visit the house, the said Sir Richard waiteth at the table as a serving man in a livery coat and cognizance'. This chamber over the parlour is immediately next to a canopy over the upper end of the Great Hall, of a similar pattern to that containing the hide at Rufford. But although the cavity is accessible, there are no signs now of a secret entrance to it.

The two known hides at Speke are both in the north wing, which was completed by Edward Norris in 1598. The larger and better known one is behind the upper part of the panelling on the right-hand side of the fireplace in the Green Room. To the left of the fireplace is the usual closet door, behind which is a modern ladder which gives access to a small loft made by putting a modern floor halfway up the chimney side space. From this, one can squeeze between the chimneybreast and the panelling of the Green Room, across to the other side of the stack, where there is a space 2.29m square and 1.55m high. Below it are two cupboards, one entered from the Green Room and the other from the King's Room at the north-west corner of the house. This place can also be approached from above, which is where the main view in Fig. 119 was taken from (it is unsafe to enter at present as it has no floorboards). The loft space at the top of the ladder shown in Fig. 119 is currently accessible from above via a short modern ladder and this is where the view of the passage way in Fig. 119 was taken from.

Assuming this space is a genuine hide, the original access to it may have been from this bedroom or from the attic above. There is no way of knowing, and neither possibility is entirely satisfactory. Climbing up to a hide is by no means unheard of but is much less common than climbing down into it. Downwards, gravity does the work and the distances involved rarely need a ladder. Ladders are awkward because they could not be left lying around outside the hide during a search. Kept inside the hide, they would occupy scarce floorspace, but there might not always be time for an assistant to dispose of one outside. (See p165 for an account of the problems of climbing up to a hide). Rope ladders are a possibility, but are hard to use in a hurry, particularly for several people. This hide could be a double or (uniquely) a tripe hide, depending on whether the fireside closet is thought to have been secret or not. Either way, there are problems: a ladder in the closet would immediately betray the loft above and the passageway across the chimney breast has no signs of a barrier concealing the hide, so any searcher reaching the loft would have merely to explore further to find the hide. Another is that the loft floor is modern and there is no certainty as to whether it even originally existed. The problem remains if we assume that the access was from above: there is still the insecure passage around the chimney breast.

Fig. 119 Clockwise from bottom left: Fireside closet, ladder, chimney passage, exit from chimney passage to hide, hide (from above).

Fig. 120 The famous cutaway drawing gives a good idea of the layout.

The other hide is a little way further along the north wing, next to the Tapestry or Haunted Room above the gateway. It is in a similar position to the first, over the cupboards in the Tapestry Room and the room next to it and has a

Fig. 121 *Tapestry Room hide interior. The above picture was taken through the modern door visible in the left-hand picture.*

trapdoor entrance from the attics directly into the hide. This hide is 1.68m by 1.98m and 1.22m high. The floor is of stone, a continuation of the chimney. There is now another entrance to it (the modern white door visible in Fig. 121), above the door of the cupboard in the room next to the Tapestry Room. This may mark the site of an original secret entrance, though it would have made the hole more liable to discovery.

Despite the Victorian renewals, I am inclined to accept both these places as genuine, though the panelled door next to the fireplace in the Green Room is unlikely to have been secret. The value of these hides is not in their ingenuity or their state of preservation but in the precise dating of the block in which they are (1598). There is said to have been a runway round the inner slope of the roof above them, and there is space in the usual triangular gap between the roof and the timber-and-plaster wall of the attics but there are no indications of use like those in the roof passages at Burghwallis and Harvington.

From the sixteenth to the nineteenth century, Lancashire continued to be the most recusant county of all. John Gerard, himself from the county, records having seen 200 or 300 people at Masses there, in contrast to the predominantly Puritan East Anglia. The 1767 House of Lords Returns, the most detailed and accurate record of Papists made in penal times, give a total of some 80,000 in the whole of England and Wales, of which the diocese of Chester (the counties of Cheshire and Lancashire) accounts for 25,000. In 1787, Bishop Mathew Gibson reported that there were 33,685 Catholics in the Northern District, 23,000 of them in Lancashire. Many recusants do not necessarily mean many priest-holes. But there are still clues to be followed up in Lancashire, and further investigation may yet yield more.

8

John Gerard in Northamptonshire and London 1597-1605

1

We left John Gerard at the end of Chapter 4, having just (July 1594) moved prisons from the Counter to the Clink. Despite occasional unsuccessful attempts at interrogation by Topcliffe and others, he there carried on an energetic ministry, until in April 1597 a renegade priest, William Atkinson, revealed that he had been transmitting letters from Rome and Brussels to Garnet through Nicholas Owen. Priesthood could be overlooked, but not communications with Garnet, whom the Government badly wanted to catch. On 12 April 1597, Gerard was moved to the Tower. Next day the Privy Council made out a warrant to the Lieutenant, Sir Richard Berkeley. 'You shall', it ran, 'by virtue hereof cause him to be put to the manacles and such other torture as is used in that place'.

However, on the night of 4 October 1597, three and a half years after his arrest, he escaped from the Tower of London. For several months, in return for suitable considerations, his gaoler had been taking out innocuous pencilled notes, unaware of the invisible postscripts written in orange-juice with a toothpick. The Countess of Arundel and her daughter, disguised as citizens of London, had penetrated to his cell in the Salt Tower. On 8 September, he contrived to say Mass in the cell of another prisoner, John Arden, in the Cradle Tower at the opposite corner of the Queen's Privy Garden. While there, he realised that it would be possible to clamber across the moat on a rope stretched from the roof of the Cradle Tower (Fig. 122) to the low wall of the Tower wharf. The escape took several

Fig. 122 Google Earth view of Cradle Tower and moat (then water filled).

weeks to set up, with one unsuccessful attempt. But at midnight on 4 October a boat pulled into the Tower Wharf, and Gerard – arms and wrists still weak from the effects of the torture - and Arden looped their rope around a cannon on the roof and made their perilous way across the moat. Horses were waiting at Garnet's house in Spitalfields, and before dawn Gerard and Owen were in the saddle.

The Wisemans pressed him to return to Braddocks, and he did in fact spend some time at their London house in the Strand. But he refused to submit them to the continuing danger of harbouring him and instead asked Garnet to move Richard Banks from Hindlip to Braddocks. Meanwhile, Gerard himself was at last able to take up a long-standing invitation to visit the Vaux house at Irthlingborough in Northamptonshire.

William Lord Vaux had died in 1595, while Gerard was in the Clink. His elder son Henry had died in 1587 and his younger son George in 1594, leaving a widow, Elizabeth (née Roper), and six children all under the age of eight. The eldest boy, Edward, was therefore the new Lord Vaux. The old Lord was chronically and chaotically in debt and had been unable to attend the Parliament of 1593 since his robes were in pawn. Sir Thomas Tresham, his brother-in-law, took time off from architecture and numerology to intervene, and the result was a series of first-class family rows. Anne Vaux sued Tresham in the Court of Chancery; Elizabeth Vaux sued him in the Court of Wards; he sued her in Star Chamber; and his niece Merill Vaux and her husband had him committed to the Fleet. Traumatised by the loss of her husband, protective of her children, and struggling to make ends meet, Elizabeth Vaux was in no mood for half-measures. As early as 1594, she had moved the entire household, including the old Lord and Lady Vaux, out of Harrowden to Irthlingborough, four miles east, which, though in a not much better state of repair than Harrowden, was at least smaller and cheaper to maintain. Here she harboured a Jesuit, Richard Cowling, the son of a shoemaker who had died in York Castle, and a first cousin of Guy Fawkes.

Cowling was a pious man and a good preacher. But he was also academic, unbusinesslike and not the character to bring Elizabeth Vaux out of her obsessive mourning. Gerard, on the other hand, appealed to her immediately and she asked him to make his headquarters there. At first, the proposal was that Cowling should remain as well, but Garnet, who had a shrewd perception of his men, insisted on moving him to Lancashire, possibly to Rufford or Martholme. Instead, after a year (in 1599) Garnet sent another Jesuit, John Percy, to Irthlingborough. Gerard had got to know Percy through secret correspondence when he was in the Clink and Percy in Bridewell, though they had never met. In 1596, Percy had escaped through the tiling of the prison, along with two other priests and seven laymen, and was now in Yorkshire, where he had earned an excellent reputation. Meanwhile there was the question of what to do about Irthlingborough and

Harrowden.

What Gerard had in mind was something like Hindlip, as near as possible to the Jesuit colleges on the Continent. Irthlingborough was too small for this and Harrowden was too dilapidated, apart from being ill-suited for defence against raids by pursuivants. So Gerard and Elizabeth Vaux began house-hunting among the stately homes of Northamptonshire and eventually, in March 1599, she took a lease of Kirby Hall, twenty miles north, for £1,500.

Kirby Hall is a beautiful Renaissance house of ironstone, now partly in ruins. In July or August 1599, Gerard and Mrs Vaux drove over to Kirby, taking with them Nicholas Owen and Hugh Sheldon, who was to help Owen in the building of the hiding-

Fig. 123 *Kirby Hall. Nicholas Owen and Hugh Sheldon were to have built multiple hides here, but the plan had to be abandoned after just one day.*

places. But one of the servants had been guilty of careless talk in London and the Privy Council knew that Gerard was now at Irthlingborough. In Northamptonshire there was gossip that Elizabeth Vaux had taken this splendid and remote mansion so that she could entertain priests freely and in large numbers - gossip, adds Gerard, that had some foundation. A search party was waiting at Kettering, about halfway between Kirby and Irthlingborough, to stop the carriage on its way back. But as luck would have it, one of the servants thought that another road back would be easier for the carriage, and the searchers waited in vain. Next morning, they raided Kirby but, even with a large force, it was too big to surround completely or even to watch all the exits. Hugh Sheldon was caught and imprisoned, but Owen, the more important quarry, slipped safely away. Realising that they had been tricked, the Justices galloped back to Irthlingborough, arriving about dinnertime. A careless porter let them in, and they were in the great chamber before Gerard and his friends knew that they had come at all. As Gerard, Percy and a Catholic layman, Roger Lee, clattered past it on their way to the hide, one of the pursuivants poked his head round the door to see who they were. But he was distracted by the noisy argument in progress in the chamber for just long enough to allow the three men to reach safety. After searching all day, the party left empty-handed.

Any move to Kirby was now out of the question. Accordingly, Mrs Vaux built an entirely new three-storey block at Harrowden, close to the old private chapel and with an unobtrusive exit to the privy garden and so through the broad walks to the fields. Gerard says that it was 'most conveniently designed' and it is almost certain that Nicholas Owen was for once able to plan a building to contain his priest-holes instead of laboriously adapting an existing one. The hide in which Gerard survived a nine-day search by a hundred men in November 1605 was probably in this block, which must have rivalled the west wing at Harvington for ingenuity. There was a library of religious books, many of which had belonged to Campion's pupil Henry Vaux, and a superbly furnished chapel with six massive silver candlesticks, a silver thurible, cruets and bell, and a golden crucifix a foot high, ornamented with the symbols of the pelican, the eagle, the phoenix and the hen gathering her chicks under her wings — the text on which Campion had preached his last sermon at Lyford. These were soon supplemented by a rare and costly ornament of gold, pearls and diamonds, representing the Holy Name of Jesus, which Elizabeth Vaux gave Gerard as a present on New Year's Day 1599. Under her management, the Vaux inheritance was evidently in a less parlous condition than it had been a few years before.

Leaving John Percy to minister in these splendid surroundings, Gerard spent much of his time riding round Northamptonshire and the neighbouring counties, converting the gentry or their wives and setting up new Mass centres. As with Oldcorne in Worcestershire, or Gerard himself in East Anglia before his incarceration, it is possible to identify some of these houses and to plot his journeyings in terms of their hides. Two of them were Waterperry and Thame Park, seven and twelve miles east of Oxford respectively and fifty miles south-west of Harrowden, so that more than one day's riding would be needed to reach them. But those to be described here are all within thirty-five miles of Harrowden, and most of them within twenty-five.

Fig. 124 Rushton Hall.

Rushton Hall, the home of Sir Thomas Tresham, is only eight miles away, on the other side of Kettering, and until his quarrel with Elizabeth and Merill Vaux there had been much coming and going between the two houses.

Now he refused to have anything more to do with them, though his son Francis, later the Gunpowder Plotter, remained on friendly terms with the Vaux sisters. Rushton, which Sir Thomas had heightened and altered as recently as 1595, is built of Weldon limestone round three sides of a courtyard, with a roof of Collyweston stone tiles. The Great Hall still has its hammer-beam roof and to the west of it, on the first floor, there is an oratory with a rather awkward plaster relief of the Crucifixion dated 1577.

In 1828, during some repairs, a door lintel was moved and a book fell out. It was one of twenty which, together with a most important collection of papers and letters, were concealed in a hole 1.5m long and 380mm wide. The papers are now in the British Library and formed the basis of Godfrey Anstruther's exhaustive family history, *Vaux of Harrowden* (1953). They had apparently been hidden by Francis Tresham at the time of the Gunpowder Plot and remained undisturbed for more than two centuries.

In the north-west corner of the park is the curious Triangular Lodge built by Sir Thomas in 1594-1597. Everything about it is directed by the number three, from the ground plan of three sides, each 10.1m - exactly one-third of one hundred yards - long, to the triangular chimney-stack, which rises from the middle of the building, with no apparent support below, to symbolise the mystery of faith. The "threes" are both an allusion to the doctrine of the Trinity and a pun on Sir Thomas's own surname. Behind the fireplace on the top floor is a windowless space which was formerly sealed off and inaccessible. It is not likely to have been a hiding-place, but the building is a good demonstration of the ingenuities of which Elizabethan designers and architects were capable.

Six miles east of Kettering and eight miles north-east of Harrowden is Drayton House, a magnificent stone mansion (used in 2023 as the filming location for *Saltburn*) which was owned by the Catholic Lord Mordaunt. A spy's report soon after the Plot lists seven priests who had made 'common resort and much abode' at Drayton, apart from various suspect laymen, including Mr Tutfield, tutor to

Fig. 125 *Drayton House.*

Mordaunt's children, who had previously held the same post at Harrowden. In the post-Plot hue and cry, Mordaunt was arrested and spent three years in Tower, dying in 1609 just after his release on payment of a £10,000 fine.

Under the floor of a closet in the north wing which he added in 1584 is a space 3.05m by 2.84m, entered by a trapdoor 910mm by 760mm. The trapdoor is modern, but part of the joist below has been cut away for the baulk of wood on the underside of the original trapdoor. The floor is of lime-ash. In the hide is a seventeenth-century chest with the letters POB marked on the lid in nails (possibly Penelope O'Brien, 2nd Countess of Peterborough, who died in 1671).

An unusual, though not unique, feature of this hide is that it has a two-light mullioned window. This appears to have been part of the original construction for the sake of symmetry and if this is a hide, not necessarily as dangerous as it sounds since glass appears black from outside unless backed by something which will reflect light. The window would certainly make that outside wall appear much less suspicious, and there are other examples in this area.

Nevill Holt, just over the Leicestershire border between Market Harborough and Corby, is a large and spectacular house of the fourteenth to nineteenth centuries. Sir Henry Nevill, who succeeded in 1633, married Ursula Clopton of Clopton, and the Jesuit Michael Alford is said to have been there from about 1629 onwards. Before that, there is no satisfactory evidence of recusancy at Holt. The cloister wing on the north front, which probably dates from after Sir Henry's death in 1665, consists of an arcaded loggia with round arches, above which is a single panelled room which may have been used as a chapel. But none of the three supposed hiding-places in the house is entirely convincing. The one in King John's Tower (which despite its name dates from about 1600) is only a void space created when a Georgian staircase was inserted. The other two, however, are at least worth recording.

At the east end of the Hall and physically continuous with it is the medieval parish church. Immediately south of the church tower and entered from it is the burial vault of the Nevills, above which is a void and windowless space. Next to this again is a gallery where there was formerly a built-in cupboard with a false floor. Beneath this was a low passage leading through a hole in the wall to a large space 5.5m by 3.35m, though only 1.37m high, between the brick roof of the vault and the timber floor of the void space above it. Escapades during the time Nevill Holt was a boarding school led to the blocking of this passage, but the place can still be reached from the other end, through a square hole in the wall of the belfry staircase. This was almost certainly an ordinary medieval window which was covered over and had its stone frame removed when the void over the vault was built up to it.

This place would have made a roomy and comfortable hide, almost

Fig. 126 Nevill Holt. House and church and cutaway view showing detail of belfry hide. The second hide is at left.

impossible to locate, since reverence for the dead would explain why the void above it was sealed off and disused - though not perhaps why it was built in the first place and provided with a boarded floor. The exit to the church tower stairs could have been covered with a movable stone, as at Scotney and Thurnham. My hesitations are caused by the engraving (Fig. 127) of 1795 which was printed in Nichols' Leicestershire, which seems to show that the

Fig. 127 Nevill Holt in 1795. Was the 'hide' present then? A recurring problem for the historian of priest holes!

gallery where the false floor was did not then exist, or at least not in its present form. But a blocked doorway high in the west wall of the church suggests that even in the fourteenth century there was a gallery there entered from the manor-house, so the details of the engraving may not be completely accurate. Although there have been a good many changes at this end of the house in superficial details like windows, gables and crenellations, the structure may be old enough for the hide to be authentic.

The other possible hiding-place is behind the top section of the magnificent fifteenth-century oriel window of the Great Hall. From inside it is not noticeable that only the lower section of the window is doing duty, for the bay has a richly carved stone vault which conveys the impression that the window ends there. But above it is another small room, lit by the top section of the window. Originally this and the great chamber to the west of it were reached by a stone newel staircase in the thickness of the wall at the south-west corner of the Hall; but most of this was destroyed in later rebuildings, and when the room was found about 1910 there was no way into it. It was almost a ready-made hide and needed only to have the doorway concealed by panelling. It has now been turned into a bathroom and is panelled, which, with pipes, bath and other fixtures, makes examination difficult. But it is the most plausible of the three places at Nevill Holt, and the use of a window for camouflage is reminiscent of Drayton House. At the time of the discovery it contained a curious old clock with the hours marked on a straight scale instead of a dial.

Nineteen miles north-west of Nevill Holt and seven miles north-east of Leicester is Priory Farm at Shoby, a remnant of the manor house of Eleanor Brooksby's father-in-law Robert Brooksby. In August 1581, the month after Campion's arrest, the Earl of Huntingdon's brother Francis Hastings wrote to the Earl of Leicester urging that it should be searched, along with the Vaux house at Ashby Magna near Lutterworth. Nicholas Yeke alias Wade, who was ordained at Rheims in 1579, was here in 1584 and seems to be the Wade who was caught saying Mass at Mr Palmer's in Kegworth in Leicestershire in 1592. More than thirty years later, in 1615, Eleanor Brooksby and Anne Vaux were living there again and harbouring a Jesuit named William Wright. This is known from the Responses of Eleanor's grandson Edward Thimelby, who was brought up there and entered the English College in Rome in 1636. Priory Farm still has a fine staircase, an upper room with a wooden ceiling patterned in stars and crosses, and Jacobean fireplaces, behind one of which Popish vestments are said to have been found. At the back, adjoining the kitchen, is a tumble-down stone building that is still called the chapel.

Fig. 128 Irnham Hall. The single round chimney is beside the hide and may have been added to provide ventilation to it, as at Hindlip (p181).

The Thimelbys' home was Irnham Hall (Fig. 128), in the south-west corner of Lincolnshire, close to Leicestershire, Northamptonshire and Rutland. Mary Brooksby, Eleanor's daughter, was born about 1579 and married Richard Thimelby while Gerard was at Harrowden. Richard Thimelby was 'a harbourer of priests and religious men, keeping one in residence in his own house.' Irnham is a large L-shaped building of grey stone, on two storeys with attics and it is likely that it once had several hides. But the Tudor north wing, which included a priest's room and a later Baroque chapel on the first

floor, was gutted by fire in 1887 and rebuilt. The fourteenth-century great hall in the west wing was drastically remodelled in the 1850s. South of it, however, in the oldest part of the house, is an important surviving priest-hole. This is in

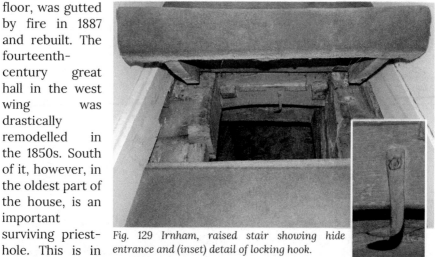

Fig. 129 Irnham, raised stair showing hide entrance and (inset) detail of locking hook.

the centre of the west block and is entered from the attics, through a step which can be raised, as at Harvington and Towneley. These steps are modern, but inside is the original iron hook to fasten them. Beneath is a space 2.45m by 1.5m and 1.7m high, which can now also be reached

through a modern door on the first floor below. It has a ventilator in the form of a circular chimney at the junction of two gables in a particularly complex part of the roof. This is now unique but can be paralleled from Hindlip, where some of the flues, 'seemingly outwardly fit for conveying forth of smoke', were found in 1606 'only to lend air and light downward into the concealments'. At Irnham, the ventilation shaft, (the top of which can be seen in Fig. 128, the only circular chimney stack on the building), runs from a void next to the hide (Fig. 130). The wall between the two has at some time been filled and then pierced again, which is where this picture is taken looking from the hide. The brick

Fig. 130 View from hide into base of ventilation shaft/chimney.

wall with a hole in it and a plaster wall behind gives into the library. This void could simply be the fireplace for that room, bricked up and repurposed as a ventilation shaft, or it could be that the shaft is entirely unrelated to the hide.

When discovered in 1844, the hide is said to have had a feeding-trap, as at Oxburgh, in the form of a narrow iron pipe. Though this is not apparent now, the same account of the 1606 search at Hindlip mentions a 'quill or reed through a little hole in the chimney', by which warm drinks had been conveyed in to Garnet and Oldcorne. Bearing in mind these parallels, and the false chimney at Harvington, it is fair to suspect the work of Owen at Irnham.

In 1929 a vaulted passage some 1.5m high was discovered, running from the great hall to a small chamber beneath a great beech tree fifty yards away, where it was covered by a slab of stone. This was obviously built as a drain, but it may have been converted in the same way as the one at Baddesley Clinton.

Fig. 131 Irnham: hide interior and (inset) view of closed trapdoor from below.

Six miles away, in the market town of Bourne, is Red Hall, named for its brickwork. It is a small, squarish building with a two-storey Jacobean Renaissance porch, a stone-tiled roof and two stone chimneystacks disguised as classical arcades. Inside, at the back, is a splendid staircase with tall finials at the newels. A report of the 1920s says that a ruinous and unoccupied room at the top of the fine stairway had a false wall of lath-and-plaster, built 900mm away from the real wall. The space so made was divided into two by a partition running from the middle mullion of a window. Each compartment was therefore lit by half a window. The larger had a door and was quite open and innocent, but the smaller one could only be reached from the garrets above.

Fig. 132 Red Hall, Bourne

Unfortunately, the lath-and-plaster divisions are long gone and upon examination in 2023 it was impossible to reconcile this description with the layout of the house, at least without creating a hide that would be glaringly obvious. Some of the details are inconsistent with others, putting us into the realm of guesswork. If access was from above, then the hide was on the first floor – but the top of the stairway is on the second floor. There would, incidentally, be plenty of space for a hide between the first and second floors in the wall on the other side of this room, which contains the chimney stacks and is well over 1m thick.

This arrangement, which amongst other things must have been extremely insecure, is worth recording for its use of a window, as at Drayton and Nevill Holt. Moreover, Red Hall was one of the houses of Sir Everard Digby, who was reconciled by John Gerard in 1602 and was later another of the Gunpowder Plotters. They had been introduced by Roger Lee and shared a common passion for hunting and hawking. Indeed, they got on so well together that Digby asked Lee whether he thought Gerard a good match for his sister Magdalen (who later became a nun at Brussels instead). In the end, Gerard converted separately and simultaneously both Digby and his wife Mary Moulsoe, who had brought Digby the magnificent mansion of Gayhurst near Newport Pagnell in Buckinghamshire, about sixteen miles south of Harrowden. There they set up a chapel and sacristy, with rich and splendid vestments, employing for their chaplain John Percy, who was replaced at Harrowden by two other priests: Thomas Strange, a Jesuit, and William Singleton, one of the Archpriest's assistants.

Sir Everard's interests were not confined to hunting and falconry. He was also an expert swordsman and skilful card-player, a useful cover in mixed company, when he and Gerard regularly staged games on the understanding that the loser got his money back afterwards and said one Hail Mary for each chip returned. He played several instruments himself and kept a consort of musicians at Gayhurst, who probably performed in the chapel as well as in the great chamber. Though only in his twenties, he was a shrewd judge of politics, well read in theology and a minor poet. Understandably, other Catholic gentry who called at Gayhurst were inspired to follow his lead by furnishing chapels and designing accommodation 'suited', as Gerard says, 'to a priest's needs' - which must imply priest-holes.

The Elizabethan rebuilding of Gayhurst House itself was begun by Sir Everard's father-in-law William Moulsoe in 1597 and was still incomplete when he died in 1602. It is a large stone house of three storeys, originally H-shaped, though the gap between the two northern wings was filled in during the eighteenth century. The main entrance, through an imposing hall porch the full height of the building, is on the south side, but there is another porch halfway along the east side, behind which was an interesting priest-hole. The loss of this place has sometimes been blamed on the second Lord Carrington, who made substantial alterations in the 1860s, but it is clear from Lipscomb's *Buckinghamshire* that it had already gone when he published his account in 1847. It was above the ceiling of the Digby Room on the first floor of the east wing, behind the porch, and was entered from the second storey through a movable section of flooring which revolved on a pivot and had a secret bolt.

It was lit by part of a large mullioned and transomed window and, according to Lipscomb, had more than the one entrance. There is a local tradition that it was discovered by putting candles in all the windows (though this assumes that the searchers already knew what to look for), and another that from a certain spot some distance away the arrangement was betrayed by some reflection or peculiarity of the light. The window is still there but the false ceiling and the hide have gone. Nevertheless, this is an important example, partly because of its use, yet again, of a window, and partly because of its precise dating. Gerard's account shows that he reconciled Sir Everard and Lady Digby after the death of William Moulsoe in 1602 but before the birth of their first child, the future Sir Kenelm Digby, in mid-1603. Since Moulsoe was a Protestant, the hide cannot be earlier than 1602 and is unlikely to be more than a few months, if that, later than 1603.

The position of the chapel described by Gerard is not known for certain, but there is a chamber in the roof known as the Oratory with a doorway which is said to have led to another hiding-place. This, however, is not mentioned by Lipscomb and may already have disappeared during the Georgian alterations of about 1750.

Nineteen miles west of Harrowden, near Daventry, is Ashby St Ledgers, which in 1598 was inherited by Robert Catesby, the ringleader of the Gunpowder Plot. In the same year, his wife Catherine died and he underwent a marked change; he left off his extravagance, swearing and wild company and returned to the practice of his religion, though still in secret. What part, if any, Gerard himself had in this conversion he does not record, but there is no doubt that he visited Ashby. He describes a wall painting which he had seen in the church there, probably the one which survives on either side of the doorway showing Death with his pick and shovel and Time with his scythe. Of the Elizabethan house only the timber and stone gatehouse and the Great Hall are left, the rest being an addition by Lutyens in the early twentieth century. According to a tradition recorded in Baker's *Northamptonshire* (1822), the panelled room on the upper storey of the gatehouse was used by the conspirators for their discussions; and it is said to have had a secret exit, though no sign of one remains today.

Ten miles south of Gayhurst, between Bletchley and Winslow, is Salden, the one remaining wing of the diapered brick mansion of the Fortescues. Sir Francis Fortescue, son of the then Chancellor of the Exchequer, was a first cousin of Roger Lee and a Church Papist. Gerard describes how in 1600 he converted Lady Fortescue (Grace Manners), after approaching her while she was winding a clock in the bay-window of the great chamber. Sir Francis came to Gerard's sermons, prepared the altar for Mass and recited the breviary every day, but would not take the final step for fear of offending his father. Salden was built on four sides of a courtyard, with fronts 60yds long, so that it was easy for a priest to live comfortably at the top of the house without his presence becoming generally known. Indeed, Gerard says that he had never come across a house in the whole of England where a priest could live so conveniently in secret. The priest in question was Anthony Hoskins alias Rivers, who was born in Herefordshire and had recently returned from Spain and remained at Salden until 1609. Lady Fortescue provided him with a suite of three rooms (for chapel, bedroom and living room) opening off a gallery 25m long (half of one front) with a view of a garden which had cost £1,000 to lay out. After Garnet's arrest in 1606 he was temporarily superior of the Jesuits in England.

Meanwhile, Gerard was meeting Lady Fortescue's cousins, the family of the fourth Earl of Rutland. The fourth son, Sir Oliver Manners, the King's Carver, was knighted with Sir Everard Digby at Belvoir in April 1603 and ordained priest in Rome in April 1611. Gerard describes how he would turn aside in the crowded Presence Chamber at court and read a chapter of *The Imitation of Christ* or stand absorbed in his own thoughts, which were not, as other courtiers imagined, of promotion or a mistress. The second son, Francis, later sixth Earl of Rutland, became a Catholic within a few days of meeting Gerard. In 1633, the Richard Broughton who had been at Hindlip in 1593 dedicated his *Ecclesiastical History* to the Earl's widow and daughter, describing himself as their 'sometime secretary'. Some letters addressed to him are still at Belvoir Castle. In 1609, Lady Rutland, the wife of the eldest brother Roger, the fifth Earl, was harbouring William Wright at Belvoir, before he moved to the Vauxes at Shoby. And her mother, Frances, the daughter of Sir Francis Walsingham and widow in turn of Sir Philip Sidney and the Earl of Essex, became a Catholic under the influence of her third husband, the Earl of Clanricarde - who was reconciled by Gerard in 1600 when he fought a duel with a relic of the True Cross under his shirt.

In 1601, the year after Hoskins' arrival at Salden, Sir Francis and Lady Fortescue had a son, Adrian, who grew up to become a Jesuit himself. He died at Huddington Court, by then the home of his nephew Sir George Wintour, in 1653, and was buried in Huddington church with a brass setting forth in Latin his attainments as linguist, philosopher and theologian. The inscription stops short of saying that he was a Jesuit, but only just. In 1630, Lady Fortescue, who had been widowed in 1624, bought Husbands Bosworth Hall, twelve miles south-west of Nevill Holt and only half a mile into Leicestershire from Northamptonshire. Despite Georgian and Victorian additions and redecorations, the early sixteenth-century brick and timber house still survives with hall and cross-wings. On the first floor of the north wing, a recess beside a fireplace is blocked off by a built-in cupboard with a round back. Behind it is a space which can be reached through the floor of the garret above. Unfortunately, the entrance is only a hole in the boards and the cupboard itself, like all the other internal fittings, is not earlier than 1700 or so. Since, however, Husbands Bosworth Hall was a Jesuit chaplaincy during the eighteenth century, it is possible that an earlier hide was reconditioned, like the false chimney at Hardwicke; and it is at least a curious coincidence that the chaplain about 1750 was Thomas Maire of Hardwicke. Even without that, there were evidently some unpredictable consequences of the winding of the little clock in the bay-window at Salden.

2

One of the most remarkable things about Gerard's activity between 1598 and 1605 is that, despite intermittent searches and spies' reports, he was able, not merely to obtain access to court, but also to maintain several houses in London which were duly provided with priest-holes. The first of these he had rented in late 1594, when he was in the Clink, engaging a Catholic widow, Mrs Anne Line, to run it for him. He kept up the lease until early in 1598, two or three months after his escape, when he gave it up because it was known to William Atkinson, whose information had led to Gerard's removal to the Tower. Amongst those who had stayed there while he was in prison were John Percy, later of Harrowden and Gayhurst; John Jones, whose leg Mrs Wiseman had poulticed in the Gatehouse prison; and John Curry, who had formerly been at Cowdray. Curry died there on 31 August 1596 and was buried in a priest-hole, since it was too dangerous to bring out a body that could not be accounted for. As the house was a 'receptacle' for young priests corning in from abroad, it must have had several other hides as well. The house, says Gerard, was conveniently sited, with a garden, and it provided priests passing through London with much safer accommodation than they could have found in taverns.

Gerard was an accomplished hide-builder: back in his time in the Clink, he had set up a chapel and built small hiding-places in his cell for papers, Massing stuff and money. On 12 April 1597, just before his transfer to the Tower, that cell was searched but without success, for he was experienced in the art of concealing items in prison. Later, in the Tower, after saying Mass for John Arden in the Cradle Tower, Gerard brought back a pyx containing twenty-two hosts to his own cell in the Salt Tower, where he must already have devised a hiding-place for it.

In the summer of 1598, Gerard and a Mr and Mrs Heywood jointly rented a large house in London, sharing the expense and using half each. In his half, Gerard set up a large and well-furnished chapel. In July 1599, just before the searches at Kirby and Irthlingborough, the house was raided while Gerard was giving a retreat there. Mrs Heywood confronted the searchers at the bottom of the staircase, her farthingale completely blocking it, while Gerard took a stool and climbed up into the hiding-place, which was built in a secret gable of the roof. He says that he closed down the little door through which he had got in, but could not open the door of the proper hiding-place inside and would have been caught if John Lillie (who had organised his escape from the Tower) had not refused to hide with him and, like Bray at Scotney, posed instead as the priest.

This was clearly a double roof hide, of the same sort as that at Huddington, and it would be interesting to know why the inner secret door was jammed. Perhaps, like those at Ufton and Mapledurham, it had a self-closing bolt. An even more vivid picture of such a place, at Mr Laurence Mompesson's in Clerkenwell (a cousin of the Perkins of Ufton), is given in an account by James Younger of a search on 12 December 1591:

> With me was also at that time another priest called William Pattinson, a Yorkshireman, some time of the College of Rheims.... We had both said Mass that Sunday, and before dinner I took the opportunity to explicate out of the English Testament a text fit for the third Sunday of Advent, when lo, there knocked at the door churchwardens, sidemen and constables, coming to know who were in that house that did not go to the church. Unawares, a maid of the house let them in; and before I could get into the secret place which we had and draw up Mr Pattinson after me, the searchers came into the place and, espying his leg to hang out of an hole, they bid him come down, which he did. I remained in an inner place made for that purpose, if so be the other place should happen to be found. They heard me go over their heads and, calling for a candle, they came up. Mr Pattinson said, 'Here are no more but myself'. Yet one fellow came up, swearing that the place were able to contain twenty. 'Yet', saith he, 'here are no more'.

Younger escaped to tell the tale to Persons; Pattinson was executed six weeks later. Earlier that same year, 1591, a breach of security by Younger had caused a raid on Garnet's cottage in Finsbury Fields. This had a kitchen and dining-room on the ground floor, and upstairs a chapel which probably served also for sleeping. It had a chimney, but no fires could be lit by day, even in winter, for fear that the smoke might be seen. In Garnet's absence, it was in the charge of Hugh Sheldon, who was later caught at Kirby Hall. After a preliminary visit by the constables, the pursuivant Richard Young demanded admittance. It took Sheldon two hours to hide the Massing stuff and Garnet's papers. In the cellar there was a hide large enough for six or seven men. Afraid that Young would sound the walls and find it, Sheldon poked the pile of coal, as if to suggest that it, the casks of beer and the stack of logs were being used to cover something. The dust drove Young back upstairs, where Sheldon offered him a drink, brushed his doublet and saw him off.

In 1598, when Gerard had to leave his former house and move in with the Heywoods, Mrs Line also rented part of another house and continued to shelter priests there. On Candlemas Day 1601 it was raided; she was arrested and, on 27 February, executed for priest-harbouring. But the priest, Francis Page, got to a hide and was not found on that occasion, though he was betrayed and executed the following year. This hide was at least on the second floor: the constables had pelted upstairs and found the congregation and the altar, but while an altercation was going on, Page dashed out and, says Gerard, 'rushed upstairs to a room where he knew Mistress Line had prepared a hiding-place and got safely into it'.

In 1602, Gerard took yet another house, in St Clement's Lane just off the Strand. This, he says, 'was a convenient and very suitable place, with private entrances front and back, and I had some very good hiding-places in it'. He used it until the Gunpowder Plot, and it seems to have been the 'house in the fields behind St Clement's Inn' where the conspirators took their vow of secrecy. An engraving of 1798 (Fig. 133) shows a ramshackle timber building of five storeys on a narrow corner site. Thousands of such buildings went

Fig. 133 John Gerard's house, St Clement's Lane. The Gunpowder Plotters met and vowed secrecy here. Engraving of 1798.

up in flames during the week of the Great Fire of London, though a surprising number survived until the early 20th century in Lime Street, Crutched Friars and Great St Helen's, and the streets of Elizabethan London are recorded for all time in Claes Jansz Visscher's engraved view of 1600 (Fig. 134). Considering such a frontage, it is easy to see that hiding places could be contrived most readily in the cellar, the chimneys and the roof. But Harvington and other houses show what could be done with an interior of timber-and-plaster partitioning, and structural alterations of plan and level were simple to make in a timber- framed house.

A similar corner house, in Lincoln's Inn Fields, owned by the Countess of Arundel, was raided early in 1598 when George Blackwell, the Archpriest, was there. He just had time, says Gerard, to escape into a hiding-place. After three days, Lady Arundel rescued him by bribing the officer in charge of the search to whom, apart from the large sum of money which she gave him then, she sent a venison pasty every Christmas for the rest of his life. It is a pity that there are no details of the hide in this agreeable story.

In 1600, Garnet rented a house called White Webbs, two miles north of Enfield, near the King and Tinker Inn at the edge of the present park. He described it as 'a spacious house, fit to receive so great a company that should resort to him thither, there being two beds placed in a chamber; but thinketh there have not been above the number of fourteen

Fig. 134 *London in 1616, from the engraving by C. J. Visscher II.*

Jesuits at one time there'. Later it was found 'to be contrived into many lodgings and rooms, with many doors, trapdoors and passages out of all sides', though the searchers could 'by no means find any secret conveyance within it'. Despite that, there must have been many. Here Anne Vaux went under the alias of Mrs Perkins and Garnet of Mr Measey, which was the name of another recusant at Ufton. It was about this time that Eleanor Brooksby's son William married Dorothy Wiseman, one of the girls who had been locked up at Braddocks during the search for Gerard in 1594, and that her daughter Mary, as already noted, married Richard Thimelby. The young Brooksbys, and in due course their two baby daughters, were part of the household at White Webbs. And here, on 24 March 1603, Garnet heard from Catesby that Queen Elizabeth was dead at last. That morning, William Weston watched from his cell in the Tower the heralds' proclamation of King James I; all that night Sir Thomas Tresham rode northwards through the rain with instructions from the Council to proclaim the new King at Northampton.

That should have marked the end of the need for priest-holes, and for a while it looked as if it would. Even before his accession, James had given Thomas Percy, later the Gunpowder Plotter, reason to suppose that Catholics would be tolerated, and soon after it Tresham was assured by Sir Robert Cecil that the King would keep his word. In July, Tresham and other leading Catholics were summoned to Hampton Court and informed that the fine of £20 a month would no longer be exacted. Between Michaelmas 1603 and Michaelmas 1604, the Exchequer receipts from these fines did in fact drop from £7,115 to £1,414. In August, the Pope reciprocated by promising, through the Papal Nuncios at Paris and Brussels, that he would countenance no insurrection of Catholics and would use ecclesiastical censures against any Catholics attempting one. During the remainder of 1603 - the first nine months of James's reign - no fewer than 140 priests entered England, the chapels of the Catholic Embassies were thrown open, and in some places, sermons were delivered in the open air to which Catholics flocked in thousands. Although the Jesuit General in Rome, Aquaviva, thought that the change was too good to be true and implored Garnet to move cautiously, others were determined that the King should move even faster. A plot to force the King to change his Councillors and servants was revealed to the government by Garnet and Blackwell, but still provoked counter-measures. On Ash Wednesday 1604, a proclamation was issued ordering all priests to leave the country.

To start with, no great attempt was made to enforce this proclamation, and in November 1604 Garnet, Gerard, Blount, Percy and other Jesuits met at White Webbs for a High Mass, with William Byrd again at the organ. Modest optimism was in order: there were now nearly forty Jesuits in England against three (Weston, Southwell and Garnet) at the time of the Harleyford conference eighteen years before. The first volume of Byrd's *Gradualia*, settings of the Latin texts for Mass on the great feasts of the year, was nearly ready for publication, to join his superb music for the English Matins and Evensong. Since this was 21 November, the feast of the Presentation of Our Lady, it is possible to suggest items from the *Gradualia* which may have been sung: *Salve Sancta Parens, Ave Maria, Salve Regina*, with one of the settings of the Mass for three, four or five voices, all of which had been printed, though without title-pages, during the 1590s. A French visitor, Charles de Ligny, mentions how Byrd played the organ 'and many other instruments' and adds: 'To that house came, chiefly on the solemn days observed by the Papists, many of the nobility and many ladies, by coach or otherwise'.

Nevertheless, there was a shadow over the celebrations. In July a priest named John Sugar had been executed at Warwick, together with a layman, Robert Grissold, who was the brother of Garnet's servant John Grissold. The pair had been arrested near Baddesley Clinton, at Rowington, the village from which the Grissolds came. Richard Blount had reported the event in a letter of 1 August. Thomas Pounde, the friend of Campion who had now been in prison for a quarter of a century, wrote to the Privy Council in protest. In November he was hauled before Star Chamber and condemned to stand in the pillory in London and Lancaster, losing one ear in each place. Although the last part was later remitted, the sentence was a grim warning that recusants should not presume on too much. By then, the thoughts of some had already turned to violence.

9
The Gunpowder Plot
1605-1606

Fig. 135 Contemporary engraving of 8 of the 13 Plotters by Crispijn van de Passe.

1

About Easter 1605, Garnet began to suspect that White Webbs had been discovered, and from then on, he visited it rarely and only for a night or two at a time. Instead, he rented the manor-house of Erith, near Dartford, which could be reached either on horseback, or by coach or by water. In London he took a room at the house of a costermonger named Bennet in Thames Street, not far from the Tower. By midsummer, Erith also was under surveillance. On 30 May, Garnet kept the feast of Corpus Christi 'with great solemnity and music' at Fremland in Essex, a house which is now at the bottom of Hanningfield Water. A week later, on 6 June, there was a solemn procession round the great garden there, after which Garnet and the rest of the party, some two dozen in all, departed. On 9 June, Robert Catesby came to see him in Thames Street with a moral problem for solution.

Under the terms of the recent peace with Spain, English Catholics were allowed to enlist in the forces of the Archdukes in Flanders. Sir Charles Percy, brother of the Earl of Northumberland, was to be Colonel of a proposed regiment, and Catesby was to be Lieutenant-Colonel. But he wanted to clear his conscience on one point. A legitimate military operation directed against, say, the leaders or commanders of the other side might involve the destruction of, say, a town or fortress containing other people who were innocent. In such a case, was the operation morally justified?

Garnet replied that a commonwealth had the right of self-defence and that the death of the innocent in such a case was permitted where it could not be avoided, so long as they were not the direct target. But he became uneasy when Catesby, on departing, urged him never to let anyone know of this conversation. Discovering in the next few days that Catesby was frequently absent from his usual recusant haunts but often in secret meetings with other young hotheads, he began to suspect that some violent scheme was in the air and determined to raise the question again next time he saw him.

The opportunity came at Fremland early in July when, apart from Garnet and Catesby, Lord Mounteagle and Sir Thomas Tresham's son Francis were also there. Garnet did his best to counsel patience, and shortly afterwards showed them letters which had just arrived from Rome, charging him in the name of the Pope to hinder any sedition or insurrection. The most that Catesby would agree to was not to take any positive action until the Pope had been briefed on the renewal of persecution in England. But perhaps he was less certain than he seemed, for in the second or third week of July he revealed the details of the Plot to Tesimond in confession, at the same time giving him leave, also under the seal of confession, to inform Garnet.

The importance of the Gunpowder Plot for this book is not merely that it led to the deaths of Garnet, Oldcorne and Nicholas Owen and to a hunt for Tesimond and John Gerard, but also that it brought together in one of the most famous and dramatic episodes of English history many of the characters, families and houses mentioned in earlier chapters. The Government did its best to represent the Plot as from first to last a Jesuit initiative; and, while that was the reverse of the truth, it is certain that no cast could have been assembled better calculated to give that impression.

According to Thomas Wintour's confession, the Plot was first put to him in a house at Lambeth in February 1604 by Catesby and John Wright. The Wright brothers, John and Christopher, came from Plowland in Yorkshire; they had been at school with Tesimond and Guy Fawkes, and through their mother, who had spent fourteen years in prison, they were related to the Inglebys and Bapthorpes. As a first step, Thomas Wintour and Christopher Wright went over to Brussels in March to see the Constable of Castile, who was negotiating the formal peace between England and Spain, 'entreating him to solicit his Majesty at his coming hither that the penal laws may be recalled'. They returned at the end of April, convinced that diplomacy would achieve nothing, and in the company of Fawkes, whom they had met at Ostend. In the middle of May, Catesby, Wintour, Fawkes, John Wright and Thomas Percy met at John Gerard's house in St Clement's Lane, where they took an oath of secrecy on a prayer-book and afterwards received communion at a Mass said by Gerard. By 24 May they had managed to get the lease of a house near the House of Lords transferred from Henry Ferrers of Baddesley Clinton to Thomas Percy. Then, since the Constable's visit to London in August might produce results after all, they 'departed several ways into the country' until October.

The mine which the Plotters attempted to dig during the winter into the foundations of the House of Lords is one of the most famous secret tunnels ever constructed, though, like so many others, it was at least partly mythical. No one ever saw it after the discovery of the Plot, and Fawkes, the only conspirator with any experience of such work, took no part in it but stood sentinel. At Christmas they went home for the holidays, after which Christopher Wright was initiated into the Plot. About the beginning of February, Robert Keyes, who was one of Lord Mordaunt's household at Drayton and since September had been in charge of the store of gunpowder in the house at Lambeth, was added to the digging force when the barrels were brought across the river to Percy's house at Westminster. But on 25 March the mining operations were abandoned altogether when Percy hired a room beneath the House of Lords which had formerly been in use as a coal-cellar. To this they transferred their gunpowder, covering the casks and barrels with firewood to allay suspicion.

Six days later, on Easter Sunday, two more conspirators were added to the circle. They were Robert Wintour and John Grant, who had married the Wintours' sister Dorothy. This meant that two more houses in the Midlands became available for the rising which was to follow the explosion: Huddington Court and the Grants' home at Norbrook, between Warwick and Stratford-upon-Avon. According to Gerard, Grant kept a priest at Norbrook and had proved such an awkward customer that pursuivants had learned not to meddle with him. Here he had a 'secret place', in which during June he laid up fifty new muskets, eight barrels of gunpowder and three new suits of armour which he had purchased in London. Norbrook no longer exists, but it was an L-shaped moated building with a long timber-framed hall-block. John Grant was a nephew of the conspirator Edward Somerville and Norbrook had been searched after the discovery of the Plot in November 1583. After the Gunpowder Plot, it was searched again, when the Sheriff found Mass books and ornaments, a chalice, and a cope in a pool nearby and 'a pair of manacles for a man's neck' in the moat.

During the summer of 1605, Ambrose Rookwood of Coldham in Suffolk was recruited to the conspiracy for his money and his fine horses, both of which were needed for the rising in the Midlands. In order to be on the spot, he rented Clopton House, near Stratford, about five miles from Norbrook. Clopton belonged to Sir George Carew, later Lord Carew and Earl of Totnes, who was a brother-in-law of William Clopton of Sledwich in County Durham. Clopton was then a medieval house built round a courtyard, but two sides of it were rebuilt in classical style in the 1660s and it was again much altered about 1830. A roof chapel survives, with a late seventeenth-century communion rail, but no hides. Since Clopton was not available until Michaelmas, Rookwood moved in with Robert Wintour at Huddington for the time being. Initially, he had grave reservations about the explosion under the

House of Lords, and it seems to have been his scruples that led Catesby to put his supposedly parallel case to Garnet in June.

Meanwhile, the Wrights also moved, from Yorkshire to Bushwood Hall, Lapworth, about six miles north of Norbrook and less than three miles from Baddesley Clinton. This was another house belonging to Catesby, who was probably born there, and it still survives with part of its moat. Robert Bates, Catesby's servant, who also joined the conspirators about this time, had been living there thirteen years before at the time when Baddesley Clinton was searched, and had been reported for bringing a 'man-child' to Mrs Brooksby's house, presumably to be christened by Garnet. Here at Bushwood, and at Huddington, Norbrook and Clopton, armour and munitions could be stored and men recruited, both under cover of the regiment being raised for Flanders. According to Tesimond, the carts of weapons were driven by Bates, the only one of the conspirators who was not a gentleman.

In June, the increasing restiveness of Catholics in the Welsh Marches broke out into open riots. In an atmosphere of such tension, Garnet was afraid that a single incident might involve the whole of the Catholic body, while Catesby was confident that once the explosion had taken place there would be widespread support for his rising.

During August, the King and Queen set out on a progress through Northamptonshire. On 3 August, they stayed with Lord Mordaunt at Drayton - where Rookwood and Thomas Wintour had been the day before. On 9 August the Queen stayed at Kirby Hall which, after Elizabeth Vaux's unsuccessful bid was now tenanted by another notable Papist, Mrs Elizabeth Mallory, and on 12 August the King spent the night at Harrowden. Their entourage included the Earls of Salisbury, Suffolk, Devonshire and Northampton and other Lords of the Privy Council, but this was a holiday: no business was transacted and the hunting was excellent. Whether John Gerard was at Harrowden as well on this occasion we are not told, but Elizabeth Vaux took the opportunity to pursue negotiations for a match between her son Lord Vaux, who was now nearly seventeen, and the Earl of Suffolk's daughter, Elizabeth - whom he did in fact marry many years later, in 1632, after the death of her first husband, the Earl of Banbury. Despite politics and religion, nobility still had its duties and privileges.

Late in August, Garnet was back at White Webbs for a few days, but since both it and Erith were under suspicion, and White Webbs was increasingly being used by Catesby and his associates, Garnet decided to spend the next few weeks in travelling to Holywell in North Wales, a traditional place of pilgrimage for English Catholics. He left White Webbs on 29 August with Anne Vaux, Eleanor Brooksby, William and Dorothy Brooksby, Nicholas Owen and some other servants. As they rode north and west, the party grew. At Gayhurst they were joined by Lady Digby, John Gerard and

John Percy, together with some of Sir Everard's servants. They stayed one night at Norbrook and the next at Huddington. From there, Ambrose Rookwood rode with them on the next stage to Kinlet, the home of Mr Lacon, where they were joined by Mrs Rookwood. Here Mass was said by 'a priest commorant [living] in the said house', probably the Wilson alias Walter who was frequenting Kinlet two years later, when he was described as 'about thirty years of age, of a middling stature, somewhat slender... and had but a small beard'. From Kinlet onwards the party was accompanied by Sir Francis Lacon and his daughter and two or three other gentlemen, who rode the rest of the way with them to Holywell. By the time that they reached the Well, the priests, gentry and servants together numbered about thirty.

The next night was spent at an inn at Shrewsbury, and the one after that at the Castell Holt, on the River Dee outside Wrexham. At Holywell they stayed 'but one night' in another inn. During the seventeenth and eighteenth centuries there were two recusant inns at Holywell, the Cross Keys, which was run by secular priests, and The Star, which was run by the Jesuits. The latter, demolished in 1802, is first mentioned in 1639, but may have been in use even earlier. For the last stretch of the journey, from the inn to the actual Well, the women in Garnet's party went barefoot.

On the return journey, they retraced their previous route, except that instead of staying in Shrewsbury they stopped at Mr Bannister's at Wem, ten miles north of Shrewsbury. Here also Mass was said by 'a priest likewise commorant there'. He was William Hughes, 'a little man, then about forty years of age... black, and did wear his hair very long. He halteth, his right leg being shorter than his left, and hath a boot made with a high heel accordingly'.

From Wem, they continued by way of Kinlet, Huddington, Norbrook and Daventry to Gayhurst where Garnet remained with the Digbys, the Vaux sisters and Owen for the next six weeks.

On Monday 7 October, Sir Everard was at Harrowden when Catesby arrived there on his way back to London from Warwickshire. Next day, as they rode to Gayhurst together, Catesby revealed the Plot to Sir Everard, overcoming his scruples by assuring him that the Jesuits had approved of the scheme. Once Sir Everard had given his consent, Catesby invited him to command the Warwickshire rising which would follow the explosion in London. It is hard to believe that such a crucial appointment was still unsettled only four weeks before the day, but perhaps Catesby had calculated that Sir Everard would not otherwise be generous enough with money for the Plot. Whatever the truth of this, Sir Everard agreed and, since he would need a house in Warwickshire, it was decided that he should borrow Coughton Court, Thomas Throckmorton having prudently gone abroad.

On Saturday 26 October, an anonymous letter was delivered to Lord Mounteagle, warning him to devise some excuse for not attending Parliament. Three days later, on Tuesday 29th, Lady Digby left Gayhurst for Coughton. With her travelled her children and servants, Garnet, Owen and the Vaux sisters, most of Sir Everard's servants, his horses and greyhounds, a cart of ammunition and other requirements. Sir Everard himself and seven servants stayed behind to close up Gayhurst. He was to follow a few days later with a trunk of clothes for himself and his wife and £300 in money. Meanwhile, he ordered one of the servants who were travelling with Lady Digby to bring back his gelding within a week, as it would be needed for hunting near Dunchurch.

2

On All Souls' Day (Saturday 2 November), John Gerard rode over from Harrowden to Gayhurst to say Mass and found 'all things hid out of the way and many of the household gone'. Comparing 'many particulars together which seemed strange', he began to ask Sir Everard questions, but was assured that he would certainly have been told of anything that he, or Garnet, ought to be acquainted with. Satisfied with this answer, Gerard parted from Digby for what would prove to be the last time and rode back to Harrowden.

Two days later, on Monday 4 November, Digby and his seven servants left Gayhurst and rode to the Lion Inn at Dunchurch near Rugby. After supper, he was joined there by his uncle Sir Robert Digby of Coleshill, by Stephen and Humphrey Lyttelton and by other friends and relatives. They had come for a hunting match on Dunsmore Heath, which was to provide cover for the kidnapping of Princess Elizabeth from Combe Abbey near Coventry and for the mustering of the force recruited in the Midlands. This began at dawn on the Fifth with Mass said by the Wintours' chaplain from Huddington, Nicholas Hart alias Hammond. By this time, Fawkes had already been arrested and the other conspirators, except Rookwood and Thomas Wintour, were already galloping northwards from London. But Digby had no means of knowing this and took the opportunity of informing the party that they might be summoned to arms later that week.

Before leaving Gayhurst, Garnet had written to Tesimond at Hindlip, asking him to come over to Coughton. Catesby had promised to be there on 31 October, and Garnet had decided to ask his permission to discuss what he had learned under the seal of confession. But the Mounteagle letter and Catesby's suspicions of Francis Tresham had kept him in London. On 1 November, while Garnet celebrated the Mass of All Saints and preached in the Tower Room at Coughton, Tresham faced Wintour and Catesby at White Webbs and convinced them that he was not the traitor. It was not until the morning of Wednesday 6 November that Garnet and Tesimond heard what had happened, when Bates arrived at Coughton with a letter from Catesby and Digby. 'They would have blown up the Parliament House', Garnet told Tesimond, 'and were discovered, and we all utterly undone'.

Bates begged Tesimond to come back to Huddington, which half an hour later he did, leaving Garnet to try and comfort Lady Digby, who had broken down, sobbing hysterically, when she read her husband's letter. When Bates and Tesimond reached Huddington, they found about three dozen gentlemen and servants there, all that were left of the conspirators and the hunting party. During the evening they were joined by Thomas Wintour, who had been last out of London and had called at his sister's at Norbrook on the way. Catesby persuaded Tesimond to ride the four miles to Hindlip and ask Thomas Habington to join them. But Habington refused 'and charged all his house to that purpose not to go unto them'. In this he was supported by Oldcorne, and the two Yorkshire Jesuits parted in some heat, Tesimond remarking, 'Thus we may see a difference between a phlegmatic and a choleric person!' He subsequently escaped from England posing as the owner of a cargo of dead pigs and, despite his choleric temperament, spent the remaining thirty years of his life teaching philosophy and theology in Italy and Spain.

Between two and three in the morning of Thursday 7th, Nicholas Hart said Mass for the remnants of the conspiracy in the roof chapel at Huddington (the room with the hide illustrated on p72). Afterwards, the Massing stuff was hidden in 'a hollow place within a wall near unto the clock-house', where a search found it a few days later.

[It included] a cross gilt with the picture of Christ and other pictures upon it, a chalice of silver partly gilt, with a little plate or cover to the said chalice, and certain boxes of singing-bread, and all other ornaments fit for a Popish priest to say Mass in, and certain Popish Mass-books, most of them in Latin and some in English, to the number of fifty or three-score, whereof some are newly printed.

This hide, unlike the other two at Huddington, has not survived; probably destruction swiftly followed its discovery.

A little before dawn, the company set out for Holbeach House in Staffordshire, the home of Stephen Lyttelton, still hoping to make their way to safety in Wales. Of the original conspirators, four rode at the front and four behind to stop the rest from deserting. They took with them a cart of weapons and ammunition and collected another cart from Hewell Grange, the home of John Talbot's brother Lord Windsor, which they passed about noon. They hoped to attract more recruits but, as Digby said, 'Not one man came to take our part, though we expected so many', and despite their precautions, throughout the wet and muddy November afternoon men continued to sneak away without being noticed. It was ten at night before they reached Holbeach.

Holbeach House, a mile north of Kingswinford, is a brick house of the early seventeenth century. The Elizabethan building was damaged and set on fire during the arrest of the conspirators, and it is unlikely that much of it is represented by what we see today. Nevertheless, two hiding places have been recorded in the chimneys, one at the front and one at the back.

Fig. 136 *Holbeach House presents a sorry sight in 2024. Used until 2022 as a nursing home, it is to be hoped that the building will survive and find a new purpose. Holes in the front stonework are said to have been made by musket balls during the shootout, but a full examination is required to identify how much of this structure is original, including whether there are any surviving hides.*

Early the next morning, Friday, Thomas Wintour and Stephen Lyttelton rode over to Pepperhill, a few miles west, where John Talbot was then staying, to attempt to win support from him. But they were driven away and on returning to Holbeach they found that some of the gunpowder, which had been spread out before a fire to dry, had ignited and badly injured Catesby, Rookwood and Grant. 'The rest of the company [had] dispersed upon sight thereof', including Digby. Robert Wintour, Bates and Stephen Lyttelton also fled, so that by the time the Sheriff caught up with them about midday there remained only six of the Plotters (Catesby, Percy, Thomas Wintour, Rookwood and the Wrights), together with five servants and one of the hunting party, Henry Morgan, in any condition to resist. Grant was still there, but with 'his face much disfigured and his eyes almost burnt out' from the explosion. The only survivors of the ensuing assault were Thomas Wintour, Grant and Rookwood. They were sent up to the Tower, where they were joined by Keyes, Digby and Bates, all of whom were picked up separately, and by Francis Tresham, who was arrested in London on 12 November. But Robert Wintour and Stephen Lyttelton remained hidden for two months in a barn close to Hagley Hall, the Lytteltons' house four miles north of Harvington.

News of the Plot and its failure had reached Harrowden before it reached the hunting party on Dunsmore Heath. A couple of months before, Henry Huddleston of Sawston and his pregnant wife Dorothy had moved to Irthlingborough as guests of Mrs Vaux. Since 24 October, Henry had been in London. On the evening of 4 November, he left London and stayed the night at The Bull in St Albans, where he met Sir Francis Fortescue of Salden. Early next morning, he was overtaken by John Wright and Catesby, and rode with them as far as Brickhill, where on stopping for something to eat they were joined by Thomas Percy and Christopher Wright. Then the conspirators continued north westwards to Dunchurch, while Huddleston raced to Harrowden with the news, arriving at about five o'clock. All the three priests (John Gerard, Thomas Strange and William Singleton) were there, and there was a hasty conference on what they should do. It was only now that Gerard realised why Sir Everard Digby had left Gayhurst the day before. Next morning, Henry Huddleston fetched his wife from Irthlingborough to Harrowden. On Thursday 7th, while the conspirators were making their grim journey from Huddington to Holbeach, Huddleston, Strange, Singleton and some servants set out to try and reach Garnet at Coughton. But that same evening they were arrested at Kenilworth, about fifteen miles short of Coughton, and interrogated. The Earl of Salisbury had known for at least two years that Gerard was being harboured by Elizabeth Vaux, and now there was evidence to connect Harrowden with the Gunpowder Plot. So, as soon as Salisbury received Henry Huddleston's examination, he gave orders that Harrowden was to be thoroughly searched for John Gerard.

The magistrate in charge, William Tate of Delapre Abbey near Northampton, arrived at Harrowden with more than 100 men soon after midday on 12 November. He posted a watch for three miles round the house, as far as Irthlingborough, which he also searched. He commandeered all the keys and went through all Mrs Vaux's papers for any evidence that she had known of the Plot. Then he examined both her and her son Lord Vaux and was favourably impressed by the answers and frank attitude of both of them. He must have told them so, since the gist of the letter which he wrote to the Earl of Salisbury the following day is given by Gerard in his *Narrative of the Gunpowder Plot*. But Tate still had a job to do, and for the next few days the house was rigorously searched, candles being used in cellars and other dark corners.

When Henry Huddleston brought the news of the Plot to Harrowden on 5 November, there had been a fourth priest there apart from Gerard, Strange and Singleton. He was Thomas Laithwaite, who also set out to reach Garnet at Coughton, though not in company with the others. He too was arrested but contrived to escape. Then, realising that he could not get through to Coughton, he returned to Harrowden on the second day of the search and was arrested again. Although he was not John Gerard, this was at least some encouragement to the searchers.

On the evening of the third day of the search, 14 November, Tate became suspicious of one part of the house, 'upon intimation given that there was a secret receptacle in the roof of the same'. But before breaking down the wall, he gave Mrs Vaux's servant the opportunity to reveal the hiding-place and so avoid the need for damage. This was agreed, and Tate was shown the secret door. 'Whereat', he reported, 'I entered and searched the same, and found it the most secret place that ever I saw, and so contrived that it was without all possibility to be discovered. There I found many Popish books and other things incident to their superstitious religion, but no man in it'. Gerard adds that Elizabeth Vaux deliberately arranged for this hiding-place to be revealed, hoping that Tate would then call off the search.

This, however, Tate did not do, and the search continued all through Friday. On Saturday 16th, Tate set out for London, taking with him Thomas Laithwaite, Lord Vaux, Mrs Vaux and some of her servants. The roads were worse than usual and the coach and horses unsatisfactory, so that they did not reach London until Monday evening. Meanwhile, Gerard had been in the house all the time, in a hiding-place where he could sit but not stand upright. But, unlike the occasion at Braddocks, he did not suffer from hunger, since every night food was brought to him secretly. This was not as easy as it sounds, for Tate had locked every door in the house and would not allow anyone to use the keys without one of his own servants to accompany them. Either Tate's servants were bribed, or Mrs Vaux had a duplicate set of keys which she did not hand over. Once Tate had departed for London on the fifth day of the search, the tension relaxed slightly, and the household were able to take Gerard out of his hole at night and warm him before a fire. All the same, confinement day after day in such a narrow space was a severe ordeal, and it was later reported to the Earl of Salisbury that 'if the watch had continued but two days longer, Mr Gerard had been pined out at Harrowden'. But on the ninth day of the hunt, 20 November, the searchers concluded that Gerard could not possibly have held out so long if he had really been in the house, and so they withdrew. Their reasoning is understandable, since the only search that lasted longer without success was the second one at Scotney, which went on for ten days, and there at least the hide was found, even if Richard Blount and Bray were no longer in it.

About Christmas, Gerard made his way to London, where he took refuge in the house of a Dr Taylor, whose son Henry later entered the Spanish diplomatic service. On Palm Sunday (13 April 1606) this house also was raided, but meanwhile at Hindlip there had been an even greater search than the one at Harrowden, in which Garnet, Oldcorne, Nicholas Owen and Oldcorne's servant Ralph Ashley had all been captured.

3

On 4 December 1605, Garnet and Owen, together with Anne Vaux, left Coughton Court and travelled the eighteen miles to Hindlip. Garnet stayed there for the next six weeks, spending most of his time in a room next to the dining room at the south-east corner of the building, perhaps the one known in the eighteenth century as the Green Parlour. (He usually had dinner and supper in the dining room with the owners, Thomas and Mary Habington.) He was not at Hindlip continuously for the whole of the six weeks. Oldcorne later confessed that on Sunday 19 January, the day before the search began, 'he met with Mr Garnet two or three miles on this side Evesham and came back to Hindlip with him'. That would indicate somewhere near Abbots Salford, and perhaps there were other such excursions. But for the most part he remained quietly at Hindlip, waiting for the storm to pass, and pass it might well have done, had it not been for yet another twist in the story.

On the night of 7 January 1606, a drunken poacher wandered into the barn near Hagley Hall where Robert Wintour and Stephen Lyttelton were still in hiding. Climbing up on the barley mow, he fell down into the hole on top of them. In the morning, he managed to escape, taking the secret of their lurking-place with him. Stephen's cousin Humphrey Lyttelton invited them to stay in the Hall itself instead, but made the mistake of telling the cook, who promptly informed on them. Next morning, 9 January 1606, Robert Wintour and Stephen Lyttelton were arrested in the courtyard of Hagley Hall. Humphrey Lyttelton escaped on horseback but was captured and within ten days condemned to death at Worcester. In an ultimately unsuccessful attempt to bargain for his life, he offered to reveal the names and abodes of 'certain Jesuits and priests which had been persuaders of him and others to these actions'. The first name he mentioned was that of Oldcorne at Hindlip.

Early on the morning of Monday 20 January, Sir Henry Bromley of Holt Castle , four miles north-west of Hindlip, arrived at the gates with 100 armed men and a set of detailed instructions for the search which had been sent to him by the Earl of Salisbury. By this time, Salisbury knew that Gerard had been at Harrowden during the search there, and he did not want the same mistakes repeated. While Bromley's men battered on the gates, the priests and their servants, together with the church stuff and many of their books, were packed away in what Gerard calls 'the most safe secret places they had'. But there was not time to hide everything, and on breaking into the house Bromley found warm beds, bundles of clothes, scholarly writings and other suspicious evidence. Thomas Habington himself was away from home, but on returning that night he assured Bromley that no such men were in his house - which he may well have believed or hoped was true, since Garnet and Oldcorne had only returned from Evesham the night before. But Bromley did not believe him, and the search proceeded.

This was not the first time that Bromley had searched Hindlip. He had been there before for three days in April 1598, when he had smashed open about twenty places in the panelling of the Long Gallery. It was on that occasion that the searchers had found a point for trussing hose which Oldcorne had dropped as he went into the hide. Failing to match it with any other men's clothes in the house, the searchers had begun to hack 'vehemently' with an axe at the panelling in front of the hide. But perhaps it was backed with a solid brick-and-timber wall, like the hide in Dodd's Library at Harvington, since it was not discovered and Oldcorne was able to escape. This time he was not to be so lucky.

Bromley had been ordered to start with the dining-room, in the east side of which 'it is conceived there is some vault'. He was also to look for any 'double lofts' or inaccessible parts of the roof space, such as Tate had been shown at Harrowden on 14 November. But nothing was found in either of these places, at least to start with, and it was not until Wednesday, the third day of the search, that Bromley 'found a number of Popish trash hid under

boards in three or four several places'. It is likely that one of these places was a hole-under-the-

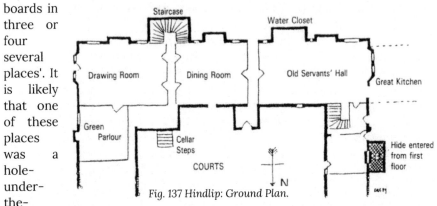

Fig. 137 *Hindlip: Ground Plan.*

garderobe which projected beyond the chimney stack of the Lady's Chamber on the first floor of the west side. This survived until Hindlip was pulled down in 1814 and was described and illustrated by the local antiquarian Peter Prattinton. He gives its dimensions as 3.38m long, 1.55m wide and 1.63m to the joists - reasonably spacious for this sort of hide. This was presumably the place that Nash had in mind when he wrote in his *Worcestershire* (1781) that 'the entrance to some [of the hides] was through necessary houses'.

Late on the Wednesday night, Bromley went back to Holt Castle, leaving his brother Sir Edward in charge of the search. He was 'much wearied' and inclined to abandon the hunt if no one was found in another day or two. But next morning, Nicholas Owen and Ralph Ashley were forced out of their hiding-place in the Long Gallery by cold and hunger, having had nothing to eat but one apple between the two of them since the beginning of the search. They had waited until the guards in the Gallery were furthest off in their patrol 'and came out so secretly and stilly, and shut the place again so finely, that they were not one whit heard or perceived when and where they came out'. But while they were making their way towards the Gallery door, the searchers turned back and stopped them. Then, realising that the pair must have been hidden in the Gallery, they began 'to break down the wainscot with which the Gallery was lined, and the walls also in a number of places'.

This hiding-place was one of two found 'in the Gallery over the gate' and described as 'cunning and very artificial conveyances in the main brick wall, so ingeniously framed and with such art as it cost much labour ere they could be found'. Presumably, one or other of these was the hide in which Oldcorne had nearly been caught eight years before. From Prattinton's drawings it is possible to make a shrewd guess where they were contrived. The outer or northern face of the gatehouse block had three large windows on the top floor, where the Gallery was: two of ten lights and one, in the middle over the gateway arch, of fourteen. Any additional thickness of walling on this side would therefore be noticeable. But the inner face of this block had only one window, and that is a bay projecting into the courtyard, so that the thickness of the main brick wall' would not be conspicuous, especially at the ends, where it joined on to the east and west blocks. It seems likely, therefore, that the hole in which Owen and Ashley took refuge was devised, like the one at Sawston, in the courtyard wall of the Gallery, and

Fig. 138 Hindlip: Western elevation.

that it was entered through the panelling or some other feature of the Gallery.

It is possible that Owen and Ashley intended to get captured, like Bray at Scotney in 1598 and John Lillie in London in 1599, to draw off the search for the two priests. But Gerard's account suggests that they were driven out by privations and hoped to get away. At all events, their capture only made the searchers keener, and on the eighth day (27 January) Garnet and Oldcorne were also found.

> Three other secret places, contrived by no less skill and industry, were likewise found in and about chimneys, in one whereof two of the traitors were close concealed. These chimney conveyances being so strangely formed, having the doors or entrances into them so curiously covered over with brick, mortared and made fast to planks of wood and coloured black like the other parts of the chimney, that very diligent inquisition might well have passed by without throwing the least suspect upon such unsuspicious places. And whereas divers tunnels usually are made to chimneys, according as they are combined together and serve for necessary use in several rooms, so here were some that exceeded common expectation, seeming outwardly fit for conveying forth of smoke, but being further examined and seen into, their service was to no such purpose, but only to lend air and light downward into the concealments, where such as was enclosed in them at any time should be hidden....

Forth of this secret and most cunning conveyance came Henry Garnet, the Jesuit sought for, and another with him named Hall [Oldcorne]. Marmalade and other sweetmeats were found there lying by them, but their better maintenance had been by a quill or reed through a little hole in the chimney that backed another chimney into the gentlewoman's chamber, and by that passage caudles, broths and other warm drinks had been conveyed in to them. Now in regard the place was so close, those customs of nature which of necessity must be done, and in so long time of continuance, was exceedingly offensive to the men themselves, and did much annoy them that made entrance in upon them, to whom they confessed that they had not been able to hold out one whole day longer, but either they must have yielded or perished in the space.

There is another vivid description of this hole by Garnet himself, in a letter to Anne Vaux written in orange-juice five weeks later, from the Tower:

After we had been in the hole seven days and seven nights and some odd hours, every man may well think we were well wearied, and so indeed it was, for we generally sat, save that sometimes we could half stretch ourselves, the place not being high enough, and we had our legs so straitened that we could not sitting find place for them, so that we both were in continual pain of our legs, and both our legs, especially mine, were much swollen, and mine continued so till I came to the Tower. If we had had but one half-day liberty to come forth, we had eased the place from books and furniture, that having with us a close stool we could have abidden a quarter of a year. For that all my friends will wonder at, especially in me, that neither of us went to the stool all the while, though we had means to do *servitii piccoli* [pass water], whereof also we were at a nonplus the day of our taking. We were very merry and content within, and heard the searchers every day most curious over us, which made me indeed think the place would be found. When we came forth, we appeared like two ghosts.

The feeding-tube and the use of the flue as a ventilator are reminiscent of Irnham, though the foul atmosphere shows either that the latter device was not efficient, or else that the searchers were generalising and that this particular hide was not so equipped, though others in the chimneys were. The 'means to do *servitii piccoli*' must have been on the lines of the latrines chiselled out of the brickwork and stone at Braddocks and Sawston, since Garnet indicates that a close stool would have made it possible to hold out for much longer. The searchers had, in fact, calculated that the priests would have to come out at intervals for 'those customs of nature', and had set a trap accordingly. Garnet's account concludes by saying that after the discovery he and Oldcorne 'desired to be led to a house of office. So I was, and found a board taken up where there was a great downfall, that one should have broken his neck if he had come thither in the dark; which seemed intended of purpose'.

The searchers described the entrance to this hide as 'curiously covered over with brick, mortared and made fast to planks of wood, and coloured black like the other parts of the chimney'. It is not clear whether this means that the hide was entered through one side of the fireplace, or through the back, or through the hearth, as at Braddocks. The last interpretation is supported by Henry Foulis in *Romish Treasons* (1671), who says that the entrance was 'by taking up the half-pace before the Hearth, whose wooden border was made like a Trap-door, to pluck up and down, and then the Bricks were laid in their Courses and Order again'. Joseph Jouvency, writing in Latin at Rome in 1710, says that Garnet and Oldcorne were found behind an elaborately decorated ceiling. That would fit the Braddocks hide, and also the stair hide at Harvington, in relation to the Great Chamber below. But both Foulis and Jouvency may owe more to imagination, and to seventeenth-century canons of style, than to accurate reports of the details.

'The whole service', Bromley concluded, 'endured the space of eleven nights and twelve days'. During it, a total of 'eleven secret corners and conveyances were found in the said house, all of them having books, Massing stuff and Popish trumpery in them, only two excepted which appeared to have been found on former searches'. Thomas

Fig. 139 Hindlip: The Courtyard, with the Gatehouse block to the right. The hides are thought to have been in the second-floor wall here.

Habington maintained stoutly that he knew nothing about any of these places, until the deeds of his lands were found in one of them, 'whereto he could then devise no sufficient excuse'. Habington was later sentenced to death but reprieved, reportedly on condition that he never again set foot outside Worcestershire. He devoted the rest of his long life to local history and antiquities, and it is said that, coming to Tardebigge church, which was right on the county boundary, he contented himself with inspecting the monuments in the Warwickshire chancel from the Worcestershire nave. A letter which he wrote in 1643 shows that there were then no remaining usable hides at Hindlip. Discussing the Shrewsbury pedigrees which had been loaned to him for his research, he said:

> I have been enforced through the outrageous tumults of this time to hide
> them in my chest of evidences, where I ever laid them, in woods and buried

in the earth.

Of the eleven hides, only the one described by Prattinton is known to have survived until 1814. But enough has been recorded to justify the Jacobean comment that Hindlip was 'the most famous house in England for entertainment of priests'. And only twelve miles away, at Harvington, it is still possible to see what it must have been like.

4

From Hindlip, Bromley took his prisoners to Holt Castle, where he treated them kindly and gave them time to recover. On 3 February they all set out for London, though Garnet was still unable to eat much and was 'a weak and wearisome traveller', despite being given the best horse. They were followed by Anne Vaux and Dorothy Habington*. Within a fortnight of their arrival in London, secret letters in orange-juice were going in and out of the Tower, with the connivance of the Lieutenant, Sir William Waad. They were intercepted, warmed by a fire to bring out the invisible writing, and deciphered. Since orange-juice stays visible once warmed, Waad had copies forged in the hands of Garnet and Anne Vaux, to be sent on to the intended recipients. The originals were kept and are now in the Public Record Office, a fraud to which we owe our knowledge of their contents, including Garnet's description of the hide at Hindlip. Waad hoped in this way to obtain evidence against Garnet, but neither the letters nor a series of examinations proved anything more than that Garnet had kept secret what he had learned in confession, and it was for this that he was eventually condemned.

John Gerard was still in London, at the house of Dr Taylor. Early in March, since his house in St Clement's Lane was no longer safe after its use by the conspirators, he rented two more houses of his own. In the smaller of these he built three 'good hiding places'. On 12 April 1606, which was the day before Palm Sunday, Dr and Mrs Taylor's house was raided. They were taken off to prison, while a priest named Thomas Everett was concealed in a hide. Fearing that he would die of hunger or else come out before it was safe and risk capture, Gerard sent some friends to the house, but Everett would not answer, even when they knocked on the hiding-place. Their voices were unfamiliar, and he suspected that it was a trick of the searchers. He stayed put until the Sunday night, when Gerard sent his friends back again, and with

---

*There is a mystery here regarding Anne's sister Eleanor (Brooksby). She was with the group at Coughton on 29th October but there is no mention of her subsequently being at Hindlip: she simply disappears from the records. Oscott College Library has a 1622 prayer book, formerly at Harvington Hall, containing the signatures of Mary and Anne Pakington, and of Eleanor ('la Baronne Brooksby'). The reader may recall that she – nervous compared to the indomitable Anne – spent the 1591 Baddesley search in a hide. Did she weather the storm at Harvington?

them the builder of the hide, who knew how to open it from outside.

Four days later, on Maundy Thursday, the smaller of Gerard's two houses was raided while Everett was saying Mass there. The Lord Mayor and his men were already into the house and on their way upstairs while Everett, with his vestments on and the Massing stuff in a bundle under his arm, was squeezing into his hiding-place. The raiding party found the congregation and the smoke from the extinguished candles but nothing else, since all three of the hides which Gerard had built a few weeks before withstood the search. But everyone else in the house was taken off for examination, and for the second time in less than a week Gerard had to arrange to have Everett rescued from confinement in a priest-hole. It was now that Gerard at length realised that London was too hot to hold him and decided to take the first chance that offered to cross the Channel to Flanders.

The hide-builder who rescued Everett on the night of Palm Sunday was not Nicholas Owen, who by this time was dead. After his capture at Hindlip and arrival in the Tower, he had been offered his life if he would talk, with the threat that if he would not, the secret would be wrested from him. There was also some mention of rewards, from the property of Catholics who could be convicted of priest-harbouring on his evidence. But it is unlikely that Owen would have been allowed to get his fingers on much of the loot. He was a poor man, with no powerful patrons, and the mercy shown to him would more probably have taken the form of a post as a servant in some great household, where he could have all the beer and bread he wanted. Or he might have been given a small and irregular pension which would enable him to take the occasional afternoon off from his carpentry to go and watch a bear-baiting. Whatever the inducements, he would not divulge what was demanded, and so, as one of the Privy Councillors put it, they had a trick for him.

John Gerard, in hiding at the Taylors', was able to find out that Owen 'hung in the torture seven hours together, and this divers times, though we cannot as yet learn the certain number; but day after day we heard of his being carried to torments'. Apart from a limp, caused by an accident with a restive horse some years before, Owen also suffered from a rupture, the result of lifting excessively heavy loads while constructing his hiding-places. It was against the law for such a man to be tortured, but this provision was ignored and as a precaution 'they girded his belly with a plate of iron'. On 2 March 1606, the inevitable happened and 'his bowels gushed out together with his life'. It was given out that he had committed suicide with a table-knife, and a ballad with a woodcut illustration was printed to encourage this rumour. But Gerard, from first-hand experience, records that prisoners under warrant for torture were not allowed knives with points; and a kinswoman of Owen's was told by his gaoler that he had not even been able to feed himself or put on his cap. 'The man is dead', the gaoler added: 'he died in our hands'.

Owen, says Gerard, 'might have made it almost an impossible thing for priests to escape, knowing the residences of most priests in England, and of all those of the Society, whom he might have taken as partridges in a net'. That was why he was put to such extremities, and why he was revered by the priests whose lives he saved at the cost of his own. Within a few months, Gerard had set down his impressions of Owen in his *Narrative of the Gunpowder Plot*, and there are tributes to him in the Jesuit historians of the seventeenth and eighteenth centuries - More, Bartoli and Jouvency. But it was not until 1871, and after strange vicissitudes, that Gerard's manuscript was at last published, and by then most of Owen's hides had been destroyed or were no longer identifiable. But enough remains for it to be clear why Owen had the reputation of a master craftsman in his strange and secret trade. The examples at Baddesley Clinton, Braddocks, Oxburgh, Sawston, Scotney, Harvington and elsewhere show an ability to handle space in order to create an illusion which is worthy of a Baroque architect, even if the materials are vernacular and the purpose more serious. It was not for this, however, that Owen was canonised as a Saint in 1970 but for a holy life culminating in a suffering and death in which he laid down his life for his friends.

The torture chamber in the basement of the White Tower has changed since 1606. The present brick vaulting was inserted about 1720; electric light has replaced the tallow dips; and visitors file through by the hundred, admiring the displays of mortars and cannon. But, for all that, it is still possible to stand there and be reminded, not merely of agony and sweat, but also of the cascading scales of Byrd's *Justorum Animae* which echoed round the Basilica of St Peter's in Rome on the day of the canonisation. 'The souls of the just are in the hand of God, and no torment shall touch them. In the eyes of the foolish they seemed to die, but they are at peace'.

10
Gunpowder Plot to Civil War
1606-1648

1

On 3 May 1606, the day of Garnet's execution, John Gerard crossed to the Continent, disguised in the livery of the Spanish Ambassador. He meant to return when the hue and cry died down, but his superiors would never allow him to take the risk. By then, Edward Oldcorne and Ralph Ashley had been executed, outside Worcester on 7 April, and Oswald Tesimond had also escaped across the Channel, disguised as the owner of a cargo of dead pigs. Hugh Sheldon, who was to have worked with Owen on the priest-holes at Kirby Hall in 1599, was arrested during 1606 in connection with the smuggling of books. William Weston, by now half blind and deaf, had been banished and was slowly recovering at Seville from the effects of his long imprisonment. The close-knit company which had provided the initiative, and much of the documentation, for the hide-building described in the last seven chapters of this book, now seemed irrevocably dispersed by death or exile.

That is probably how the Earl of Salisbury saw the position, and certainly it is how he would have liked it to be. The propaganda effects of the Gunpowder Plot did last until the nineteenth century and beyond, with No-Popery sermons, an order of service which Queen Victoria did not suppress until 1856, and the annual burning of effigies of the Pope as well as of Guy Fawkes. But after the first crisis, recusants themselves were hurt more in their pockets than in their persons. The number of convictions for recusancy shows a dramatic increase, though this is not fully reflected in the Exchequer receipts, since many recusants were farmed out to courtiers or officials as profitable speculations. But the numbers of executions declined steadily.

During the 1580s there had been a hundred-odd, during the 1590s sixty-odd. During the first decade of the seventeenth century there were thirty-odd, and during the second only ten. In the 1620s there were three, and in the 1630s there were none at all. Meanwhile, the number of priests at work in England and Wales rose from 300 (plus fifty or sixty Marian survivors) in 1596 to 400 in 1610, and to nearly 800 in 1642, a figure which was still being maintained in 1667. In other words, the network pioneered by Garnet and Southwell in the 1580s and 1590s had been durable enough not only to survive the shock of the Gunpowder Plot but to extend after it.

There were also political reasons. King James himself, as a connoisseur of theology, disliked settling arguments by violence. Before 1608, his consort, Anne of Denmark, had been received into the Roman communion by Richard Blount. After the death of the Earl of Salisbury in 1612, influence was increasingly exercised first by the Howards and then by the Villiers, both of which clans had Catholic leanings. Towards the end of his life, James entered into negotiations for the marriage of his heir Charles to a Spanish princess and then, that failing, to Henrietta Maria of France. In 1623, William Bishop, formerly one of the Appellants and later a scholar in Paris under the patronage of Cardinal Richelieu, became the first Catholic bishop in England since the Reformation. In the same year, Inigo Jones designed the Chapel Royal of St James for the Catholic Princess of Wales, Henrietta Maria. It had a staff of French priests, an organ on the south side, and a choir which sang Masses and Vespers to which the public were admitted. By the time that John Gerard died in Rome, in 1637, there were Papal diplomats in London and discussions were being held about the possible union of the Roman and Anglican churches.

But this easing of restrictions on Catholics was gradual, patchy and never complete. In the early years after the Gunpowder Plot, things went on much as in the last years of Elizabeth. In the roof of Holywell Manor in Oxford there is a hiding-place formerly entered by a door covered with plaster, as at Ufton and Huddington. It is at the junction of two gables on the side nearest the road and has the distinction of being the only previously unknown hiding-place that I have discovered myself. Holywell was the manor-house of the Nappers, one of whom, George Napper, was executed nearby in 1610 for his priesthood. But the hide is probably much earlier than that: even in 1591 Cardinal Allen noted that a priest would be 'well provided for in Oxford with Mr Napper'. According to the seventeenth-century antiquarian Anthony à Wood, William Napper rented land at Cowley to 'one Badger, a mason living in St Peter's in the East, and a Roman Catholic as Napier was; who built a house thereon, about the latter end of Queen Elizabeth, for a hiding-hole of a priest or any other lay-Catholic in times of persecution'. It seems likely that William Badger also built this hiding-place at Holywell, and there would certainly have been a use for it up to 1610 and beyond.

Even in the 1620s, priests were still liable to searches, imprisonment and condemnation, although the sentences were rarely carried out. In November 1621, a Jesuit named John Sweet was arrested in Exeter with a bag containing his Massing stuff, which he had hidden 'over the tester of the bed in the chamber where he was apprehended'. It included 'Popish books, a chalice with a crucifix on the foot thereof, a silver plate parcel gilt to carry the wafer cakes, a casket of silver wherein are three little silver boxes of oil, and other superstitious things tending to Papery. And in his pocket we found a Mass book and a box of wafer cakes, most of them with the impression of a crucifix'. Sweet was imprisoned in London, but in 1623 he took part in a famous series of debates between Catholics and Anglicans, contributions to which were made both by the King and by William Laud, later Archbishop of Canterbury. Sweet's colleague on this occasion was John Percy, formerly of Harrowden and Salden, who was now living on parole in the house of the Countess of Buckingham.

Similarly, there was George Fisher alias Muscote, whose Massing stuff was found to include a brass pistol and a false beard. He was sentenced to death in 1629 but reprieved at the Queen's intercession. For the next twelve years he remained in prison in Newgate and the Clink, conducting a vigorous ministry and writing lengthy reports on it to Rome. In 1641, he was chosen to be President of Douai College and released to take up this appointment. There he overhauled the finances and died peacefully four years later.

It seems likely, therefore, that the construction of hiding-places continued, especially in London, but with less urgency as the years went by. As early as 1617, what William Johnson betrayed to the governor of York Castle was 'all the *old* [my italics] hiding-places' in the Northern houses where he had been received as a priest. When the Civil War broke out in 1642, there is a strong impression of old hides being hastily refurbished, or of no hides at all being available. In 1643 John Worthington wrote that at Blainscow Hall in Lancashire he had 'a secret hiding-place in which *for many years'* [my italics] he had been safe, but that in the more troubled times of the War he had found the coal shed less liable to search. Of the hiding-places used by King Charles II after the Battle of Worcester in 1651 (to be described in detail in the next chapter), one was 'formerly made in times of persecution' and another was 'an old well-concealed hiding-place' made by the then owner's recusant ancestors. I have already mentioned in the last chapter how Thomas Habington, who in 1606 had kept his deeds in one of the eleven hides at Hindlip, was reduced in 1643 to keeping valuable borrowed documents buried in a chest in the garden.

Even so, and despite the lack of a continuous narrative like John Gerard's, there are hides which can be dated, sometimes quite closely, within the reigns of James I and Charles I. A discussion of a dozen or so will indicate the range.

Mapledurham is on the banks of the Thames, two miles above Reading. An H-shaped Jacobean building of diapered brickwork, its exact date was unknown until analysis by Dr Dan Miles of the Oxford Dendrochronology Laboratory showed that was built with timber felled between 1608 and 1611. The Eystons, descendents of the Blounts who built it, still live there. During the 1960's the house was skilfully and exquisitely restored and the Georgian chapel, in Strawberry Hill Gothick, is again in use.

There are three hides at Mapledurham, two with Ufton-style bolts leading off the same first-floor bedroom and a third, only discovered in 2003, within the chimney breast of the same room and now accessed from the room above it.

The first hide (Fig. 140) is a small one under a cupboard floor. The second (Fig. 141), under the garderobe closet, is 2.13m long and 1.22m wide, though only 1.02m deep. It has a boarded floor and one of the most perfectly preserved trapdoors in the country, made of three layers of oak planks, for solidity and to muffle

Fig. 140 Mapledurham: small hide.

sound. One end of it is fastened to the joist below with iron 'butterfly' hinges of the same pattern as those in one hide at Harvington. The hinges of both hides are so positioned that the end of the trapdoor tucks under the wall when the hide is closed, leaving no break in the boards to catch a searcher's eye. The hide is not very comfortable to sit up in, but there is room to lie full length. This is the other house, along with Ufton Court (p21) where spring bolts are found, and this hide has a refinement compared with Ufton: the oak pulley wheel to prevent the cord fraying.

The date of the house means that these bolts are around 25 years later than those

Fig. 141 Large hide open and (inset upper) closed and (lower) detail of bolt showing pulley wheel and nails that formerly held spring.

at Ufton, leaving open the possibility that more examples of this builder's work are still to be found within Oxfordshire. The bolt in the smaller hide does not have a spring or a pulley wheel, but as the hide is too small for human occupancy, there must originally have been some mechanism to operate it from outside. It is possible to do so with a piece of bent wire.

Fig. 142 Chimney Hide closed, open and view down inside. The entrance is a modern conjectural reconstruction following that at Braddocks.

The third hide, whose existence had been something of a family legend was finally rediscovered during repair work in 2003. This is within the chimney stack wall between the bedroom containing the two previously known hides and the room above. The space is 440mm wide for most of its length, tapering to only 330mm at the south end. Here the width is reduced by a bulge representing the flue from the cellar fireplace. At this end there is a narrow step or seat in the brickwork, also plastered. To sit on it is a tight squeeze, but more comfortable than squatting on the bottom of the hide. The length of the hide is 1.57m, the same as the fireplace above. At the other (north) end there is a gap running diagonally through the outside brickwork and providing some light and air. The depth, as indicated by the plastering, is 900mm, below which clearing of the rubble has revealed signs of a timber floor. It had been sealed up after fire damage in the 19th century and the original access is no longer known, However, as access from above is more common, this was chosen for a conjectural reconstruction in which the entire hearth slides forward on runners.

The positions of all three hides (red) are shown in Fig. 143. The first-described two are accessed from the room traditionally known as the Priest's

Room (green outlined window). The small hide is the lower one in the chimney stack and the large one is under the floor of the dressing room (blue

rectangle) off the Priest's Room. The chimney hide is the upper red rectangle and is now accessed via the hearth in the room (yellow) above the Priest's Room, raising the possibility that this room was the Jacobean secret chapel. As the house dates from around 1608-11 it is possible that these hides were designed into the original structure rather than being later additions.

Naworth Castle, near Brampton in Cumberland is a fourteenth-century circuit of walls and towers, altered by Thomas Lord Dacre about 1520. In 1604, through the marriage of a Dacre heiress, it came to Lord William Howard, who was a

Fig. 143 Mapledurham: positions of all three hides.

half-brother of Philip Howard, Earl of Arundel, William Weston's friend; a full brother of Thomas Howard, Earl of Suffolk; and a nephew of Henry Howard, Earl of Northampton. He was 'a known recusant dwelling in the remote parts of England northward, unto whom the recusants of greatest note do daily resort'. One of his sons became a Franciscan; one of his daughters married Sir Henry Bedingfeld of Oxburgh; and he himself kept a Benedictine priest named Hungate at Naworth Castle.

Fig. 144 Naworth Castle.

Among alterations which Lord William carried out at the Castle was the reconstruction of what became known as Lord William's Tower. Here he

had his bedroom, library and chapel, and here he spent much of his time. The chapel, on the top floor, contains a richly decorated screen from nearby Lanercost Priory, and a German painting dated 1514 representing the Scourging, Crucifixion and Resurrection of Christ. To the left of the altar, a section of panelling at the bottom of a projection, together with a trapdoor in the floor, can be opened to reveal seven steps of a newel staircase leading down to a space beneath the altar about 1.5m high and 1.68m square. There is a boarded floor, but this, the trapdoor and the panelling are all comparatively recent and seem to be part of the reconstruction carried out by Anthony Salvin after a fire in 1844. There is a small window, made by blocking up part of a larger original one. At the level of the third step up are pieces of wood in the walls,

Fig. 145 Naworth Castle hide.

which look as if they supported a shelf. The nineteenth-century alterations make it impossible to be sure, but it seems likely that this place represents a genuine hide, constructed as part of Lord William's work after 1604.

It is possible to be more precise about Carlton Towers, near Goole in Yorkshire. The main part of the mansion is an imposing series of Victorian state rooms, but the ivy-covered wing to the left is the original Carlton Hall begun by Elizabeth Stapleton in 1614 and later slightly Gothicised. This is a compact three storey block with the chimneystacks in the

Fig. 146 Carlton Towers. The ivy-covered wing at left is the original house containing the hide, which is concealed by the right-hand one of the (unusually) internal chimney stacks.

middle, instead of projecting from outside walls, and the result is an interesting variant on the usual hole-under-the-closet. The hide is 1.8m high, 2.45m wide and no less than 4.3m long. It is beneath the closet and the back third of a top floor bedroom, with the chimney-stack occupying part of the space. Since the stack is in the middle of the building, the hide does not begin until 4.3m back from the outside wall, and so it cannot be located from outside. The entrance is through a modern trapdoor, with

Fig. 147 Bedroom with closet and hide entrance.

one original joist, down a modern ladder. The original floor of lime-ash has survived, and there is a modern plaster ceiling to part of the hide, which may replace an original.

Beneath the hide is a passage with a stone arch to support the section of the stack in the hide. On either side of this arched passage are bedrooms with fireplaces on their inner walls, so that the flues join in the arch. Further along the block, the similar chimney stack has its fireplaces back-to-back in the middle of the house, with no passage or arch or consequent hidden space between them. This would be extremely difficult to engineer as an alteration and implies that the hide was designed into the house from the beginning and is therefore also datable to 1614.

The top floor, from which the hide is entered, was originally the Long Gallery and was not divided into separate rooms until 1842. The account books of Sir Miles Stapleton for 1664 include items 'for making the new chapel in the Gallery', with rails, a

Fig. 148 Hide interior (picture from 1983).

wooden tabernacle, a carved and coloured canopy, and vestments and frontals of pink and crimson silk. The altarpiece was 'a great picture' of the Crucifixion. A priest named Thomas Thwing was at Carlton by 1662, though it is not certain whether he was the Thomas Thwing who was executed at York in 1680. The chapel in the Gallery was replaced in 1778 by a much more ambitious one in the east wing, whose pedimented altar-piece, framing a Nativity by Theodore de Bruyn, is now on show in the room from which the hide is entered. When the Gallery was divided in the 1840s the hide was not tampered with and remains in its original condition.

Fig. 149 *View into hide from trapdoor.*

Visitors to the house are informed of the existence of a second hide behind panelling in the private family apartments, but no further information is available about this.

By 1622, the Jesuit mission in England had expanded to about 150 priests and was promoted to the status of an independent province of the order. The papers giving effect to this change mention three major Jesuit houses, in London, Staffordshire and South Wales, the last of which had been specially constructed with enough hiding-holes for forty priests. Since this building outdid even Harvington and Hindlip, it is worth trying to identify it.

From 1615 to 1625, the home of the Jesuit superior in Wales, John Salisbury, was Raglan Castle, in the middle of the triangle formed by Monmouth, Abergavenny and Usk. Although this magnificent structure was slighted after the Civil War, large parts of it still stand and there are detailed descriptions of the interior. It was built around two courtyards, the Pitched Stone Court and the Fountain Court, which were divided by the Great Hall and a chapel with the Long Gallery above it. Outside the main Castle was a five-storey hexagonal tower-house, the Yellow Tower of Gwent, which could be reached only by a high-level bridge from the Withdrawing Room off the Great Hall. A windowless stone enclosure projecting into the basement kitchen of the Yellow Tower may have been the Marquess of Worcester's strong-room at the time of the Civil War, as this Tower was 'where his Lordship did use to keep his treasure'. His father, the fourth Earl of Worcester, who owned the Castle from 1589 to 1628, held many offices under both Elizabeth I and James I but was nevertheless a known Catholic and a patron of William Byrd, who dedicated the first volume of his *Gradualia* (1605) to him. Elizabeth remarked that 'he reconciled what she believed impossible, a stiff Papist to a good subject'. So it is tempting to think Raglan is the site of the hide for forty men.

Unfortunately, the Castle was not 'specially constructed' by the Jesuits, and it was under the protection of a powerful lord, which the documents say this house was not. A more likely site is The Combe or Cwm, four miles north of Monmouth and just into Herefordshire, which was another centre associated with John Salisbury. Already in 1605 a report had mentioned 'Mr William Griffiths of The Combe... with whom Richard Griffiths alias Fleming alias Watson, a Jesuit, remaineth. Thither also repaireth very often Morris alias Jones'. It was alleged that while Robert Wintour and Stephen Lyttelton were in hiding at Hagley, Edward Oldcorne had met this Jones at Huddington Court and asked him to guide them to The Combe. At the time of the Oates Plot in 1678, a library was found behind a secret plaster-covered door at The Combe, but the present building dates only from the Regency.

Treowen Court, four miles north-east of Raglan, was the home of Sir Philip Jones (1602-1660), who married a first cousin of the Marquess of Worcester, Elizabeth Morgan of Llantarnam. It contains a splendid Jacobean open-well staircase which goes up all four storeys of the north block. Under the first-floor corridor next to this staircase is a space 1.37m high, 1.5m wide and 1.83m long.

Fig. 150 *Treowen Court Hide*

The entrance is through a trapdoor in the corridor floor, which was renewed in 1932. The hide now has a modern floor, replacing some worm-eaten boards found laid across the joists. In it was found a seventeenth-century picture of St Mary Magdalen on a piece of parchment measuring just under 75mm by 100mm. Since in 1678 Lady Jones was accused of harbouring 'Thomas Powell, a reputed Popish priest', it is likely that this place was well used and, as at Harvington, its construction suggests that it was built at the same time as the adjoining staircase.

The Jesuit house in Staffordshire may well have been Boscobel, which will be described in the next chapter in the context of Charles II's escape in 1651. The one in London was probably Hunsdon House in Blackfriars, the residence of the French Ambassador, Comte de Tillier. On 26 October 1623, while Fr Robert Drury was preaching to a congregation of some 300, the floor collapsed and he and nearly 100 others were killed. The accident, which became known as the Doleful Evensong, caused a considerable stir and was described in a pamphlet by a Puritan divine, Samuel Clarke, who had been one of the survivors. In 1627, the Jesuits instead took a large corner house in Clerkenwell belonging to the Earl of Shrewsbury. In March 1628 the pursuivant Humphrey Cross raided it, having observed lights showing in what was supposed to be an empty house. By the usual delaying tactics, 'they within the upper rooms got advantage to retire themselves by secret passages into their vaults or lurking places, which themselves called their securities, so as when the officers came up they found no man above stairs, save only a sick man in his bed, with one servant attending him'. But when he went down into the cellars, 'Cross espied a brick wall newly made, which he caused to be pierced'. Behind it they found five priests, and next day 'in the like lurking place' they found a sixth. A great quantity of papers and church stuff also fell into the pursuivants' hands. Cross's information and the mention of the 'newly made' wall enable us to date these two hiding-places to 1627; and the Secretary of State, Sir John Cooke, was left in no doubt that the house was 'really hired and used for a College of Jesuits'.

About the same time, a Jesuit named Henry Floyd who, like John Percy, had been lodging with the Countess of Buckingham, was arrested in Nevill's Alley off Fetter Lane 'in a private place, between a chimney and a wall curiously contrived'. He was released and in 1629 was reported to be 'much at Yaxley Hall by Eye in Suffolk', a house which contained a hide until a fire in the 1920s. In 1633, after a visit to Rome, he was arrested again, this time at the manor-house of East Cheam, whose owner was 'never without a priest or Jesuit' and had 'a private place in his house to convey them into upon any search'. Floyd, it appeared, had had himself arrested for debt and then, armed with a note from a recusant doctor, had obtained a warrant from the Privy Council to take the air for the good of his health. This warrant meant that he could go where he liked without being stopped and examined, and he had made full use of it. When arrested, he 'gave out many peremptory and threatening speeches', asserting that the houses he went to were protected and that if the pursuivant waited till next day there would be three or four more priests with him. Floyd was sent to the Fleet prison but let out again on parole for the good of his health in 1637. He died in London in 1641 at the age of eighty.

In 1623, another important Jesuit centre was established at St Anthony's, three miles from Newcastle on the Northumberland bank of the Tyne. This was the dower-house of a devout widow, Mrs Dorothy Lawson, and became the new headquarters of Richard Holtby, who was now seventy. In 1624, he was sent a young assistant, Henry Morse, who, after being arrested and exiled three times and having worked as an army chaplain in Flanders and among the plague-ridden slums of London, was eventually executed at Tyburn in 1645. St Anthony's was a new house, with a chapel, library, private entrances and hiding-places, which, as at Carlton, could be allowed for in the designs.

An informer's report of 1615 shows that there was already an effective Catholic underground in Newcastle, run from a shop on Sandhill where a widow in a four-cornered cap sold ropes, red herrings and salt fish. Upstairs there was a priest named William Southern, and a red chest at the left side of the chamber, containing hosts in a painted box, books and rosaries. But as a result of this report Southern was arrested and hanged in Newcastle in 1618. The King was not pleased: he was in the middle of delicate negotiations with the Spanish Ambassador for the marriage of Prince Charles and swore that whoever was responsible would feel his indignation. The responsibility, or at least the blame, fell on Lord Sheffield, who, having been appointed to the Council of the North for his enthusiastic part in the search of Grosmont in 1599, was now removed from its Presidency for being too enthusiastic. Mrs Lawson had been living near Newcastle, at Heaton, since 1605, but St Anthony's was even closer to the river and, as her biographer put it, 'most commodious for pleasure and pleasant for all commodities'.

When Mrs Lawson first came to Heaton, it had the only chaplaincy and the only set of Massing stuff in the neighbourhood. By the time that she died in 1632, 'there was not one heretic family, and six altars were erected for divine service'. At St Anthony's she maintained an elaborate round of liturgical ceremonies, with sung Compline every afternoon at four o'clock and the full services of Holy Week. She also had elaborate arrangements for smuggling. Some of these came to light on 1 April 1626, when Anthony Vandenhaupt, a Flemishman from Mechlin who had come over in the *Flying Hart*, was arrested with a large 'fardel' (bundle) addressed to Holtby. It contained 'beads and relics of Papery', letters to several priests, and more than eighty books of theology, canon law, Scripture and devotion. Like other smugglers before and since, Vandenhaupt disclaimed knowledge of the contents of the fardel and of the man to whom it was addressed. A week and a half later, the *Sea Horse*, a collier bound for Dunkirk, was stopped under the guns of Tynemouth Castle. On board, disguised as seamen, were found Morse and a boy, John Berry, whom he was taking across to school at Douai. They had embarked as the *Sea Horse* passed St Anthony's and warned by Vandenhaupt's misfortune, had brought the minimum of luggage: 'each of them a pie, two loaves of bread, one cheese, a cloak-bag, and a few eggs'.

At the end of April, another collier, the *Fortune* from Enkhuizen in Holland, was searched by the customs officers at Newcastle. Aboard it was another schoolboy in the charge of a man who called himself Zachary Vanderstyn and claimed to understand only Dutch and French. But some of the crew had heard him speaking English during the voyage, and he had a chest containing a further consignment of theological books. His real name was John Robinson, and on 1 May he joined his fellow Jesuit Henry Morse in gaol at Newcastle. Soon after, both were moved to York Castle. Bishop Neile of Durham organised a series of searches in houses both north and south of the Tyne. But on each occasion the suspects were absent (or in hiding), and the Bishop was reduced to proposing that recusants should not be allowed to live near the river. How this was to be effected he did not say. In 1627 he was translated to Winchester, while on Tyneside the recusant smugglers carried on as before.

Fig. 151 Kirby Knowle.

Mrs Lawson was a daughter of Sir Henry Constable (1556-1607) of Burton Constable, the great Elizabethan house near Hull*. Sir Henry was a Church Papist, and the wealthiest of them in Yorkshire, but his wife Margaret and his brother Joseph were active priest-harbourers. Near Thirsk, the family owned two castles of the fourteenth century, Upsall and Kirby Knowle, within a mile of each. other.

Thomas Clark, whose confession has already been quoted in Chapter 7, was arrested at Upsall in 1593, and in 1598 it was reported that Kirby Knowle had 'vaults and secret passages both above and below ground', making it a safe place for priests to hide in. Eleven years later, in 1609, more priests were caught at Upsall, which was said to have a maze of vaults beneath it as a means of escape into the open countryside.

Nothing now remains of Upsall. Kirby Knowle was damaged by fire in 1568 and rebuilt by Sir Henry but was half-ruinous again by 1653, when John Constable was unable to redeem a mortgage on it and it passed to one James Danby. He reconstructed it as the present tower-house of dark grey stone perched dramatically on a steep hill backed by trees. The interior was altered again later. But until the nineteenth century there survived a remarkable hiding-place entered through a narrow passage in the thickness of the east wall. This was concealed by a cupboard with a false back. The hide was 1.07m square and 1.83m high, at the junction of two walls. It was originally a corner

---

* Not to be confused with Constable Burton, the classical house by John Carr near Leyburn

closet with a little window. When it was converted into a hiding-place the gap was filled by a stone angle-piece with an iron handle, which could be removed from inside the hide to admit light and air. This device was 250mm long and nearly 180mm on the two faces of the angle, and nothing like it has been recorded anywhere else.

About 1620, the Jesuits also acquired 'a building of mean appearance' somewhere in Lincolnshire. In 1644, the Jesuit John Hudd was arrested there. One of the Parliamentarians who searched it, taking a last look round 'an obscure room', found a rope hanging from the ceiling, which proved to open a trapdoor. Hudd was hiding in the roof, along with his Massing stuff, and in his hurry had forgotten to pull the rope up after him. There are no further details of the hide, but the date can be fixed at between 1620 and 1644 and is likely to be nearer to the earlier date than the later.

One of the last hiding-places made before the Civil War was at Lulworth Castle in Dorset, which was burnt out in 1929. This Castle was a Jacobean fancy built by Thomas Howard, Lord Bindon, who first mentioned it in a letter of 1608. It is an exact cube, 24.3m (80 feet) each way, with a round tower at

Fig. 152 *Lulworth Castle.*

each corner, 9.1m in diameter and rising 4.9m above the surrounding walls. Apart from the basement there were three storeys in the main building and four in the towers. The chapel was in the north-west tower, at any rate by the eighteenth century.

In 1641, Lord Bindon's grandson sold Lulworth Castle to Humphrey Weld, Cupbearer to Queen Henrietta Maria. He was a recusant and must have been responsible for the hiding-place beneath the floor of the muniment room in the north-east tower. Although no full description survives, it seems to have been entered by a trapdoor with a flight of stone steps beneath, and to have been unusually spacious. Perhaps it extended the full diameter of the tower, for with ceilings 5.5m high it would be easy to create the necessary illusion in the room below by artful design of the cornice and plasterwork. Inigo Jones is said to have worked here, and he was both a recusant and a master of stage perspective. At all events, the hide was a wise precaution, for within a year of Weld's purchase of the Castle the Civil War had broken out and such holes were now needed not only for priests but also for fugitive Cavaliers.

2

Hiding places of the Civil War are usually alleged to have been used after the battles of Marston Moor (1644) and Worcester (1651). But so many private rivalries, minor skirmishes and amateur sieges were caught up into the greater conflict that such datings should be taken with a pinch of salt. The best documented hiding-places are those used by King Charles II after Worcester, which will be discussed in the next chapter. Of the following sample of escapes by less exalted fugitives, none can be precisely dated.

One of the best such stories concerns Colchester Castle, from which Sir John Trevanion is supposed to have escaped after receiving this letter:

> Worthie Sir John - Hope, that is the beste comfort of the afflicted, cannot much, I fear me, help you now. That I would saye to you, is this only: if ever I may be able to requite that I do owe you, stand not upon asking me. 'Tis not much I can do: but what I can do, bee you verie sure I wille. I knowe that, if dethe comes, if ordinary men fear it, it frights not you, accounting it for a high honour, to have such a rewarde of your loyalty. Pray yet that you may be spared this soe bitter, cup. I fear not that you will grudge any sufferings; only if bie submission you can turn them away, 'tis the part of a wise man. Tell me, as if you can, to do for you any thinge that you wolde have done. The general goes back on Wednesday. Restinge your servante to commande. R.T.

These were admirable sentiments, and Sir John spent a whole day pondering them. In the evening he asked to be taken to the chapel. This was on the second floor of the keep, at the south-east corner. It has now mostly been destroyed, but apparently had an arcade and ambulatory, like the chapel of St John in the White Tower at the Tower of London. Since it had only one door and narrow windows high in the walls, Sir John's gaolers were willing to leave him there alone. But when they returned, he had disappeared. The third letter after each punctuation mark in the message formed the words: 'Panel at east end of chapel slides'. The walls of the sub-chapel below are 4.5m thick, so that there would have been ample room within the walls of the chapel itself for a mural passage or staircase - presumably part of the Norman or medieval construction which had been covered up and turned to other uses. The only Sir John Trevanion known to have served in the Royalist Army died of battle wounds in 1643, five years before this story is supposed to have happened but the story is well known in cryptology and this technique is called the Trevanion Cipher.

In Corvedale, south of Shrewsbury, is Wilderhope Hall, a small manor-house of about 1586 built of grey limestone with a steep stone-tiled roof and three massive brick chimney stacks. The Smallmans of Wilderhope were recusants, and in several of the ceilings the initials of Francis and Ellen Smallman, the builders, repeatedly figure beside the Tudor rose and portcullis, fleurs-de-lis and the word *Jesu* on a heart. On one occasion during the Civil War, Major Thomas Smallman was captured by Parliamentary troopers and shut into an upper room at Wilderhope. He contrived to escape down the garderobe flue, seized a horse and galloped away. But his captors pursued him and cut him off at the dizzy height of Wenlock Edge. Rather than surrender, he put his horse to the cliff and leapt over it. The horse was killed, but Smallman's fall was broken by a crab-apple tree: he escaped back to Shrewsbury on foot and lived to see the Restoration of the Monarchy.

The governor of Shrewsbury during the Civil War, and the most prominent Royalist in Shropshire, was Sir Francis Ottley of Pitchford Hall, the finest black-and-white house in a county that is full of them, which

Fig. 153 Pitchford Hall from north.

contains a hiding-place nicknamed 'Pope's Hole'. Although Mary Ottley was a recusant in 1635-1636, it is perhaps more likely to be a Royalist hide.

It is in the east wing (the right-hand block of Fig. 153), between the library and the drawing room and above the ceiling of a low passage on the ground floor. It is entered from a bedroom above, where part of one of the vertical rails in the panelling can be moved slightly sideways. This opens a bolt behind and allows a section of

Fig. 154 Secret door in panelling.

the panelling, the size of an ordinary door to pivot open. This device is a restoration but may follow an original. Beyond is a small closet with a trapdoor in the floor, which covers an inner hide some 4.6m deep. The

bottom of this is lit by the top three lights of the square window seen on the left-hand side of Fig. 155. The lower part of the window lights the passage below, as at Gayhurst and elsewhere. A drawing of the same view in 1825 shows a doorway in that location, and the hide itself contains what

Fig. 156 (above) Hide interior. The owners would be pleased to hear from anyone who can explain what these drawers were for!

Fig. 155 (Left) Pitchford: hide location.

can best be described as a built-in chest of drawers of 18th or 19th century appearance, so it seems likely that a Victorian owner modified an existing space to make a store for valuables or documents.

An even more famous escape than Major Smallman's was that of Captain Arthur Jones at Chastleton in Oxfordshire. The estate had belonged to Robert Catesby, but the present lovely Jacobean house of stone was built by Walter Jones, a clothier of Witney, from 1603 onwards. The traditional hiding-place, now a panelled dressing-room, is over the porch, concealed by a dummy row of window-lights. The twelve-light window of the hall is balanced by one in the porch, but the ceiling of the porch is lower than that of the hall, at the level of the second transom up. Behind the top row of lights is a blank wall, and behind that again is the dressing-room.

According to the story, the captain was concealed here by his wife, who entertained the search-party with plenty of beer. When they were all snoring, she stole into the bedroom from which the hide was entered and released her husband. By morning, when the soldiers awoke, he was over the hills and far away. A thorough search would have revealed this place but it would have been safe enough for one night and there are hides over porches in other houses, like Benthall in Shropshire and Barlborough in Derbyshire

The Joneses were not recusants, so the hide must belong to the Civil War period. The same can be said for two other Royalist houses which had hides, though at neither does the secret place now survive. One of these was at Claydon House near Aylesbury, which is now notable for its eighteenth-century rococo state rooms. The older building contained a hiding-place in the great central chimney, entered, like the one at Lulworth, through a trapdoor in the floor of the muniment room. That it was not a priest-hole is clear from the anger of Sir Edmund Verney and of his son Sir Ralph when, in 1639, a widowed cousin first married a Catholic, William Eure, and then became one herself. Sir Edmund was killed three years later at the Battle of Edge Hill, and Sir Ralph was driven into exile in France. One of his letters home in 1645 mentions a copy of Foxe's *Book of Martyrs*, so confirming his Protestantism. The hide can therefore be dated with some certainty to the 1640s.

Broughton Hall in Staffordshire, an imposing black-and-white house of 1637, formerly had a hide in the chimney of the Great Hall, entered from the adjoining staircase. It was blocked up during extensive repairs and alterations in 1927, as the cavity was weakening the chimney stack. The entrance is said to have been covered by a portrait of a man known from his costume as Red Stockings. Sir Brian Broughton, who inherited Broughton in 1648, was created a baronet at the Restoration for his loyalty to the King, but was no recusant: indeed, as a magistrate in the 1660s he was active in harassing Dissenters. Here again, the hide can be dated but no longer exists.

The suppression of Anglican worship by the victorious Roundheads, along with the smashing of unscriptural ornaments like rails and organs and the expulsions of incumbents, meant that the Church of England had to acquire some of the arts which had been familiar to Catholics for eighty years. Pepys describes attending illicit celebrations of the Prayer Book services in London in terms which echo those of many recusant accounts; and there were even Anglican secret chapels. At Elmbridge in Worcestershire, the Laudian altar table and rails were removed by one of the churchwardens to his own house, Purshall Hall, and set up in a private chapel in the roof. The arrangement was so similar to that of a recusant chapel that it was in fact adapted for Catholic use in 1742, at a cost of £3 10s 8d. At that time, a hole was cut in the table top for an altar stone, which was, of course, not required for Anglican use. In 1947, after an absence of 300 years, the table and rails went back to Elmbridge church, where they can now be seen in a side-chapel.

11
The Escape of Charles II, 1651

S tuart sovereigns had more experience than most of disguises and evasions, what with the escape of Mary Queen of Scots from Lochleven in 1568, the attempted escapes of Charles I from Carisbrooke Castle in 1648, the flight of James II to France in 1688 and the wanderings of Bonnie Prince Charlie after Culloden in 1746. But their most dramatic adventure, which deservedly became one of the most famous episodes in English history, was the escape of Charles II in 1651 after the Battle of Worcester.

1

The story of the King in the oak-tree has been in print continuously for more than 300 years, and his hide at Boscobel has been on show to the public for almost as long. But remarkably little has been written directly on this and the other hiding-places to which he owed his life during those hazardous six weeks. It is not for lack of material: the 'Boscobel Tracts', the various printed and manuscript accounts of the affair, are together as long as Gerard's *Autobiography of an Elizabethan* and *Narrative of the Gunpowder Plot*. From these it is possible to plot the complicated movements of the King and of the other characters in the story, not merely day by day but often hour by hour. They also furnish a good deal of useful, if discreetly worded, information about the hides.

By far the most detailed and reliable account was published immediately after the Restoration by Thomas Blount, a lawyer from a Staffordshire recusant family. In 1680, at Newmarket, the King dictated his own story to Samuel Pepys, who then made it his business to collect the versions of as many other participants as he could. So for each stage of the journey, in addition to the two continuous accounts of Blount and the King himself, there are vivid local reminiscences of what happened at Boscobel or Moseley, in Dorset or in Hampshire. But fascinating as they are, they need careful reading if they are to yield all the information that they contain.

Right at the beginning there is a problem. When the Battle of Worcester was hopelessly lost, why was Boscobel chosen as the royal refuge? And when it had been chosen, why did the King ride all night to within a mile of it, but not go there until two days later, and then only after two changes of plan? And when he did go there, why did he spend all day in an oak tree, rather than in one of the hides which he says himself were the reason for choosing Boscobel in the first place?

If he had known where he was a few minutes after the decision was taken, as he rode past the lane to Harvington Hall, he might have saved himself another thirty miles in the saddle and had his pick of the finest hides in the country. A week later, he was still only a dozen miles from Harvington. But in the confusion, it happened that one of the Giffards of Chillington, near Wolverhampton, was in the party riding with the King and offered to guide him, though not to Chillington or to Boscobel. The suggestion of Boscobel came not from Giffard but from the Earl of Derby – and was 'humbly' discouraged by Giffard, who instead proposed White Ladies, less than a mile from Boscobel.

This is odd when one considers that the Earl's suggestion was based upon recent practical experience. Twelve days earlier, on 22 August, the force which he had raised for the King in Lancashire had been defeated near Wigan and the Earl himself had been wounded. He had made his way south for eighty miles in the direction of Worcester with two servants and Colonel Edward Roscarrock, who had also been wounded. At a house in Shropshire he had been recommended to the caretakers at Boscobel, William and Joan Pendrell. There he had been hidden for two days. Blount, who tells this story, describes Boscobel as 'a very obscure habitation', but does not add that it was a Jesuit house, though this must be what *A True Narrative and Relation* (which draws on the reminiscences of the Pendrells) alludes to in the discreet expression: 'Several other Gentlemen before had used this for their Sanctuary'. Nor does he mention that Boscobel Wood had been the scene of a Royalist defeat three years before. But the Roundhead troop at Codsall, three miles away, must have known of Giffard's recusancy, which would account for the prompt search of the surrounding woods on the Thursday, the day after the Battle.

An account published in 1660, *The History of his Sacred Majesty's most Wonderful Preservation*, says that 'to the end the company might not know whither his Majesty directly intended, Mr Giffard was required to conduct his Majesty to some house near Boscobel, the better to blind the design of going thither'. That sounds sensible and has been repeated in most accounts since. But it does not square with what actually happened. As soon as the party reached White Ladies, Colonel Roscarrock had sent to Boscobel for William Pendrell, and, when he arrived, Derby had entrusted the King to him and his brother Richard Pendrell. Why, then, once Derby and the others had ridden off to Tong Castle and the King had been disguised, did he not go to Boscobel, only fifteen minutes' walk away, instead of sitting all day in the rain in Spring Coppice?

The King had told Lord Wilmot, who was to be his companion throughout the adventures of the next six weeks, that they would meet in

London, at the Three Cranes in the Vintry. But during the day he decided to make for Wales instead, and in the evening, when Richard Pendrell came to fetch him, he asked if there was any recusant Royalist who could help him to cross the Severn. Richard suggested Mr Wolfe of Madeley and set out with the King, leaving a message for his brother John Pendrell (who had undertaken to guide Wilmot) that the original plan was off and Wilmot could make his own way to London. But when, in the small hours of Friday morning, 5 September, the King reached Madeley, he was told that the Severn crossings were guarded, that there was a troop of horse in the village, and that the hides in the house had been found.* After spending the day in a barn, he set out that night on the return journey with Richard Pendrell, who took him to Boscobel because there was nowhere else to go. At Boscobel they found Colonel Carlis, a local man who had made his way back there after fighting in the rear-guard action at Worcester. Meanwhile, John Pendrell had found quarters for Wilmot at Moseley, eight miles away, with Mr Whitgreave, whose chaplain, Father Huddleston, he had met on the Wolverhampton road on the way back from buying a parcel of shirts. But William Pendrell at Boscobel knew only that Wilmot and John Pendrell had gone, not where. It was already light, and so, 'after a short conference and but inchoated counsel of the King's probablest means of escape... Colonel Carlis brought and led the King to that so much celebrated Oak, where before he had himself been lodged'. There, with a bottle and some bread and cheese, they stayed until the evening, when, after a supper of roast chicken, the King slept in a hide in the house.

All this explains why he had not gone to Boscobel before. Clearly, William and Joan Pendrell, who had more experience in these matters than the Earl of Derby, did not think that their hide would be proof against a search in daylight, though it was safer than a bed at night. It also explains why Carlis (who was, according to the King, 'a Roman Catholic also') suggested hiding in the oak, as 'it would be very dangerous for me either to stay in that House or to go into the Wood'.

Boscobel House is a timber-framed building of two principal storeys apart from cellar and attics. It is L-shaped, with a sixteenth-century block to which a taller hunting-lodge was added in the 1620s. It may be the house described in the Jesuit deeds of 1622 as in Staffordshire and with enough accommodation for ten men, though in fact it is just on the Shropshire side of the boundary. Originally, the timber-framing was exposed but by the end of the eighteenth century most of it had been rendered with stucco. Blount

---

* The Wolfes' house was Upper House in Church Street, a 17th century building of stone and timber-framing. It still stands, though without any hides. Not to be confused with Madeley Court, an Elizabethan house of sandstone with a large formal garden and an astronomical sundial, which was the home of another recusant, Sir Basil Brooke.

says that it was given its name by Sir Basil Brooke of Madeley 'from the Italian Bosco-bello... because seated in the midst of many fair woods'.

In the main bedroom on the first floor, sometimes known as the Squire's Room, is the usual fireside door, which opens on a closet built within the chimney stack and lit by a small window on the south side. In the boards of this closet is a trapdoor

Fig. 157 Boscobel, exterior showing garden door and above it the location of Squires Room closet and hide (Fig. 158). All the other "windows" on the chimney stack are painted decorations.

Fig. 158 Squire's Room hide – a familiar type.

covering a space 840mm deep between the joists, the same area as the closet itself. Below this space, but not connected with it, is another cavity within the stack, 1.8m high with a plastered ceiling, entered from the garden by four steps leading up to an old door in the stack. There is a tradition that the space under the closet and the cavity below that were formerly joined, so that a man could get from the bedroom to the garden and the dense woodland round the house by way of the little door and the four steps. It is much more likely that the door and steps were a short cut to the garden from the Parlour on the ground floor, the panelling in which was substantially altered about 1800. But they would go some way towards camouflaging the hide, by creating the impression that there was not enough room for it between the ceiling of the ground-floor cavity and the presumed floor-level of the closet above. It has also been stated that the closet itself was once secret, but that is unlikely, since its window is already shown on the engraving in Blount's first edition of 1660.

The other hide at Boscobel is entered through a trapdoor at the top of the attic staircase. The space below is 1.22m by 1.14m and 1.6m deep. It was concealed by building a false wall built across the small room below, disguised as the underside of the stairwell. Nothing but accurate measurements and the making of a sectional drawing would have disclosed it, so craftily is it situated. It still has part of its original lining of coarse reddish hair-plaster (though this has been repaired) and part of a false ceiling made by nailing planks to the underside of the joists. The trapdoor is not the original, but it is clear from the rest of the flooring that it formerly consisted of two boards, like other examples elsewhere. The room to which the stairs lead was the secret chapel, but it is also known as the Cheese Room, and there is a legend that on one occasion the pursuivants brought bloodhounds, which were put off the scent by the cheeses stored there. This is an

Fig. 159 View down into King's Hide   *Fig. 160 Hide entrance.*

embroidery of a search here at the time of the Oates Plot in 1678-1679, when bloodhounds were used.

There are four reasons for thinking that this is the hide in which the King spent the night of 6-7 September 1651. First, it is more cunningly designed and would be safer. Second, the antiquarian William Stukeley was told so when he visited Boscobel in 1713, only a dozen years after William Pendrell's death and when his grand-daughter Catherine Howe was still living at Boscobel. Third, the *True Narrative and Relation*, which, as already mentioned, draws on the Pendrells' recollections, describes the King's hide as 'a place made between two walls, on purpose for secrecy, contrived at the building of the house', a description which fits this hide, with its false wall, better than the one under the closet. Fourth, there is Blount's description of the Sunday morning. 'His Majesty got up early', he says, 'his dormitory being none of the best nor his bed the easiest, and near the secret place where he lay had the convenience of a gallery to walk in, where he was observed to spend some time in his devotions, and where he had the advantage of a window which surveyed the road from Tong to Brewood'. The only window that answers this description is in the attic from which the hide is entered and which, since it runs the full length of the wing, could fairly be called a 'gallery'. However, one night in such a cramped space was more than enough for the King, and before his departure the following night 'they laid him a sorry Bed upon the Staircase, as they used to do for strange Woodcutters, that the meanness of his lodging might secure him from suspicion'.

At dawn on Sunday, Colonel Carlis stole out to a neighbouring sheepfold and stole a sheep to provide mutton for the King's breakfast. Meat was an unusual luxury for the Pendrells, and questions would have been asked if they had tried to buy any. After demonstrating his skill with the frying-pan, the King spent most of the day in a summerhouse on the mound in the garden, quietly reading. John Pendrell, who had been startled to learn, on arriving back from Moseley on Saturday night, that the King was actually in the house and not in Wales, trudged back to Moseley first thing on Sunday morning. He returned in the afternoon with good news. He had found Lord Wilmot and Mr Whitgreave, and the King could be moved from Boscobel that very night.

2

On the Sunday night, therefore, the King, escorted by all five Pendrell brothers and their brother-in-law Francis Yates, rode the eight miles from Boscobel to Moseley on Humphrey Pendrell's mill-horse. The scene is incised in black marble over the Parlour fireplace at Boscobel. About midnight, the King arrived safely at the Moor Close, a field with a stile near Moseley, where Father Huddleston met him and brought him through the orchard, in at the back door and up the newel staircase to the King's Room (then known as Mr Huddleston's Room), where Lord Wilmot was waiting. Here, for the first time since the Battle, the King was able to wash, change into clean clothes and sleep between sheets, in the bed which can still be seen there with its original hangings of yellow moreen. He stayed in this room for most of the next two days.

Like Boscobel, Moseley Old Hall was a timber-framed building, though about 1870 it was entirely refaced with brick. Since 1963 it has belonged to

the National Trust and has been regularly open to the public. Despite long neglect and damage caused by subsidence due to coal mining during the nineteenth

Fig. 162 Moseley Old Hall. Above in 2024 and

Fig. 161 (right) as it originally looked.

century, it still has much of its original panelling and oak flooring. It is now furnished with seventeenth-century pieces, and the walls are hung with prints, proclamations and broadsheets concerning the King's adventures. The red and blue bricks of the facade are still an eyesore, but the interior is admirably kept.

As soon as Whitgreave and Huddleston had kissed hands, the King asked where the hide was, 'which being already prepared and showed him, he went into it, and when came forth, said it was the best place he was ever in'. Despite this regal commendation, it is in fact another hole-under-the-closet, 1.5m long, 1.45m wide and 1.07m high. The trapdoor is the original, and the beam which supports it has a slot cut in one side in which a bolt could engage. The actual closet is open on the far side, forming a short passage to another bedroom, like the one from which the Withdrawing Room hide at Harvington is entered. The door to it from the King's Room swings back over the secret trapdoor, preventing it from being opened unless the door is shut first. On the King's Room side, this door is covered by a modern outer 'secret door' of deal and hardboard, painted to look like the plaster on either side. This has been inserted in deference to a tradition that there was formerly a camouflaged door at this point, but is most unlikely to represent an original.

After a glass of sack and some biscuits, the King dozed fitfully on a palliase dragged into the hide. In the morning all the servants were sent out to work in the fields except the cook, Elizabeth Smith. They were told that Huddleston was not well, and that no one was to enter his room except Whitgreave and his mother. Huddleston's three pupils were released from their lessons and told to keep watch from the top windows for priest-hunters. Mrs Whitgreave supervised the preparation of a meal by Elizabeth Smith. When it was ready, Mr Whitgreave carried the dishes upstairs, Mrs Whitgreave carved the joint, and Huddleston waited on the King and Lord Wilmot. Clearly, Whitgreave was no novice in matters of security, and his precautions ensured that no one outside the group of the Whitgreaves, Huddleston and Wilmot even suspected that the King was in the house.

Fig. 163 Moseley: King's Hide entrance and original trapdoor.

For most of the day, the King rested on the bed in Huddleston's room or discussed the situation with Wilmot and the others. Colonel Lane of Bentley Hall, about five miles away, had a sister, Jane, who had obtained a permit for herself and a groom to visit Abbots Leigh, near Bristol, where a friend of hers, Mrs Ellen Norton, was expecting a baby. It was agreed that the King would be the groom. At first, when the King was believed to be safely on the way to Wales, it had been suggested that Wilmot should be the servant, but he had readily agreed to stand down. In any case, Charles himself records that throughout their adventures Wilmot would never wear any disguise, 'saying that he should look frightfully in it, and therefore did never put on any'. His Sacred Majesty was more down-to-earth.

Next morning, Tuesday 9 September, the King was less exhausted and, though he again spent most of the day 'reposing upon his bed' in Huddleston's room, he also spent some time with Huddleston 'in the window of a closet in the next room, just over the porch of the door which enters the hall'. This closet over the hall porch still exists and fixes beyond any question the location of Huddleston's room, and with it the identification of the hiding-place. From the closet window the King watched stragglers from his army at Worcester making their way northwards. Among them he recognised several Highlanders from his own regiment. They had been stripped nearly naked, even to their boots, and many were wounded. They were so desperately hungry that they were gnawing cabbage stalks and other refuse thrown out for pigs. Mrs Whitgreave fed them and dressed their wounds, while the King's conversation turned to the Scots and his march with them to Worcester.

That afternoon, when he was back in Huddleston's room, Elizabeth Smith came running to the foot of the newel staircase shrieking 'Soldiers! Soldiers are coming!' They included one Southall, 'the great priest-catcher'. Whitgreave did not make the mistake of locking and barring the doors. Instead, having seen the King safely hidden, he went down to the garden-gate to face the intruders, leaving instructions that all doors were to be left wide open. When the soldiers saw him, he says, 'they were ready to pull me in pieces... saying I was come from the Worcester fight'. But the neighbours confirmed that he had been too ill to take part in the Battle, even if he had wanted to; and no one was tactless enough to mention that Huddleston was not only a priest but a former chaplain in the Royalist army as well. While this argument was going on in front of the house, Southall had made his way round to the yard at the back. There he found a blacksmith shoeing horses and offered him £1,000 if he would say where the King was. By this time the Roundheads knew that the King had been at White Ladies on the Thursday morning, and an experienced pursuivant might easily have guessed that he had been passed on to another recusant house nearby. But Whitgreave's prudence paid off. The smith had not the slightest idea that the King was anywhere in the neighbourhood, and even Southall became convinced that he was wasting his time. Whitgreave waited until he was quite sure that the searchers would not return, and then went upstairs to release the King.

After the Restoration, Elizabeth Smith petitioned for a pension on the grounds that when the alarm was given she 'rubbed softly your Majesty upon the feet and legs to wake your Majesty and warn your Majesty thereof, and provided sweet herbs into the private place ere your Majesty went therein'. It is apparent from Whitgreave' s version that she was not even allowed to see the King and only shouted up the stairs. But she deserves some marks for imagination, and she raises the question, not suggested by any other document, whether priest-holes were ever perfumed with sweet herbs to counter the foul atmosphere that so much annoyed the searchers at Hindlip.

That evening, Charles asked Huddleston to show him the chapel, 'saying he knew he was a priest, and he need not fear to own it to him, for if it pleased God to restore him to his kingdom, we should never need more privacies'. This chapel, which remained in use until 1825, is in the usual position in the attics. The walls are decorated with a seventeenth-century design in grey in imitation of panelling, part original and part restored. One section of the ceiling still has an eighteenth-century pattern of gold stars on a blue ground. On the altar was a crucifix, which may be the mid-seventeenth-century Spanish one that stands there now. The King remarked on it, adding that he too had an altar with a crucifix and silver candlesticks 'until my Lord of Holland brake them'. Altogether, he thought, the chapel was 'a very decent place'. Thirty-four years later, there was a sequel to this conversation. When the King lay dying in Whitehall Palace, Huddleston was brought up the back stairs to minister to him and was greeted with the words, 'Father, you who once saved my body are now come to save my soul'.

There is said to have been a hiding-place or camouflaged exit in the roof of the chapel. There are no signs of one now, but there is no doubt about the place nearby in the apex of the gable over Whitgreave's closet and the hall porch. This is 1.1m wide, 1.9m long and 900mm from the joists to the angle of the rafters. It is awkward to climb up to, a man could only crouch or lie full length in it, and since it is directly under the tiles he would be roasted in summer and frozen in winter. It is therefore almost certain that this roof-hide was for the Massing stuff. The siting of the two hides would then be entirely logical: one for the priest off the room where he spent most of his time, and one for the chalice and vestments close to, but not in, the attic chapel where they were used.

The entrance is a diamond-shaped gap between the beams, now closed by a clumsy wooden door. Both the door and its hinges are ancient, but neither is original to this place. Hinges on the outside of the doorframe, as these are, would be far too conspicuous, and the door itself does not fit the gap between the timbers. Often it is hard to be sure how much movement of a timber frame has taken place, but here all the joints of the diamond are tight and snug - and the door does not fit. Moreover, all round the inside edge of the door frame there are chases cut into the timbers, which prove that the original door fitted against the inner face of the frame, not the outer, as at present. There are no signs of hinges on the inside, and unless the level of the ceiling below had been altered, there would not be room for any hinged door to swing. A more likely form of entrance is a section of plaster which could be lifted or slid into place.

Fig. 164 Moseley attic 'secret corner'. The door is not original.

3

At midnight, a few hours after Huddleston had shown him the chapel, the

King left Moseley for Bentley Hall. Since Colonel Lane was a Protestant, there were no hides at Bentley - which was the reason why Wilmot had declined an offer of hospitality there. But Charles was only there for a few hours, and on Wednesday morning, a week after the Battle, he set out for Bristol with Jane Lane and Colonel Lane's Cornet, Henry Lascelles. For the first day they were accompanied by Jane's sister and brother-in-law, Withy and John Petre, who were travelling back to Horton in Buckinghamshire and were not in on the secret. For this reason, and presumably also to avoid the neighbourhood of Worcester, they were to ride first to Stratford-upon-Avon, where they would cross the river, and stay overnight with the Tomes at Long Marston. Colonel Lane and Wilmot were to follow by a different road and spend the night at Packington, between Birmingham and Coventry, the home of Sir Clement Fisher, whom Jane later married. In 1679-80, Sir Clement faced Packington Old Hall with brick and added plasterwork and a new staircase, so that it now appears to be wholly of that date. But the core of it is Elizabethan or Jacobean, and it contains a hide.

This is a space beneath the attic floorboards measuring 2.46m by 2.26m and 1.45m high to the underside of the joists. It has a boarded floor secured by the usual iron nails. The entrance is by a modern trapdoor and a fixed ladder. It is the sixth, and so far the last, example of a hiding-place camouflaged by a window, the others being at Gayhurst,

Fig. 165 *Packington Old Hall, showing location of hide and the part of the window that lights it.*

Red Hall, Drayton, Nevill Holt and Pitchford. The window in this case is the upper left pane of the window indicated in Fig. 165, with the floor of the hide at the level of the window transom. The lower left pane lights a corridor and the two right hand panes a room. From the window mullion to the back wall of the hide there runs a partition wall, resting on the floorboards and dividing the hide from the habitable space next to it. The fact that neither this wall nor the corresponding one at the other end of the hide are bonded into the rest of the brickwork shows that this space was not simply left over from the original construction but was the result of a subsequent alteration. Unless it was intended for occupation, the flooring would be pointless, and there are no signs of an entrance except through the boards above. It is therefore acceptable as a hide, even though the Fishers were not recusants.

The King, Lascelles and Jane Lane stayed the night of Thursday 11 September at an inn, The Crown at Cirencester, and reached Abbots Leigh on the evening of Friday 12th. Here they remained for four days while Wilmot caught up with them and the butler, John Pope, tried to find a ship for France. In this Pope was unsuccessful and, since he was worried that others might discover the secret, arrangements were made for Jane to be summoned back to Bentley and for the King to move to Trent Manor, on the borders of Somerset and Dorset.

The owner of Trent, Francis Wyndham, was a Royalist colonel who had been governor of Dunster Castle during the Civil War, when Charles was in residence there, and had subsequently come into possession of Trent by marrying the heiress to it, Anne Gerard. In 1651, his wife was still only nineteen, two years younger than the King. These Gerards were distant cousins of John Gerard, and Trent had been sequestrated in 1590 for the recusancy of William Gerard of Trent and Clerkenwell, whose wife Mary was also convicted. Anne Gerard's sister was Mrs Winter of Dyrham Park in Gloucestershire, where Wilmot had spent the night of Friday 12 September. He owed this hospitality to the lucky chance that on his way from Packington that morning he had met and been recognised by one of his former officers, Captain Thomas Habington, a friend of John Winter of Dyrham. Accordingly, it was agreed that Wilmot should arrive at Trent first, on the evening of Tuesday 16 September, to warn Colonel Wyndham that the King would be following the next day. As it turned out, Charles stayed as long at Trent as he did in all his other refuges put together, for most of the three weeks from Wednesday 17 September to Monday 6 October.

There was a hiding-place at Trent, which Blount describes as follows:

> During his Majesty's stay at Trent (which was above a fortnight) he was for his own security forced to confine himself to the voluntary imprisonment of his chamber, which was happily accommodated (in case the rebels had searched the house) with an old well-contrived secret place, long before made (for a shelter against the inquisition of pursuivants) by some of the ancient family of the Gerards, Colonel Wyndham's lady's ancestors, who were recusants and had formerly been owners of that house.

This hide still exists (Fig. 166) and is another hole-under-the-closet. Next to the panelled room where Charles relieved the tedium of waiting by cooking his own meals and boring holes through gold coins, there is a small chamber with the usual fireside closet. Beneath the floorboards of this closet is a space only 685mm deep and 1.5m square – almost the same dimensions as those of the similar hide at Boscobel. The joists on either side of the (modern) trapdoor have been shaved down for easier access, as at Huddington and elsewhere. As at Moseley, the King approved of the hide and 'was much pleased that upon the least approach of danger he could thither retreat with an assurance of security'. Anne Wyndham records that he did so at least once, on the evening of Friday 26 or Saturday 27 September, when she saw a troop of horse 'clap silently' into the neighbouring town of Sherborne.

In the room actually used by the King, behind the panelling on the right of the fireplace, is a shallow secret recess. It was perhaps for Massing stuff or prohibited books and recalls the 'hole in the wall, not very big', over the fireplace in the Gallery room at Towneley Hall. It has two small secret panels which work on pivots and have interior latches, so that at one time they could only have been opened by pulling a concealed string, like the hides at Ufton. It is impossible to guess what other secret places there may once have been, as the remainder of the house has been entirely reconstructed and modernised.

Fig. 166 Trent Manor: King's Hide.

4

Although the King's enemies had completely lost track of him, there was still the problem of finding a ship for France. Next morning, Thursday 18 September, after Lascelles and Jane Lane had left for Bentley, Colonel Wyndham rode over to the Strangways at Melbury, ten miles south. Colonel Giles Strangways was sympathetic and gave Wyndham £100 in gold for the King, but

> was not able to serve his Majesty in procuring a Vessel according to expectation..., all that were formerly of his acquaintance in Weymouth being for their loyalty banished and gone beyond the sea; and in Poole and Lyme he was a mere stranger, having not one Confidant in either.

But on Friday Wyndham got in touch with a merchant and former Royalist captain in Lyme Regis, William Ellesdon, one of whose tenants, Stephen Limbry of Charmouth, intended to take his ship over to St Malo early the following week. It was arranged that Limbry would take the fugitives off Charmouth beach in the small hours of Tuesday. On Saturday, Wyndham's servant, Henry Peters, was sent to book rooms at the inn at Charmouth, the Queen's Arms. In case the hostess wondered why the party might be leaving in the middle of the night, Peters spun her a story that his master (Wilmot) was eloping with a beautiful young lady (Wyndham's cousin Juliana Coningsby), whose relations were opposed to the match. As before, the King was the young lady's servant. On the Monday, he, Wilmot, Wyndham, Juliana and Peters met Ellesdon at a remote farm a few miles from the coast, where the arrangements were confirmed.

Ellesdon then returned to Lyme, and the others rode to Charmouth. About an hour after they got there, Limbry arrived at the inn and reported that all was well: the long-boat would fetch them off about midnight.

But when Limbry reached home, his wife became suspicious of this sudden excursion across the Channel. She had been at Lyme Fair that morning and had heard the proclamation about the King's escape. When Limbry went into the bedroom to pack his sea-chest, she locked him in and threatened that if he did not stay where he was, 'she would forthwith go to Lyme and give information both against him and his landlord to Captain Macy, who had then the command of a foot company there'. So there he stayed. At first light on Tuesday, when it became obvious to the royal party that he was not coming, the King, Wyndham and Juliana set out for Bridport, five miles away (which they found full of Parliamentarian soldiers), while Wilmot and Peters stayed behind to find Ellesdon and Limbry. As soon as they had done so, they followed the others to Bridport.

Meanwhile, the ostler at the Queen's Arms had become suspicious too. While Peters had gone into Lyme to find Ellesdon, Wilmot discovered that his horse had cast a shoe and told the ostler to have a new one put on. The smith looked at the horse's hooves and remarked that the other three shoes had been set in three different counties, one of them in Worcestershire. That confirmed the ostler's suspicions, and he hurried off to the minister, Benjamin Westley. After a lengthy delay while he finished his prayers, Westley went to a local Justice, who refused to act on such an unlikely story. The ostler then informed Captain Macy, who immediately set out in pursuit. But soon after leaving Bridport, the royal party turned off the Dorchester road into the hills, with the intention of working their way back to Trent. Macy and his men rode straight on to Dorchester, where they made a thorough search of the inns and ale-houses, before returning to raid several Royalist houses in the neighbourhood, including that of Wyndham's uncle, Sir Hugh Wyndham, at Pilsdon.

That evening, the King and his friends reached Broad Windsor, only two or three miles from Pilsdon, where the landlord of The George, whom Wyndham knew slightly, gave them rooms in the attics. But about nine o'clock a detachment of a Roundhead regiment arrived at the village and requisitioned all the empty rooms in the inn. During the night, one of the camp-followers went into labour on the kitchen floor and was delivered of a child. That caused 'the constable and overseers for the poor of the parish to come thither at an unseasonable hour of the night, to take care that the brat might not be left to the charge of the parish'. But, as Anne Wyndham points out, 'this quarrelsome gossiping was a most seasonable diversion, exercising the minds of those troublesome Fellows, who otherwise were likely to have proved too inquisitive after the Guests in the house'. The party upstairs used their enforced isolation to discuss what should be done next, and it was agreed that the King, Juliana and Wyndham would return to Trent next morning (Wednesday 24 September), while Wilmot, guided by Peters, would go to Salisbury and take up his quarters at the King's Arms. The landlord there, Henry Hewitt, was a staunch Royalist. Here Wilmot would contact a kinsman of Wyndham's, John Coventry. After the alarms and excursions of the last two days, the King would remain at Trent until a ship had been secured.

The King's Arms at Salisbury is just outside the Cathedral Close, by St Ann's Gate. No hides are known there now, but there must have been several. Wyndham, who with 'many of his friends had been sheltered [there] in the times of troubles...desired the Lord Wilmot to be confident of lying concealed'. But just across the road is Malmesbury House, which may have been Coventry's home at the time. In an attic staircase, the second riser from the top slides out past the newel-post, and behind is a small space known as the 'pistol-hole'. Two other hides are known to have existed, in one of which was found a Tower musket with a bayonet in a leather sheath. And in the orangery in the garden is a remarkable example of the utilisation of apparently non-existent space.

Just inside this building, on the left, one of the panels is hinged to form a cupboard-door. The right-hand side of this cupboard, which is 360mm deep, is a secret door, masking a narrow way up into the roof. Foothold can be gained on the brickwork of an old chimney, for hidden between the panelling and the outside wall is a

Fig. 167 Malmesbury: Summerhouse.

a Entrance to hiding place
b Hiding Place

disused fireplace, a remnant of an older structure. It is said that the secret door was kept in place by a removable shelf in the cupboard, and that it had an iron hook and staple to fasten it on the inside. The roof consists of three low gables, each 4m long and 1.27m wide but only 760mm high. At the far end of the first gable there is a slight gap, through which it is possible to see the other two gables running parallel to the first but not (for me) to crawl into them. The external walls of the summer-house are carried up higher than the base of the gables, and on the two sides facing the garden they are surmounted by large pediments which completely mask the gables behind. The other sides are screened by trees and by the north wall of the Close, against which the orangery is built. The gables can be seen from the upper windows of Malmesbury House, but at that angle they do not look high enough to conceal a man, even if such a light-hearted structure had been suspected anyhow.

When this place was found, about 1870, it contained an embroidered blue velvet cushion and a mattress, both of which fell to pieces on being handled. There was also a horn tumbler with its metal rim missing, but this is not the sort of object that can be precisely dated. The plasterwork of one pediment, the rusticated stonework and the sash-windows with their heavy glazing-bars all indicate that the building was at least refaced at a date later than 1651. The trellis glazing of the doors resembles that of the back door of No. 68 The Close, which is said to have been built in 1718. Mr John Cornforth has suggested that 'perhaps James Harris [who altered Malmesbury House between 1745 and 1749] improved an existing building to provide a prospect from the windows of his drawing room and library'. The bayonet found in the house was marked GR and so we may assume that a third period of usefulness was found for the hiding-place. While, therefore, it is likely that this was originally a Cavalier hide, we cannot altogether rule out the possibility that it was a Jacobite one. Such places were built, and several will be described in the next chapter.

5

On arriving in Salisbury on Thursday 25 September, Wilmot got in touch with John Coventry and also with Colonel Robert Philips, a younger son of the family at Montacute House, six miles west of Trent. On Saturday 27th, Philips went to see a merchant from Southampton named Horne and told him 'that he had occasion of a bark to carry him and a friend or two into France'. After considering, Horne said that he knew a trustworthy man, whom he would bring to meet the Colonel the following afternoon. On Sunday it was arranged that the ship would be ready on Wednesday night, when Philips would meet the captain at the Bear Inn, just outside Southampton. He then returned to Salisbury to tell Wilmot of his success and sent his brother Edward Philips to Trent to tell the King. Since Trent was inconveniently far from Southampton, both Colonel Philips and John Coventry wanted the King to be closer at hand. So on the Wednesday, 1 October, Coventry's chaplain, John Sellick, was sent over to Trent with a letter proposing that the King should move to Heale House, three miles north of Salisbury, the home of Mrs Amphillis Hyde. The letter was 'rolled up into the bigness of a musket-bullet, which the faithful messenger had order to swallow down his throat in case of any danger'.

But the King, cautious after his experience at Charmouth, wrote back that 'he desired all diligence might be used in providing a vessel, and if it should prove difficult at Hampton, trial should be made farther; that they should be ascertained of a ship before they sent to remove him, that so he might run no more hazards than what of necessity he must meet with in his passage from Trent to the place of his transportation'. The King's caution was justified by events, since the same day, on meeting Horne and the captain at The Bear, Philips was informed that 'his bark was pressed to carry provisions to the fleet which then lay before Jersey under the command of General Blake'.

This was the expedition on which the soldiers at Bridport and Broad Windsor had also been bound. In consultation with Dr Humphrey Henchman, former Precentor of the Cathedral and later Bishop of Salisbury and London, Philips and Coventry decided to abandon the Hampshire coast altogether and try in Sussex. They agreed to approach Colonel George Gounter of Racton, near Chichester, whose wife was a sister-in-law of Mrs Hyde of Heale, and whose family had been recusants since the 1570s. Philips wrote a letter to be delivered by Mrs Gounter's nephew, Lawrence Hyde of Hinton Daubnay in Hampshire. But Wilmot, who was perhaps tired of 'lying concealed' at the King's Arms, where he had now been for a week, decided to deal with the matter himself. Accompanied by his servant Robert Swan, who had been with him ever since the Battle of Worcester, he set off for Hinton Daubnay, where he arrived on the evening of Monday 6 October. There he found Gounter's brother, Captain Thomas Gounter, in whose company he reached Racton on the night of Tuesday 7th.

Meanwhile, Philips had ridden over to Trent to urge the King again to move from Trent to Heale. This time Charles agreed, and on Monday 6th he, Philips, Juliana Coningsby and Henry Peters rode across the downs, reaching Heale just before dark. There they were met by Dr Henchman. Mrs Hyde told the King that 'she had a very safe place to hide me in', but that she could trust nobody but herself and her sister. Next morning, on her advice, the King left with Philips and rode up to Stonehenge. Mrs Hyde then gave all the servants leave to go to the fair in Salisbury, and the King and Philips 'returned back again to Heale... about the time she appointed; where I went up into the hiding-hole, that was very convenient and safe, and stayed there all alone (Robin Philips then going away to Salisbury) some four or five days, sometimes Mrs Hyde and sometimes her sister bringing me meat'.

Heale House is now a late seventeenth-century building of brick and stone, skilfully extended in the original style in the 1890s. There are no descriptions or inventories to show what it was like in 1651, and the King's account is the only one of the primary sources to mention the hiding-place. Blount, who is usually so informative, says merely that the King 'appeared no more in public but had meat brought him privately to his chamber, and was attended by the good widow with much care and observance'. But the five days from the evening of Tuesday 7 October to the evening of Sunday 12th, when Philips arrived to report that Colonel Gounter had secured a boat from Brighthelmstone (now Brighton), were by far the longest period of concealment that the King had to endure. Such a time would have been physically impossible in the holes at Boscobel and Trent and almost unendurable at Moseley. This place at Heale must have been far more commodious. The Earl of Clarendon later described it as 'a little room which had been made since the beginning of the troubles for the concealment of delinquents, the seat always belonging to a malignant family'* The phrase 'a little room' suggests something larger than the normal priest-hole, perhaps like the place at Chastleton. The only other hint about it comes from Colonel Gounter, who on Wilmot's arrival at Racton asked him if the King was well and safe, 'and gave him a reason for his question: if he should not be secure, he doubted not but he could secure him till a boat could be gotten'. Wilmot, who did not know that the King had moved to Heale the day before, replied that

> he hoped he was out of danger at present, but intended to be at his house with him on the Wednesday... Upon the hearing of this, the Colonel's thoughts were much raised in expectation of such a guest, until he was better informed, as he was soon after to his good content and satisfaction, knowing the house well and the conveniences thereof, and the worth and fidelity of the persons.

In such a context, 'the conveniences thereof' must mean the facilities for hiding, as it does in Blount's phrase, 'a great convenience of concealment at Boscobel House'. In other words, Gounter had a hiding-place at Racton, but he knew that the one at Heale was safer.

The King stayed at Heale until Monday 13 October. That night he slept at Hambledon, at the house of Gounter's brother-in-law Thomas Symonds. On Tuesday night he was at The George at Brighthelmstone, and at two in the morning he and Wilmot went on board. On Thursday morning they landed at Fécamp in France.

---

* 'Delinquent' and 'malignant' were Parliamentarian terms for their opponents.

12

Restoration to Regency: Tradition and Truth

1

In 1660, nine years after his escape from Worcester, King Charles II returned to his kingdom, amid scenes of ecstatic rejoicing which made him wonder out loud why he had ever left it. The story of Boscobel immediately became a national epic, and the sign of the Royal Oak is still a familiar feature of villages and towns all over the country, however remote from the course of his youthful wanderings. The escape came to be spoken of as a miraculous preservation, explicable only by direct divine intervention; and the hiding-places that had played such an important part in it made a powerful appeal to the imagination, especially as ingrained caution made their owners still unwilling to divulge their exact whereabouts. While hiding places for religious and political fugitives continued in use for a century after the Restoration, there was at the same time the beginning of a literary and antiquarian interest in them, which was undoubtedly prompted by the events of 1651.

No priest was executed for the first eighteen years of Charles's reign, and a great many, perhaps a majority, of those recorded on the Recusant Rolls of the 1660s were Quakers and other Protestant Dissenters. Few priest-holes can have been built during these years, though there is one at Capheaton, Northumberland, which, as the building accounts show, was not begun until 1668. On 25 August 1678, the diarist John Evelyn dined at Ham House, Weybridge, with the Duke of Norfolk, who 'made no scruple of showing me all the *latebrae* and hiding-places for the Popish priests, and where they said Mass, for he was no bigoted Papist'. Clearly, Norfolk thought that the need for such precautions had gone. But only five weeks later, Titus Oates announced the discovery of his Popish Plot to murder the King, stage a French invasion and massacre all good Protestants. In the ensuing frenzy, which led to a fresh batch of executions, several hiding-places, including that at Boscobel, came back into use for priests and there are stories of hunts and escapes from 1678 to 1681 as vivid as anything from the 1590s. The panic was followed by a reaction, and after the Rye House Plot of 1683 it was the Whigs' turn to lie low. Lord Howard of Escrick was found in his house at Knightsbridge 'behind a tall cupboard where was a chimney', while a report on Toddington Manor in Bedfordshire, then the retreat of the Duke of Monmouth, drew attention to 'that vastness and intricacy that without a most diligent search it's impossible to discover all the lurking-holes within it, there being several trapdoors on the leads and in closets into places to which there is no other access'.

Hiding-places for priests were needed again at the time of the Glorious Revolution of 1688: indeed, sporadic priest-hunts and references to hides continued into the 1720s, though the penalty for Roman orders had been commuted to life imprisonment by an Act of 1698. According to the letter of the law, Catholic chapels were illicit until 1791, but throughout the eighteenth century there was much toleration in practice, and some odd contrasts. Richard Challoner, who was Catholic bishop of the London District from 1741 to 1781, presided openly in periwig and mitre at the chapel of the Sardinian Embassy, which in effect served as his cathedral. But he also said Mass in garrets guarded by burly labourers and preached in the Ship Tavern in Holborn to congregations sitting with pint-pots before them to deceive any constable who looked in. Some Catholic chapels of this period were built to look like mills or warehouses; others, like those at Thorndon, Wardour or Lulworth, were superb works of architecture with elaborate classical altar-pieces and even organs. At Giffords Hall in Suffolk, the Rev. Sir George Mannock, baronet and Jesuit, dressed in the height of fashion with silk or velvet coats, ruffles of the finest lace, bag-wig, diamond ring, pin, buckles and sword. But off the library was the little chapel where he said Mass, and he refused the offer of a dispensation from his vows that would allow him to marry and continue the line. He was also patron of the Anglican living* and on the best of terms with the parson, whom he once rescued from a No-Popery mob, assuring the rioters on the word of a gentleman that his friend was no Jesuit.

One reason for increasing toleration was that by the time of George III's accession in 1760 Catholics had come to accept the Hanoverians as lawful sovereigns. But for many years after 1688 most of them still regarded the Stuarts as the rightful dynasty, and some hiding-places which were no longer needed for priests now concealed Jacobites and their papers and equipment. In 1694, at the time of the Lancashire Plot, Standish Hall in Lancashire was used by two of the ringleaders, Colonel John Parker and James Lunt. In 1752, a builder discovered a bundle of old papers sealed into a hole in a wall there. They proved to be a copious correspondence, dated 1692-93, between Parker and Jacobite exiles at Saint-Germain, together with lists of supporters and fifty blank commissions for officers in the rebel army. After the rising of 1715, Nicholas Blundell of Crosby in Lancashire described in his Diurnal how he

---

*Some Anglican parish priests are appointed not by the local bishop but by a patron – a local landowner, or a Trust etc. Cases where the patron is the local Catholic priest must be rather rare.

'set all day in a strait place for a fat man' while the house was searched for him. Since a fire in 1887 this hide has existed only as an ordinary cupboard but just qualifies as a surviving place mentioned in a contemporary document. But the fire did reveal that under the hide was a 'secret corner' for vestments and church plate, in which a rosary was found.

At Danby in Yorkshire, cavalry equipment concealed for the 1715 rebellion in a hide in a chimney-stack was found about 1800 in such good condition that the harness was used on the farm and the weapons distributed to the local yeomanry at the time of the Napoleonic invasion threat. At Capheaton, two cartloads of Lord Derwentwater's papers were hidden in 1715 in a place 'between two walls behind a chimney'. There they were discovered thirty years later by a Presbyterian slater named Walton who was repairing the roof. He informed the Deputy Lieutenant, who 'was observed to measure exactly the outward space between the windows, and then the inward. When he found the place described by Walton, he broke the wall and met with the old records above named, which he seized and sent off to London'.

Stonyhurst in Lancashire has been the site of the famous Jesuit school since 1794. The original mansion of the Shireburns, begun in 1592, was quadrangular, with a magnificent gatehouse on the west, a great hall on the east and a long gallery on the first floor of the south block. But educational rebuildings in the nineteenth century have left only the south and parts of the east and west blocks. In the armoury are several horse-pistols found in a hide in the gateway tower, and about 1800 another place was discovered which contained a bed and mattress, a hoard of James II guineas and a bottle of rum. There is still a hide over the bay in the long gallery, entered through a trapdoor in the window seat above, rather as at Parham in Sussex. Others are mentioned briefly in the college records but were destroyed by the alterations that revealed them. Although it is likely that at least some of them were of Elizabethan origin, the only evidence for their use is in Jacobite times, which is why they are mentioned here.

In Scotland there were Jacobite hides from the 1745 rebellion as well, though the places which sheltered Bonnie Prince Charlie himself during the five months after Culloden were mostly caves and fissures in the rocks of the Highlands and Western Isles. At Fetternear, fifteen miles north-west of Aberdeen, are the ruins of the sandstone mansion of the Leslies, a late seventeenth- and early eighteenth-century building with fine heraldic decoration. Here there was a hide entered through the sliding back of a large fixed bookcase with glazed doors. Also in Aberdeenshire, near Aboyne, is Balnacraig, an E-shaped laird's house built in 1735. It was the home of the Innes family, who were prominent Catholics and Jacobites, and contains a hiding-place which was entered through a panel at the back of a box-bed. When it was found, in the late nineteenth century, there were some Jacobite papers and a curious old armchair in it. Even in the Midlands of England, at

Worksop in Nottinghamshire, a deponent in 1745 swore that nine years earlier he had seen two secret rooms entered by a trapdoor from the leads above the Long Gallery, one of which was full of arms.

At Leith, near Edinburgh, one Jacobite, the Chevalier James Johnstone, was lucky enough to find shelter at the house of a Mr Blythe, who had had several hiding-places built during alterations 'for concealing the contraband goods which he used to bring from foreign countries'. But most smuggling hides were caves or other forms of natural cover, and artificial places of concealment are not easy to find. The most convincing that survive are those at the Three Mariners in Quay Street, Scarborough, a late seventeenth-century inn a few yards from the old harbour. The Mariners is a tiny house, with only two rooms on each of two floors, together with cellar and attic, but it nevertheless contains two spacious hides, both entered through doors in the Queen Anne panelling of the upstairs rooms. One of them is 4.6m long and 1.3m wide, with a secret door at each end.

Fig. 168 *The Three Mariners, Scarborough*

Fig. 169 *Secret spaces at the Three Mariners*

It is built over the ground-floor passage, which has a kink in it to allow for the staircase; and since the inn is cheek-by-jowl with other buildings in Quay Street and has a back door to an alley off Sandside, it would not have been so easy to measure up and plot as its size might suggest.

Also in Yorkshire was the White House at Saltburn. This was owned by the notorious smuggler John

Andrews, who died in 1835. In the last stall of the stables, on the seaward side, was a false floor giving access to the cellar in which Andrews' gang stored their barrels. If the place was searched, they would put in that stall a mare which could be trusted to kick viciously at any stranger.

In 1961, four casks were found concealed in the window-sill of a front room at the Hastings Arms in Hastings. They were about 900mm high, long and narrow, with a removable panel in front and so arranged that when the sill was closed the casks were completely hidden. The house is mentioned as a rendezvous of the smugglers by John Campbell, who after being a smuggler himself eventually became a police inspector and wrote his reminiscences.

In the West Country, there is a well-known example at Chambercombe Manor, near Ilfracombe. Here, in 1865, the farmer discovered a narrow low-ceilinged room containing a handsome carved bed, on which lay the skeleton of a woman. The room had a double floor, and it seems likely that the space between was used for contraband.

Smugglers were not above using the old priest-holes on occasion. When the English nuns from the Teresian convent at Antwerp were driven back to England by the French invasion in 1794, Lord Arundell of Wardour offered them a house at Lanherne in Cornwall, which is still a convent today. They found that only three rooms of it were habitable and that it had been used for storing contraband. One of the nuns met a smuggler in the house in the middle of the night, and years later bottles were discovered in holes under an old staircase.

Meanwhile, honest folk continued to have hides built for valuable possessions. A fine example is at Bell Hall, Naburn, in Yorkshire, which was built in 1680. A section of panelling above the door of a first-floor room slides down between the posts to reveal a space between the ceiling of the passage outside and the floor above. At Leche House, Chester, there is a small place high up on the right-hand side of the ornamental plasterwork of the hall fireplace. A more unusual example is at Woodham Mortimer in Essex, the home of the Chamberlens, who during the seventeenth and eighteenth centuries had a reputation as obstetricians, based on a form of short forceps which was kept a family secret. When the hide was found in 1813, it contained four varieties of these forceps and other instruments, which are now on show at the Royal College of Obstetricians and Gynaecologists in London. It is a shallow space about 1.5m square between the floor and ceiling of the top storey of the porch. The trapdoor was kept shut by two metal strips which pivot on nails and could be locked by turning what from outside appear to be two nail-heads. Peter Chamberlen (1601-1683), was physician to Charles I and Charles II, and in addition to devising the forceps may also have constructed these locks to suit these special conditions. The place had apparently been forgotten since Hope Chamberlen sold the house in 1715, since, apart from the obstetric instruments and various letters and trinkets, it also contained a New Testament with a manuscript note on the flyleaf dated 1695.

2

The first hiding-places to be displayed to the public were, not surprisingly, those at Boscobel. As early as 1686, Robert Plot stated in his *Natural History of Staffordshire* that the King had spent a night at Boscobel (6-7 September 1651) 'in a privacy behind the chimney in one of the chambers'. No previous account had been so explicit about the location of any of the hides connected with the escape. But Plot seems not to have been told the whole truth, as that is a description of the hole-under-the-closet on the first floor. As explained in the last chapter, it is more likely that the King was in fact hidden in the more cunning place under the attic stairs. Perhaps the then owners, Brian and Jane Fitzherbert, were willing to admit to the existence of the less useful hide while still keeping quiet about the really secure one, which had, after all, been needed at the time of the Oates Plot, only seven years before Plot's book was published. Thirty years later, in 1713, when Boscobel was still the headquarters of the Staffordshire Jesuits, the stair-hide was shown to the antiquary William Stukeley as the King's, while the closet hide now came into the story as the place where 'his bed was artfully placed behind some wainscot that shut up very close'. At a time when some hides were still in use, others such as these were already being viewed by tourists, and legends were beginning to accumulate about them.

During the reigns of George II and George III, county histories and other antiquarian publications began to include accounts of hiding-places apart from those used by Charles II. In 1735, for instance, Ezra Cleaveland mentioned one in his account of Powderham Castle in Devon. Sir William Courtenay V (1554-1630), he says, 'did receive into his house and harbour the Jesuits and other Popish priests which came secretly into England and spent a great deal of money in maintaining of them. For there is a tradition that in a dark secret room which is in Powderham Castle many Popish priests lay concealed'. Five years later, in 1740, Francis Peck published an eminently Gothick discovery made about thirty years before at the now-ruinous manor-house of Minster Lovell in Oxfordshire:

> Upon occasion of new laying a chimney... there was discovered a large vault or room underground, in which was the entire skeleton of a man, as having been sitting at a table which was before him, with a book, paper, pen &c, and in another part of the room lay a cap, all much mouldered and decayed. Which the family and others judged to be this Lord Lovell, whose exit hath hitherto been so uncertain.

The reference is to the Lord Lovell who was a favourite of Richard III and disappeared after the Battle of Stoke, near Newark, in 1487. In 1621,

Francis Bacon had recorded a rumour that Lovell had not been drowned in the Trent but 'that he lived long after in a cave or vault', and this discovery seemed to confirm it. Presumably, Lovell had entrusted himself to the care of a retainer who had been imprisoned or otherwise prevented from returning, and so had been left to starve.

Such a picture consorted agreeably with the Georgian fashion for grottoes, which had begun with Alexander Pope's at Twickenham in the 1720s. In 1737, Thomas Goldeney of Bristol 'finished the subterraneous passage to the grotto and began upon the grotto the same year', though he did not finish it until 1764. Other grottoes followed at Stourhead, Oatlands, St Giles House in Dorset and so on, the finest perhaps being those at Hawkstone in Shropshire (1783-87), which Dr Johnson described as 'abounding with striking scenes and terrific grandeur'. The most notorious are Sir Francis Dashwood's caves at West Wycombe; but the sober fact seems to be that they were dug about 1750 to obtain material for a new road. There is little evidence that they, rather than Medmenham Abbey seven miles away, were used for the wining and wenching of the Order of St Francis of Wycombe, otherwise known as the Hell-Fire Club. Nevertheless, this is a site where rumour and tradition have been more influential than documented fact.

In 1747, Horace Walpole, younger son of Sir Robert, , bought a house at Strawberry Hill on the banks of the Thames, which he began to convert into what he called 'a little Gothick castle'. In 1764, after a disturbing dream, he wrote in two months the fantasy which was published as *The Castle of Otranto*. The plot is rambling, the characters mere dummies and the dialogue absurdly stilted. ('Oh transport!' said Isabella, 'here is the trapdoor'.) But what mattered was the atmosphere and the setting, of castle, church, caverns and vaults, and *Otranto* was followed in due course by an army of admirers and imitators, notably William Beckford's *Vathek* (1786), Anne Radcliffe's *The Mysteries of Udolpho* (1794), Matthew Lewis's *The Monk* (1796) and Charles Maturin's *Melmoth the Wanderer* (1820). The secret passages and hiding-places which were essential properties of these novels undoubtedly encouraged a renewed interest in authentic examples, or what were thought to be such. In 1781, Treadway Russell Nash included in his *History of Worcestershire* Sir Henry Bromley's detailed narrative of the great search at Hindlip in 1606. In 1791, John Collinson, in *The History and Antiquities of the County of Somerset*, described the discovery in the prior's house at Bath Abbey of a walled-up apartment containing 'the copes, albs, chesiples and other garments of the religious'. Jane Austen must have known of this when she wrote *Northanger Abbey*. In 1800, the *Gentleman's Magazine* reported an underground passage from Kendal Castle to a house known as Castle Dairy in Wildman Street. In 1801, at Sparrowe's House in the Buttermarket at Ipswich, above a carved plaster ceiling of about 1670 there was found a void space with a fifteenth-century hammerbeam roof, which was assumed to be proof of ecclesiastical use. In 1814, as Hindlip was being pulled down, Peter Prattinton of Bewdley made his detailed record of it, with drawings, measurements and a plan of the one surviving hide. How much he was in accord with contemporary taste can be seen from the account of Hindlip published the same year in *The Beauties of England*:

> Whoever has wandered with the writers of modern romance, through towers, turrets, winding passages, creaking staircases and dark closets, would here find themselves at home: there is scarcely an apartment that has not secret ways of going in or going out; some have back staircases concealed in the walls; others have places of retreat in their chimneys; some have trapdoors; and all present a picture of gloom, insecurity and suspicion.

By this time, the extravaganzas of the Gothic novelists were being made to seem old-fashioned by the more plausible fictions of Sir Walter Scott, who, though an inveterate user of secret devices, was at least aware of some of the archaeological foundations for them. The 'Laird's Lug' at Castle Fraser in Aberdeenshire, which he used in *The Fortunes of Nigel* (1822), still exists today: a hole-under-the-closet which allows of eavesdropping on conversations in the oriel window of the hall. The hinged portrait in *Woodstock* (1826) is based on one at Lyme Park, Cheshire: an early nineteenth-century whimsy but in a house which contains a genuine hiding-place. In *Redgauntlet* (1824), Scott explained to his readers that the smugglers' den with its secret devices was copied from the similar establishment of a real gang leader named Richard Mendham, at whose execution Scott, as Sheriff of Selkirkshire, had himself been present. Scott and his successors, like Harrison Ainsworth and Bulwer Lytton, undoubtedly fostered some awareness of history in their readers. But they also encouraged a deep rooted credulity about two-mile secret passages from castles, monasteries and ancient houses which hindered a just appreciation of the authentic historical examples.

One consequence of this was that some Victorian owners carried out reconstructions of hiding-places which owed more to their reading of novels than to study of the documents (which in any case did not become generally available in print until the 1870s and 1880s). At Aston Hall in Birmingham (1618-1635) there is a space under the bottom flight of the great staircase which can only be reached by swinging round a large carved porter's chair fastened to the wall by hinges. From 1818 to 1848, Aston Hall was the home of James Watt, son of the famous engineer, who carried out extensive and sensitive repairs. It was in his time that the hole was first described as the 'secret place', and it is highly unlikely that it was any such thing.

At Clarke Hall, Wakefield, there is a space in a chimneystack entered through the top of a wall-cupboard and with a communication trap in the form of a sliding panel in the overmantel. But all this seems to be an elaborate reconstruction of about 1900, utilising space created by a lath-and-plaster addition of about 1850. At Little Moreton in Cheshire, perhaps the most famous black-and-white house in England, a sliding section of panelling was 'restored' in 1936 in accordance with a description in Henry Taylor's *Old Halls of Lancashire and Cheshire* (1884). But the room beyond is an ordinary bedroom, with a garderobe and two windows. Other considerations apart, it is too large ever to have been secret.

Fig. 170 Victorian "Hides" at Clarke Hall, Wakefield *(above) and Little Moreton Hall, Cheshire*

These apocryphal examples were at least in houses of the right date. But some completely new Victorian houses had hiding places built into them. One such is at Kinloch Castle on the Isle of Rhum, which was completed for Sir

George Bullough in 1897. Plans of that date reveal that the pretty dining-room alcove was originally a little secret room, entered by a door in the fireplace alcove in the hall. At Garrowby in Yorkshire, which is in essentials of 1892-3, the second Viscount Halifax had no fewer than three hiding-places constructed for his children to play in. One of these was entered through a hinged portrait, another through a chest with a false bottom, and the third through a movable set of false shelves, copied from the genuine place at

Abbots Salford. Robert Hugh Benson, who was a guest at Garrowby, incorporated all three devices into 'Stanfield Place' and 'Maxwell Hall' in his novel *By What Authority?* (1904), and so one form of fiction acquired literary distinction in another.

The most recent example appears to be Agecroft Hall in Virginia, USA, where a near-replica of the Abbots Salford hide has been built, in a genuine Tudor manor transported across the Atlantic in 1928, albeit here the reason was for educational purposes.

Fig. 171 *replica hide at Agecroft Hall, VA, USA.*

In these circumstances, it is understandable that after the First World War, when archaeology became a scientific profession and it was fashionable to debunk Victorian assumptions, anyone with an academic reputation to lose would be very cautious about accepting anything so nebulous and romantic as a priest-hole. Recusant historians, who knew at least some of the documents, tended to fight their own little corner and to be happier with the evidence of paper and parchment than with that of brick and timber, which were thought perhaps to be insufficiently spiritual. But since the Second World War a constant stream of books, films and television programmes on escapers and evaders has made everyone familiar with recent and authenticated equivalents to the work of Nicholas Owen and his compeers. It is taken for granted that smugglers need their caches, terrorists their safe houses and governments their concealed headquarters in case of nuclear devastation. Secret hiding-places can no longer be loftily dismissed as fictions which could not have happened.

The remainder of this book can therefore be devoted to considering how this fascinating and neglected form of architectural evidence can be used in writing the history of Elizabethan and Jacobean England.

3

First of all, there is the obvious point that a hiding-place is good evidence, and may well be the only evidence, that a house was being used for secret worship under Elizabeth I and James I. The Recusant Rolls can reveal that so many gentry, butchers, bakers and candlestick-makers were convicted of recusancy in a given county but they cannot by themselves reveal where these people went for the spiritual solace which they could not find in their parish churches. Still less can they throw any light on those who were absent but were never convicted. Even if a family are known to have been recusants, it does not necessarily follow that they harboured priests, and it is unusual to find names of priests at particular houses until the reign of Charles I, sometimes much later. If none is recorded at Stonor between 1590 and 1667 and none at Coughton between 1605 and 1671, it is hardly surprising if evidence is even sparser at less famous houses. The copious documentation of Hindlip, where it is possible to construct a detailed clerical directory from 1590 to 1606, is very much the exception. In any case, Gerard's *Autobiography* proves that a house could be used for Mass even if it was owned by a Church Papist, like Salden, or a Protestant, like Kirby. Conclusions about Massing centres and the harbouring of priests in the most dangerous period are therefore likely to contain a wide margin of error if they are based only on the surviving documents.

A hiding-place, on the other hand, is strong evidence that a priest was sheltered in the house, even if there is no written evidence at all. Obviously, it is necessary to make sure that the place existed in the seventeenth century and is not merely the result of Victorian romantic imagination or (as at Melford and Nevill Holt) Georgian reconstruction. But if it survives that common-sense test, it is much more likely to be a priest's hiding-place than a Cavalier's, since even Charles II relied entirely on the old priest-holes. Almost all accounts of Harvington published before the 1950s asserted that the Pakingtons had been Protestants until 1631 and that Mary Pakington, who inherited the Hall in that year, only became a Catholic on her marriage to the recusant Sir John Yate. From that it followed that the hides could not have been built before the 1630s, and to account for their quality it was even conjectured that Nicholas Owen might have had an apprentice in Worcestershire who carried on his trade after his master's death in 1606. Squiers, with only the evidence of the hides to go on, suspected that the Pakingtons must have been Catholics at least thirty years earlier and he was eventually proved right.

In the second place, the study of priest-holes discourages the assumption that numbers and importance are the same thing. It is tempting to think of the recusants as forming a single Catholic community, to which the more populous counties made the most important contributions. But it is just as true to say that there were at any given date several hundred English Catholic communities, which might survive for anything from a few months to four centuries, and whose significance did not depend on the existence of other such communities close by. Throughout the period from the sixteenth to the nineteenth century, Sawston was the only recusant centre in the whole of Cambridgeshire, and even there few families were presented apart from the Huddlestons. Statistically, therefore, Cambridgeshire recusancy is insignificant. But the Owen hide at Sawston is perhaps the finest in the country; and there is no reason why one of similar quality should not turn up in Cumberland or Devon or Powys. I have no doubt that in such a case it would be possible to trace a link, through marriage or kinship or education together at Oxford, between the Elizabethan owner and some other house in which Owen had worked. But a house isolated geographically can nevertheless contain a brilliantly-constructed hide. Conversely, it does not follow that all the best hides ought to be in Lancashire; and in fact, apart from the one at Thurnham, the surviving examples there do not compare with those in some less recusant counties. Statistics of population are useful, but they are not the whole story.

In the third place, it should be clear by now that recusancy after the Armada was much more than an unimportant postscript to something that really belongs to the 1580s. It is true that the executions of priests took place predominantly in the 1580s; but the importance, and still more the success, of various phases of a campaign is not to be measured simply by the number of casualties incurred in them. During the 1590s and 1600s there were more seminary priests at work in England than there had been in the 1580s, they were better organised, and they had a higher chance of surviving. That was due to the coherent and on the whole successful strategy initiated by William Weston and carried out after 1586 by Garnet, Southwell, Gerard, Holtby and their colleagues. There is adequate and consistent evidence for the conclusion that most hiding-places were built after 1586 as part of this strategy; it is no accident that Nicholas Owen, the most famous and the most ingenious builder of hides, was at work from 1588 to 1606.

That brings us to the character and achievement of Owen himself. Even in the seventeenth century he had become a figure of mystery and legend. The Jesuit historian Mathias Tanner, whose work was published at Prague in 1675, speaks of Owen's 'incomparable skill in conducting priests to a place of safety along subterranean passages, in hiding them between walls, in burying them in impenetrable recesses and in entangling them in labyrinths and a thousand windings'. It would, however, be incautious to do as some writers have done and take too literally the labyrinths and underground passages, despite Baddesley Clinton and perhaps Irnham. Tanner's Latin is strongly reminiscent of the language used about Daedalus in Virgil's *Aeneid* and Ovid's *Metamorphoses* and is probably meant as an elegant Baroque tribute to a craftsman worthy to be compared with the predecessor who built

> The labyrinth of subterranean Crete,
> A legend for evasion and deceit;
> Where blind partitions wove a baffling maze,
> And sly devices turned a thousand ways.†

It was inevitable, however, given the secrecy of Owen's work, his violent death and the lack of a corpus of authenticated examples, that legend and supposition would continue to flourish. Only now has it become possible to disentangle the thousand windings.

The starting-point must always be the hide at Braddocks, the only (indisputable) surviving one for which we have Gerard's statement that Owen built it. Fortunately, however, it is also precisely datable, from John Frank's deposition, to Christmas 1592. Family connections make it reasonable to group with it the hides at Oxburgh and Sawston, as all being consequences of Gerard's work in East Anglia between 1588 and 1594, a conclusion reinforced by the similarity of the seats and latrines at Braddocks and Sawston. All of these places are away from outside walls and show an ability to think in three dimensions, and especially to exploit changes of level and the twist of staircases, which is much superior to the conventional hole-under-the-garderobe on an outside wall. The direct comparison at Sawston leaves no doubt that two builders were at work, and that Owen must have been the later of the two. At this point, it is justifiable to bring in Gerard's statements that the searchers used to begin by noting any unexplained stretches of wall on the outside and that Owen strove to make his hides of several fashions in several places. Both of these are well illustrated at Braddocks, Oxburgh and Sawston and we are entitled to draw the further conclusion that holes-under-the-garderobe, even the one used by Charles II at Moseley, are not the work of Owen. The similarities of the hide at Snore to those at all three of the houses already mentioned in East Anglia would justify adding it to this group.

In Warwickshire and Worcestershire, the same pattern emerges at Baddesley Clinton, Hindlip and Harvington. There is the same contrast between commonplace and ingenious hides, similar connections with the Jesuit network and evidence for dating within the period of Owen's activity. The similarity of Hindlip and Harvington and the friendship of their owners suggests that the same builder was at work; the style of the staircase at Harvington suggests a date of soon after 1600; and the Papal ruling of 1602 requiring the seculars to set up their own organisation provides a good reason for constructing about that time a second Hindlip only ten miles from

---

† *Aeneid* V, 588-91, tr. *Michael Hodgetts*

the first one. The hide at Abbots Salford and the larger one at Huddington may also be by Owen, but not the one in the gatehouse at Coughton, though that does not rule out the possibility that other hides by Owen there have since been destroyed.

In the south-east, the hole under the stairs at Scotney shows the same trade-marks of detail and siting; there is documentary evidence to link it with a Jesuit, Richard Blount, and its use in the search of 1597-98 confirms that it is of the right date. Owen must have built many other hides in this region, thanks to Southwell and his cousins, but the only known surviving plausible claimant, apart from Scotney, is the one at Twyssenden, and even that is disputable.

How much hide-building in the north was Owen's, rather than Richard Holtby's, may never be known. Gerard does say that Owen 'laboured in all shires and in the chiefest Catholic houses of England', but after the destruction of Grosmont and Thornley and of all but one of the hides at Towneley the only hides surviving in the north of comparable quality to these examples in East Anglia, the Midlands and the south-east are those at Hardwicke and Thurnham, of which the one at Hardwicke must be by Holtby. The similarity between the swinging beam hides at Grosmont and Harvington is intriguing, and so is that between the hinged stones at Scotney and Thurnham and the false chimneys at Harvington and Hardwicke. The six-monthly Jesuit meetings would have provided convenient opportunities for Owen and Holtby to swap ideas, and perhaps this is what Gerard means by saying that Owen 'sometimes had occasion to discourse of the fashion of them for the making of others'. All the same, using Gerard's distinction between 'devising' hides and 'framing' them, it can be said that, whatever hints Holtby may have picked up from Owen regarding design, his actual construction must have been of the highest quality for the story to get about that no pursuivant ever found one of his hides. The obituary circulated by his fellow-Jesuits in 1640 says that he continued building hides until he was an old man; and, while that is unlikely to mean until his death at the age of eighty-seven, it does suggest that through him the style and technique of Owen continued in the North, at St Anthony's and elsewhere, at least until the 1620s.

John Gerard's work in Northamptonshire and London after his escape from the Tower in 1597 yields a fair list of houses where Owen certainly or probably worked, but not much in the way of surviving hides which can be ascribed to him. lrthlingborough has been demolished; Harrowden is now mostly Georgian; and at Kirby, which might have rivalled Harvington or Towneley, Owen and Hugh Sheldon were interrupted after only one day's work. The hide at Irnham, with its false chimney flue and feeding-trap like those at Oxburgh, Snore and Hindlip, may well be one of Owen's, and that at Gayhurst is almost certain to have been. The date of the latter, 1602-3, is the same as I have suggested for the later hides at Harvington and it is a great pity that it was destroyed. The surviving wing of Salden is now a farmhouse and no hides are known - though it should be remembered that none was known at Braddocks, also a farmhouse, until Squiers excavated the Owen hide there at Easter 1931. It is a curious coincidence that of the six known hides that make use of a window four (Gayhurst, Drayton, Red Hall and Nevill Holt) are in this area and two belonged to Sir Everard Digby. But this feature is not so remarkable as the spring-bolts at Ufton and Mapledurham, and it is not clear whether or what conclusions should be drawn from it.

In London, there are no survivors of the many houses used by Gerard and the other Jesuits but two features are worth comment. The first is the datable use of double hides at Mr Mompesson's in Clerkenwell (1591) and in the house which Gerard shared with the Heywoods (1598-9). Both of these, incidentally, were roof hides. The second is the information that Gerard himself built three 'good hiding-places' in the smaller of his last two houses between the beginning and the end of Lent 1606 (early March to mid-April). This is the nearest we have to a contemporary indication of the time required for building a hide, but is not, of course, exact, as we do not know how soon the hides were finished, what else Gerard was doing while he built them, or how large they were, except that one sheltered Fr Thomas Everett on Maundy Thursday. One or both of the others may have been only big enough for papers, books and Massing stuff. Oswald Tesimond's Italian narrative of the Gunpowder Plot, based on Gerard's but with some additional details, can be taken as stating that Owen built two or three hides a week. But the passage, in Tesimond's imperfect Italian, is ambiguous: it says that he always began work by confessing and communicating, 'which he usually did two or three times a week', where the relative clause is more likely to refer to the sacraments than the hide-building. For exact records of the necessary man-hours we must go to modern examples.

These modern parallels are, in fact, very illuminating, and not only at Colditz, where the prisoners were confronted with the solid stone walls of a medieval and Baroque castle. Even now, when searchers have infra-red heat-detectors and miniature television cameras that can be pushed through walls on probes, the problems of the hide-builder are much the same as they were in the sixteenth century and will remain so, at least until we all live in transparent geodetic domes. The requirement is for a hidden space, large enough for an adult to survive in and entered through a floor, a wall or a ceiling. Whatever variants of detail there may be, all secret entrances must come under one of these three headings, and the inevitable cracks must be concealed by being made to coincide with the edges of some normal feature of the room. An escapers' tunnel may extend for a considerable distance behind the entrance, but to start with it needs the same techniques as a priest-hole. That is why between 1940 and 1944 many of the devices of the

1590s were re-invented, even the hole-under-the-garderobe or, as in one famous instance at Colditz, the tunnel behind the urinal making use of an ancient garderobe flue. Of roof hides, the two most famous are probably two at Colditz also - the glider workshop and the radio shack, which was still intact when four former inmates returned to the Castle in 1974. It was under the tiles, as at Hardwicke, entered through a floorboard under the slope of an attic roof, as at Sawston or Snore, and lined with grey blankets to stop light shining through, as at Ripley. The contents are now in the Imperial War Museum.

Speculations about what might have happened are proverbially unsatisfactory but are unavoidable in considering priest-holes and the Gunpowder Plot. Almost all that is known about Nicholas Owen comes from Gerard's *Autobiography* and *Narrative,* one of which was occasioned directly and the other indirectly by the Plot. Without these two works it would be impossible to construct a chronology of the subject; there would have been none of the vivid documentation available in the confessions and examinations that followed the discovery; and, while Owen might have lived on in busy obscurity for another ten or fifteen years and the hides at Hindlip might still exist, there would be nothing to link the one and the other. Owen's work might have been known only by a single reference, like that of old Green in Northamptonshire or William Badger in Oxford. It was only his savage death and Gerard's need to defend himself against the charge of complicity in the Plot that have made this book possible. The most difficult chapter to write was, in fact, that on the years between the Gunpowder Plot and the Civil War. Although a dozen or so examples can be dated to this period, only those at Mapledurham, Carlton, Clerkenwell and perhaps Lulworth can be fixed to within a year or two, and of these only Mapledurham and Carlton survive. Casual references to hiding places are not uncommon, but for anything like a connected narrative the sources simply do not exist. It is here that this book is most likely to need revising by future historians of the subject[‡].

The escape of Charles II faces us with the opposite problem. Instead of there being too little evidence, there is if anything, too much. That makes it possible to tell the story with a wealth of colourful detail but without noticing the questions which it provokes. It is clear that Giffard, Carlis and the Pendrells did everything they could to keep the King away from Boscobel, and the most plausible explanation seems to be that the Earl of Derby had unwittingly invited his sovereign to stay in a nest of Jesuits which had already come under suspicion. Of the other houses associated with the escape, Moseley is of outstanding importance as containing an extant hide used in a

---

[‡] When these words were originally written, Mapledurham was believed to have been built in the 1580s. The general point about the paucity of evidence stands.

datable search. The great loss has been at Heale, where the hide must have been unusually commodious for the King to be able to spend five continuous days in it. Despite the Earl of Clarendon's statement that it had been made since the beginning of the troubles, it is worth remembering that Mrs Hyde was a Tichborne, and so one of a well-known recusant family. Perhaps, therefore, the hide was built before 1642. The splendid example in the summer-house at Malmesbury House in Salisbury Close raises the opposite difficulty, that the stonework, pediments and sash-windows point to a later date than 1651, perhaps about 1700. It is important for the chronology of the whole subject, and it is certainly one of the most ingenious in the country.

The Oates Plot and the Glorious Revolution have left us some exciting stories but very little in the way of identifiable hides. It seems more likely that old hides were hastily refurbished than that new ones were built for these sudden and short-lived crises, at least outside London. In the State Trials there is a detailed and dramatic account of the arrest of the Jesuit George Busby at West Hallam, near Derby, in 1681. But his hiding-place, 'near unto a stack of three chimneys' and entered through 'a wooden door and a little iron hinge' camouflaged with tiles, could have been built at any time during the previous century, since Campion had stayed with the Powtrells at West Hallam early in 1581. In 1688, at Courtfield in Herefordshire, another Jesuit, James Richardson, spent ten days hiding in the woods and then seven weeks in a disused lime-kiln, which hardly suggests that the house was adequately furnished with priest-holes. Although hiding-places for valuables, weapons and contraband continued to be built throughout the eighteenth century, and for that matter are still being built today, the great period of hiding-places for fugitives in this country ends with the escape of Charles II, anything after that being in the nature of an appendix and even an anti-climax.

With the death of the last generation to need them, many priest holes were lost and forgotten. For them to remain known, the secret had to be passed on from one owner to the next every twenty-five years or so, and for various reasons this might not always be possible. Ursula Towneley's list of 1710 or so suggests a certain anxiety on this point, perhaps prompted by the deaths of father and son within six years of each other. It seems likely that several of the hides at Harvington were forgotten when Lady Yate died in 1696 and was succeeded by her grand-daughter Mary Throckmorton, her son and grandson having already predeceased her. During the eighteenth century there was a marked concentration of landed estates into fewer hands. In consequence, many manor-houses too antiquated for Georgian society passed to distant cousins, who demolished a wing or two to avoid window tax and leased the remainder to a tenant farmer. If the house was sold, or the heir was a Protestant, or the mission was moved elsewhere, there would no longer be a resident priest to provide another thread of continuity.

Over the years, a vague memory of secret worship and secret devices would be garbled into a local legend of a secret passage to the parish church. The Gothic novels and the occasional discovery of an Elizabethan sewer during repairs or landscaping would do the rest. How widespread and tenacious this belief had become is shown by the fact that in an area of Somerset only ten miles square there have been recorded no fewer than sixty-seven stories of subterranean passages.

Nowadays, people are less credulous, at least in this respect. Squiers pointed out robustly that 'The simplest and smallest passage that a man could conveniently traverse for two miles [a favourite supposed length] would require the minimum excavation of four thousand tons of earth and several men to accomplish it. Work out for yourself the masses of stone or brick required for the lining and then say if such a place could ever have been considered secret, even in the days of the constructor's great-grandson'. Since these words were written, standards of historical and architectural knowledge at country houses have become immeasurably higher, among customers as well as custodians, so that wild and unverifiable rumours are now much rarer than they used to be, though they are not quite extinct. The melancholy Arthurian twilight which many Victorian owners thought appropriate to an ancient building is difficult to combine with central heating, a modern electrical installation and a thriving tea-room.

All the same, there is a great deal still to be discovered about priest-holes. The 180 or so houses mentioned in this book are a sample of perhaps a quarter of the field. Further investigation would undoubtedly turn up others, some of them important. The false chimney at Harvington was not found until 1954, the hide at Ripley Castle until 1963, the Little Attic at Stonor in 1964 and the Chimney Hide at Mapledurham in 2003. It would be rash to suppose that no more will ever come to light, even though the discard rate of those reported in local newspapers is very high.

Such discoveries are nearly always made in the course of repairs or renewals of services, when walls are pierced or floors taken up. An investigator of priest-holes spends very little time knocking on wainscot or fumbling among oak carvings for the secret catch, and much more examining places which have already been found, perhaps a century or more ago, and which may have been repaired or worse still, 'reconstructed'. Most of it is spent in libraries and record offices on the necessary drudgery of documentation. But with hindsight and practice it is possible to acquire a sense of where such places may be found and, even more useful, where they are not likely to be found.

The way to begin is the way that Gerard says the pursuivants used to begin, by walking round the outside of the house looking for unexplained stretches of blank wall. That was how I guessed, correctly, where the hide at

Compton Wynyates was, some years before I actually saw it. Better still is an attempt to imagine what the building would look like with one wall taken off, using the chimneystacks as clues to the internal partitions. Elizabethan chimneystacks are normally in projections along the outside walls, frequently combined with garderobes; and, except in long galleries, there is likely to be an internal division between one stack and the next. Staircases are normally also in projections and may be indicated by windows that are smaller or staggered. The central staircase hall is a development of the later seventeenth and eighteenth centuries.

If the house is built round a courtyard, the hall will be in the block at the back, opposite the gatehouse, with the domestic offices on one side and the parlour and other family apartments on the other. If the courtyard is open, with only three sides, the gatehouse is omitted and the disposition of the other three blocks remains the same. A porch to the hall makes this into an E-plan, and moving the hall forward so that the wings project in front and behind it makes an H-plan. In any of these plans, the space taken up on the ground floor by the hall tends to push the staircases outwards to the angles. The vertical stroke of the E or the horizontal of the H will be the longest, and if there is a long gallery it will be on the top floor there.

In a house which is internally of timber-and-plaster framing, partitions can be freely added, subtracted and altered, without much reference to windows or chimneystacks. The west wing of Harvington is a fine illustration of this point, and the wall paintings prove that it has not been altered since around 1600. Access was usually from one room to another and continuous corridors are often later alterations, but not always, as is shown by the Mermaid and Nine Worthies Passages at Harvington. The end bedroom of a series is therefore the most private and the most suitable for a hole-under-the-garderobe.

Hiding places on the ground floor are very great rarities and there is no point in wasting time on them. The roof space, while immune from redecoration according to changing fashions, is likely to show evidence of structural repairs and alterations since the survival of the entire building depends on keeping it watertight. Replacement of common rafters and scarfing of new timber on to defective trusses cause no confusion but the insertion of ceilings, sometimes at several levels, and of partitions of various dates from the seventeenth to the nineteenth centuries can make the original layout very hard to establish. It is possible to discover 'hiding places' in almost any large and complex roof, and here, more than anywhere else, it is necessary to insist on adequate corroborative evidence before claiming a space as secret.

Between the ground floor and the roof-space come the two or three floors which are most likely to contain hiding-places. If the attic chapel and the priest's room can be identified, it is likely that there was a hide near one or both. They are usually close together and might even be a single room used for both purposes. At Sawston, the chaplain was apparently still living in the attics in 1769, and the chapel there, described in 1757 as 'a gloomy garret and in no way ornamented', was not replaced by a more dignified room on the ground floor until late in the eighteenth century. But at Moseley, admittedly a small house, even in 1651 the priest's room with its hide was on the floor below the chapel and at the opposite end of the building. At Harvington, Sir John Throckmorton spent more than £100 in 1796-8 on modernising the North Tower as a 'House of the Incumbent of Harvington Hall', and it seems likely that it was then that the Elizabethan rooms on the top floor of the west wing were abandoned. That was late enough for their former use to be remembered and recorded in the nineteenth century but often there are no such clues. Wall paintings, as at Moseley and Althrey, or plaster arches and coved ceilings, as at Woollas Hall, are most unusual survivals and cannot be expected as a matter of course.

If the chapel and priest's room cannot be identified, it is not possible to get very far without a measured plan of the whole building. Stone walls are often thick enough to have spaces quarried out of them, as at Sawston; in timber or brick buildings, like Braddocks, that can only be done in the chimneys. But plans can tell the whole story only if floor and ceiling levels are consistent throughout the building, which is most unlikely. Even if sections are taken, it is often difficult to account for all the space round a staircase, especially when there is a chimney-stack close by, as at Braddocks, Snore and Scotney. It is a chastening thought that after Harvington had been unsuccessfully searched in the 1890s by the then authority on the subject, Allan Fea, the hide behind the swinging beam was found by a young man sheltering from a shower. Hide-hunting is a sport with a large element of luck.

Plans need to be interpreted in the light of the architectural history of the building. With rare exceptions like Capheaton, it is a waste of time to search a house, or part of one, which is later than 1620 or so. Windows and decoration are not reliable indications of date; many Georgian houses in the north, for instance, incorporate medieval peel towers which only show on the plan as unusually thick walls and puzzling changes of level. The surroundings of the hide at Towneley are now almost completely Georgian but seem to have been done carefully so as to preserve an earlier hide which might still be needed. On the other hand, where the space of the 'hide' itself was created by a later alteration, as at Melford, Nevill Holt or Clarke Hall, it must be discarded, however historic the rest of the building may be. Since even the summer-house at Malmesbury House, Salisbury, shows evidence of at least two phases of building, possibly three, it is wise to be cautious about larger structures which may have been altered at frequent intervals for the last four or five centuries.

It is still true that at Hindlip some of Owen's contrivances withstood the search for more than a week, despite the ruthless methods of over 100 men. A modern pursuivant cannot expect things to be any easier. A perfect hide is, by definition, one which baffles detection. A cavity in brick or stone which has once been filled up or covered over is likely, barring accidents, to remain a secret until the house is demolished. Subsequent tenants of the house which Anne Line ran for Gerard in London must have been completely ignorant of the priest-hole in which John Curry had been entombed in 1596. Only the clues in Gerard's *Autobiography* could have prompted the two days' work with hammer and chisel which led to the rediscovery of the hide at Braddocks. Much of the fascination of the subject lies in this pitting of one's wits against a three-dimensional puzzle designed by a man long since dead, where the penalty for losing was once arrest, torture and perhaps death. What Squiers wrote in 1933 is still an accurate summary and is likely to remain so:

> Many of these places were only discovered when the houses were pulled down. Some are known, but their entrances have been covered over. Many more must still remain to be found, though some of them - like their remarkable builder - will hold their secrets for ever.

Appendices

The following two papers describe some broader aspects of recusant life. *The Layout of Elizabethan Recusant Houses* explains how illicit worship was possible within the recusant houses and *The Elizabethan Underground* describes how priests were brought into the country and transported to safe houses. Both originally appeared in *Midlands Catholic History*, and were standalone papers, so there is some repetition of material, both among them and between them and the book.

I: The Layout of Elizabethan Recusant Houses

The country house', wrote Geoffrey Tyack in 1980, 'was more than simply a family home. It combined some of the functions of a museum, a local government office, a farm and a hotel'.[1] If it was a recusant house, it was also a church, a presbytery and something of a thieves' Alsatia. A century and a half before that, John Kirk had commented that the chapel at Moseley Old Hall, 'like many others, while the penal laws hung over our heads, was a part of the garrets and had no other approach to it than through the house. Yet to this inconvenience did the family willingly submit, to accommodate their tenants and the neighbouring Catholics'.[2] The conflicting requirements of security and access to the attic chapel for family, servants and outsiders had, however, to be reconciled with the complex functions of an Elizabethan great house and with the other activities of gentry, servants and visitors, many of them not Catholics. How this was done had implications for the entire building, not merely for one or two rooms on the top floor and is worth examination in its own right.

In a note on Sir Everard Digby's Buckinghamshire house at Gayhurst, Philip Caraman wrote that 'First consideration . . . was to be given to the siting of the chapel and the priest's quarters. An elaborate system of hiding-holes had to be arranged throughout the house irrespective of the convenience or privacy of the occupants. Also there had to be easy access to the open country in the event of a sudden raid.'[3] But some distinctions should be made. An elaborate system of hides throughout the house was only needed in a 'receptacle', such as Harrowden, where several priests might have to be hidden at the same time. The intrusion on privacy at Moseley was caused by the fact that it is a small house: in great houses like Gayhurst a priest could have his own quarters in what Robert Persons called 'some part retired from the rest'.[4] The 'access to the open country' which John Gerard mentions at Harrowden[5] was more for unobtrusive comings and goings on pastoral work than for escapes from searches, when it would be much safer to use a hide. And the most serious problem, which Caraman did not mention, was that of keeping the secret from all but a few trusted servants.

Gentry, Servants and Priests

On the ground floor, any medieval or Elizabethan manor-house followed a common plan, with the hall in the middle, the kitchen and buttery at the lower end and the private rooms of the owner at the upper end. This can be seen alike in small houses like Moseley and in great palaces like Raglan Castle, where the upper and lower ends have each become complete courtyards, with the hall dividing them. But the division into family and servants' wings was not so tidy upstairs. For reasons of warmth the master bedroom was often above the kitchen, as Sir Thomas Holte's was at Aston Hall, Birmingham. Moreover, the servants necessarily had access to other parts of the house; even if a priest had a room on the top floor, he had to go out and come in on the ground floor; and there is evidence that chapels were often approached by staircases at the lower end of the hall. Half a dozen examples may illustrate these points.

In 1582 Roger Ogden, a servant of Richard Bold of Bold Hall in Lancashire, deposed that he had seen a priest, Richard Smith,

> as he came over the dam-head at Bold, and three or four with him, and he was cunningly conveyed at a back gate into the garden over the drawbridge into the house. And he hath seen meat go forth of the kitchen and forth of the dairy house into his chamber, over what is called Sir Thomas Gerard's chamber.[6]

This strongly suggests that the layout there was like that at Harvington, where above the kitchen are the South Room, with a garderobe and hide, on the first floor and the Priest's Room on the second floor, both reached by a newel staircase opposite the buttery. In the same way, according to a spy's report of 1595 on Derbyshire,

> [At] Mr Wittall's house near Ashbourne [Yeldersley Hall], four miles from Alkmonton, is Robert Showell, a seminary priest with a bald head, having one leg shorter than the other; and at the buttery door go up a pair of stairs to the chamber where they say Mass often. .... [At] Rawlins' house at Roston, three miles from [Yeldersley], before the parlour door is a spence [buttery] where priests and church stuff are to be found.[7]

At Gouthwaite in Yorkshire it was alleged that

As [Robert Joye] was working in the hall at Golthwaite [*sic*] in the summer before the Powder Treason, about the later Lady Day in harvest [the

Assumption, 15 August], Marmaduke Lupton, the steward to Sir John Yorke, came to him and told him it was my lady's pleasure he should remove out of the hall and work in the buttery. Whereupon he removed into the buttery and Lupton put the door to. Whereat he, marvelling, pulled open the door a little and saw Lupton bring in a reasonable broad man. And the Lady Yorke came out of the parlour and met him in the entry that goeth to the kitchen and up the stairs to the garret. She said, 'Welcome, Mr Gerard!', which this examinate perfectly heard, for there was but an inch board between. Mr Gerard was carried up to the garret chamber and there remained for a month, not openly coming down. Heard Lupton, Grange and Almond many times severally ask the cook secretly whether Mr Gerard's meat were ready.[8]

At Hindlip in January 1606,

There is two or three necessary to be examined, for that they will not confess anything here. The one is the horse-keeper [William Glandish] that receiveth all strangers' horses; the other is one [Edward] Gerrard, Mrs Dorothy Abington's man, that ever attendeth on these priests, bringeth them up their victuals and hideth them when there is occasion.[9]

And at Winchester House in London on Candlemas 1651, 'having by some treachery previously gained all details, [the searchers] made at once for the back stairs, and would have gone direct to the chapel and the Father's room, had not the Marquess himself for some time detained them'.[10]

Apart from the lady's gentlewomen and those in the nursery, the laundry and the dairy, the servants would be men.[11] 'An note of the household servants of Mr Thomas Throckmorton Esquire', probably made in 1593 when Coughton was searched, names twenty-three men and only three women.[12] At Harvington, there are Jacobean references to several men-servants but only two women: an unsatisfactory laundry-maid who had left and 'Catherine, who supplied the place for the making of white m[eats ?] and malt'.[13] In 1606, one of John Wintour's servants at Huddington, Thomas Lowe, was imprisoned in irons at Stafford. His widowed sister, Agnes Walworth, wrote to the Earl of Salisbury on his behalf, reminding him that she 'was once your Lordship's laundress and one of the first women servants that your honour entertained'.[14] So such households were predominantly masculine establishments, even when, like the court, they were headed by women.

Ground Floor

Many manor-houses were surrounded by moats, which obstructed sudden raids. At a Jesuit house in Kent, perhaps Scotney Castle, on a Christmas Day in the 1640s, the searchers were able to get in all the same because the moat had frozen over.[15] In any case, a quadrangular building would have some form of gatehouse. There are hides in gatehouses at Coughton, Oxburgh and perhaps Stonyhurst; there are chapels in gatehouses at Coughton and perhaps Tamworth Castle. In 1593 searchers in York Castle 'broke open several places, including the ceiling over the outgate and in the new chamber above'.[16] On the far side of the courtyard was the porch to the hall. Because the ceiling of the hall was higher than that of the porch, there might be a hidden space between the ceiling of the porch and the floor of the closet above it. Examples can be seen at Benthall in Shropshire, Water Eaton in Oxfordshire, Woodham Mortimer in Essex, Barlborough in Derbyshire and Coldham in Suffolk.[17] They may owe their origin to the use of the closet as a study, where there might be private papers: at Moseley, Mr Whitgreave referred to the closet over his porch as 'my studie'.[18] At Chastleton in Oxfordshire the twelve-light window of the hall is balanced by a twelve-light window in the porch, but the ceiling of the porch is lower than that of the hall, at the level of the second transom up. Behind the top row of lights is a blank wall, and behind that a panelled dressing-room which is said to have been a Royalist hide. At Little Malvern and at Cothay in Somerset the top storey of the porch served as an oratory; in 1584 Ralph Miller, who had been tailor at Rheims, deposed that at Lord Vaux's house in Hackney the priest

> lieth in a chamber beyond the hall, on the left hand the stair that leadeth to the chambers, and the Mass is said in the chapel, being right over the port entering into the hall; and the way into it is up the stair aforesaid, on the left hand, at the further end of the gallery; and there is a very fair crucifix of silver.[19]

The 'gallery' would have been that at the lower end of the hall, as still at Cothay and at Little Malvern until the 1960s.

The hall itself was used for ceremonial entrance; as the servants' dining room and common room; for estate business, local government and administration; for household prayers and for plays.[20] But the gentry would normally eat in the great chamber or the parlour. Sir Thomas Holte's moral reflections in the hall at Aston in Birmingham were for his servants, not his guests, to digest along with their food and drink.

At the lower end of the hall there was a screen, with the gallery above. It seems to have been here that at Rushton in 1828 a hiding-place was found in which were concealed the Tresham papers used by Anstruther for his *Vaux of Harrowden* (1953).[21] The elaborate screen at Burton Agnes in Yorkshire includes carvings of the twelve sons of Jacob, Peace and Concord, the Evangelists, the Apostles and the Heavenly City.[22]

The parlour was on the ground floor at the upper end of the hall and was for informal use by the family or for upper servants. Sometimes there might be two or three parlours, one of which might contain a shovelboard or, as at Hindlip in 1582,'a pair of playing tables'.[23] At Lyford in 1581, the spy George Eliot was given a mug of ale in the buttery and then taken through the hall, past the 'dining parlour' and so upstairs to 'a fair large chamber', where Campion was saying Mass. This would have been the great chamber and may survive as the upper half of the present (1959) staircase hall.[24] A great parlour might be as elaborately decorated as a great chamber (like those at Aston and Speke), but was still on the ground floor.[25] At least two of the three hides known to have been entered from the ground floor were entered from parlours, which were about the only rooms on that floor private enough for that purpose.[26] At Tusmore in Oxfordshire there was 'a neatly furnished room below ground for hiding the priest in cases of emergency; the entrance was by a trapdoor constructed in the window-seat of a parlour, which turned on a pivot and rose or fell with the weight of a person'.[27] At Sledwick in County Durham the Cloptons

> had an excellent place which was made all the length of a little garden under-ground and could have held a dozen priests. The going into it was by a device in the parlour, and it had another going forth beyond the said little garden, where, if the secret place should be descried on the inside, they might get forth on the outside and make haste to step into great woods or copses.[28]

A parlour might in any case have a porch leading out to the garden, as at Speke (1613), and this appears to be the origin of the outside door in the parlour chimneystack at Boscobel.

Beyond the lower end of the hall were the domestic offices: buttery, kitchen, brewhouse, pantry, wet and dry larders, bakehouse, dairy and so on. At Abbots's Leigh near Bristol in 1651, Charles II in disguise as Will Jackson went to the buttery for his breakfast (bread and butter, with 'very good ale and sack'), and was recognised by the butler, John Pope, who had trained in the royal household.[29] It seems likely that the constant comings and goings around the buttery made comings and goings up and down the adjacent staircase to the chapel less noticeable, as at Abbot's Salford in Warwickshire and Ufton in Berkshire.[30] Often there were hides in the massive chimneys of this part of the house but they were always entered from above, not from the offices themselves. This comes out in the best contemporary description of the most common form of hide, from Breccles in Norfolk:

> In Breccles house, where Mrs Woodhouse dwelleth, there is a chamber over the bolting-house, whereunto there is a way by a door which is in the floor of a privy-house; which door is covered with mats and is so close that it cannot easily be found out; and, the door being opened, there standeth a ladder to go down into a close chamber, and no other way into it; which can be discovered on the outside.[31]

This hide, and others like it, could be found from outside because privies were built on to chimneystacks, which projected from the outside of the building, so that the missing space showed as a blank wall. The King's hide at Moseley is safer because there the chimneystack is in the middle of the house, between the brewhouse and the buttery, but there could not then be a privy built on to it, as an outside wall was needed for the drain. Moseley was described as 'new' in 1602; at Carlton in Yorkshire, which was built in 1614, the large and commodious hide is again in a chimneystack in the middle of the house, off the former Long Gallery, which was furnished as a chapel in the 1660s.[32] It seems that builders of hides and houses had learned and adapted.

First Floor

Off the first landing of the great staircase was a suite of rooms for entertaining and display: in order, the great chamber, the withdrawing room and the best bedchamber. Here or on the floor above there might also be a long gallery. The uses of these rooms have often been obscured by a confusion of names: the great chamber might also be known then as the 'great parlour' or (as at Aston in 1654) the 'great dining room' and in the nineteenth century as the 'banqueting hall' or the 'withdrawing room'. But the most common designation, and that used by Shakespeare, was 'great chamber'.

> Why, then may you leave a casement of the great chamber window, where we play, open; and the moon may shine in at the casement. . . . Then there is another thing: we must have a wall in the great chamber.[33]

> Away with the join-stools, remove the court-cupboard, look to the plate. . . . You are looked for and called for, asked for and sought for, in the great chamber. . . . We cannot be here and there too.[34]

Whatever its name, it was the first, the largest and the most accessible of the three rooms and was used for dining, music, plays and masques, and lyings in state. It was often, as at Benthall, above the hall, so that the hierarchy of gentry and servants was visibly expressed in the plan of the house. Dishes might be brought up the great staircase from the kitchen (which at Montacute is seventy yards away) in a formal procession with trumpets and shawms.[35]

At Thame Park in Oxfordshire, Gerard describes how he was at dinner with Lady Wenman in the (surviving) great chamber when in walked George Abbot, then Master of University College, Oxford, and later Archbishop of Canterbury.[36] From a room so open no hides could be entered, though the hide at Braddocks in which Gerard spent four days in April 1594 is high up and to the left of the fireplace in the great chamber.

In 1599 Irthlingborough in Northamptonshire was raided at dinner time. A careless porter let the justices in and they were up in the great chamber before Gerard and the Vauxes knew they had arrived. Fortunately, Mrs Vaux was indisposed and they were about to eat in Gerard's room, not in the great chamber. But the only way to the hiding-place passed the door of the chamber. One of the searchers looked out as the fugitives were passing but was distracted by the noisy argument behind him and did not challenge them.[37] This house has been demolished, but the layout must have closely resembled that at Harvington, with its Great Chamber, South Room and hide in Dodd's Library.

The withdrawing room was between the great chamber and the best bed-chamber. Originally, and still in the sixteenth century, it was an antechamber to the bedchamber where a servant might sleep but was now also the room to which you withdrew (if invited) from the great chamber or for private meals. Withdrawing rooms unattached to bed-chambers began to appear soon after 1600 but were unusual until well into the eighteenth century.[38] At Hardwick, the ruined Old Hall (1580s) has two great chambers, both on the second floor and named after the views from the windows: the Forest at the east end and the Hill at the west. The New Hall (1590s) also has two. On the first floor is the Low Great Chamber (or 'Dining Room') with its Withdrawing Room (across the hall gallery) and the Ship or Cut Velvet Bedchamber; on the second floor, the High Great Chamber with the State Withdrawing Room, Green Velvet and Blue Rooms and the Long Gallery.

Because admission to the withdrawing room was by invitation of the owner, it was safer to have a hiding-place there than in the great chamber. But only one example seems to have been recorded, at Harvington. This may be because other withdrawing rooms have later been used as bedchambers, libraries or boudoirs and been renamed accordingly. Or it may be because at Harvington the Elizabethan Withdrawing Room and adjoining Gate Room were the solar wing of the much smaller medieval house and the hide may have been constructed before the great enlargement of the 1580s.[39]

A long gallery might be on the middle floor or the second. The Owen hide at Sawston is high up behind the panelling of the Long Gallery and is entered from the top of the adjoining newel staircase. The hide at Hindlip used by Nicholas Owen and Ralph Ashley in 1606 was off what Gerard calls 'a long and fair gallery, four-square going round about the house' and 'lined with wainscot'.[40] According to Oldcorne,

> upon the 19th of January last he and Mr Garnet met together near unto Evesham . . . , and they riding together two or three miles, they met with an old man, sometime servant unto old Mr Habington, on horseback also; and three or four miles before they came to Mr Habington's house, the old man took their horses and they went there on foot. And when they came to the house, they were carried into a gallery by that old man; and because they were afraid to be troubled, they were showed to the place into which after they went.[41]

But according to the contemporary account of the search the hide was next to a chimney and sustenance had been passed into it from the hearth in another room.[42] The inventory of 1582 mentions 'the Lady's Chamber' and 'the

Maidens' Chamber', but it is not clear if either of these was the room meant by the searchers. According to a Jacobean account printed by Foley, during a previous search in April 1598, the searchers 'broke about twenty places of the wainscot in the galleries' and almost found Oldcorne; according to Oswald Tesimond, the hide that Oldcorne used on this occasion was also the one in which he and Garnet were found in 1606.[43]

The answer, here and elsewhere, may be that 'a gallery' or 'the galleries' might not be the long gallery or that above the screens passage. Blount in 1662 refers to the attic chapel at Boscobel as 'a gallery'; at Breccles the report already quoted continues: 'There are also many secret places about the gallery . . . which they used and do use (as it is thought) their Masses' (sic). At Henwick near Newbury in Berkshire in 1591,

> If he [the priest Oliver Almond] be not in the house, you shall find him in a gallery going through the hall at the table end: on the right hand up a great pair of stairs there is the gallery where his [Mr Winchcombe's] sons doth lie; there is a press where all the church stuff is.[44]

And at Haddon Hall in Derbyshire, the Earl's Bedroom, which is also off the great staircase, 'now has the character of a gallery and it seems to have been constructed as such by Sir Henry Vernon' about 1500 but 'became redundant for its original purpose when the Long Gallery was created a century later'.[45]

Hiding-places off bedchambers, on the other hand, are common; the King's hide at Moseley is only the best documented of many. On 26 December 1593 Bullocks at Northend in Essex was raided in search of a priest named Brewster, 'a tall man with a waxen beard', who was 'hid in a privy place in a chimney in a chamber'.[46] At Drayton House in Northamptonshire, on which there is a detailed report of 1606,[47] a hide in this position still contains a seventeenth-century trunk marked POB on the lid in nails: it was probably used for storing the vestments. The trapdoor here has been replaced, but the originals survive at Moseley and off the South Room at Harvington: to deaden sound, the latter is of three layers of boards, of which the topmost runs the full length of the closet so that there is no betraying break in the floor. At Mapledurham there are two, both with original bolts on the trapdoors.

Second Floor

On the top floor (or in the attics) were the servants' sleeping quarters, the nurseries, and, in a recusant house, also the chapel and the priest's rooms. Most servants were male: upper servants would have their own room; lower servants would share a dormitory, like Dick's Garret at Aston. For this reason, at Abbot's Leigh the Nortons were told that 'Will Jackson' was recovering from a quartan ague, so that he could have a truckle bed in the chamber of his 'master' Cornet Lascelles and not have to sleep with the other servants. In 1583 Sir Thomas Tresham was confined for six months to 'a cottage, erst a tippling ale-house,' at Hoxton, where he contrived a hiding-place on the excuse that 'his serving men lay in that chamber and his son in the next chamber', and therefore he had barred up the doorway between them. What he had also done was to turn one bay of the roof on the son's side into a hide which was used by two priests during a search. How this was done can still be seen at Chambercombe Manor on the outskirts of Ilfracombe. Here in 1865 the farmer discovered a secret room containing a carved bed on which lay the skeleton of a woman. It had escaped notice till then, despite its bricked-up window, because it is the fourth of five rooms on the upper floor, of which the first three were reached by a staircase at one end of the building and the fifth by a staircase at the other (kitchen) end. And if Tresham's ale-house had only one staircase, it would be simple to cut an opening in the attic floor at the servants' end and put in a crude ladder. There was no ceiling, at least in the kitchen, which was below Sir Thomas's own room.

The chapel and priests' rooms had to be separated from the servants' accommodation, but the congregation had to have access to the chapel. For this, there must have been precise household regulations about who could use which stairs. At Aston, apart from the great staircase and its counterpart (the 'Oak Stairs') at the lower end of the hall, there were also newel staircases in turrets in both wings. At Ufton in Berkshire outsiders came in by the brew-house and had to climb a staircase to the first floor, cross a landing and then climb another staircase to the second floor. At Braddocks, at the top of the stairs to the great chamber, there was 'a great trapdoor by which the upper part of the house could be entirely shut off'. At Harvington there was a door on the top landing of the newel staircase, so that the chapels were accessible from it but not the priests' rooms.

The nursery might not seem to have much to do with harbouring priests, and that label for the room at Harvington between the two chapels is not recorded before the nineteenth century. But at Heaton, near Newcastle, about 1605 Mrs Dorothy Lawson had a conforming husband and at first was served by an itinerant priest who called once a month, and even then 'she went monthly abroad, as if she had wanted the conveniences [of the sacraments] at home. . . . She was forced to convey the priest into the house by night, and lodged him in a chamber which, to avoid suspicion, was appointed by grant from her husband only for the children to say their prayers'. Perhaps such excuses were made elsewhere. At Moseley in the early seventeenth century one of the few upstairs rooms must have been used as a nursery for young Thomas Whitgreave (later 'The Preserver') and his six elder sisters, and in 1651 Father Huddleston's three young pupils must have shared one of these rooms. But in neither case is there any clue to which it was.

Whereas a medieval manor-house would have its chapel on the ground floor, with an entrance above to a gallery for the family and another from the courtyard for the servants, recusant chapels were necessarily in the attics. Compton Wynyates in Warwickshire, begun about 1480, has its original chapel on the ground floor and its secret one in the roof. Often the decoration of these rooms is the only clue to their former use. At Moseley there is a seventeenth-century design in grey in imitation of panelling, and one section of the ceiling still has an eighteenth-century pattern of gold stars on a blue ground. This was a recusant equivalent to the painted firmaments in churches like those at Compton Wynyates and at Bromfield in Shropshire.[48] At Todd Hall in Lancashire there is a crude mural of the Crucifixion, with the two Marys in farthingales. At Harvington in Worcestershire, the smaller of the two chapels is painted with red and white drops, for the blood and water of the Passion, and the larger with vines, lilies and pomegranates. At Althrey Hall Farm, Bangor-on-Dee, are the sacred monograms IHS and INRI in the gable-ends, with the sun beaming over the battlements of a castle on one side and the moon on the other, done in black, grey and greenish yellow. Even more elaborate is the decoration at Bumpits, near Lynsted in Kent, which was built by Sir John Roper, first Lord Teynham, in 1587. Here what appears to be only a conventional strapwork design conceals a cross, eagles, peacocks, a wounded heart, a chalice in the form of a lily and other recusant symbols.[49]

The celebration of Mass requires plate and vestments, which, for all that they had to be hidden away between uses, were often highly elaborate. At Sir Thomas Tresham's house in Hoxton in 1584, there were found 'a new-fashioned picture of Christ in a great table and a tabernacle of sundry painted images with leaves to fold, serving, as it should seem, for a tabernacle or screen to stand upon an altar'.[50] A month later, there was 'a very fair crucifix of silver' in the chapel over the hall porch at Lord Vaux's house in Hackney.[51] At Stonyhurst are some remarkable vestments worked by Helen Wintour, daughter of Robert the Gunpowder Plotter. The red chasuble and cope are decorated with parted tongues in gold thread, together with the Wintour arms and the motto *Orate pro me Helena de Wintour*. Another chasuble is worked with pomegranates in silver and gold, and in two sets of vestments there are altogether four hundred and seventy-one pearls.[52] Three others passed to Mary Wintour, Helen's niece by marriage, who died in 1697, and are now at Kemerton, near Tewkesbury.[53] At Coughton there is a purple velvet cope and at Cleobury Mortimer in Shropshire a dark blue chasuble formerly at Coughton, which were made up in accordance with the will of Catherine of Aragon from gowns which had belonged to her. Both are decorated with floral patterns, winged figures on wheels (from Ezekiel), seraphim, fleurs-de-lys (symbols of the Trinity) and scrolls. Both are likely to have been in use in the Tower Room at Coughton during the 1590s and 1600s and must have made a magnificent splash of colour against the bare Tudor brickwork. The collection at Plowden Hall in Shropshire includes an early-sixteenth century frontal of blue cut velvet; a chalice veil with Elizabethan embroidery in gold and silver thread; a chasuble with Jacobean stumpwork embroidery of pears, strawberries, grapes and carnations; and a seventeenth-century ivory-coloured Italian frontal showing the Annunciation and birds in sprays of flowers worked in silver thread and blue, red and green silks.

The chapels are often mentioned, at least by implication, in inventories. In 1575 at Little Malvern there were coffers, caskets, andirons and bed-linen in 'the chapel chamber', which was probably the gallery leading to the chapel over the porch.[54] At Speke Hall in 1624 there were 'the chapel chamber', 'the new little chapel', 'the old chapel', and 'the chamber over the old chapel, called Sir Thomas Gerard's chamber'. Here 'the old chapel' was clearly on the ground floor and is supposed to have been what later became the servants' hall in the north (gatehouse) wing.[55] Since, however, this wing was not built until 1598, a ground-floor chapel there is unlikely and would not have been very 'old' in 1624. An inventory of 1633 from Chideock Castle in Dorset records the contents of 'the chapel and the chapel chamber' in one of the towers.[56] But this chapel may have been the medieval one, as at Nunney Castle in Somerset.[57]

Even under persecution, the liturgy in these chapels could be remarkably elaborate. At least down to the Civil War, there are records of two priests and two Masses a day, of Vespers or Compline, of the complete offices of Holy Week including Tenebrae, and of Christmas Midnight Mass preceded by carols or Matins. Sometimes services were sung with 'the music of the house', which might include viols, wind instruments and organs (probably short-compass table-organs).[58] Such celebrations must have been known to everyone in the house, and the candles for Midnight Mass must have been visible from outside. How these risks were countered is unclear, but somehow they must have been.

The accommodation for the priests varied. At one extreme, they might be confined to a single room, unable to go out except after dark and walking carefully along the line of the joists so that the boards would not creak.[59] At Gouthwaite in 1605, 'Mr Gerard was carried up to the garret chamber and there remained for a month, not openly coming down'. At the other extreme, Mrs Vaux built a new three-storey wing at Harrowden for Gerard and his Jesuit colleague John Percy, with its own way out to the garden and so to the fields.[60] At Salden in Buckinghamshire there were three rooms for the priest off a gallery eighty feet long which overlooked a formal garden.[61] Two of the three priests' rooms at Harvington, as well as both chapels, still have their original wall-paintings. Whatever the room or rooms were like, there would have to be a hide close by, as there was sometimes next to no warning of searches. At the Heywoods' in London in July 1599:

The justices came upstairs with [Mrs Heywood]. . . to the room where we were. But straight opposite was the chapel, with a door facing the door of my room on the other side of the passage. The magistrates saw the chapel door open, went in and discovered a beautifully furnished altar with Mass vestments laid out. . . . Meanwhile, . . . there was no hiding-place in the room, and the only way I could get out was along the passage where the searchers were. While we were discussing what to do, the searchers came to my room and knocked. We made no answer and, as there was no bolt or lock on the door, we pressed down the latch with our fingers. Then they knocked again, and we heard [Mrs Heywood] saying, 'Perhaps the servant who sleeps here has taken the key away with him. I'll go and look for him'. . . . They went downstairs [and] . . . I opened the door of the [next] room and as quietly as I could took a stool and climbed up into the hiding-place, which was built in a secret gable of the roof. [62]

This layout can still be seen at Harvington, with the important difference that there the three priests' rooms have interconnecting doorways as well as a passage outside, so that from any of them it is possible to reach a false chimney and so a hide in the roof.

Barns, Lodges and Caves

Lastly, there were buildings and other spaces outside the house which were sometimes used for worship or concealment. At Lyford in 1581 Edward Yate was hidden in the dovecote; at Standon Lordship in Hertfordshire in 1678 the third Lord Aston was also hidden in the dovecote and a box of his jewels at the bottom of the River Rib, which flows through the park.[63] At Crosby Hall in Lancashire in the 1620s the sermons of the Jesuit John Layton drew so many hearers that it was hard to find a barn that could hold them all; John Gerard records that in Lancashire he had himself seen more than two hundred present for Mass and sermon, which again points to the use of a barn, rather than anywhere in a house.[64] Of concealments in barns the most famous is that of Charles II at Madeley Upper House on 5 September 1651, where the barn still exists.

Away from the house there was often a lodge, which might be used for keeping 'secret house' (when less ceremony was observed), either during the summer holidays or at other times while the main house was being cleaned.[65] For harbouring priests it had the advantage that the owner did not live there usually and could therefore claim not to know what might have been going on there. Boscobel was ostensibly a hunting-lodge; otherwise, the best examples that survive are the two in Northamptonshire built by Sir Thomas Tresham: Rushton Triangular Lodge, which is emblematic of the Trinity, and Lyveden New Beild, which is emblematic of the Passion and is surrounded by gardens which may represent Calvary and the Mount of the Ascension.[66]

(Benson provided 'Stanfield Place' with a garden house which combines elements from both of these and is reached by a secret passage which seems to be based on the sunken approach to the domestic offices at Lyveden.)[67] In 1586 it was reported that 'at the lodge in Samlesbury Park [in Lancashire] there be Masses daily and seminaries divers resort thither [sic], as James Cowper, Harrison, Bell and such like'.[68] In 1592 there was a search both of Samlesbury Hall and of the Lodge. On this occasion, the magistrate in charge found various images and other items 'in a secret vault over the dining chamber and another chamber', and listed the names and jobs of all the servants, both at the Hall and the Lodge. At the Lodge were John Wright, his wife and children and one servant, Elizabeth Southworth; at the Hall were four gentry, more than thirty men-servants and three women servants. [69] About 1870 at the Lower Hall (which may have been on the site of the earlier Lodge) a hiding-place was found in a late-seventeenth century staircase, which is now in a farmhouse at Grimsargh, about a mile away.

Sometimes it might not be easy to tell between a small lodge, like the Triangular Lodge (which was used by Sir Thomas Tresham's warrener),[70] a banqueting house, like that at Lacock Abbey, and a summer-house, as in I *Henry* IV, III.1.158, which Hotspur thinks of as somewhere for 'feeding on cates', in other words, as a banqueting-house (in the Elizabethan sense). At Rushock Court, two miles from Harvington, in 1595 there was 'a fair garden containing two acres and a half . . . with a fair banqueting house at the west end thereof', which may have been larger than what would now be called a summer-house.[71] The late-seventeenth century building in the garden at Malmesbury House in Salisbury (by St Ann's Gate) has an ingenious hide in the roof,[72] and perhaps this was not the first or the only time that such a trick was played.

Beyond the gardens and the fields there might be caves used for concealment. In 1593 Anthony Atkinson, the customs searcher at Hull, wrote that whenever priests were searched for in the six Northern counties, 'they [were] conveyed into caves in the ground or secret places not possible to find them'.[73] Such caves can still be identified five hundred yards from Hardwicke Hall in Co. Durham and on the Little Orme at Llandudno. The second of these was used in 1587 for the printing of *Y Drych Cristianogawl* (*The Christian Mirror*, the first book printed in Wales), when it was the scene of a well-documented search.[74] In 1590 the Privy Council wrote to the Sheriff of Shropshire about 'William Hanmer, taken in the cave in the Park [apparently Park Hall, near Oswestry], together with the hamper and two little barrels with divers leathern bags full of stamps and letters in metal for printing, with other instruments and tools for that purpose'.[75] At The Cwm, near Monmouth, in 1678 the Bishop of Hereford reported that there were two houses 'seated at the bottom of a thick-woody and rocky hill, with several hollow places in the rocks wherein men may conceal themselves, and there is a very private passage from one of the houses into this wood'.[76]

After 1660

With minor changes, such as Dutch gables, 'Elizabethan' houses continued to be built under James I and Charles I; Aston Hall was not finished until 1635. But after the hiatus of the Civil War and the Commonwealth, houses built from the 1660s onwards were markedly different, not only in their classical dress but also in their internal planning. The hall became the ceremonial approach to a saloon behind it and contained the grand staircase. So the servants now ate in a separate hall downstairs and had access to the upper floors by a complicated series of back stairs, corridors and closets. There were fewer servants, with different titles and functions, and in such a house they could be kept out of sight of the quality except when wanted.[77]

A fine and accessible example of Restoration planning is Belton House in Lincolnshire, which is now owned by the National Trust. This was not a Papist house, but among others like it that were are Wootton Wawen and Foxcote House, both in Warwickshire, and Capheaton Castle and Nether Witton, both in Northumberland.[78] Powys Castle which also belongs to the Trust, is a medieval stronghold turned into an Elizabethan mansion in the 1590s and then altered again in the 1660s. Two priests, Norris or North and Wilson or Walter, were calling there by 1603;[79] later, the Castle was a Jesuit chaplaincy until 1748. Both Capheaton and Nether Witton contain hiding-places;[80] Wootton Hall (whose builder married a daughter of the Earl of Powis at Powys Castle) is said to have had 'chapel, priests' rooms and the customary artifices of concealment'.[81] At Ham House, Weybridge, in August 1678, just before the 'discovery' of the Oates Plot, the sixth Duke of Norfolk unwisely showed the diarist John Evelyn 'all the *latebrae* and hiding-places for the Popish priests, and where they said Mass, for he was no bigoted Papist'.[82] But how recent these hides were is not clear.

The changes to houses and their functions must in any case have affected arrangements for priests. Further exploration of this topic might start with the papers of the Throckmortons, who by 1705 were keeping priests in four houses,[83] each with a different architectural history. Coughton was badly damaged and set on fire in 1643 and repaired and altered by Sir Francis Throckmorton in the 1660s, when, at least for a time, his estranged wife lived there but he did not. Under James II, the hall opposite the gatehouse was used as a chapel but destroyed by a mob in 1688: it is not known when the later chapel in the south wing, now the Saloon, was first used.[84] At Harvington, half the house was pulled down about 1700 and a new chapel was created in 1743 on the upper floor of a range of farm-buildings within the moat. But the priest seems to have stayed on the top floor of the

Hall until 1797, when Sir John Throckmorton spent over £100 on furnishing rooms for him on the middle floor.[85] Weston Underwood in Buckinghamshire, where the Throckmorton baronets usually lived, was originally a quadrangular Elizabethan building with twenty-two hearths, but about 1700 the then Sir Robert rebuilt the north front. The chapel, of which there is an inventory of 1749, seems to have remained in three attics knocked together in the west wing until the house was demolished in 1828, when the best of the panelling was moved to Coughton.[86] Meanwhile, however, in the 1750s, another Sir Robert (1702-91) had built Buckland New House, a superb classical house which included 'an almost free-standing cruciform chapel with a fine domed interior', and Buckland Old House, where in 1592 Hopton had conveyed himself into his hole, had been adapted as its stables.[87] Coughton and Harvington, the two of these houses now open to the public, do not by themselves tell the whole story.

II: The Elizabethan Catholic Underground

I t is easy to get the impression that there was little contact or movement between recusant houses, and that priests spent most of their time 'lurking' in garrets. Some had to, but others did not.[88] In 1609 John Gerard recorded that towards the end of his time in England (1588-1606) he rarely had to stay at inns during a journey of a hundred and fifty miles because he had so many safe houses along the way.[89] Another Jesuit, James Sharpe alias Pollard, wrote in 1610:

> Among my friends and acquaintances, the most of them, if not all, being gentlemen of good account, I can travel from this side Lincoln to York, and so thirty miles further, which is above eighty miles, and within every six miles come to a Catholic house, and for the most part within three miles, all or the most of them gentlemen or gentlewomen's houses of good account; and for all this I will not in all the way go six miles out of the ready and nighest way.[90]

This picture is confirmed by other evidence. In 1587 Swithin Wells had ridden from Ufton Court in Berkshire to Warblington Castle on Chichester Harbour and so to Slindon and Michelgrove near Arundel.[91] The Jesuits who were hidden in 1591 at Baddesley Clinton in Warwickshire[92] had come from all parts of the country: Edward Oldcorne only from Hindlip in Worcestershire but Gerard from Braddocks in Essex, Richard Holtby from Grosmont, near Whitby, Thomas Stanney from near Winchester and John Bennet from Holywell. In 1590 Stanney had landed at Whitby and Bennet at South Shields, after which both had got in touch with Holtby at Grosmont, and Stanney had been escorted to Hampshire by Wells.[93] Between 1591 and 1594 Gerard travelled from Braddocks to Staffordshire, Yorkshire and Lancashire.[94]

An appreciation of these journeys and their itineraries is necessary for an understanding of Elizabethan and Jacobean recusancy. But the sources are fragmentary and scattered, apart from a few exceptional episodes such as Wells's journey of 1587, Campion's travels through the North in 1580-1[95] or Henry Garnet's pilgrimage to Holywell in 1605.[96] We know all four houses at which Wells stayed between Ufton and Michelgrove; we do not know any of the dozen or fifteen at which he must have stayed in the three hundred miles between Grosmont and Hampshire. But it is clear that there were elaborate and well-practised procedures for smuggling boys, girls and priests in and out of the country and for escorting them from house to house within it. These can usefully be considered under four headings: 'landing', 'receptacles', 'leaders of priests' and 'itinerant priests'.

Landing

There were five colleges beyond the seas for secular priests: in order of foundation, at Douai, Rome, Valladolid, Seville and Lisbon. The first, the nearest to England, and always the largest, was that at Douai, which was founded in 1568 by Dr William Allen, later the Cardinal. Douai (or Douay or Doway) was then in the Spanish Netherlands and in 1576 it became unsafe because of the Dutch Revolt against Spain. So Allen took as many of the students as he could to Rheims in France and sent the rest to Rome, where another college was set up in the buildings of the English hospice for pilgrims in the Via di Monserrato, where it still trains priests for England. The college at Rheims returned to Douai in 1593 and remained there until the French Revolution. The college at Valladolid was founded in 1589; Seville was founded from Valladolid in 1592 and merged with it again in 1768. Lisbon was considerably later—1628. In addition, there was a school at Douai and another, run by the Jesuits, at St-Omer in France, which is now at Stonyhurst in Lancashire. The Jesuits staffed the English colleges in Rome, Valladolid and Seville and also had houses of their own at Liège, Ghent and elsewhere on the Continent. In 1580 Arthur Faunt (1554-91) from Foston in Leicestershire was teaching at the English College in Rome, but he died eleven years later in Vilnius in Lithuania.[97] Oswald Tesimond, having escaped from England in 1606 disguised as the owner of a cargo of dead pigs, spent the rest of his life teaching at Valladolid, Naples and Messina. The Jesuits had a chaplaincy, the *missio castrensis*, for English volunteers in the Spanish army in Flanders, such as Guy Fawkes; from 1634 they also had a mission in Maryland. Apart from that, from the 1590s onwards there were English convents on the Continent;

after 1600 there were Continental houses of English monks and friars: Benedictines, Franciscans and Dominicans. All of this made for a considerable illicit traffic across the Channel and for lengthy journeys on the other side.

In 1615 the future martyr Arthur Francis Bell travelled from St-Omer to Valladolid by way of Paris, Orléans, La Rochelle, Bordeaux and San Sebastian, partly on foot, partly by boat and from Arras to Amiens by coach. The journey, of more than 1000 miles, took him from 27 July until 22 September.[98] In 1633 Humphrey Price and Francis Victor walked from Douai to Lisbon, leaving on 9 May and arriving on 4 July.[99] From Rome to Worcestershire is twelve hundred miles: by land across the Alps, by sea across the Bay of Biscay. From 1578 to 1589 priests returning from Rome mostly used the 'French route', by way of Mont St-Cénis, Lyons and Paris (as Gerard, Oldcorne and their companions did in 1588). After that, because of war in France, priests used either the 'imperial route' (Milan, the St Gotthard Pass, the Rhine and the Netherlands) or the 'Spanish route' (by ship to the east coast of Spain, and then overland to Bilbao or another northern port).[100] As one Roman student said in 1636, either was 'difficult and dangerous'. In 1657 three young priests and a student from Rome were drowned off Leghorn.[101] In 1654 a ship from Lisbon with a priest, Daniel Fitter, on board was intercepted off Ostend by a Spanish privateer. A shot from it detonated the powder magazine; Fitter was blown off the deck and landed in the ship's boat, breaking a leg and three ribs. But the Spanish crew, on learning that he was a priest, set him ashore, where he recovered. He worked in Staffordshire for more than forty years, dying at St Thomas's Priory, near Stafford, in 1700. There is an inventory of his church stuff there; under James II he opened a chapel in Stafford itself.[102]

The shortest passages across the Channel were to Dover, Rye or Newhaven or to London, but these were also the most dangerous. Customs officials had descriptions of priests, supplied by spies in the colleges: a list made in 1580 by one of them, Charles Sledd, contains a hundred and eighty such descriptions.[103] Everard Hanse, on landing in 1581, went to the Marshalsea to contact other priests, where a gaoler noticed that his shoeshad been made in France.[104] So illicit passengers might disembark before the ship reached harbour (or embark after it had left). In April 1606 a spy reported to the Earl of Salisbury:

> The priests of the country commend such youths as they make choice of unto [Richard Fulwood, a servant of the Jesuit superior Henry Garnet], who placeth them in some blind alley near the water until wind serves for passage; which fitting, the vessel (which is some old hoy or suchlike, to avoid suspicion) goeth down empty towards Gravesend, and he provideth a pair of oars and boats, the passengers and carriage, and ships them in the bark, commonly beyond Greenwich, and conveys the money which belongs unto them afterwards himself. They ship them to Gravelines or Calais and take

forty shillings for the passage.[105]

Another way was to disembark further west or north. In 1586 a ship carrying four priests ran aground off Littlehampton at the mouth of the Arun.[106] Robert Southwell had left England in 1576 by way of Warblington Castle.[107] From 1585 there is a survey of landing-places along the Hampshire coast, which shows that the Privy Council was suspicious about their users.[108] In April 1591 William Warford landed 'in an out-creek near Plymouth'.[109] In 1602 it was reported that at Chickerell in Dorset 'there were nine priests at one time in Mrs Jessop's the widow's house'.[110] It is likely that at least some of them had just been put ashore, either at Weymouth, two miles to the southeast, or at Fleet, a mile to the south-west behind Chesil Bank, which was later said to be much used by smugglers.[111] On the east coast, William Weston landed in 1584 on a beach between Lowestoft and Yarmouth, and Gerard and Edward Oldcorne in 1588 on a beach near Happisburgh, between Yarmouth and Cromer.[112] Further north, many priests landed at Whitby and Newcastle. But the most daring ploy was that of some priests from Valladolid who in 1591 came back to Portsmouth disguised as sailors captured during Essex's attack on Cadiz. When two of them were taken up to London and interrogated by Admiral Lord Howard in person, they were able to convince him that they were what they said they were—and were accordingly sent off to claim the Queen's bounty for distressed seamen.[113]

Receptacles

On 29 November 1593 Edward Pemberton deposed that a priest named Richard Broughton alias Rowse, whom he had known at Douai, was

> 'sent, as this examinate thinketh, for Worcestershire, because he told this examinate that he should find him, the said Rowse, at Mr Habington's house at Hindlip with Mrs Habington. He is a tall man, with black hair and a black beard with some white hairs, cut close. . . . Mr Rowse said he would go to his friends in Derbyshire and afterwards into Worcestershire'.[114]

The whole of this deposition gives a vivid picture of the Catholic underground, but this detail illustrates a remark of John Gerard about Edward Oldcorne, who was at Hindlip for sixteen years from 1590 until his arrest there in 1606. This is that Oldcorne 'stationed priests in many places' and (in St Jerome's phrase about St John) 'he founded and governed all the churches in those parts'.[115] Hindlip was a 'receptacle', a house where incoming priests could be held until arrangements were made for them, where priests already posted could meet for conferences and retreats—and which therefore had more priest-holes than a manor-house where only one was being harboured.

Hindlip was described by an acquaintance of Oldcorne as 'the most famous house in England for entertainment of priests'.[116] Only two such houses have survived in working order with their hides: Harvington, which has eight and had connections with Hindlip; and Ufton Court, which has four and was the scene in 1599 of a copiously documented search on a warrant for the arrest of Gerard and Garnet. But a couple of dozen other receptacles can be identified, most of which seem to have been established, like Hindlip, by Garnet and his fellow-Jesuits from 1586 onwards.

In Lancashire, Towneley Hall had nine hiding-places, which are detailed in a list of about 1700, though only one survives.[117] From Lincolnshire there is a report of 1597 on Twigmore, near Scunthorpe, which was 'like a Popish college, for traitors in the north parts are there harboured. It joins upon Humber, and great woods, caves and vaults thereunto belonging'.[118] Garnet was there at Easter 1604, and priests were still hiding there at the time of the Oates Plot.[119] Drayton House in Northamptonshire also has only one hide now, but a report of 1606 names seven priests who had made 'common resort and much abode' there; it seemed to be 'a receptacle of most dangerous persons . . . [with] continual concourse between it and foreign seminaries'.[120] Kirby Hall, also in Northamptonshire, would have become another such house, but was raided the very day that Owen began work on the hides there.[121] In 1605 two of the Gunpowder Plotters, Robert Wintour and Stephen Lyttelton, approached Oldcorne with a request to get them to The Cwm, near Monmouth, which also remained a major centre for harbouring priests until 1679 and may be the house in south Wales which was said in 1622 to contain enough hides for forty men.[122] The report on the nine priests at Chickerell adds that 'the place is solitary by itself and the house hath conveyances in it to hide the priests and Massing priests in', which implies that it also was a receptacle.[123]

In the south-east there were Warblington Castle, from which Robert Southwell crossed to France in 1576; Battle Abbey, where the dowager Lady Montague had a choir and pulpit in her chapel; and perhaps Scotney Castle, which is now owned by the National Trust. According to a deposition of 1598,

> There are three priests to come over: by name, Fr Charles Tancred, Fr Cooper and another Father whom I have forgotten; they will repair to Scotney, as they said. . . . For Oliver Almond, the priest, I should find him about Eynsham [near Oxford] or at Scotney, and he would also bring me to some other Papists who should relieve me and help me in anything.[124]

Of these, Charles Tancard was at the English College in Rome from April 1583 until January 1584, joined the Jesuits at Naples in February 1584 and was ordained before 1592. By 1593 he was at the English College in Seville and from 1596 at Valladolid, where he died in 1599.[125] John Cooper was ordained at Rheims in 1592, joined the college at Valladolid in 1593 and was sent to Seville in October 1594.[126] Oliver Almond was born in Oxford, educated at Brasenose College, Rheims and Rome and ordained in Rome in 1587. He left for Seville in 1589 and came back to England in 1591, where he worked in Oxfordshire and the neighbouring counties for more than thirty years.[127] Two months after the report of 1598, Scotney was raided and searched for ten days for Richard Blount, one of the 'distressed seamen' of 1591 and later the Jesuit provincial. Although it was a Jesuit chaplaincy much later, Blount himself moved elsewhere: it seems likely that in the 1590s it had been a receptacle for priests landing on the south coast, but that it was no longer safe to use for that purpose.[128]

In the north-east there were five important houses, all associated with Richard Holtby, a skilled needleworker who made his own vestments and a skilled carpenter and mason who made his own priest-holes.[129] At Abbey House in Whitby, Sir Henry Cholmley

> married Margaret, daughter to Sir William Bapthorpe. This wife at this time was a Roman Catholic and, he living then at Whitby, it was a receptacle to the seminary priests coming from beyond seas and landing frequently at that port; insomuch as I have been told there have been in his house three or four at a time, and, most coming bare of both clothes and money, have, at his lady's charge, been sent away with a great supply of both, some in scarlet and satin with their men and horses, the better to disguise their professions. All which Sir Henry connived at, being a little then in his heart inclining that way, though he went to church.[130]

A few miles up the Esk from Whitby was Grosmont, where in 1593 Thomas Clark met a dozen or so other priests and which he described as 'a place where they are specially directed when they come over from Rheims'.[131] In 1599 it was searched, when

> 'divers valtes of strange conveyance weare fownd oute, amongst which one at a staire's head, within a thick stone wall, was covered with a great post of the bignes of a man's body, which semed to beare the howse but indeed did hinge onely and was removeable to and froe'.[132]

This is a remarkable parallel to the hide in Dodd's Library at Harvington. After landing at South Shields, Clarke and another priest had gone first to Thornley in Co. Durham, 'where they met with Richard Holtby, a Jesuit, to whom they were specially directed'. At Sledwick, also in Co. Durham, the Cloptons 'maintained always one [priest] of residence in their house, besides receiving those who came, so that at one time there hath been no less than a great table full'.[133] And in 1614 the widowed Mrs Dorothy Lawson built a new house called St Anthony's at Byker, three miles downstream from Newcastle, which in 1623 became Holtby's headquarters. Apart from the neighbouring congregation of a hundred, it also served 'sea-faring men of other nations' but was burnt down in 1644 to deny the Scots army the use of it.[134] There are descriptions of it—but not of its hides.

'Leaders of Priests'

To reach receptacles and other houses, priests had to be guided. The phrase used for this heading is from a list of 1583 which includes under Oxfordshire: 'Fordes eldest son of Garsington: A common leader of priests about the country'.[135] But the first mention of such 'leaders' is in 1580-1, for the journeys of Campion and Persons. Between July and October 1580 Persons was escorted by George Gilbert through the shires of Northampton, Derby, Worcester, Hereford, and Gloucester;[136] between January and May 1581 Campion went on a journey through Derbyshire, Yorkshire and Lancashire. For the first stretch of this he was accompanied by Gervase Pierrepoint from Holme Pierrepoint near Nottingham; for the second by a Mr Tempest, probably the Robert Tempest of Holmeside in Durham who was ordained at Soissons in 1584.[137] While Persons was in the Welsh Marches, Campion seems to have travelled round Oxfordshire, Buckinghamshire and Berkshire: it was later alleged that he had been harboured at Lowches in Long Wittenham, near Dorchester, by Henry Russell, a former colleague at St John's College in Oxford, who was at Lyford Grange when Campion was arrested there and later inherited Little Malvern Court in Worcestershire and married Elizabeth Pakington, a sister of Humphrey Pakington of Harvington.[138]

From then on, there are reports of such 'leaders' from all over the country. In 1582, Thomas and Rhys More, watermen of Ripple in Worcestershire, were described as 'poor men but very dangerous. . . . Many Papists resort to their house (as it seemeth) to hear Masses and to have other conference'.[139] It seems likely that they ran a ferry across the Severn. Also in 1582, at Bold Hall in Lancashire, Richard Smith 'came over the dam-head . . . , and three or four with him, and he was cunningly conveyed at a back gate into the garden over the drawbridge into the house'.[140] In 1586, a priest named Richard Brittain was 'conveyed' from Westby, near Blackpool, to Speke Hall on the northern shore of the Mersey by William Norris, son of the then owner of Speke.[141] As the crow flies, the distance is thirty miles but, allowing for the crossing of the Ribble, it would be at least forty on horseback. They may have stayed a night on the road, perhaps at Rufford, which was owned by the recusant Heskeths and is about halfway between Westby and Speke.

In the south, there is the curious episode of the arrest on 28 February 1585 of Nicholas Owen's brother John.[142] On Saturday 13th he had left London and at Putney Ferry was overtaken by two gentlemen named Bray and Roger Brierton. They rode to Kingston, where they drank together. Then Bray and Brierton turned aside to Hampton Court Park to watch some of Lord Montague's servants coursing a doe, while Owen continued to Guildford 'in the company of one of the Lord Montague's men'. A note in the State Papers about this time includes six named servants of Lord Montague among 'knaves, Papists and harbourers of priests'.[143] When Bray and Brierton reached Guildford, they found Owen with two other men called Williams and Triver. All five stayed in Guildford for the Saturday night and at the White Horse in Winchester for the Sunday night. On the Monday, Brierton, Triver and Williams went to Salisbury, returning to Winchester on Friday 19th; on Sunday 21st, Brierton rode to Mr Fitzjames's at Cambourne, a justice who was 'vehemently suspected' and had a son who was later a priest. On Sunday 28th, Owen was arrested at Mrs Warnford's in Winchester with a certain Walter Treveven, who claimed that he had come from Mawgan in Cornwall 'to bring certain congers and other dry fish' to Elizabeth St Aubyn, then living with Mrs Warnford. He did not explain why her fish had to come two hundred miles from Cornwall, rather than fourteen miles from Southampton. It is hard to avoid the conclusion that these encounters were not accidental, especially as Treveven 'forgot' at first to mention that two other women in Mrs Warnford's household were his mother and sister.

From Jacobean Worcestershire there are four suggestive fragments. First, in 1604 Walter Cowarne, a nephew of Henry Russell, went to St Omer's and then on to Valladolid to study for the priesthood. He was seen off from London by Humphrey Pakington and by Dr John Halsey, who was another of the 'knaves and harbourers' listed with Lord Montague's men twenty years before.[144] Second, on 30 January 1606 Sir Henry Bromley wrote from Hindlip to the Earl of Salisbury reporting the capture of Garnet and Oldcorne and adding that he was also examining 'one [Edward] Gerard, Mrs Dorothy Habington's man, that ever attendeth on these priests, bringeth up their victuals and hideth them when there is occasion'.[145] This Gerard may or may not be the 'old man, sometime servant to old Mr Habington,' whom Garnet and Oldcorne met near Evesham on the day before the search began and who took their horses and 'carried [them] into a gallery' at Hindlip.[146] Third, if Robert Wintour and Stephen Lyttelton *had* persuaded Oldcorne to get them from Hagley to The Cwm, they would have been escorted by 'one Charnock, now prisoner in Worcester gaol'.[147] And fourth, about 1620 Thomas Habington's son William, who was born on 5 November 1605, went to school at St Omer's.[148] Thomas Lister, a Jesuit who was at Hindlip in 1605, had been at Warblington Castle in 1603:[149] perhaps young Habington went the same way as young Southwell had done. All of these give hints of the secret comings and goings which lie behind bald entries in registers that, for instance, Samuel Smallman was ordained in Rome on 24 August 1603 and buried at Chaddesley Corbett, the parish of which Harvington Hall is the manor-house, on 15 May 1613.[150]

In 1651, Charles II owed his escape after Worcester fight largely to the five Penderell brothers. The precautions taken by them, by the Woolfes at Madeley and by Thomas Whitgreave at Moseley show that they knew what they were doing. At Whiteladies, the King's horse was led into the hall, so that no one outside should see it. The King's face was blackened with soot, his hair was cut, the embroidered tops of his stockings were cut off, and he was disguised in a greasy steeple hat, a green jump-coat, an old leather doublet and an old pair of shoes. On the way to Madeley, Richard Pendrell several times corrected the King's gait, which was not that of a countryman, though he quickly adopted the local accent. At Madeley, what was left of the white stockings was hidden by another pair in old green yarn, and Mrs Woolfe made an infusion of walnut leaves because the King's hands were too white. At Boscobel, Col. Carlis had hidden in the oak before, and must have done so with the help of William and Joan Pendrell.[151] At Moseley, Lord Wilmot's horses were stabled at a neighbour's and their distinctive saddlery and harness hidden in the priest-hole; when the searchers arrived, Whitgreave ordered that all the doors were to be left open.[152] All this implies significant previous experience of dealing with fugitives.

Nearly thirty years later, at the time of the Oates Plot, several suspects were committed to Worcester Castle. One, William Tremeere, had been arrested at Droitwich with 'a concealed letter directed to the Lady Yate [Humphrey Pakington's daughter at Harvington], the contents not to be understood but by her Ladyship or the person that wrote it'. Another, Thomas Palin from Dearnsdale in Staffordshire, was arrested at Pixton Ferry on the Severn, having 'convey[ed] a Popish priest out of this country' (meaning 'county'). This was Henry Barnesley, whom Palin had brought from Blackmore Park to Cookhill, near Coughton, and who was arrested in Warwickshire and taken to London.[153] Clearly there were still 'leaders of priests' a hundred years after they are first heard of.

Itinerant Priests

Some priests lived in country houses, posing as upper servants or cousins of the owner. Others were itinerant and constantly on the move. By the eighteenth century they were known respectively as 'in-priests' and 'out-priests', and there was an official Latin term for the out-priests— *circumforanei*,[154] 'round-the-markets men', in other words, 'travelling merchants'. But the practical distinction goes back to the 1560s, when some of the 'old' Marian priests left their benefices rather than accept the Act of Uniformity and the Elizabethan Prayer Book. Some, even then, were sheltered in great houses, others travelled between such houses. From 1574 onwards they were joined by the 'young' priests ordained abroad, who at first were mostly itinerant, 'rarely spending more than a night in each house'.[155] According to the spy and playwright Anthony Munday, 'There is no long tariaunce in one place for a priest, but he must shift styll, least he be taken'.[156] At Lawshall in Suffolk about 1584 a priest explained that he 'did for three years before teach [the] two sons' of Mr Henry Drury, because he was 'unable to travel continually', as if this was not usual.[157] From the mid-1580s onwards, as the hunt became hotter, in-priests became more usual, but there were always out-priests as well. The same man might work in both ways, like St Ambrose Barlow, who in the 1630s spent three weeks of each month at home at Morleys Hall, near Manchester, and the fourth 'on circuit, sometimes to several places in a morning'.[158] Or priests might be paired, as at Osgodby in Yorkshire, where about 1608 there were 'continually two priests, one to serve and order the house at home, the other to help those who were abroad', or later at Madeley Court in Shropshire, where in 1692 there were 'one for the family [household], the other for the country'.[159] At Wolverhampton in the eighteenth century there is a reference to 'the junior or out-priest',[160] and this is likely to have been the division of labour elsewhere, since the life of an out-priest was physically more demanding.

Examinations and spies' reports give glimpses of these priests and their disguises. Here two will have to serve: those of George Snape in 1592 on Oxfordshire and the neighbourhood and of Richard Bubb in 1607 on the Welsh Marches. Snape, 'a little man, palsied', was born about 1555, ordained at Rheims in 1582 and sent to England in 1583. In 1592 he was arrested at Great Shefford in Berkshire and gave his interrogators 'the names of certain seminary men and the places of their abode',[161] among whom were Richard Chapman, John Filby and William Hopton:

Chapman . . . useth in divers shires, but chiefly in these, viz. Buckingham, Oxford and Berkshire. He used to the recusants of Kirtlington in Oxfordshire very much and is a great man with them, but the place of his abode is at Addington in Buckinghamshire, where dwells an old gentlewoman, if I have been rightly informed, named Mrs Windsor. He is a man of a mean stature, square and well set, of swarf complexion and black beard, and he looketh a-squint. He goeth sometimes on horseback but most commonly on foot, in white fustian with a long pikestaff in his neck, like a grazier.

Filby . . . is now with Mr Belson of Ixell [Ixhill] Forest in Buckinghamshire. From whence he was once chased away by the pursuivants, and their church stuff and books, amounting to the value of twenty marks, were found in a box with a false bottom; after which disaster he refrained the house for a space but now repaireth there again very often. This man is of mean pitch, of a phlegmatic complexion, black-bearded, and commonly travelleth afoot in a white [frieze] or otherwise, in very plain and simple attire. He hath frequented Oxford any time this twelve or fourteen years.

Hopton . . . lieth most usually, and hath since these many years, at Buckland in Berkshire, at Mr Yates his place. . . . In this lieth all Hopton's stuff and books, hidden in a secret corner. It hath been told me of a truth that Mr Hodgkins the pursuivant came on a time to search the house, about Candlemas last (as I have heard it reported), when Hopton in great haste, casting off his gown upon his bed, conveyed himself into his hole; which gown Mr Hodgkins, coming incontinent into the chamber, did find, and felt the same warm as yet under the arm-pits from his body. And he knocked at the ceiling behind the which Hopton was hidden, so that there was no more but the bare ceiling betwixt the pursuivant and him. This Hopton is a tall man, of a sanguine complexion and a yellow beard, handsome and well-set and gentlemanlike in his apparel and behaviour. He rideth altogether and never goeth or travelleth afoot. . . . He hath used about Oxford in the shires thereabout these ten or twelve years at the least.

Richard Bubb's 'calendar and description' of twenty-three priests in the Welsh Marches was taken at Ludlow Castle on 16 December 1607, though most of the information in it was then about four years old.[162] Again, three extracts will give the flavour of it: those on Robert Holland alias Jones (his real name), William Hughes and one named Dunne. Jones (1564-1615) became Jesuit superior in England in 1609; neither Hughes nor Dunne can be identified.

Robert Holland. Alias Powell, alias Morgan, which is thought to be his truest name; of the age of fifty-four or fifty-five years; known to the said Bubb four or five years past; of stature tall, broad-faced, high-foreheaded, great–eyed, his hair then turning from Abram colour. He is to be known by a sword-blade put in a rapier hilt. He frequenteth the house of Edward Morgan of Llantarnam in Monmouthshire, whose wife is a recusant and whose eldest son married the Earl of Worcester's daughter; likewise the house of John Aubrey of Muckland [? Monkland] in Herefordshire, tenant to Mr Blount the Councillor, and the house of Richard Clarke of Wellington in Herefordshire.

William Hughes. Known to Bubb about four years past. A little man, then about forty years of age (as Bubb thinketh), black, and did wear his hair very long. He halteth, his right leg being shorter than his left, and hath a boot made with a high heel accordingly. He frequented the house of Mr John Edwards of Chirk in Denbighshire, and . . . after Bubb did know him [did] frequent the house of Gittins, a schoolmaster in Shrewsbury. And the said Bubb about the same time going towards Bishop's Castle met Hughes, who told him that he oftentimes frequented Red Castle in Montgomeryshire, where the Lady Herbert did then lie, and also the house of Mr Bannister of Wem in Shropshire.

Dunne, who was known unto Bubb about four or five years past, then about fifty years of age, of a middling stature, swarthy-complexioned, pale and seemed sickly, and wore a knit nightcap; his hair naturally black but turned partly white, his beard somewhat round and full. He frequented Sir Basil Brooke's at Madeley and the foresaid Mr Aubrey.

Of these houses, 'Red Castle' was Powis Castle, which is now owned by the National Trust, and 'Sir Basil Brook's at Madeley' was Madeley Court, which is now a hotel, with an astronomical sundial in the Great Garden. In the 1620s it was one of the places to which Bishop Richard Smith travelled on visitation, in a coach and accompanied by nine or ten priests.[163] Bubb also mentions two priests who were resorting to Plowden Hall in the south-west corner of Shropshire, one of whom, Walter alias Wilson, also frequented Powis Castle.

A cowl does not make a monk or white fustian a grazier. Disguised priests had to act the parts they had assumed, and some were better at this than others. Robert Southwell could not remember the technical terms for hawking, with which, of course, any gentleman would be familiar from boyhood.[164] On landing at Rye in 1582, William Bishop (later Bishop Bishop) claimed to be a merchant but could not say what merchandise he dealt in. On the other hand, the 'sailors' who landed at Portsmouth in 1591 must have been thoroughly coached in their parts, and some later priests were in fact what they claimed to be. Charles Powell (1591-1650) had been a doctor before he was ordained and got permission from Rome to continue in practice when he returned to England in 1628 as long as he did not charge. In the 1660s, Thomas Read (1606-69) was an advocate of Doctors' Commons and a surrogate for Sir William Meyrick, judge of the Prerogative Court of Canterbury, which dealt with the probate of wills. And Edward Booth (1638-1719) combined being chaplain at houses in Yorkshire and Lancashire with being a leading member of the Clockmakers' Company in London.[165] At Stonyhurst is a mid-seventeenth-century pedlar's box which was found walled up at Samlesbury Hall: it contains Massing stuff under a pink bonnet and other items of women's clothing. So at least this priest had the right props for his part. Perhaps the plays at the English College in Rome gave students acting experience which would be useful back in England.[166] Prof. Maurice Whitehead has suggested that the Earl of Worcester's Men (after 1603 the Queen's Men) at the Red Bull Theatre in Clerkenwell provided cover for Robert Jones when he was in London, and that his aliases of Draper and Holland were chosen to imply connections with Anne Bedingfeld (born Draper), who owned the site of the theatre, and with Aaron Holland, who was one of its shareholders.[167]

All the same, however well disguised and rehearsed they were, out-priests were exposed to constant risks. In June 1586 William Weston and a companion had to retrieve a trail of altar-breads which had been dislodged by the jogging of one of their horses and had blown along a village street and into the fields for nearly half a mile.[168] When William Freeman was arrested near Alvechurch in 1595, his breviary was found under his hat[169]. In 1612, when George Napper was arrested in Oxfordshire, the constable found his breviary and holy oils, which was enough to convict him[170]. At Harvington there is an exhibition of plate, vestments and books, which includes miniature chalices and an abbreviated missal printed for itinerant priests. It is worth bearing in mind that such items could bring their possessor to the gallows[171].

---

[1] Geoffrey Tyack, *Warwickshire Country Houses in the Age of Classicism, 1650-1800* (Warwickshire Local History Society, 1980), p. 31.

[2] [John Kirk], 'Catholic Chapels in Staffordshire', *The Catholic Magazine and Review* 5 (1834), p. 394, reprinted with original pagination in *Staffs. Catholic History* 14 (1974).

[3] *John Gerard: The Autobiography of an Elizabethan*, ed. Philip Caraman (1951, 1956; reprint with new introduction by Michael Hodgetts, 2006), pp. 254-5.

[4] Richard Simpson, *Edmund Campion: A Biography* (2/1896), p. 233, from Persons, 'Of the Life and Martyrdom of Father Edmund Campion', Book II, Chap. 1; also quoted by Evelyn Waugh, *Edmund Campion* (1961), p. 124. This account, in Stonyhurst *Collectanea* P, was printed between the two editions of Simpson in [*Jesuit*] *Letters and Notices* 11 (1877), pp. 219-242, 308-339; 12 (1878), pp. 1-68.

[5] Gerard, *Autobiography*, pp. 160-1.

[6] SP 12/153/62, in V.C.H. *Lancashire* III, p. 402. Sir Thomas was the Jesuit's father and Bold's father-in-law; cf n.63 below.

[7] SP 12/151/13-14, printed in Foley IV, pp. 470-1.

[8] John Morris, *The Condition of Catholics under James I* [introduction to John Gerard, *Narrative of the Gunpowder Plot*] (1872), p. cclvii. For Gerard's actual movements at this time see Hodgetts, 'Henry Garnet's Pilgrimage to Holywell, 1605', M.C.H. 26 (2019), pp. 12-30.

[9] Sir Henry Bromley to the Earl of Salisbury, 30 January 1606: SP 14/18/52 (Foley IV, pp. 76-77).

[10] Foley II, pp. 515-6; Jerome Betts, *Blessed Peter Wright* (1997), pp. 111-113. Wright could have withdrawn to 'a secure hiding-place' but preferred to hide on the leads—carelessly leaving the window open.

[11] Girouard, pp. 27, 28, 139, 142.

[12] Warwick R.O., Throckmorton MSS (CR 1998), Box 86, Folder 1, nos. 2, 11; cf Hodgetts, 'Coughton and the Gunpowder Plot', in Peter Marshall & Geoffrey Scott edd., *Catholic Gentry in English Society: The Throckmortons of Coughton from Reformation to Emancipation* (2009), pp. 93-121, on pp. 102-3. The servants may have been those at Weston Underwood. But a return of recusants of 14 March 1605/6 (*Worcs. Recusant* 18, p. 32) includes for Coughton: Humphrey Palmer, yeoman; Edward, his son, yeoman; Anthony Palmer, yeoman; Anne, his wife; Mary, wife of William Parsons, yeoman; and Margery Parsons, widow. This list of Thomas Throckmorton's servants includes a Thomas Palmer and a William Parsons.

[14.] Worcester R.O. (The Hive), Berington Collection 576(14) and 569(8). The second is printed in Aileen M. Hodgson & Michael Hodgetts, *Little Malvern Letters: I* (C.R.S. 83, 2011), no. 96.

[14] C.R.S. 53, pp. 182-3.

[15] Foley I, pp. 213-214; 'Index III', no. 320.

[16] *Troubles* III, p. 163; 'Index III', no. 393.

[17] 'Index I', nos. 17 (Barlborough), 109 (Benthall), 125 (Coldham); 'Index III', no. 313 (Woodham Mortimer); Granville Squiers, *Secret Hiding-Places* (1933), pp. 110-111 (Water Eaton).

[18] In William Matthews, *Charles II's Escape from Worcester* (1967), p. 120.

[19] SP 12/173/64; 'Index I', no. 76.

[20] Girouard, pp. 88-89.

[21] Now British Library Add. MSS 39828-38.

[22] Pevsner & Neave, *The Buildings of England: York and the East Riding* (1995), pp. 366-370. Cf 'Index III', no. 385.

[23] Malcolm Wanklyn ed., *Inventories of Worcestershire Landed Gentry, 1537-1786*, Worcs. Hist. Soc. N.S. 16 (1998), p. 61.

[24] Hodgetts, 'Lyford Grange, 1581-1681', *Midland Catholic History* 22 (2015), pp. 9-20.

[25] Girouard, pp. 102-104.

---

[26] At Thornley, also in County Durham, Richard Verstegan recorded a hide below ground which was big enough for six men but does not say how it was entered. Morris, *Troubles*, III, p. 114; cf Hodgetts, 'Elizabethan Priest-Holes: V', *Recusant History* 13 (1975-76), pp. 256-8.

[27] 'Index II', no. 253 (from John Dunkin, *History and Antiquities of the Hundreds of Bullingdon and Ploughley* (1823), II, p. 94n.).

[28] Index I', no. 31 (from Adam Hamilton ed., *The Chronicle of the English Augustinian Canonesses of [St Monica's at] Louvain*, I: 1548-1625 (1904), pp. 244-6).

[29] Richard Ollard, *The Escape of Charles II* (1966), pp. 63-66.

[30] For Ufton see the plans in Hodgetts 1989, pp. 24, 26, 28, or in *Recusant History* 12 (1973-74), pp. 107, 109, 111.

[31] Norfolk R.O., Frere MSS, K.11(a).

[32] J. Charles Cox, 'The Household Books of Sir Miles Stapleton, Bart', *The Ancestor* 2 (July 1902), pp. 17-39, esp. pp. 20-27.

[33] *Midsummer Night's Dream* III.1.49-51, 55-56.

[34] *Romeo & Juliet* I.5.5, 10-11.

[35] Girouard, pp. 88-94, 114-118, Plate VII (Sir Henry Unton's musicians in his great chamber).

[36] Gerard, *Autobiography*, p. 170.

[37] Ibid., 159-60. For 'great chamber' Caraman has 'dining-hall' the first time and 'great hall' the second. But if the searchers were 'up' in the room before Gerard and the others knew, it was on the first floor: a great hall was on the ground floor, and see above

[38] Girouard, pp. 94-100.

[39] Hodgetts, 'Elizabethan Priest-Holes: IV—Harvington', *Recusant History* 13 (1975-76), pp.18-55 esp. pp. 19-20, 26-29.

[40] *Narrative*, p. 153.

[41] SP 14/216/187, printed in Foley IV, pp. 223-4.

[42] British Library, MS Harleian 360, f. 101.

[43] Foley IV, p. 216; Francis Edwards ed., *The Gunpowder Plot: The Narrative of Oswald Tesimond alias Greenway* (Folio Society, 1973), p. 167.

[44] SP 12/238/62, printed in Foley I, pp. 379-382. For 'where his sons doth lie' Foley has 'where [h]is souse [? hose] dothe ley'. But 'souse' for 'sonse' is an easy misreading.

[45] Keith H. Mantell, *Haddon Hall* (English Life, Derby, 1968), p. 19.

[46] Morris, *Condition of Catholics* (n.9 above), p. xli (= SP 12/247/3); 'Index I', no. 42.

[47] *Hatfield Calendar* XVII, p. 626; 'Index I', no. 96.

[48] John Newman & Nikolaus Pevsner, *The Buildings of England: Shropshire* (2006), p. 173; *Compton Wynyates* [guidebook, c. 1960], p. 20: 'The ceiling of one aisle was painted with the sun and clouds to represent Day and that of the other with the moon and stars to represent Night; but in 1912 the plaster became dangerous and had to be removed, only a small piece of each, representing the sun and moon, being kept, and these have almost entirely lost their colour'. (Not mentioned in Pevsner & Wedgwood, *Warwickshire* (1966), pp. 242-3, or in V.C.H. *Warwks.*, V, pp. 66-67.)

[49] Information from the owner, Mr Anthony Vaughan, 2001.

[50] Godfrey Anstruther, *Vaux of Harrowden* (1953), p. 150.

[51] Ibid., p. 153.

[52] W. Sterry-Cooper, 'Badgecourt', *Worcs. Arch. Soc. Trans.*, N.S. 28 (1951), pp. 23-33, and Plates VII-VIII between pp. 28-29.

[53] Christine Collins, *St Benet's Church, Kemerton: A History, 1843-2006* (2006), pp. 4-11 with colour photographs.

[54] C.R.S. 83, pp. 45-46.

[55] Liverpool City Library, 920 NOR 1/395, in *Lancs. & Cheshire Hist. Soc. Trans.* 96-97 (1945-6); Hodgetts 1989, pp. 135-8, with plans. This Sir Thomas (cf n.7) was the Jesuit's brother.

[56] Foley III, pp. 427-8; 'Index I', no. 24.

[57] 'Index I', no. 115; S. E. Rigold, *Nunney Castle* (H.M.S.O., 1957), p. 14.

[58] Hodgetts, 'Recusant Liturgy, 1559-1791', pp. 2-3.

[59] Foley III, pp. 1-16 (a Jesuit report of 1616).

[60] Gerard, *Autobiography*, pp. 160-1.

[61] Ibid., p. 162.

[62] Gerard, *Autobiography*, pp. 151-2. 'Sir Clement Fisher and his company lately searched in Warwickshire at Mrs Heywood's alias Smith's for Greenway [Tesimond] or Gerard. A Gerard and a priest was in the chamber where they searched and so continued three days whilst the house was beset, yet escaped': William Udall to the Earl of Salisbury, 19 June 1696, in P. R Harris, 'The Reports of William Udall', *Recusant History* 8 (1965-66), p. 214. But 'Heywood' may be a mishearing for 'Hugford' or for 'Henwood', the Hugfords' house two miles east of Solihull and five miles south-west of Great Packington, where Sir Clement lived. Lucy Holte, a sister of Sir Thomas Holte of Aston, married John Hugford about 1596, and their sister Mary Holte married George Smith of Wootton Wawen. See Hodgetts, 'The Holtes of Aston', *Midland Catholic History* 9 (2002-3), pp. 13-16; *V.C.H.* IV, p. 216; Anstruther II, pp. 337-8.

[63] 'Index III', no. 217; Edwin H. Burton, *The Life and Times of Bishop Challoner* (1909), I, pp. 214-5.

[64] Foley II, p. 1108; Gerard, *Autobiography*, p. 32.

[65] Girouard, pp. 76, 106.

[66] Girouard, *Lyveden New Beild* (National Trust, 1990); Girouard, *Rushton Triangular Lodge* (English Heritage, 2004); 'Index II', no. 245; 'Index III', no. 348; and Alix Wilkinson in *The Garden* (journal of the Royal Horticultural Society), January 2000, with a plan on p. 28.

[67] *By What Authority?* (see n.22), pp. 365, 425-8 (Part III, Chaps. 4, 10).

[68] British Library, MS Harleian 360, f. 32v.

[69] C.R.S. 60, pp. 37-41.

[70] Girouard, *Rushton Triangular Lodge*, pp. 16, 25-26.

[71] *Midland Catholic History* 10 (2004), pp. 1-8.

[72] Squiers (n.18), pp. 228-230 ; Hodgetts 1989, pp. 210-212 and Plate 39.

[73] C.R.S. 5, p. 211, from SP 12/245/131.

[74] 'Index I', no. 169, from SP 12/200/31.

[75] 'Index II', no. 259, from *Acts of the Privy Council*, 22 September 1590.

[76] 'Index I', no. 49; Foley IV, pp. 462-70; cf Hannah Thomas, 'Missioners on the Margins: The Territorial Headquarters of the Welsh Jesuit College of St Francis Xavier at The Cwm, c.1600-1679', *Recusant History* 32 (2014-15), pp. 173-194.

[77] Girouard, Chap. IV ('The Elizabethan and Jacobean House') and Chap. V ('The Formal House, 1630-1720').

[78] In 1687 Bishop Leyburn confirmed 240 candidates at Nether Witton and 440 at Wootton Wawen. J. A. Hilton, A. J. Mitchinson, Barbara Murray & Peggy Wells edd., *Bishop Leyburn's Confirmation Register of 1687* (North-West Catholic History Society, 1997), pp. 68-72, 241-7.

[79] SP 14/28/122/i, in *Worcs. Recusant* 47 (June 1986), p. 31, nos. [21-22].

[80] Squiers (n.18), pp. 138, 140; 'Index I', no. 100 (Capheaton); 'Index II', no. 247 (Nether Witton); Hodgetts 1989, pp. 216, 218, 236.

[81] Donald G. Graham, 'The Affair of James Clifton, Vicar of Wootton Wawen [1676-1703]', *Worcs. Recusant* 24 (December 1974), pp. 2-17, on p. 4.

[82] Evelyn's *Diary*, 25 August 1678.

[83] J. Anthony Williams, 'The Distribution of Catholic Chaplaincies in the Early Eighteenth Century', *Recusant History* 12 (1973-74), pp. 42-48, on p. 43: '2 C[lergymen] & 2 M[onks]'.

[84] Geoffrey Scott in Peter Marshall & Geoffrey Scott edd., *Catholic Gentry in English Society: The Throckmortons of Coughton from Reformation to Emancipation* (2009), p. 175

[85] Hodgetts, 'The Throckmortons of Harvington, 1696-1923', *Recusant History* 26 (2002-03), pp. 143-168, esp. pp. 150-1.

[86] George Lipscomb, *History and Antiquities of the County of Buckingham*, IV (1847), pp. 403-4, 407; Warwick R.O., Throckmorton MSS (CR 1998), Box 66, Folder 8, no. 1 (Hearth Tax, 1685-9); Throckmorton MSS, Large Carved Box, no. 60 (inventory, 1748-9, including the chapel and vestry).

[87] Roderick O'Donnell, 'The Architectural Setting of Challoner's Episcopate', in Eamon Duffy ed., *Challoner and his Church: A Catholic Bishop in Georgian England* (1981), pp. 55-70, on p. 56; cf Scott in Marshall & Scott (n.95), pp. 205-7. The Elizabethan house (now known as Buckland Manor House) has been converted back into a dwelling, with what Marcus Binney has described as 'the character . . . of an 18th-century castellated folly' (*The Times*, 21 January 2005, 'Bricks and Mortar', p. 4).

[88] Foley III, pp. 1-16 (a Jesuit report of 1616).

[89] *John Gerard: The Autobiography of an Elizabethan* (tr. and ed. Philip Caraman, 1951, 1956; new impression, Family Publications, Oxford, 2006, with introduction by Michael Hodgetts), p. 40.

[90] John Morris ed., *Troubles of our Catholic Forefathers*: III (1877), p. 467.

[91] Catholic Record Society 5, p. 133 (SP 12/206/77), where 'Vveton' (= Ufton) is printed as 'Weton'. Cf Hodgetts, '*Mille Maeandris*: Nicholas Owen, 1606-2006', *Recusant History* 28 (2006-07), pp. 177-191 (on pp. 180-1).

[92] Gerard, *Autobiography*, pp. 41-43.

[93] Godfrey Anstruther, *The Seminary Priests, I—Elizabethan* (1968), p. 332; C.R.S. 5, p. 200; Richard Challoner, *Memoirs of Missionary Priests* (ed. J. H. Pollen, 1924), pp. 591-3, 595; Foley III, pp. 294-300.

[94] Gerard, *Autobiography*, pp. 37-39.

[95] Campion's itinerary in the North was first worked out by Richard Simpson in *Edmund Campion* (2/1896, pp. 263-6), mostly from British Library MS Lansdowne 30/78. See also Hodgetts, 'Campion in Staffordshire and Derbyshire, 1581', *Midland Catholic History* 7 (2000), pp. 52-54.

[96] Hodgetts, 'Henry Garnet's Pilgrimage to Holywell, 1605', *M.C.H.* 26 (2019), pp. 12-30.

[97] Foley II, pp. 286-9.

[98] Bell's 'Autograph': Latin and Spanish text in C.R.S. 1 (1905), pp. 117-122; English translation in Richard Manners, 'A Worcestershire Martyr: Arthur Bell', *Worcs. Recusant* 53 (July 1989), pp. 4-16.

[99] Anstruther II, pp. 256, 329.

[100] Michael E. Williams, *The Venerable English College, Rome, 1579-1979* (1979), pp. 7-8.

[101] C.R.S. 55, no. 765 (*Responsa* of Hugh Owen, 1636); Anstruther II, pp. 179, 228, 311.

[102] Anstruther II, pp. 109-110; C.R.S. 72 (*Lisbon College Register, 1628-1813*), pp. 52-53; Michael Greenslade, *Catholic Staffordshire, 1500-1850* (2006), pp. 153-4; cf p. 163.

[103] Printed in C.R.S. 53 (1961), pp. 193-214

[104] Challoner, *Memoirs of Missionary Priests* (see n.6), p. 587.

[105] Foley I, p. 499; Gerard, *Autobiography*, p. 240 (SP 14/20/47); cf C.R.S. 54, pp. 76, 78.

[106] Anstruther I, pp. 48, 94, 189, 338.

[107] Christopher Devlin, *Robert Southwell, Poet and Martyr* (1956), pp. 13-17, 27-28.

[108] SP 12/182/20, 18 September 1585.

[109] Foley IV, pp. 575-6 (SP 12/239/11).

[110] Anstruther I, p. 174.

[111] Granville Squiers, *Secret Hiding-Places* (1933), pp. 243-4; E. Meade Faulkner, *Moonfleet* (1898).

[112] Augustus Jessopp, *One Generation of a Norfolk House* (1879), pp. 134-6, 147-8.

[113] Devlin, *Southwell*, pp. 255-6; Morris, *Troubles*: I (1872), p. 190.

[114] SP 12/246/18.

[115] *Autobiography*, p. 45.

[116] Foley IV, pp. 213-216.

[117] Hodgetts, *Secret Hiding-Places* (1989), pp.129-132.

[118] *Hatfield Calendar* VII, p. 300, Anthony Atkinson to Sir Robert Cecil, 12 July 1597.

[119] Caraman, *Henry Garnet and the Gunpowder Plot* (1964), pp. 316-7, from SP 14/20/45; Foley V, pp. 621-2; cf Squiers, *Hiding-Places*, p. 88.

[120] *Hatfield Calendar* XVII, p. 626; Hugh Ross Williamson, (1951), p. 80, quoting *Hatfield Calendar* XVIII, p. 421.

[121] Gerard, *Autobiography*, pp. 148-9, 158-60.

[122] Thomas M. McCoog, 'The Establishment of the English Province of the Society of Jesus', *Recusant History* 17 (1984-85), p. 121-139, esp. pp. 135-7.

[123] Anstruther I, p. 174. He prints 'conveniences' but 'conveyance' was the usual Elizabethan word for a hide big enough for a man, as opposed to a 'secret corner' for vestments, plate or books. At Hindlip in 1606 'eleven secret corners and conveyances were found in the said house': British Library, MS Harleian 360, f. 101.

[124] SP 12/268/82 in Foley II, pp. 242-3: examination of John Stanley, 18 October 1598, in connexion with Squire's Plot; cf Anstruther I, pp. 153-4. The Stanleys lived at Eynsham; one of them was the celebrated beauty Venetia Stanley who married Sir Kenelm Digby (1603-66), son of the Gunpowder Plotter Sir Everard. In 1613 Sir Edward Stanley of Eynsham (and Tong Castle) and his daughters Frances, Petronella and Venetia were returned as recusants: C.R.S. 60, pp. 226, 232, 238, 240

[125] C.R.S. 75, p. 309.

[126] Anstruther I, pp. 86-87.

[127] Anstruther I, pp. 6-7.

[128] Morris, *Troubles*: I (1872), pp. 187-215.

[129] Foley III, p. 16.

[130] *Recusant History* 13 (1975-76), p. 262.

[131] SP 12/244/5: extracts in *Recusant History* 13 (1975-76), pp. 256-7.

[132] SP 12/271/71.

[133] Adam Hamilton, ed., *Chronicle of St Monica's at Louvain*: I (1904), pp. 244-6.

[134] Caraman, *Henry Morse: Priest of the Plague* (1957), pp. 32-33.

[135] 'The names of certaine persons noted in sondrie counties to be Receauors and entertayners of Jesuits and Seminaries': SP 12/168/33, f.77r.

[136] C.R.S. 2, p. 27. Since some of these counties do not adjoin each other, the list is incomplete.

[137] Anstruther I, pp. 349-350.

[138] Hodgetts, 'Campion in the Thames Valley, 1580', *Recusant History* 30 2010-2011), pp. 26-46; 'Lyford Grange, 1581-1681', M.C.H. 22 (2015), pp. 9-20; *Little Malvern Letters*: I (C.R.S. 83), pp. xv-xvi.

[139] SP 12/156/29, in J. D. Crichton, 'Rushock, the Russells and the Moores of Ripple', *Worcs. Recusant* 4 (December 1964), pp. 34-37.

[140] V.C.H. *Lancs.* III, p. 402, from SP 12/153/62.

[141] British Library, MS Harleian 360, ff. 32-33.

[142] SP 12/177/3, discussed in 'The Owens of Oxford', *Recusant History* 24 (1998-99), pp. 415-430, esp. pp. 418-9.

[143] SP 12/195/107.

[144] C.R.S. 83 (*Little Malvern Letters: I*), no. 66; Berington 562(46). See C. D. Gilbert, 'John Halsey, Recusant Physician', M.C.H. 2 (1994), pp. 4-7, and the index to C.R.S. 83.

[145] Foley IV, pp. 76-77 (SP 14/18/52).

[146] Foley IV, pp. 223-4 (SP 14/216/187).

[147] Foley IV, p. 223 (SP 14/216/183); cf M.C.H. 12 (2006), pp. 22-27.

[148] C.R.S. 69 (*St Omer's & Bruges, 1593-1773*), p. 122.

[149] Foley III, pp. 501-520; VII/2, p. 714.

[150] C. D. Gilbert, 'The Death of Samuel Smallman', M.C.H. 18 (2011), pp. 44-46.

[151] Boscobel may have been the Jesuit house described in 1622 as in Staffordshire and with accommodation for ten men. McCoog, *Recusant History* 17 (see n.39 above), pp. 136-7.

[152] In Richard Ollard, *The Escape of Charles II* (1966), pp. 26, 27, 34-35, 36, 47-48, 54. In his *Brief Account*, Fr Huddleston recorded that 'the necessaries they used not were secured in the Secret': William Matthews, *Charles II's Escape from Worcester* (1967), p. 104.

[153] C. D. Gilbert, 'Worcestershire and the Popish Plot—[I]', *Worcs. Recusant* 46 (December 1985), pp. 1-10, esp. pp. 1, 2; 'Worcestershire and the Popish Plot—II', *Worcs. Recusant* 48 (December 1986), pp. 31-34; Anstruther II, p. 17.

[154] Estcourt & Payne, p. 339.

[155] C.R.S. 39, p. 77 (Persons, 1580).

[156] *The English Romayne Life* (1590), in *Harleian Miscellany* VII, quoted in Christine Kelly, *Blessed Thomas Belson* (1987), p. 33.

[157] SP 12/175/75 in Foley II, p. 590.

[158] 'The Apostolicall Life of Ambrose Barlow', *Downside Review* 44 (1926), pp. 143-6.

[159] Morris, *Troubles*: III, pp. 467-8; C.R.S. 9, p. 114.

[160] [John Kirk], 'Catholic Chapels in Staffordshire', *The Catholic Magazine and Review*, 5 (1834), p. 307, repr. with original pagination in *Staffs. Catholic History* 14 (1974).

[161] SP 12/229/78, printed in M.C.H. 15 (2008), pp. 1-6; cf SP 12/238/62; Anstruther I, p. 324.

[162] SP 14/28/122/i. See also the report of Bishop Robert Bennet of Hereford to the Earl of Salisbury, 22 June 1605 (SP 14/14/52-53, printed in C.R.S. 2 (1906), pp. 289-297).

[163] Foley I, p. 138, from SP 16/99/19.

[164] Gerard, *Autobiography*, p. 15.

[165] Anstruther I, p. 37 (Bishop); II, p. 252 (Powell); II, p. 262 (Read); III, pp. 19-20 (Booth).

[166] Suzanne Gossett, 'English Plays in the English College Archives', *The Venerabile* 28/1 (1983), pp. 23-33.

[167] Maurice Whitehead, *Piety and Patronage: The Venerable English College, Rome, the Earls of Worcester and Links with Wales, 1578-1679* (First Schwarzenbach Lecture, 25 May 2014, English College, Rome, 2016), pp. 24-29.

[168] Philip Caraman ed., *William Weston: The Autobiography of an Elizabethan* (1955), pp. 65-66, 68.

[169] Challoner, *Memoirs of Missionary Priests* (ed. Pollen, 1924) pp. 308-9

[170] This article is based on a talk given, with local variations, to the Oxford Newman Society in 2002; to the English Catholic History Association at Downside Abbey in 2004; to the Winchester Catholic History Group in the Milner Hall in 2006; and at Harvington in 2003, 2014 and 2022. I am grateful to Mr Vincent Burke for help with some of the references.

[171] C.R.S. 5, p.350

Index of People and Places

The book text is available as a fully searchable ebook: please email thepriestholesite@gmail.com

236, 245
Millington Heref, 79
Minster Lovell Oxon, 228
Mitcham Surrey, 80
Mompesson Mr Laurence, 31, 146, 165, 237
Monk Hesledon Co. Durham, 126
Monmouth Duke of, 224
Monmouthshire, 269
Montacute House Som, 115, 220, 250
Montague see also Browne family, 6, 17, 35, 111, 114, 263, 265, 266
Moor Close Moseley Staffs, 210
Mordaunt Lord, 155, 171, 172
More Thomas, v, 80, 111
More, Henry (Jesuit Historian), 123, 126, 186
Morgan Elizabeth Lady Jones, 196
Morgan Henry, 177
Morley Derbys, 82
Morris priest alias Jones, 196
Morris William alias Hartwell, 25
Morse Henry, 197, 198, 275, 297
Moseley Old Hall Staffs, vii, 205, 207, 210, 215, 216, 222, 235, 238, 242, 245, 246, 248, 249, 252, 253, 254, 266, 297
Mostyn Thomas, 33
Moulsoe family (Lady Mary (Digby), William), 161
Mounteagle Lord, 68, 170, 174, 175, 295
Mountjoy Lord, 60
Mrs Whitgreave, 213
Mulgrave Castle Yorks, 129
Munday Anthony, 7, 76, 267, 295
Mundesley Norfolk, 39, 68
Muscote alias of G. Fisher, 189, 297
Mush John, 15, 100, 120, 123
Naburn Yorks, 227, 297
Nanfan, Elizabeth, née Southwell, 79
Nanfan, Giles, 79
Napper family (George, William), 188, 270
Nash Treadway Russell, 229
Nash, John, 113
Nash, Treadway Russell, 181
Naworth Castle Cumberland, vii, 192
Neile Richard Bishop of Durham, 198
Nelson John, 127, 296
Nevill Holt Leics, 156, 158, 161, 163, 215, 233, 237, 242, 296
Nevill, Sir Henry: wife Ursula née Clopton, 156
Neville Sir Henry, 25

Newbuildings Place Sussex, 113, 295
Newcastle-upon-Tyne, 123
Newell William, 11, 15, 54, 55, 56, 57, 69, 79, 82, 293, 295
Newgate prison London, 104, 189
Newmarket Suffolk, 205
Newport Pagnell Bucks, 161
Nichols John, 157
Norbrook Warwicks, 171, 172, 173, 174, 175, 296
Norfolk, vii, 18, 31, 39, 40, 46, 47, 48, 68, 223, 249, 272, 275, 294
Norfolk Dukes of, 223, 258
Norris family, Rycote, Oxon: Sir Henry, 82; Sir Thomas, 82
Norris family, Speke: Edward, 147, 148; Elizabeth, 146; Sir Richard, 148
North Riding of Yorks, 127, 132
Northampton, 167, 173, 177, 265
Northampton Earl of, 192
Northampton, Marquesses of, (Comptons), 27
Northamptonshire, iv, ix, 2, 5, 43, 111, 151, 152, 153, 154, 158, 162, 163, 172, 236, 238, 250, 252, 256, 263
Northend Essex, 54, 60, 252
Northern District, 150
Northumberland, 123, 144, 197, 223, 258, 298
Northumberland, Earl of, 169
Norton Mrs Ellen, 212
Norwich, 39, 47, 48
Norwich Bishop of, 48
Norwich Cathedral, 40
Nottingham, 18, 35
Nottingham Grammar School, 35
Nottinghamshire, 6, 226
O'Brien, Lady Penelope, 156
Oates Titus, ix, 14, 196, 209, 223, 228, 239, 258, 263, 267
Oatlands Surrey, 229
Ogleforth York, 119
Oldcastle Sir John, 7, 79, 293
Oldcorne, Edward, 266; and Garnet, 69, 76; and Tesimond, 70, 175; arrest, 182; at Hindlip, 68; examination after arrest, 76, 179, 251; execution, 187; first Hindlip search, 14; landing in Norfolk with Gerard, 39; new centres in Welsh Marches, 70; search at Baddesley, 61; stations priests in Worcs, 69; travels in Europe, 261

Pollard James alias Sharpe, 135, 259, 293, 295, 296
Poole Dorset, 217
Pope, Alexander, 229
Pope, John (butler), 216
Popes the, 170, 187; Clement VIII, 100; Paul V, 167
Popham Sir John Attorney-General, 10
Pounde Thomas, 5, 7, 168
Powderham Castle Devon, 228
Powell Thomas, 196, 269, 270, 276
Powtrell family, 239
Pracid Fr, 122
Prague, 234
Prattinton Peter, 180, 181, 184, 230
Preston Lancs, 144, 146
Priory Farm Shoby Leics, 158
Puckering Sir John Lord Keeper, 36
Pugh Robert, 35
Pulborough Sussex, 112
Purshall Hall Worcs, 204
Racton Sussex, 221, 222, 297
Radcliffe Anne, 229, 298
Raglan Castle Mon, 195, 196, 246, 297
Rationes Decem, 25
Reading, 18, 19, 20, 189
Reading Abbey, 19, 20
Red Hall Bourne Lincs, 160, 161, 215, 237
Redhead Robert, 122
Reigate Surrey, 118
Rheims France, iv, 4, 5, 39, 43, 44, 103, 110, 123, 128, 158, 165, 248, 260, 263, 264, 268
Rich Lord, 60
Rich, Lady Penelope, 54, 60
Richard III King, 228
Richardson James, 239
Richelieu Cardinal, 188
Richmondshire, 123, 297
Ripley Castle Yorks, 12, 71, 130, 132, 238, 240, 296
Ripple Worcs, 80, 265, 276
Rivers Sir George, 105
Rivers, alias of Anthony Hoskins, 163
Rivers, alias of Anthony Whitehair, 115
Robinson John, 198
Roffey Sussex, 17, 114
Rookwood family: Ambrose, 77, 172, 175, 176; Edward, 48; Robert, 49
Rookwood, alias of Thomas Garnet, 49
Roscarrock Col. Edward, 206
Rothwell Market House, 5

Roughey see Roffey, 114, 296
Rowington Warwicks, 63, 168
Rowse alias of R. Broughton, 69, 262
Rufford Old Hall Lancs, 146
Rugby Warwicks, 174
Rushton Hall Northants, 154
Rushton Triangular Lodge, 5, 256, 273
Russell Henry, 49, 78, 82, 100, 265, 266, 294
Russell John, 78, 79
Russell, priest, 79
Rutland family (4th,5th, 6th Earls, Countess, Francis, Grace, Lady Fortescue, Sir Oliver), 162
Sacheverell family: Abigail, 82; Henry, 82
Sackville family, 112
Sackville, Thomas, Lord Buckhurst, 109; d-in law Margaret, 109
Saffron Walden Essex, 49
Sager Edward, 145
Saint-Germain France, 224
Salden Bucks, 162, 163, 177, 189, 233, 237, 255, 293
Salisbury John, 195, 196
Salisbury Wilts, 219, 220, 221, 239, 242, 247, 257, 261, 266, 271, 273, 276
Salisbury, Earl of, 177, 178, 179, 187, 188
Salisbury, Earl of, 46, 172
Saltburn Yorks, 226, 298
Salvin Anthony, 193
Samlesbury Hall Lancs, 145, 257, 270
Sandhill Newcastle-upon-Tyne, 198
Sandringham Norfolk, 47
Sardinian Embassy chapel London, 224
Sawston Hall Cambs, 58, 60, 99, 131, 177, 181, 183, 186, 234, 235, 238, 242, 251, 294
Scarborough Yorks, 226, 297
Scotland: Highlands, 225; Western Isles, 225
Scotney Old Castle Kent, iv, vii, ix, 14, 103, 104, 106, 109, 110, 118, 142, 144, 157, 165, 179, 181, 186, 236, 242, 247, 263, 264, 293, 295
Scott Sir Walter, 230
Sebright William, 82
Seely Robert, 25
Selkirkshire, 230
Sevenoaks Kent, 109
Seville Spain, 187, 260, 263
Shambles The York, 120, 130
Sharpe alias of J. Pollard, 135, 259, 296
Sheffield Lord, 129, 198

Sources

Almost all the secondary and many of the primary sources have been digitised and can be read free of charge online. I recommend the Internet Archive search on http://www.archive.org/. Searching for the book title, e.g., "The Condition of Catholics under James I" will bring up the book.

The architectural information on the houses included in this book is from seven main sources: Pevsner's *Buildings of England*; *Country Life*; the reports of the Royal Commission on Historical Monuments (RCHM); the Victoria County Histories (VCH); guidebooks to houses which are open to the public; the folio county histories of the eighteenth and nineteenth centuries; and articles in the transactions of local archaeological societies. References are normally given only to the last two of these, the others being easily traceable. For the historical information the following abbreviations are used.

Anstruther	Godfrey Anstruther, OP, *The Seminary Priests*: I, Elizabethan (1968); II, Early Stuarts (1975)
CRS	Catholic Record Society
Devlin	Christopher Devlin, *The Life of Robert Southwell, Poet and Martyr* (1956)
Foley	Henry Foley, SJ, *Records of the English Province of the Society of Jesus*: I-VII (2) (1875-1884)
Garnet	Philip Caraman, SJ, *Henry Garnet (1555-1606) and the Gunpowder Plot* (1964)
Gerard	*John Gerard: The Autobiography of an Elizabethan*, tr. Philip Caraman (second ed. 1956, repr. 2006)
Hodgetts I – VI	Michael Hodgetts, 'Elizabethan Priest-Holes: I-VI', *Recusant History* 11 (1971-2), pp. 279-298; 12 (1973-4), pp. 99-119, 171-197; 13 (1975-6), pp. 18-55, 254-279; 14 (1977-8), pp. 97-126
Hodgetts Index I – III	Michael Hodgetts, 'A Topographical Index of Hiding-Places' I-III, *Recusant History* 16 (1982-3), pp. 146-216; 24 (1998) pp. 1-54; 27 (2005), pp.473-520
Narrative	John Gerard, *A Narrative of the Gunpowder Plot*, ed. John Morris (1872) under the title of *The Condition of Catholics under James I*
SP	State Papers Domestic: /12 (Elizabeth I); /13 (Elizabeth I Additional); /14 (James I)
Squiers	Granville Squiers, *Secret Hiding-Places* (1933, repr. 1934)
Troubles	John Morris ed., *Troubles of our Catholic Forefathers* I-III (1872-1877)
Vaux	Godfrey Anstruther, OP, *Vaux of Harrowden* (1953)
Weston	*William Weston: The Autobiography of an Elizabethan*, tr. Philip Caraman (1955)

Chapter 1: Harleyford, 1586

1. Introduction (pp. 1-5). Notes and Queries, First Series 11 (1855), p. 437. Sir John Oldcastle: Chronicle of Thomas Walsingham (Rolls Series) II, p. 307.
2. Harleyford (pp. 5-12). Weston, pp. 69-79; Devlin, pp. 113-117; Gamet, pp. 32-37; Hodgetts I, pp. 279-283; Hodgetts II, p. 99; CRS 53, p. 209 (Sledd's description of Persons).
3. The building of priest-holes (pp. 12-17). Hodgetts I, pp. 281-3; SP 12/151/10 (Worsley and Newell); SP 12/163/55 (Somerville Plot); Devlin, pp. 131-5 (Arundel House); George Eliot, A True Report of the Taking of Edmund Campion (1581), printed in A.F. Pollard, Tudor Tracts (1903), pp. 451-474; Devlin, pp. 123-6 (Hackney); Vaux, pp. 169-171 (Hackney); Gerard, pp. 195-6 (Harrowden Massing stuff), 162 (Salden), 160-1 (new block at Harrowden); Foley VII (1), pp. xvi-xvii (1616 report); Gerard, p. 206 (Maundy Thursday 1606). For the loca secretiora which had become known by mid-1581, see Recusant History 19 (1989 pp386-395).
4. Searches (pp. 17-20). Narrative, pp. 36-37; Gerard, pp. 41-43 (Baddesley Clinton), 58-63 (Braddocks); Narrative, pp. 150-155 (Hindlip, and cf chapter 9 below); Cobbett, State Trials VIII (1810), col. 534 (West Hallam, 1681); SP 12/229/78 (Buckland); Troubles III, p. 163 (stones down chimneys), pp. 114-115 (Thornley); Troubles I, p. 213 (Scotney); Foley IV, p. 216 (Hindlip); Troubles III, pp. 114-115 (searchers' tricks), 401 (Margaret Clitherow); Adam Hamilton ed., The Chronicle of St Monica's in Louvain (1904) II, pp. 165-6 (Frances Burroughs); Corrie ten Boom, The Hiding-Place (1972), pp. 83-85; Foley III, p. 754 ('gone away').

Chapter 2: Garnet and Southwell, 1586-1588

Introduction (pp. 21-22). Devlin, pp. 10-16, 117-119, 127-129; *Vaux*, pp. 149-153, 163-4, 179-181; *Garnet*, pp. 38-49.

1. Ufton and Mapledurham (pp. 23-33). Hodgetts II, pp. 99-115.
2. Stonor (pp. 33-35). Hodgetts Index, no. 107 (pp. 182-3); R. J. Stonor, OSB, *Stonor* (1951), pp. 243-260, 265-270, 367-8 and pedigree between pp. 240-1; Anstruther I, pp. 309-310; CRS 18, p. 251; CRS 57, pp. 121-2, 125.
3. Compton Wynyates and Coughton (pp. 35-40). Hodgetts II, pp. 116-117; Hodgetts Index, nos. 10, 136, 138-9 (pp. 152, 193-6); *Vaux*, p. 121; *Weston*, p. 77; CRS 4, p. 70; *Garnet*, pp. 33, 64; Devlin, pp. 18-21, 58, 114, 340; Foley IV, pp. 288-330 (Southwell's panegyric on Edward Throckmorton); *Acts of the Privy Council* 24 (1592-3), p. 148 (the search at Coughton, which is, however, misprinted as 'Laughton'); Hodgetts, 'Park Hall, Castle Bromwich', *Worcestershire Recusant* 40 (December 1982), pp. 40-41.
4. Little Orme (pp. 40-41). Douglas B. Hague, 'Printed in Wales', *The Countryman*, Winter 1962, pp. 805-810; *Garnet*, pp. 100, 247, 298; Anstruther I, p. 31; Hodgetts Index, nos. 168-9 (pp. 204-5); Penry Williams, *The Council in the Marches of Wales under Elizabeth I* (1958), pp. 87, 97, 240; David Rogers, 'Popishe Thackwell and Early Catholic Printing in Wales', *Biographical Studies (Recusant History)* 2 (1953-4), p. 37; Foley IV, pp. 497-516; Foley VII, p. 50.
5. Padley (pp. 41-44). *Garnet*, pp. 1-3, 15, 72-73, 175-7; Bede Camm, OSB, *Forgotten Shrines* (1910, 1936), pp. 1-74; Cuthbert Fitzherbert, *Padley* (1933, 1968); James Fidler Hargreaves, *Padley and its Martyrs* (1946); Hodgetts Index no. 20 (pp. 155-6); *Martyrs of England and Wales: A Chronological List* (Catholic Truth Society H.163, 1960); P. R. Harris, 'William Fleetwood, Recorder of the City, and Elizabethan Catholicism', *Recusant History* 7 (1963-4), pp. 106-122.

Chapter 3: John Gerard in East Anglia, 1588-1594

1. Grimston and Oxburgh (pp. 45-48). *Gerard*, pp. 9-23; *Narrative*, pp. 278-282; Augustus Jessopp, *One Generation of a Norfolk House* (1879), pp. 130-153; Hodgetts III, pp. 171-2; Squiers, pp. 178-181; Foley V, p. 565n, quoting the *Orthodox Journal* of February 1833, the first published description of the hide at Oxburgh. English Heritage report on Oxburgh: https://historicengland.org.uk/research/results/reports/22-2006 plus private communications between PH and Adam Menuge. For descriptions of Gerard, see Jessopp, pp. 145, 221, and *Gerard*, p. 286.
2. Nicholas Owen (pp. 48-51). *Narrative*, pp. 182-6; Anstruther I, pp. 263-4; *Garnet*, pp. 98-99; *Vaux*, p. 252; *Weston*, pp. 72, 252; P.R. Reid, *Colditz* (1962), pp. 564-580, with John Watton's drawing of the interior of the glider hide, p. 578; Squiers, p. 26.
3. Hides in East Anglia (pp. 51-59). Hodgetts III, pp. 172-4; Squiers, pp. 181-3, 206-208, 210-213; Jessopp, *One Generation*, pp. 138-144; *Gerard*, pp. 18-36, 220-227. Anmer: Jessopp, p. 111, quoting Bartoli, *Inghilterra* (1676), p. 413. Breccles: *Country Life* 26 (1909), p. 677; George Crabbe, 'Robert de Grey, Recusant', *Norfolk Archaeology* 9 (1880-1884), p. 283. Coldham: *Narrative*, pp. 85-86. Hengrave: CRS 22, p. 120; Foley II, pp. 277-285. Lawshall: Anstruther I, pp. 147-8. Melford: Hodgetts Index, no. 126 (pp. 189-190); Stevenson and Salter, *The Early History of St John's College*, Oxford Hist. Soc. N.S. 1, passim; Aileen Hodgson, 'A History of Little Malvern Court: II', *Worcestershire Recusant* 39 (June 1982), pp. 2-31, for Henry Russell. Sawston: T. F. Teversham, *History of Sawston* II (1947); Hodgetts, 'A House with Three Priest-Holes', *Country Life* 131 (1962), p. 662. Gerard (p. 33) says that Henry Huddleston was reconciled before he married Dorothy Dormer. The settlement for this marriage was drawn up on 29 May 1592. Snore: CRS 22 (1921), p. 61; CRS 53 (1961), p. 113.
4. Search at Braddocks (pp. 59-64). *Gerard*, pp. 51-115; *Narrative*, xi-xiv, ccliv (=SP 12/243/95 and /244/7); Squiers, *Broadoaks: The Story of an Essex Manor- House* (1933).

Chapter 4: Baddesley Clinton, 1591: Warks and Worcs

1. Search at Baddesley Clinton (pp. 65-70). Hodgetts III, pp. 174-184; *Garnet*, pp. 128-135; *Vaux*, pp. 183-192; Squiers, pp. 28-34; SP 12/229/78 (George Snape on Buckland and the house in Warwickshire); Anstruther I, p. 324; Hodgetts Index, nos. 2, 4; Bodleian Library MS Top. Warw. C.2, ff. 18-23 (survey of Ladbrook Park); Thomas Throckmorton's private Act of Parliament, 1603 (1 Jae. I, no. 60). I owe the last two references to Mr John Tobias.

2. Oldcorne and Hindlip (pp. 70-75). Devlin, pp. 274-290; *Narrative*, pp. 282-5; *Gerard*, pp. 44-48; Hodgetts ill, pp.184-195; Squiers, pp. 34-36; CRS 53 (1961), pp. 127-9 (Bishop Bilson, 1596); Hugh Ross Williamson, *The Gunpowder Plot* (1951), pp. 138-9 (Tesimond).

3. Warwickshire and Worcestershire (pp. 75-81). Squiers, pp. 38-41, 64-72; SP 12/151/10 (Worsley and Newell); *Worcestershire Recusant* 1 Oune 1963), pp. 20-23 (John Felton's examination). Abbots Salford: British Library MS Lansdowne 153, f. 129 (recusancy of Eleanor Alderford and Charles Stanford); Eanswith Edwards, OSB, *Wares. Recusant* 27 (June 1976), pp. 2-18; Anthony Munday, *Brief Discourse of the Taking of Edmund Campion*, quoted in A.F. Pollard, *Tudor Tracts* (1903), pp. 462-3 (similar hide at Lyford). Birtsmorton: Devlin, p. 7; CRS 57 (1965), p. 191; St Helen's RO, Worcester, MS Lechmere 899/169/B.8; VCH Worcs. IV, pp. 29-33.
Buckenhill: SP 12/151/10; CRS 18 (1916), p. 138; SP 14/28/122/i.
Cleeve Prior: John Humphreys, *Studies in Worcestershire History* (1938), pp. 167-8; H. H. Spink, *The Gunpowder Plot and Lord Mounteagle's Letter* (1902), p. 303; Ross Williamson, *Gunpowder Plot*, p. 151. ; current situation private correspondence between PH and Cleeve Prior Historical Society
Elmley Castle: V.C.H. Worcs. III, p. 340; James Lees-Milne, *Shell Guide to Worcestershire* (1964), p. 36.
Grafton Manor: V.C.H. Worcs. III, pp.123-7; Humphreys, *Studies in Worcs. History*, pp. 87-114, 174-187; Humphreys, Birmingham Arch. Soc. Trans. 44 (1918), pp. 1-125; *Worcs. Recusant* 8 (December 1966), pp. 15-32.
Harborough: C.R.S. 53, p. 129; C.R.S. 57, p. 195.
Huddington: Hodgetts Index, no. 149; Ross Williamson, *Gunpowder Plot*, p. 178 (description of Hart).
Little Malvern: Aileen Hodgson, 'History of Little Malvern, I-III', *Worcs. Recusant* 38, pp. 4-18; 39, pp. 2-31; 40, pp. 25-36 (December 1981-December 1982); S.P. 12/195/107 (Lumley, Compton and Halsey).
Woollas Hall: Philip Panter, *Worcs. Recusant* 6 (December 1965), pp. 1-6.

Chapter 5: Harvington Hall

Hodgetts IV, pp. 18-55; Lionel and Veronica Anderton Webster, 'The Pakingtons of Harvington', *Recusant History* 12 (1973-4), pp. 203-215; Hodgson, 'History of Little Malvern, II-ill', *Worcs. Recusant* 39, 40, as above for Little Malvern; Hodgetts, 'Seventeenth-Century Priests at Harvington', *Worcs. Recusant* 35 (June 1980), pp. 8-11; Hodgetts, 'Harvington Hall, 1929-1979: A Study in Local Historiography', *Worcs. Recusant* 37 (June 1981), pp. 3-25. Squiers, pp. 73-80; Bede Camm, OSB, *Forgotten Shrines* (1910, 1936), pp. 253-274. Henry Sacheverell: British Library, MS Lansdowne 30, no. 78; SP 12/151/14, quoted in Foley V, p. 470, Squiers, p. 87, and *Vaux*, pp. 253-5; Anstruther I, p. 152; CRS 53 (1961), p. 187. Hodgetts *Life at Harvington* 1250-2000 pub. 2002
Inventories of 1797 and 1826: *Worcs. Recusant* 38 (December 1981), pp. 19-30, and 45 (June 1985), pp. 16-31.
Chapel inventory of 1696-7: *Worcs. Arch. Soc. Trans.* N.S. 39 (1961), pp. 11-12. Inventory of 1714: Birmingham Archdiocesan Archives C.260.

Chapter 6: Scotney Castle, 1598: The South-East

1. Scotney (pp. 100-106). Devlin, pp. 255-6; *Troubles* I, pp. 187-215; Christopher Hussey, *A History of Scotney Castle* (1955, 1963); Squiers, pp. 261-8.

2. Hides in the south-east (pp. 106-115). Squiers, pp. 251-260, 269-275; Devlin, pp. 10-14, 127-9; 214-219; Hodgetts Index, nos. 46, Mapledurham (Hants); 47, Winchester; 131, Sutton Place; 132, Cowdray (add VCH Sussex IV, p. 76); 134, Michelham.
Ashington and Wappingthorn: CSPD 1591-4, p. 510. (Index no. 85 is an error.) Battle: A.C. Southern ed., *An Elizabethan Recusant House* (1954).
Benton's Place, Newbuildings Place and West Grinstead: Foley III, p. 538n; Timothy J. McCann, 'West Grinstead: A Centre of Catholicism in Sussex, 1671-1814', Sussex Archaeological Collections 124 (1986), pp 193-212; VCH
Sussex VI, pt 2, pp 91, 102-4, 116-117; British Library Add. MS 5686, f.74; West Sussex RO Ep.1/37/1, no. 10. (I owe this last reference to Mr McCann.) Hellingly: cf Culworth (Northants), Hodgetts Index, no. 95; VCH Sussex II, p. 25. Ightham: SP 121182/26 and 34, in C. E. Woodruff, *Archaeologia Cantiana* 24 (1900), pp. 197-9;

Anstruther I, p. 206; CRS 22 (1921), p. 120.

Knole: Devlin, pp. 198, 215, 231-2, 246, 257; *Troubles* I, p. 197. Parham: VCH Sussex II, pp. 25-26.

Roughey: Devlin, pp. 230-2; SP 121193/25; Anstruther I, pp. 320-1. Warblington: Camm, *Forgotten Shrines*, pp. 75-90; Devlin, pp. 13-17, 27-28; Anstruther I, p. 21.

Chapter 7: Grosmont Priory, 1599: The North

Hodgetts V, pp. 254-279 (Birchley, Duckworth, Thornley, Hardwick, Whitby, Grosmont, Towneley, Samlesbury, Rufford, Speke).

Hodgetts Index, nos. 27 (John Nelson = *Gamet*, p. 168); 28, Esh; 31, Sledwich; 33, Waterhouses; 63, Thurnham; 162-4, York.

Squiers, pp. 115-161; Winifred Haward, *Secret Rooms of Yorkshire* (1956) and *Secret Rooms of North-West England* (1964); *Gerard*, pp. 32-33, 37n.

Anstruther I, pp. 29-30 (Thomas Bell), 326-8 (Christopher Southworth); *Troubles* III, p. 467 (James Pollard alias Sharpe).

Ripley Castle: Sir Tho Ingilby, *A Personal History of Family Life from 1300* (*Guidebook to Castle and Village*) York Castle: *Troubles* III, p. 163 (account by Holtby); J. C. H. Aveling, *Catholic Recusancy in the City of York* (CRS Monograph 2, 1970), pp. 61-65, 102, 104, 114.

Chapter 8: John Gerard in Northants and London, 1597-1605

Gerard, pp. 116-196 (chaps. 16-22); *Vaux*, pp. 217-259 (Part 2, chaps. 5-6); Squiers, pp. 54-63, 89-90.

Hodgetts Index, nos. 70, Nevill Holt; 71, Shoby; 72, the Mompessons'; 74, the Clink; 75, Finsbury Fields; 79, Lincoln's Inn Fields; 80, the Marshalsea; 83, St Clement's Lane; 86, Anne Line's; 87, the Heywoods'; 88, Anne Line's; 96, Drayton; 97, Harrowden; 98, Irthlingborough; 99, Kirby Hall.

Ashby St Ledgers: *Narrative*, p. 55.

Gayhurst: VCH Bucks. IV, p. 346; George Lipscomb, *History and Antiquities of the County of Buckingham* IV (1847), p. 158. The time within which Lady Digby was reconciled is given by *Gerard*, pp. 165, 167.

Husbands Bosworth: VCH Leics. II, pp. 62-63.

Irnham: *Vaux*, pp. 256,388; CRS 55, no. 691; T. B. Trappes-Lomax, 'The Owners of Irnham Hall', *Lines. Architectural and Archaeological Society Trans.* N.S. 9, Part 2 (1962), pp. 164-177.

Nevill Holt: VCH Leics. II, p. 63; Bernard Elliott, 'The Nevills of Nevill Holt: I, *Recusant History* 17 (1984-5), pp. 173-180.

White Webbs: *Vaux*, pp. 255, 257, 281-2; *Garnet*, pp. 264, 317; Hugh Ross Williamson, *The Gunpowder Plot* (1951), pp. 143-5.

Sugar, Grissold and Pound: *Vaux*, p. 263; Ross Williamson, pp. 115-116; J. H. Pollen ed., *Acts of English Martyrs, 1578-1642* (1891), pp. 321-2.

Chapter 9: The Gunpowder Plot, 1605-6

1. The summer of 1605 (pp. 159-165). *Garnet*, pp. 318-329 (chap. 34); Ross Williamson, *Gunpowder Plot*, pp. 124-165; *Narrative*, pp. 49-94 (chaps. 3-6); *Vaux*, pp. 260-278, 287-290.

   Erith, Thames Street and Fremland: *Garnet*, pp. 319-320; Ross Williamson, pp. 131-4; *Vaux*, pp. 275-6.

   Norbrook, Clopton and Bushwood: Ross Williamson, pp. 128-9, 141-3; *Narrative*, pp. 86-87; SP 12/163155 (search of Norbrook after the Somerville Plot); VCH Warwks. III, p. 92 (search of Norbrook after the Gunpowder Plot); illustration of Norbrook in Burgess, *Historic Warwickshire* (1876), p. 259; certificate of Warwickshire recusants, SP 12/243/76, ed. Hodgetts, *Wares. Recusant* 5-6 June-December 1965); Hodgetts Index, no. 137; Squiers, p. 39 (Clopton).

   Royal progress through Northants: *Vaux*, pp. 289-290.

   Holywell pilgrimage: *Garnet*, pp. 324-5; Ross Williamson, pp. 143-6; *Vaux*, pp. 286-7; Hodgetts, 'Shropshire Priests in 1605', *Wares. Recusant* 47 June 1986), pp. 24-36, incl. transcripts of SP 14/216/ii/21 and 153.

   Sir Everard Digby: Ross Williamson, pp. 148, 161-2; *Narrative*, pp. 87-90, 137-8; *Vaux*, p. 280; *Wares. Recusant* (as above) 47, p. 28.

2. November-December 1605 (pp. 165-169). Ross Williamson, pp. 162-5, 173-182; *Vaux*, pp.

290-310; Hodgetts Index, no. 149 (Huddington). Search at Harrowden: *Gerard*, pp. 197-9; *Narrative*, pp. 138-141; *Vaux*, pp. 311-322. Dr Taylor's in London: Hodgetts Index, no. 89.

3. Search at Hindlip, January 1606 (pp. 170-177). Hodgetts III, pp. 184-192; *Narrative*, pp. 148-160 (chap. 10); *Gerard*, p. 200; *Garnet*, pp. 330-341 (chap. 35); *Vaux*, pp. 333-340; Squiers, pp. 34-36. Oldcorne later stated that he had sent for Garnet to come from Coughton to Hindlip 'about St Barbara day' (4 December): Foley IV, p. 225.

4. London, February-March 1606 (pp. 177-179). *Garnet*, pp. 342-440 (chaps. 36-45); Ross Williamson, pp. 208-243; *Narrative*, pp. 185-9 (Owen's death); *Vaux*, pp. 340-351 (secret correspondence between Garnet and Anne Vaux); Foley IV, pp. 259-260 (Owen's examinations); Hodgetts Index, nos. 89-90 (Thomas Everett).

Chapter 10: *Gunpowder Plot to Civil War, 1606-1648*

1. Hides under James I and Charles I (pp. 180-191). Hodgetts Index, nos. 25, Lulworth (Squiers, p. 241); 49, The Cwm; 73, Clerkenwell; 81, Nevill's Alley;
105, Holywell, Oxford (Squiers, p. 110); 108, Wroxton (Squiers, pp. 111-112);
127, Cheam; 173, Raglan Castle; 176, Treowen.
T. M. McCoog, 'The Establishment of the English Province of the Society of Jesus', *Recusant History* 17 (1984-5), pp. 121-139, esp. pp. 136-7. Anstruther II, pp. 102-109 (Fisher alias Muscote); Foley II, p. 641 (Hudd); Anstruther I, p. 192; Foley III, p. 121 (William Johnson); Foley IV, pp. 647-652 (Sweet).
Blainscow: Squiers, p. 159; Foley II, p. 82.
Carlton: Squiers, pp. 116-118; John Martin Robinson, 'The Priests' Hiding-Hole at Carlton Towers' (leaflet obtainable at the house, 8 pp., n.d.). On John Edisford (Squiers, p. 118) see Foley V, pp. 682-4.
Hunsdon House, Blackfriars: Foley I, pp. 76-97.
Kirby Knowle and Upsall: Squiers, pp. 127,131; William Grainge, *The Vale of Mowbray* (1859), pp. 234-248, 275-6; Anstruther I, pp. 242, 289; Aveling,
Northern Catholics (1966), pp. 161, 168, 238, 247. In 1593 Thomas Clarke admitted saying Mass 'once or twice at the Lady Constable's, wife to Sir Henry Constable, at Upsall in Richmondshire' (SP 12/244/5).
Naworth: Squiers, pp. 142-3; Howard S. Reinmuth Jr, 'Lord William Howard and his Catholic Associations', *Recusant History* 12 (1973-4), pp. 226-234. St Anthony's: Philip Cararnan, SJ, *Henry Morse: Priest of the Plague* (1957),
pp. 32-52.
Yaxley: Squiers, p. 187; Foley I, pp. 503-513.

2. Civil War hides (pp. 191-195). Hodgetts Index, nos. 36, Colchester Castle; 103, Chastleton; 113, Wilderhope; 116, Broughton
Claydon: Squiers, p. 105; Frances Parthenope Verney, *Memoirs of the Verney Family during the Civil War* I (1892), pp. 3, 6, 281-8.
Pitchford: Squiers, p. 172; VCH Shropshire VIII, pp. 119, 124 (Mary Ottley's recusancy).
Purshall: Camm, *Forgotten Shrines*, pp. 269-271, 277-280; Squiers, p. 70; *Wares. Recusant* 15 (June 1970), pp. 2-15, and 38 (December 1981), p. 45; cf Hodgetts Index, no. 145 (Badge Court).

Chapter 11: *The Escape of Charles II, 1651*

Hodgetts VI, pp. 97-126; Allan Fea, *After Worcester Fight* (1904); William Matthews, *Charles II's Escape from Worcester* (1967); A.M. Broadley, *The Royal Miracle* (1912); Richard Ollard, *The Escape of Charles II* (1966); Squiers, *Moseley Old Hall* (guidebook, 1950).
For the recusancy of the Counters of Racton see VCH Sussex II, p. 25; CRS 22, p. 81.

Chapter 12: *Restoration to Regency: Tradition and Truth*

1. Hides from 1660 to 1800 (pp. 216-220). This and the next section are condensed from my article in *Eighteenth-Century Life* (Williamsburg, Virginia), N.S. 9, part 2 (January 1985), pp. 36-50.
Hodgetts Index, nos. 1, Toddington; 21, Worksop; 78, Knightsbridge; 100, Capheaton; 129, Ham House, Weybridge.
Squiers, pp. 125-6, Danby; 128-9, Scarborough, Three Mariners; 130-1, Bell Hall, Naburn; 138-9, Capheaton; 158, Standish; 159-160, Crosby; 164, Leche

House, Chester; 192, Gifford's Hall; 208-9, Woodham Mortimer; 248, Chambercombe.
Balnacraig and Fetternear: Allan Fea, *Secret Chambers and Hiding-Places* (1901),
pp. 243-4, 247-8. Since then, Fetternear has been gutted by fire and it is not possible to
go beyond Fea's description.
Capheaton: Eneas Mackenzie, *An Historical, Topographical and Descriptive View of the
County of Northumberland* II (1825), p. 340n.
Crosby: F. Tyrer ed., *The Great Diurnal of Nicholas Blundell of Little Crosby* II (1712-
1719), Lanes. and Cheshire Record Soc. 112 (1970), p. 152.
Gifford's Hall: Foley V, pp. 549-552.
Hastings Arms, Hastings, and White House, Saltburn: G. Bernard Wood,
Smugglers' Britain (1966), pp. 33, 111. Lanherne: Foley V, p. 976.
Leith: James Johnstone, *Memoir of the 'Forty-Five*, ed. Brian Rawson (Folio Society 1958),
pp. 197, 200.
Standish: Jane Garrett, *The Triumphs of Providence: The Assassination Plot* 1696 (1980),
p. 53 and Plate 1, facing p. 84 (quoted from Lanes. and Cheshire Record Soc. 115, pp.
91-106).
Stonyhurst: Squiers, pp. 146-8; John Gerard, *Stonyhurst Centenary Record*
(1894), pp. 78, n.2, 95; *Stonyhurst Magazine* 9 (February 1906), pp. 271-2, 295;
16 (June 1922), pp. 276-7; 18 (February 1925), p. 9; 21 (June 1932), pp. 551-2;
33 (July 1957), pp. 522-3; 35 (October 1966), p. 226.
Woodham Mortimer: J. H. Aveling, *The Chamberlens and the Midwifery Forceps*
(1882), pp. 218-226; Walter Radcliffe, *The Secret Instrument* (1947).
2. Tradition and Truth (pp. 221-225). Hodgetts Index, nos. 15, Little Moreton; 110, Boscobel (cf
Hodgetts VI, p. 103); 114, Bath Abbey; 154, Garrowby.

Illustration Credits

Every effort has been made to trace ownership, and the publisher apologises for any oversight or omission and would be delighted to include any corrections in future editions.

Most hide photographs are new, but Wikimedia Commons has been used to source pictures of building exteriors and a handful of monochrome images used have been colorized.

Editor's images of NT interiors reproduced by kind permission of the National Trust.

The Making of *Secret Hiding Places*

172 (Right) Phil and Paul covered in plaster and brick dust at Braddocks. After the owner stopped laughing, she kindly lent us a broom.

173 (Above) Michael at Oxburgh: we think this was in the 1980s.

174 (Right) There's a huge thrill in going into these spaces. (Clockwise from top left): Phil at Braddocks, Ufton and Abbots Salford. Sadly, there are no pictures of either of us exiting the latter, a process of leaning forwards and wriggling with outstretched arms to land in a heap on the floor outside.

175 Cobwebs, dirt and sometimes mud. R – Paul at Baddesley and (L and below) Hardwicke is now a hotel: Trish was more interested in the gin selection.

176 Rachel's classic 2023 photo of the scene of John Gerard's dramatic escape from the Tower of London.

177 Large hides make useful store rooms.

178 Smaller assistants are needed to access the tightest spaces.

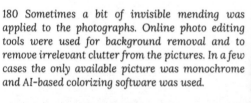

179 In modern times, the most frequent users of hides are electricians.

180 Sometimes a bit of invisible mending was applied to the photographs. Online photo editing tools were used for background removal and to remove irrelevant clutter from the pictures. In a few cases the only available picture was monochrome and AI-based colorizing software was used.

Printed in Great Britain
by Amazon

43381042R00175